Living in the Lap of the Gods

Lynn Roach

First published 2022
by Rowanvale Books Ltd
The Gate
Keppoch Street
Roath
Cardiff
CF24 3JW
www.rowanvalebooks.com

A CIP catalogue record for this book is available from the British Library.
ISBN: 978-1-913662-89-9
ebook ISBN: 978-1-913662-90-5

I would like to dedicate this book to everybody who has helped me on my journey through life. John Sherwood, who first tried to teach me to write. Anita Hughes, the author of No Half Measures, who encouraged me to tell my story. John Davis, who helped start my adventure. Bowmer, for all the advice on sailing and for being a friend for the last twenty years. And all the people I have met who have supported and helped me.

And last of all, the most important person in my life, who has spent thousands of hours correcting her dyslexic "Sun's" badly written English: my mother.

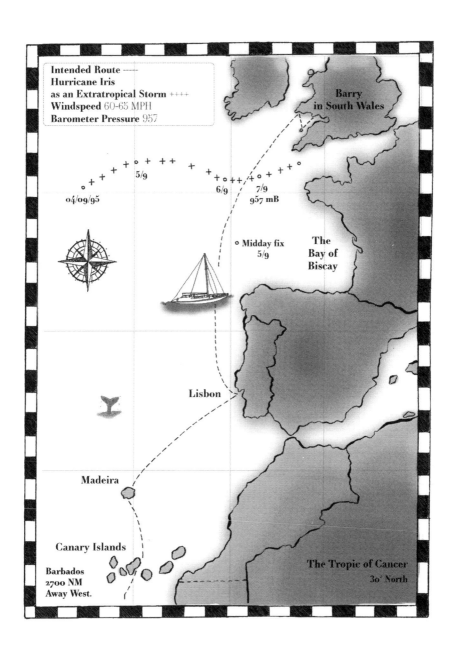

Intended Route ----
Hurricane Iris
as an Extratropical Storm ++++
Windspeed 60-65 MPH
Barometer Pressure 957

Barry
in South Wales

5/9

04/09/95

6/9

7/9
957 mB

Midday fix
5/9

The
Bay of
Biscay

Lisbon

Madeira

Canary Islands

Barbados
2700 NM
Away West.

The Tropic of Cancer
30° North

Why I Wrote This Book

One evening after work, my mother suggested that we find a pub and eat out for a change. I decided to drive along the coast, but every pub we came to had a sign saying: 'Closed for food on Mondays'. Finally, after stopping at five different pubs, I found one that had a sign saying: 'Open for food, senior citizens menu. Please come in and enjoy our open fire.'

Walking in, I saw a group of men sitting at a long table. Mum found a table opposite them, close to the big, open fire. Returning from the bar with drinks in hand, I sat next to her. We chatted away, waiting for our food to arrive, when our attention was drawn to the conversation at the table opposite us. We could not help but overhear one of the men telling a story about sailing a yacht to Lundy Island twenty years ago, picking up two hitchhikers and giving them a lift to Nayland in West Wales. He could not remember the hitchhikers' names. I could. I finished his story for him by saying, "Then you hopped in your car and gave them a lift back to Barry."

Mum and I were in a random pub in the middle of nowhere on a Monday night, and a person I didn't know was telling a story about something I did twenty years ago.

Mum said, "Lynn, you should write a book."

From a very early age, I knew I had only one life and one chance to have a look around this planet we all call home.

This is my account of my look around. I hope you enjoy the read, the humour in it, and best of all... IT'S A TRUE STORY.

A ships barometer

Introduction
When Dreams Turn to Nightmares

8th day at sea
Tuesday 5th September

Only by holding my small radio to my ear could I hear (between the static *CRRR*) parts of the Radio 4 shipping forecast. "Severe gale—*CRRR*—force 10—*CRRR*—Sole, Plymouth, visibility poor, wind backing—*CRRR*—Sea areas Finisterre, Biscay, Trafalgar—*CRRR*—low pressure 980mb—*CRRR CRRR*—12. Hurricane Ir—*CRRR CRRR*—imminent—*CRRR CRRR*."

I thought, *what a nightmare*. Only eight days after leaving Wales, the forecast was not what I wanted or expected. 'Imminent' meant the hurricane would be with me in the next six to twelve hours, which wasn't good news at all. The situation I had found myself in did not help. I was single-handedly sailing a forty-one-foot wooden yacht with no engine, built in 1936, designed to sail the calm, flat waters of the Baltic Sea.

Looking at the chart, I saw one bit of good news: my midday GPS fix put me a hundred and eighty nautical miles off the north coast of Spain, approximately in the middle of the Finisterre shipping forecast area, which gave me a lot of sea room to play with—or so I thought.

I had experienced bad weather the previous night and survived. At least I knew a bit about what to expect. But what scared me the most from listening to the weather forecast was that I hadn't even known that the Beaufort scale went past force 8. To gain a bit more knowledge, I looked up the Beaufort scale description in my ocean passage planner book, and to be honest, I wished I hadn't.

Beaufort 8. Gale. Winds: 34 to 40 knots. Wave height: 18ft. Sea conditions: Large waves with foam blown off crests.

Beaufort 10. Storm. Wind: 48 to 55 knots. Wave height: 30ft. Sea conditions: Very high waves with overhanging crests.

Beaufort 12. Hurricane. Wind speed: 64 knots plus. Wave height: 46ft plus. Sea conditions: Giant waves, air full of foam and spray.

All I could do was pray that the BBC had got the forecast wrong and watch the barometer needle for any indication that a storm was coming my way. The needle was pointing to 1008mb and, to my dismay, dropping rapidly. I could hear the voice of my astronavigation teacher telling the class:

"If your barometer drops three points in an hour, you are in for bad weather."

I wondered what he would say if he was looking at my barometer. I know what my mate Bowmer would have said, with a laugh in his voice:

"Roachy, if I was in your position, I would have changed my underpants by now."

I had expected an easy trip of sunny days with calm, downwind sailing. And that was definitely not what was coming my way.

After I had prepared the yacht for a few more rough days at sea, I cooked some food and ate it while the going was still good. While drinking a coffee, I wondered what to do. I debated whether to carry on sailing south in the hope of finding better weather or west to gain more sea room. The one thing I could not do was to sail east towards the danger of land. Sailing along a lee shore before an imminent storm was out of the question.

All afternoon, I had been sailing south with the fresh south-easterly breeze, watching the swallows and the swifts flying east towards land. They'd known something bad was coming. My mood was further dampened by the fact the moon had a big ring of cloud around it: another sign I was about to see some really bad weather.

The wind slowly started backing to the south-west and increasing in strength. The cold front was approaching. I knew the Radio 4 shipping forecast was pretty accurate and the swifts weren't daft either: they knew something was afoot. I tried, but I couldn't pick up the 1700 hours shipping forecast.

I put a third reef in the mainsail and changed the no.2 genoa to my storm jib, as I didn't want to be messing around on the bow of the yacht in the oncoming storm. After I set the sails and made sure George, my self-steering, was happy, I went back below deck. I got all my anchor warp and spare rope and tied them together to use as a drogue, just in case I needed to slow the yacht down later.

Looking out to the west, I saw dense black clouds forming. There were periodic rumbles of thunder and huge forks of lightning. I could also see a lot of rain, and the swells were getting bigger as the wind speed increased.

The worst thing was looking at the barometer and watching the hand continue to drop towards the word 'stormy'. It had dropped ten points during the afternoon and still kept dropping. This was not good. I kept tapping the barometer with the back of my hand, in the hope this second-hand barometer I had bought at the Beaulieu yacht jumble was stuck and the hand would move back up. It didn't.

23:00

The wind had picked up to force 7/8. The barometer was down to 990mb; the hand was pointing to the 'm' in stormy— another eight points, not good. The waves were getting really big, forty or fifty feet in height, and the sets were getting a lot closer together!

***

9th day at sea
Wednesday 6th September

02:30

The waves were starting to break, and there was a lot of white water. The air was full of foam and spray, and as I sailed over the top of each wave, I got the full force of the howling wind. All I could see in this chaos was the next huge wall of water coming towards me. It's funny; even in those dangerous conditions, there was no point in me being scared. I had to rely on fate, George and my workmanship in rebuilding the yacht. There was no way I could fight Mother Nature in her very angry mood.

The conditions were so dangerous I could no longer go on deck, as there was no deck to be seen. It was continuously underwater. I stayed in the cabin and relied on George, who, despite the conditions, seemed to be coping very well.

I tried to get some sleep, but it was impossible with the sound of the waves crashing over the yacht and the wind screaming through the rigging. If that wasn't enough, there was also the crashing and banging of items in the cabin, not to mention the pots and pans clattering about in the cupboards. I had to hang on to my bunk to prevent myself from being thrown across the cabin with the rest of my things.

As difficult and miserable as those conditions were, I had no option but to bide my time and ride out the storm. While pumping the water out of the yacht every half hour.

06:00

At first light, I checked the barometer, and wished I hadn't. The hand had passed the 's' in stormy and read 975mb. Checking back through the ship's logbook, the barometer pressure had dropped 33mb over the last 24 hours.

Outside, the wind was blowing harder and the waves looked a lot bigger. In fact, they were enormous—it was like looking up at a multi-storey building. I had at least one boat length of water stretching ahead of me when I looked up the wave and another behind to the trough.

Sitting on top of my cabin steps with my diving mask on was the only way I could see anything; there was so much foam and spray being blown around. All I could see was broken white water.

Watching George steer the yacht in those conditions was amazing. How he did it, I don't know—which just confirmed to me that I had done a good job in designing and building the system. At the top of the wave, we got the full force of the storm; George would steer into the wind, luffing the yacht for a few seconds. As the wave passed under the yacht, the bow would fall off and we'd sail down the back of the wave into the next trough, where we would momentarily lose the wind. George would then start the whole process over again, hour after hour.

12:00

The wind had increased yet again, and by this stage, the waves were monstrous. *Seefalke* began to struggle to sail up the faces of the oncoming waves.

Several times, she would start up the wave and then stop before reaching the top. It was a horrible sensation when the yacht would slowly start to slide backwards.

My worry was the yacht would be pooped, meaning the bow would be pushed over the stern by the wall of water. Luckily for me, the stern dug into the face of the wave, stopping our backward slide, letting the wave pass, so *Seefalke* could sail over the crest and down its back. Getting pooped would have been fatal.

Five times, *Seefalke* sailed up only to start sliding backwards down those huge waves. It was getting way too dangerous, and so I had no option but to turn the yacht around—not an easy job, with plenty that could go wrong.

I knew sailing downwind with the mainsail still up would pose a number of problems: the yacht speed would massively increase, which I didn't want, and it would be all too easy for the yacht to gybe, which could damage the mast. With all my storm gear on and making sure I was clipped to the jackstay, I ventured on deck. After the first wave, I was drenched. Nevertheless, crawling to the mast, I waited for a lull in the trough and then dropped the mainsail as quickly as the conditions would permit. Once it was on the deck, I quickly lashed the sail to the boom.

To turn the yacht around safely, I needed to be in the trough of a wave. Ending up beam on, just below the crest of a breaking wave, with the full strength of the wind hitting *Seefalke* would be very dangerous. Luckily for me, I had no problem turning the yacht around.

13

With the wind now coming from behind, the yacht began surfing down the faces of the huge waves. The danger now was pitchpoling, which happens when the yacht races down the face of a wave, the bow digs in at the bottom of the trough and then the wall of water pushes the stern over the bow. Getting pitchpoled would be as fatal as being pooped.

Back in the cockpit, I set the storm jib up on the centre line of the yacht. By pulling both sheets in tight, I kept the yacht sailing downwind and down the faces of those monstrous waves.

Getting the anchor warp and the other ropes that I had tied together earlier, I fastened the two ends to the main genoa winches before heaving the whole lot over the stern. I was amazed at how much drag all the warps created. They acted as a superb brake, slowing the yacht down to a safe speed. This was a major success, and I could start to relax a little bit.

My next problem was that I was sailing east towards the coast. I had a day's grace before I would run out of sea room and hit land.

Now that *Seefalke* was settled and more comfortable, I had time to look for something to eat that I didn't have to cook. I found a lump of cheese, a packet of peanuts and a Mars bar. I managed to make myself a coffee by hanging on to the kettle while the water boiled.

The yacht was leaking badly, and pumping her out was an ongoing job. A small leak was not unusual, but the amount of water coming in had increased dramatically. There didn't seem to be any water coming from the bow or cabin, and so the only place left to look was the 'counter'—the very back of the yacht. There was only one way to check. Torch in hand, I crawled down the quarter berth, which was like a long dark tunnel taking me under the cockpit. I started thinking to myself that if the yacht pitchpoled, I was definitely in the wrong place. Thankfully, I found the leak; the water was coming in through the rudder stern tube at the top where it joined the deck. Every time a wave hit the yacht's counter, water sprayed me like a shower. I was happy I had found the leak, but I couldn't fix it while the storm continued to rage.

For the last eight hours, I had been sailing in an easterly direction. I tried to get a GPS fix to check my position, without any luck. Maybe the waves were too big or the yacht was rolling around too much. Anyway, something was stopping my new six-satellite GPS from getting a signal, so I didn't have a clue where I was.

By my dead reckoning, I had sailed forty miles during the previous eight hours, and I was concerned that if I went much farther, I would start to sail into shallower water on the continental shelf. The barometer had quickly risen to 990mb, and the waves weren't breaking quite so much, so I decided to alter course and start sailing south once more.

Back on deck, the wind was still blowing gale force. I pulled in the trailing warps before I crawled to the mast to rehoist the mainsail. I managed to get part of the sail up, but for some reason, it jammed. I could not move it up or down; it was stuck. With the boom sitting in the gallows, (gallows are on top of the cabin roof and stop the boom swinging around and sweeping the deck at my head height) all I could do was secure the loose sail as best I could with sail ties.

Sitting safely in the cockpit, I set the sails and George up so we could start heading south. My new course enabled me to sail diagonally across the waves, going over them at a thirty-degree angle, which was a lot more comfortable and safe. As we approached the top of a wave, the wind would increase and George would respond by luffing the yacht until she was over the crest, and then we would sail safely down the other side.

***

10th day at sea
Thursday 7th September

03:00

My batteries had gone flat. This was a nightmare—now I had no radio, cabin lights, automatic bilge pumps or navigation lights, leaving the yacht invisible to any shipping. Making this trip south harder still.

When I'd left Wales, the last thing on my mind was storms at sea. Now that I was in a big one, all I could do was deal with what was in front of me. To distract myself from thinking, I concentrated on pumping the yacht out every half hour, which was hard work and tiring, but essential, if I wanted to live to follow my 'dream'.

06:00
Overall, the yacht coped well during the night despite the setbacks. In daylight, I could see what the mainsail had been catching on but decided to leave everything as it was until the weather improved. The barometer continued to move up, pointing to a better weather outlook. The waves were still big, though they were decreasing in size all the time, but the wind was still in the south-west and blowing hard. I had expected the wind to start dropping as my barometer rose, but it hadn't. I put this down to the fact that the barometer had been rising quickly, which is just as bad as it falling quickly.

12:00. Pos. 44°08'N 009°46'W
My GPS came back to life for the first time in two days. Looking at my midday position plotted on the chart, I saw I had sailed a hundred and thirty miles south and forty miles east during the storm, putting me on the same latitude as the north of Spain, and only twenty miles off the longitude of Cape Finisterre. If the storm had lasted one more day, or even six more hours, I would have been kissing the beaches of northern Spain, like all the poor sailors who have died on that dangerous coastline. Frightened by that thought, I started working my way back out to sea, tacking into the still very large waves and against the wind to try to get back some of the sea room I had lost.

15:00
I fixed the problem with the mainsail track: a screw had worked itself loose in the track, preventing the sail from being hoisted. I tied myself to the mast using my safety line, and standing on the mast winches, hanging on with one hand, I managed to reach up and remove the offending screw, solving my problem.

I had been keeping an eye on the barometer; it was back to 1005mb and rising slowly, which was a good sign. As the weather improved, the wind started to drop. I managed to haul the mainsail back up, still with the third reef in. I needed to clean up the yacht and give myself a break before setting more sail. The last few days had been brutal. I was absolutely exhausted from the lack of sleep and the physical exertion of pumping the yacht out every half hour.

The weather got better by the hour until finally, I had blue, clear sky, and a warm afternoon sun on my back. Sitting in the cockpit, I wrote in my logbook that I had not seen a ship for days. As I did, *Seefalke* went over the top of a wave, and when I looked forward over the bow, I could see a supertanker two or three miles away. *Seefalke* went down into the next trough, and the ship disappeared from view. I expected to get another glimpse of the ship as we sailed over the next wave. To my surprise, the horizon was clear. I never caught sight of that ship again.

The yacht and I seemed very small in comparison to those very large swells. It was really amazing to me how quickly I had got used to the Atlantic waves. All were far larger than anything I had ever encountered before, and I hoped I would never see weather like I had just experienced ever again. Sunny days and downwind trade-wind sailing were all I wanted from then on.

Chapter 1
Dreaming of Adventure

My story starts on a cold and wet November morning in a council house where my parents lived with my grandparents. That house was in Cardiff, South Wales, and I was born there in 1958.

My love of travelling started when my parents decided to move to Australia. We went on what was known as a ten-pound assisted passage. Basically, it was a ferry to Australia. It was a bargain then and sounds an amazing price now. On arriving in Oz, we became known as 'ten-pound poms'. After only three years of my first great adventure, we returned home to sunny Wales.

My parents bought a new house in a small village in South Wales overlooking the Bristol channel. It was a great place for me to grow up; I had a new adventure every day—rock climbing or swimming. I very soon learned to respect the sea, because of the weather and the very high tides in the channel.

Over the school holidays, my grandmother would look after me. Most days, we would go for long walks across the beach with the dog. When we got to Nan's favourite spot, we would sit down and she would tell me about the adventures of her father, an old sailing ship captain, which I loved to hear.

One day, sitting on a rock looking out to sea, Nan said to me, "One day you will go to sea, as you have my father's soul in you. He will be looking after you."

The family summer holiday was always somewhere in Europe. It was on these holidays that I first met people of different cultures, and my love of travelling really took off.

I confess I found school utterly boring. Despite my lack of interest, I was good at maths, physics and anything that involved using my hands, i.e., metalwork and woodwork. I was, however, useless at English. In one school report, the English teacher placed me thirty-ninth in the class, which made me laugh as there were only thirty-eight of us.

I left school with a Certificate of Secondary Education qualification (CSE) in metalwork, woodwork, physics and maths grade 1. I failed my English, which was no great surprise. On leaving school, I was now free to travel with the money I had saved from my paper round; I packed my rucksack and was off to see the world. Just as I was walking out through the front door, however, my mother was walking in. Mum stopped me and said I couldn't go travelling until I was eighteen and had a trade.

Luckily for me, I found an apprenticeship. The company made medical parts: artificial knees and hip joints.

After four years of hard work, I was just about to finish my time as a qualified toolmaker. So, it was a bit of a surprise when I was called into the personnel office. I thought they wanted to talk about my excellent exam results—I had achieved one credit and two distinctions in maths and physics. To my surprise, I was told the company were not keeping on any apprentices. This didn't make any sense to me at all. The company had spent four years training me, only to let me go just as I completed my apprenticeship—it seemed complete madness.

There was nothing I could do about my employer's decision. However, I saw a silver lining. I was free to travel, if I could find a job abroad.

Looking in the back of *The Sun* one day, I saw there was a job advertised for a toolmaker in Germany. After a quick chat on the phone, I picked up my first contract working in Germany, followed by a contract in Canada, where I learned to scuba dive. Seeing a steam train underwater on my first dive really got my interest and imagination going.

There is only one place in the world to enjoy diving: Australia, with its warm, blue waters. Luckily for me, my last contract abroad took me to Oz. I had a year there, diving most weekends, which I enjoyed immensely.

Back in the UK, I finally found work in Milton Keynes. The job involved machining parts for the restoration of a World War Two Spitfire MK 11a for the RAF's memorial flight, which I thoroughly enjoyed, as it was very interesting work.

My landlady at the time would say, every three or so weeks, "Lynn, it's time you went home, I can tell you are missing the sea." She was right.

After I drove home, my first job was to take my dog, William, a West Highland White Terrier, down to the beach. One evening as the sun was setting, I saw a yacht sailing down the channel and wondered where it was heading. For some reason, it sparked the thought that if I had a yacht I could live on, I could sail anywhere I wanted. Diving off the yacht sounded like a fun thing to do, and drinking beer in the sun, sailing around the world, seeing different places full time sounded like a good idea to me. All I had to do was learn to sail, and buy a yacht—easy.

At home one weekend, I was told my father's mother had died. I decided to make myself scarce as this was an upsetting and stressful time for my parents. I left them and went to see a friend in West Wales.

Walking to the pub, Paul said, "What's wrong, Lynn? You look down."

"I'm okay," I told him. "I've just had some sad news: my grandmother has died."

Halfway through my pint, Paul said, "Finish your pint and let's go and see Penelope. She'll cheer you up."

"Who's Penelope?" I asked, thinking it was one of his girlfriends.

"Come on, I'll show you."

As Paul drove, I asked, "Where is she?"

"You'll find out soon," he said.

Driving into the docks at Milford Haven, Paul stopped the car and pointed out a long, white, sleek-looking yacht with a tall wooden mast, lying very low to the water on the opposite side of the harbour.

"That's *Penelope*."

The yacht had the same shape as *Endeavour*, a yacht I had seen on the dock in Southampton a few years earlier. *Endeavour* was one of the one-hundred-and-thirty-foot long,

J-class yachts designed by Charles Nicholson for Tom Sopwith, built by Camper and Nicholsons to challenge for the America's Cup in 1934 and 1937. I'd fallen in love with the shape of that yacht then and wished I'd had the money to buy and restore her at the time.

Looking at *Penelope*, the only difference I could see was she was a pocket-sized version of a J-class yacht at forty feet long. She had the same graceful lines, looked so elegant in the water. And yes, she did cheer me up.

"Can we get a better look at her?" I asked Paul.

"Yes, let's walk around the harbour to her."

I had to get a better look at this lovely yacht. We scrambled down the dock wall to the deck. On closer inspection, I could see she was quite rough in places; there was lots of rot in the coach roof. The deck had been sheathed in fibreglass, which was lifting in places, and it was evident that rainwater was getting trapped underneath, causing more rot. It did not take much effort to find a way into the yacht through the forehatch. It was light inside, but very narrow. I could touch both sides of the cabin with my arms outstretched and I could just about stand up without hitting my head. I was surprised to find very little water inside, considering the state of the deck. I could see some of the frames were cracked and would need to be replaced. The engine was an old two-stroke petrol that I didn't think would ever run again. She really needed a lot of tender loving care, which I thought I could do slowly over a few years.

After spending an hour on the yacht, I had to buy it. Paul reckoned I could pick it up for three thousand pounds, as she had been on the market for a long time.

Back in the pub over another pint, I asked Paul to tell me her history. He explained, "*Penelope* is a fifty-square-metre yacht built in Germany before the Second World War for the German Armed Services, for the purpose of training their personnel. After the war, when the British army entered Kiel, they found a fleet of yachts. These were commandeered as spoils of war and brought back to the UK. They became known as Windfall yachts."

That night, I could not sleep; I just kept thinking of *Penelope*. Early the next morning, I got in contact with the yacht broker.

I made an offer of three thousand pounds, which was accepted by the owner. I wrote a cheque to pay the ten percent deposit and arranged for the yacht to be taken out of the water and surveyed.

The survey took place in Milford Haven Dock. Reading the report, there was not too much wrong with her, apart from the deck, which I already knew about. My plan was to buy the yacht and do a little bit of work, say a thousand pounds' worth a year, and slowly, over a few years, restore her.

I was going to the Southampton Boat Show that weekend. I decided to take all the paperwork for the yacht with me and try to get a loan with the Marine Mortgage Company. It worked; I got the loan.

I decided to get the restoration project started straight away and arranged with a local boat builder for *Penelope* to be lifted out of the water and taken to his boatyard. I asked the boat builder to take the fibreglass off the deck so I could inspect the damage underneath. Once this was done, I could make a plan for what to do next.

***

Description of Penelope

The yacht had a carvel hull, constructed of mahogany planks fastened on to oak frames. She was built for the German Luftwaffe in 1936 by the very famous Abeking & Rasmussen boatyard near Bremen, North Germany, to the design of H. Rasmussen.

The yard and designer were celebrated for the beauty of their yachts, and Penelope was no exception. The yacht had a nicely formed spoon bow, and this was balanced by a most beautiful and elegant counter stern, so often a feature of Abeking & Rasmussen's yachts. The yacht had a shallow forefoot, running smoothly aft to a triangular underbody, ending at a moderately sloping sternpost.

The rudder and rudder stock were constructed of wood; the stock ran up through the counter. The yacht had a low and nicely designed superstructure of mahogany with three deadlights on each side and a full six feet standing headroom below.

Penelope *was a Bermudan Sloop, with a three-quarters rig. Her Sitka spruce mast was keel stepped with two sets of stays on each side. Above deck, the mast was supported by two sets of spreaders and a set of jumper stays on the forestay diamond fitting.*

Dimensions:
Length overall: 41.6 feet.
Length of waterline: 28 feet.
Beam: 8.6 feet.
Draft: 6 feet.
Sail area: 538 square feet (50 square metres).
Sail number: 390.
Previous Names: Seefalke *but renamed* Sea Soldier *by the British Royal Marines.*

***

I thought at the time that classic wooden yachts would get as popular as classic cars, and I had just bought a real classic.

The next time I saw *Penelope*, I was in shock. The boat builder had stripped the whole deck off her and removed the top two planks on the hull and most of the deck beams. When I was given the bill for the work so far, I was not a happy bunny. I'd had no intention of doing that much work so early on in the project. I decided from that point forward I wasn't going to pay for any more work to be done on my yachts; I could learn to do it myself.

At least now I had a good understanding of what needed to be addressed—most of the damage had been caused by sheathing the deck in fibreglass. Unfortunately, the survey hadn't picked up on the fact that the tops of all the frames were rotten, as were the ends of the deck beams. This was going to cost a lot of money to fix, which I did not have.

To save some money and start restoring the yacht, I had to get it closer to home, so looking in the phonebook, I found a boatyard in Barry and decided to go and talk to Ray, the boatyard owner. I showed him the photos of *Penelope*; he was extremely interested in the yacht, and we talked for over an hour on the best way to restore her. Very quickly, I decided to move the yacht to Barry.

When the big day came to move *Penelope*, I drove down to West Wales to watch her being loaded onto the road trailer for the trip to Ray's boatyard in Barry Docks.

My problem was I now had a loan to pay off. My job in Milton Keynes had finished, and I could not find work in Wales; instead, I found a job in Reading making parts for F1 cars. I rented a room from a work colleague, Martin Sage. We became good friends; he was tall and well-built with a very easy-going attitude to life. However, he did have one annoying habit: he would always let his food go cold before eating it. Every time I watched Martin eat his cold food, or drink cold tea, I had my mother's voice in my head saying, "Eat it while it's hot."

The highlight of my job in Reading was making a part for the Ayrton Senna F1 car.

Driving from Reading to Barry to work on the yacht at the weekends was a waste of time and money. Instead, I concentrated on working all the overtime I could to try to save some money to kick-start the restoration project. It was a year before I went to see Ray again, and all I had done was pay the storage bill.

To my surprise, Ray had built a big steel shed and moved the yacht inside it. We spent an hour inside the hull looking at the damage that had been caused by the yacht being out of the water, the road trip to Barry and being exposed to the elements outside for over a year. The yacht had definitely deteriorated; the hull had dried out, and consequently, all the frames had become loose. Most of the frames had rotted in their ends and some were cracked. We decided to replace all fifty-four frames, which was going to be a mammoth job.

To get the job started and to speed things up, I got a quote from Ray to laminate new frames for me. This wasn't a job I fancied tackling myself, as I lacked the tools, and fitting them would be a two-man job. The quote was an eye-watering two thousand pounds, and that was to replace only half the frames in the yacht.

While thinking about Ray's quote, on a Wednesday, I met up with my old friend John at the folk club held in the local pub.

Over a few pints, I told John about how I wanted to get the yacht restoration project started, and that I needed two thousand pounds for new frames. John had always been interested in the yacht and immediately said he'd lend me the money, which he did.

When my contract in Reading came to an end, luckily, I found work in Caerphilly, just north of Cardiff. Now I could start to focus on *Penelope*'s restoration.

I planned to start work on the yacht in the evenings. Ray told me that it wouldn't be a problem, as he had just started to build a steel yacht for himself and would be working on it most evenings. To save more money, he told me I could camp out on one of the abandoned yachts in the yard if I wanted to, which I agreed to do. Ray was happy with this arrangement, as he now had a security guard in the yard.

The last piece fell into place when I joined Barry Yacht Club and got use of a shower. All in all, this was great news for me.

Every evening after work for the next month, I'd work on the yacht with a hammer and chisel. I broke up and prised one or two frames off the hull each night. This left the copper rivets exposed; there were two per plank. The head of each rivet had to be cut off before it could be punched out of the hull, taking the wooden blanking plug with it. There were thousands of rivets, and this was a painstaking job. It took two months of hard work to remove half the frames.

Once every other frame had been removed, the job of making new frames could begin. First, I had to make a pattern of the hull shape for Ray to make a new laminated frame. On a typical evening, I would make the patterns for the two frames to be made the next day. I then cleaned off the excess epoxy resin from the frames that had been made that morning. I used a hand plane to clean off the epoxy, which set really hard. The plane blade would go dull very quickly and so I used two planes, one for roughing and the other for finishing. This meant I only needed to re-sharpen the roughing plane blade three times to finish each frame, then use the other plane to smooth off any minor imperfections in the wood. Once the frame was planed to the right thickness, I'd used a small block plane to put a 5mm radius on the outside edges. The final step was to give the frame a light rub-over with some sandpaper, and then it was ready for fitting.

25

My finished frames were then screwed into place. Once the frame was in its correct position, it was fastened in three places along its length. This was a two-man job. One of Ray's boys stayed inside the yacht and made sure the frame didn't move while another one fitted the screws from the outside of the hull.

My next job each evening was to refasten the planks to the frames, using inch-and-a-half silicon bronze screws. I fitted the screws by using a carpenter's hand drill known as a brace with a screwdriver bit attached to the chuck. Each plank was fastened with two screws.

At the end of each night, I would walk up the hill to the Marine pub, where I usually fell asleep with a pint in my hand. I nearly got thrown out a couple of times, until the landlord realised I was not drunk, just physically exhausted. Once I finished putting the first half of the new frames in, I started to remove the other half, ready for the whole process to start again.

I finally finished the restoration of the hull, with a galley chart table and sleeping berths fitted. I moved *Penelope* out of Ray's shed for the first time in three years and changed all the keel bolts and rehung the rudder. She was finally taking shape, but I still had a lot of work to do.

The name of the yacht had bothered me ever since I bought her. As she was finally coming back together, I realised she did not look like a *Penelope* to me. Changing the name of a yacht was deemed to bring bad luck, so to get around this, I reverted to the yacht's original name, *Seefalke*—"sea eagle" in German—which I was happy with.

Chapter 2
Mast, Boom and Sails

The mast had been sitting in a mast rack in Ray's shed for the best part of four years. Given that the yacht came with a wooden mast, and I had no idea how old it was or when the rigging had last been changed, I needed to strip the mast of all the fittings and have the whole lot checked by someone who knew what they were doing. This was important for the future integrity of the rig and for insurance purposes. This would also give me the opportunity to scrape the mast back and apply fresh varnish. It took six people to carry the mast out of the shed and place it on trestles I had set up in the boatyard.

I'd finished stripping the rigging and fittings off the mast one evening when three people walked into the boatyard and asked if they could look around. I gave them a tour of *Seefalke*. As they were leaving, I said jokingly, "If you're ever bored and need something to do, you're always welcome to come and give me a hand." To my surprise, the next day one of them turned up to help me strip the varnish off the mast.

He introduced himself as Justin and asked what the mast was made of. I explained that it was hollow, made of spruce, and was fifty feet long. Without the heavy rigging, the mast was very light; the two of us could pick it up easily.

As a thank you for his help, I bought Justin a beer in the yacht club. Justin was six feet tall, well-built with lots of charm, and very good-looking. Over a pint, I asked him what he did for a living, and to my surprise, he said, "I'm a ballet dancer, currently performing in the West End in a production of *The Phantom of the Opera*."

We soon became great friends. Justin helped me on the yacht every time he was back in Barry, and it didn't take me long to realise that Justin was a real magnet for the ladies.

At around the same time, I became close friends with Karl, the local sailmaker, who I met through Barry Yacht Club. Karl was younger than me; he was a wiry, athletic-looking guy with a receding hairline which made him look older than his years. He was very friendly, incredibly laid-back. We did have a lot in common: drinking beer, playing the guitar and sailing. He was also into classic yachts, which was why he showed a lot of interest in the restoration of *Seefalke*.

Over a pint in the yacht club, I asked Karl to have a look at *Seefalke*'s rigging. The rigging was made of old galvanised wire and bottle screws, which had seized up with rust. My heart sank and I quickly experienced an empty feeling in my stomach on receipt of Karl's condition report. In the space of fifteen minutes, he condemned the whole lot. I didn't have the money to replace the rigging, which I quickly pointed out.

"No problem," he said. "I've just replaced the rigging on a forty-five-foot racing yacht. The rig had to be changed for insurance reasons—as far as I can tell, there's nothing wrong with the wire. Let's go to the sail loft and have a look at what we can use."

We laid my old rigging on the sail loft floor alongside the rigging from the racing yacht. There was plenty of length in the replacement wires, which were all marine-grade stainless steel. Karl cut the fittings off each end of the wires (the weakest point of any rigging stay) and new eye terminals were swaged onto one end of each wire with his swaging machine (his hydraulic press for crimping terminals onto the end of wires). We intentionally left the rigging longer than required so the wires could be individually measured and cut once the mast was back in the yacht.

My new rigging was attached to the newly restored mast fittings; new blocks and halyards were fitted. I also replaced the mast-head navigation light and fitted a VHF radio aerial and cable. By the time I had finished, the rig had received a complete overhaul and was ready to be lifted back into the yacht for the first time in years.

Karl was on hand to help Ray and his boys, and with the use of a crane, we lifted the mast vertically above *Seefalke*.

This was an incredibly exciting, yet anxious, moment. Karl guided the mast as it was slowly lowered through the deck and onto the mast step, which lay on top of the forward part of the keel. Just before the mast was seated, I remembered to place an old pound coin under the heel—a long-standing tradition to bring ships good fortune.

With the mast in place, Karl and I quickly attached the rigging to the chain plates. Once the forestay was attached to the bow, I had a standing mast in the yacht. Karl spent the rest of the evening up the mast, sorting out the spreaders, clamping and taping the ends off to stop them catching on the sails. His last job was to run the electric cables for the mast-head light and the VHF radio down the backstay.

With Karl up the mast, I fitted the mast chocks. These specially cut wooden wedges were banged into place at intervals around the mast to keep it in the centre of the hole where it passed through the deck. To finish the job, a rubber boot was wrapped around the mast and clamped in place using long jubilee clips to provide a watertight seal between the mast and the deck.

Next, my attention was drawn to the boom, which was nineteen feet six inches long and eight inches in diameter, made from a single piece of Douglas fir. It was heavy—two people could only just lift it. After I had checked and inspected the boom, I applied fresh varnish and put it back on the mast. It felt like the project was finally coming to an end.

My thoughts turned to the sails. There were two no.2 genoas that were in decent condition considering their age. The mainsail was rotten; it ripped as soon as Karl touched it so went straight in the bin. There was one final sail bag marked "storm sail". I dragged it out and spread it on the sail loft floor. Looking at it, the sail had a thick, heavy rope sewn around the edge; it was also very baggy and stretched. Karl took one look and said, "That looks like a whale's foreskin!"

How Karl knew what a whale's foreskin looked like was beyond me, although he was right—the sail looked terrible. I had to laugh.

Karl had a collection of old sails in the loft. He found a mainsail that was the right length for the mast, but five-foot short on the foot. I didn't mind this one bit, as Karl agreed to sell it for fifty quid, which was a bargain. Karl also agreed to restitch all the seams to make sure it was as good as it could be. The only thing I had left to do was cut the slides off my old sail and reattach them to the luff of my new mainsail to ensure that it could be hoisted using the existing mast track. What a result! I had a decent set of sails for the yacht for the princely sum of fifty pounds and a few hours of hand sewing.

With my new mainsail fitted to the boom, the sail could be hoisted up the mast. For the safety of myself and the yacht, and to ensure that the yacht didn't become 'over-pressed' in winds above a force 5 on the Beaufort scale, I needed to have a quick and effective method of reefing the mainsail—reefing being the term used for reducing the sail area. The new mainsail was designed for slab reefing, but my boom was the old style for roller reefing—a more traditional and less efficient method of shortening the sail. With Karl's help, I converted the boom to slab reefing by fitting three blocks along its length and a small winch at the mast end, which meant I would be able to drop the mainsail and put a reef in it at the mast.

I had put the deck on *Seefalke* without building in any cockpit lockers, or washboards into the main cabin, as I wanted to keep any seawater coming over the deck out of the bilge. For any water that came below, I fitted two manually operated bilge pumps, one I would be able to use from inside the yacht, as well as two twelve-volt electric fifteen-hundred-gallon-per-hour automatic bilge pumps. All the bilge pump hull fittings I kept above the waterline.

The only other hull fitting was for the sink, which was the only skin fitting below the waterline. All the hull fittings were fitted with a gate valve so I could isolate them if I needed to. As an added precaution, I tied wooden bungs to each valve so I could quickly plug a major leak in the event of a catastrophic failure.

So I could keep the hull fittings below the waterline to one, my plan was to have no fixed toilet or shower. Instead, I was given a portable chemical toilet like the ones used for camping, and I planned to use a solar shower on deck.

A twelve-volt control panel was fitted above the chart table and connected to two twelve-volt batteries. The first things

I wired up were the automatic bilge pumps. Next was the lighting.

The local lifeboat coxswain told me once that a red light was important for maintaining night vision. He said it could take up to half an hour for night vision to fully return if your eyes inadvertently became exposed to bright white lights, so I followed his advice. A big red and white light was fitted over the chart table for me to use when navigating at night.

Once the navigation light and VHF radio were installed and the cables connected to the control panel, cabin lights were fitted around the saloon. I bought a nice big deck compass off a yacht club member and fitted it just in front of the main hatch, once I'd connected the small light up to the main electric control panel, so I would be able to steer a course at night.

For cabin furnishings, I had been given some soft cushions, which I made good use of, even though they didn't fit properly. But as the saying goes, beggars can't be choosers.

One of my last jobs was to paint the deck. I mixed sand in with the paint to create a non-slip application. This would enable me to work on deck with confidence even in the slipperiest of conditions.

The rest of the yacht was painted and the mahogany varnished; my new laminated tiller was bolted to it, and a spare tiller was safely stowed away. Finally, with all the deck winches and genoa tracks in place, and the most important part—the mainsail sheeting horse—fitted over the tiller, *Seefalke* was ready to go back in the water.

In the summer of 1992, *Seefalke* was launched for the first time in five years.

She promptly SANK!!!

Chapter 3
Getting Help from Friends

I had been working really hard on *Seefalke* with the help of some very good friends. Martin from Reading, Karl and Justin, and the rest of the members of Barry Yacht Club—all of us were very keen to see the yacht back in the water.

With *Seefalke* being out of the water for so long and the weather being so hot, the hull planking had opened up due to the wood drying out. Prior to the launch, Barry had experienced hot, settled weather for about six weeks, which was odd for South Wales. I knew the fine weather could cause me a problem, as *Seefalke* was a tight-seamed 'Built Yacht', which meant each plank was touching edge on edge. Each plank was perfectly shaped and fitted to the planks next to it. Once the planks were immersed in water, any slight imperfections were 'taken up' by the swelling of the wood to form a watertight seam.

To help the wood swell or 'take up' prior to launching, I had been throwing large buckets of seawater into *Seefalke*'s bilge to allow the planks to swell. I also used a hose to spray water on the hull every night and placed wet hessian sacks on the inside of the hull to further aid the taking-up process. These were all tried and tested methods, and I was confident that once *Seefalke* was launched any leaks would quickly stop.

There was only one way to be sure.

***

Launch day

Martin had driven down from Reading to help on the big day. At 9:30 a.m., Ray Harris threw the switch to the winch that started to lower *Seefalke* into the water. As we hit the water, Ray stopped the winch to enable us to check the bilge for leaks. We stopped the winch three or four times as the water level rose around the yacht. There were several small leaks but in line with what I expected, and I was confident that the bilge pumps would easily keep up.

With the yacht floating, I jumped into the water. I swam around the hull and marked a line four inches above the waterline. The plan was to quickly lift her back out and antifoul the hull to this water line.

As I swam around the yacht, Martin was pumping the bilge, trying to keep pace with the water coming in. We were working on the principle that the longer the hull was in the water, the less the yacht would leak.

I'd finished marking the waterline when I noticed that the plywood pads that had been resting against *Seefalke*'s hull had floated away. These pads were important as they provided protection from the four sharp metal uprights that stopped *Seefalke* from falling over when she was sat on the trailer. Without the pads, one of the exposed metal pipes could easily puncture the hull.

Meanwhile, Martin was shouting that the electric bilge pumps had stopped working and he couldn't keep pace with water coming into the yacht.

I swam ashore and had a quick chat with Ray. We decided to float *Seefalke* off the trailer and bring the launch platform back out of the water, remove the trailer, lower the platform back in and let *Seefalke* sit on her keel.

Directly in front of the slipway were some old wooden posts, the last reminders of a bygone age when people would flock to the harbour to enjoy a trip on a paddle steamer. The posts had formed part of the gangway structure, which had long since rotted away. I rowed over and secured a line to a post, and with the other end secured to *Seefalke*, we pulled her clear of the trailer.

It was at this point that my parents turned up. I had told them we had planned to launch at 10:30 a.m., expecting the yacht to be floating by then. Looking up at them, I noticed that a large group of people had gathered. There were over fifty standing around watching what was going on.

I jumped back on board, picked up a five-gallon bucket and tried to bail the water out through the forehatch while Martin continued on the bilge pump. Ray had managed to get the trailer out of the way, with help from the crowd.

Ray lowered the launch platform back into the water, and as we got *Seefalke* positioned over it, she was picked up by a small wave. All the water in the bilge ran to the bow; I saw a two-foot wave inside the hull, which pushed the bow underwater. At the same time, the yacht started to list to port.

Standing on the deck, I saluted to the large crowd as I expected to go down with the ship in true captain style. I spotted my mother in the crowd; she had a look of horror on her face and was crying.

Just at the last moment, we had a bit of luck. Ray managed to get the launch platform back under *Seefalke*. It was the only thing that stopped her sinking altogether. Still stood on the bow, I was waist-deep in seawater; only the cockpit remained out of the water. At that moment, I saw two maroons go up, signifying a launch request for the R.N.L.I. All-Weather Lifeboat. I could also hear the wail of two fire engines; I remember thinking to myself that someone was having a worse day than me.

The lifeboat motored roughly a hundred yards across the harbour and tied up next to the old paddle steamer posts. I shouted over to the coxswain to see if they had a water pump on board—"No" was the answer. After making sure there was no risk to life, and with not much else they could do to help, the lifeboat returned to its station.

Shortly afterwards, the two fire engines I had heard earlier stopped outside Ray's yard with the lights and sirens still blaring away. Both sets of fire crews started to argue, resulting in a fight between the two of them. Only in Barry— you couldn't write a book about it. Once the fighting stopped, the crews, working together, started rigging their large and not-very-portable water pump down the dock to get as close to *Seefalke* as possible.

Their Venturi pump had a three-inch hose. I fed the intake through *Seefalke*'s forward hatch. The firefighters engaged the pump and started sucking water out of the yacht. Slowly but surely, *Seefalke* was brought back from the brink of total disaster.

Eventually, enough water was pumped out to allow us, with the help of the crowd, to pull her upright. As she started to float, we seized the opportunity and quickly secured her to the launching platform. Ray started to bring her very slowly out of the water, but due to the shape of the keel, she slowly fell forward, ending up bow down. After two hours of heart-stopping excitement, *Seefalke* was safely back ashore. What a nightmare.

All the trouble I had gone to in soaking the hull prior to the launch had been in vain.

After we had helped Ray move the yacht back into the yard, Martin and I went for a shower at the yacht club. Once showered and changed, we went for lunch and a few beers with my parents, who were still in a state of shock.

Martin and I spent the rest of that afternoon walking around Barry Docks looking for all the bits that had floated away during our morning's fun.

I spent the next month washing the inside of *Seefalke*, getting rid of all the salt, and salvaging as much of the electrics as possible.

Martin drove back down from Reading for *Seefalke*'s second launch. I told him I was confident she would float this time, as over the last month, the weather in Wales had been much more of what was expected—a lot of rain and cold, all good for the wooden hull of *Seefalke* to take up. He wasn't convinced.

Oh, Martin of little faith.

This time, I kept launch day a complete secret and didn't tell a soul. Given all the trouble with the trailer last time, we decided to put *Seefalke* straight onto the launch platform. We also supported her so she wouldn't nosedive. This time, *Seefalke* floated straight away, with hardly any water coming in. Half an hour later, I was happy she wasn't going to sink. What a difference a few weeks made. With Martin below deck, checking the bilge, I swam around the hull marking the waterline again. Ray brought *Seefalke* back out of the water, and we quickly gave her two coats of antifoul to prevent weeds and other marine organisms taking hold on the underside of the yacht.

We were able to put *Seefalke* back in the water on the same tide. With Martin on the helm, I borrowed Ray's dinghy, and with a rope attached to the bow, I rowed her out to a mooring in the middle of Barry Harbour. For peace of mind, I fitted a small solar panel to keep the batteries charged, which in turn ensured that there was power to the automatic bilge pumps should they be needed.

I left *Seefalke* happily floating on her mooring for a week before we went sailing. The first few times Karl and I took her out in the evenings, she sailed beautifully, well-balanced. I could sail the yacht with only a very light hand on the tiller.

Karl wanted to start racing *Seefalke*. I knew nothing about yacht racing, but I was willing to learn. I knew *Seefalke* had beautiful lines but how quick she was, I had no idea.

There was only one way to find out, and that was to race other yachts. So, to have a bit of fun, I entered her into the Thursday evening race series at Barry Yacht Club. To be able to compete, I first needed to agree on a suitable handicap number for the yacht. Handicaps are used to enable yachts of different sizes and speeds to compete against each other in the same race. Because *Seefalke* was a one-off with no previous racing pedigree, the race committee didn't know how to rate her. So, for our first race, I was given a provisional Portsmouth Yardstick number of 1020, which Karl told me was really good. I knew nothing about the handicap system, but it sounded fair to me.

For my first race, my crew consisted of Karl and Spud, who worked for Karl. I knew Spud; he too was a member of Barry Yacht Club, younger than me, a keen sailor with his own small racing yacht. Spud was very capable on a yacht, and with a 'rock star' crew had won most of the local yacht races and was a revered helmsman—just what I needed.

Spud was keen and turned up early, but Karl was nowhere to be seen. He did eventually turn up when the ten-minute warning gun was fired. Ideally, we should have been in position near the start line and not half a mile away in the harbour still on the mooring. Once Karl was on board, we sailed off the mooring and crossed the start line five minutes late—once again, Karl had lived up to his nickname of 'Deadloss'. On rounding the first marker buoy, we were still in last place, but then, we started to catch and overtake the rest of the fleet. With only two legs to go, we were up to third place, which was not bad for our first outing. On the last windward leg, we rounded the final mark of the course and took the lead. I was blown away by my yacht's sailing performance.

We held our position and were first to cross the finishing line. Karl and Spud suggested we 'buzz' the other yachts as they finished, which we did. This is a technical term for sailing around each yacht. Our little endeavour certainly upset a few people and proved not to be the best approach to making friends with the rest of the racing yacht crews. At least I learnt something. Thanks, Karl.

When we got back to the yacht club, we found we had been disqualified from the race for using our engine ten minutes before the start. Karl, Spud and I laughed; we pointed out to the race committee that we did not have an engine. Once this was sorted out, *Seefalke* was reinstated and awarded first place. Our bandit handicap was promptly reassessed and dropped to 980—in simple terms, the lower the number, the faster the yacht. Thanks once again, Karl.

I felt truly rewarded for the painstaking effort I had put in over the years. To get here, I had poured every penny I had into the yacht. From the first minute I set eyes on her, I knew she was right and finally I had confirmation. Thank goodness her sailing performance bore resemblance to a Ferrari and not that of a Morris Minor.

Karl, Martin from Reading and I enjoyed hours of fun sailing *Seefalke* around the Bristol Channel most weekends that summer, despite the fact that I still had tons of work to do to finish the yacht off.

At the end of the summer, I moved *Seefalke* back into Ray's yard. For the first time since I had bought the yacht, I could live on her. Ray's yard was not quite the Caribbean, but my dream was finally bearing fruit and coming together.

My 'to do' list still seemed endless, including: painting the inside, finishing the fiddly woodwork trim and mouldings, putting hinges on doors and finally fitting the stainless-steel bow roller I had made for the anchor. On deck, I managed to make and fit a pull pit, which as the name suggests, prevents people from falling over the bow. Additionally, I fitted all the stanchions on to their bases.

Once I had stanchions, I had to fit a safety line through them and fit jackstays or lifelines. These are all fundamental to the safety of the crew. For shorthanded sailing, they are a non-negotiable part of the yacht's inventory, as they enable people working on deck to attach a safety line from their life jacket, safety harness or foul-weather jacket to the jackstay. Once attached, you can then move freely up and down the deck with peace of mind. In the unfortunate event that you find yourself falling over the side, you will remain attached to the yacht. That's the good news. The bad news is, if you're sailing single-handed, getting back on board will be another problem.

Once again, my sailmaker friend Karl said he would help me. One evening, he called over with some rigging wire and his hydraulic swager. Working together, we made and fitted the jackstays, which ran down both side decks and were fastened at both ends to strong points on the deck.

On arriving at the shed one night after work, I discovered that a new yacht had been brought in and placed alongside *Seefalke*. Ray introduced me to its owner, Steve, and explained that Steve would be working on his yacht in the evenings for a while so I would have some company. Over the next few weeks, I got to know Steve well. It was great to be able to help each other, particularly on the awkward jobs where an extra pair of hands made life so much easier.

It turned out Steve was a schoolteacher, and one evening while we were chatting, I asked him what he taught.

"Metalwork," he answered.

What a result, I thought. I asked him if he could get the boys in his class to make a mould from one of *Seefalke*'s fairleads and one from a deck cleat. I then asked if this were possible, could he get his class to cast eight more?

To my delight, Steve agreed.

Steve and his yacht had long since left the shed by the time I was ready to fit the cleats and fairleads. Although these jobs were a fair way down my list, both items were essential to the mooring up of the yacht. When you tie a yacht to the dock, all the warps (by warps, I mean mooring ropes) pass through the fairleads, which prevent chafing, before being made fast to a cleat, which has hopefully been bolted through some strategically reinforced pads on the deck.

I once tried casting bronze myself but with absolutely no success. Now that I wasn't in regular contact with Steve, I kind of thought the prospect of getting my bronze fittings made was looking slim. However, my faith in human nature was fully restored when one night, Ray handed me a big, heavy bag, saying, "Steve asked me to give you these."

I looked in the bag, and to my sheer delight, I could see eight sets of bronze deck fittings. They still needed to be finished, which was not a problem—I finished them at work. With the bronze fairleads and cleats screwed in place, the deck was finished.

On a slightly less sophisticated note, I found an old pig-iron five-pound weight which I connected to a long piece of line with knots tied at six feet intervals. This became my cheap, cheerful, yet highly functional depth gauge.

To find the depth, all I had to do was drop the weight over the side and wait for it to hit the bottom, then simply retrieve the pig-iron and count the knots. This is how the old-timers used to do it, and if it was good enough for them, it was good enough for me.

Last but not least, I was given an old trailing log so I would be able to work out my distance sailed and yacht speed through the water.

Chapter 4
Getting to Know the Boys

One evening, as I returned to the boatyard from work, Karl was waiting for me. He was in a real panic and looked incredibly stressed.

He said, "I promised a customer that I would have his mast finished by tomorrow, but the new aluminium extrusion has only just turned up."

When I asked Karl why the extrusion had only just turned up, I got the usual, "Errr..." before he admitted he had only ordered it last week. This was classic Karl; he was a complete nightmare. Karl went on to say that he had just started working on it and had already "cocked up" and could I give him a hand?

Giving Karl a hand wasn't a problem; I owed him a mass of favours.

In the sail loft, the thirty-foot mast was laid out on three trestles. Karl had marked out where he wanted the fittings to go. I could see he had tried to cut one hole in the mast. It was a mess. With a bit of care, I sorted the hole out.

Before I carried on, I asked Karl if he was happy with what I had done so far.

"Yes, Lynn, that's brilliant, keep going."

"Okay," I said. "Just leave the mast to me."

"Great." He smiled with relief and handed me a bag of mast fittings.

Looking around the loft, I noticed Karl had acquired a lot of angle iron, steel bars and a welding set. Being curious, I asked what the steel was for.

"The loft has been broken into three times this month," Karl said. "Each time the kettle has been stolen, but strangely nothing else."

This could only happen in Barry, I thought.

"It's costing me a fortune. So, I bought the steel to make the loft burglar-proof. I want to stop the little bastards stealing my kettles," said Karl.

Fair enough.

I slowly worked my way around the mast, drilling and tapping the holes, putting *Tef-Gel* paste on each screw to stop galvanic corrosion, before attaching the mast fittings. As I had never worked on a mast before, I needed to concentrate.

Karl started to cut the angle iron and the steel bars ready to fit to the windows. He was using a chop saw, which was really loud, and as he cut the metal, hot sparks flew everywhere. I found the whole experience very off-putting, particularly as most of the structure and floor of Karl's loft was made of wood. After a while, he stopped cutting the metal and started to try and weld the parts together. Although not noisy, I now had to contend with even more hot metal sparks flying everywhere. To protect my eyes, I turned my back on him.

At one point, Karl asked me to come over and have a look at his weld. I told him that in my honest opinion it looked like chicken shit and he shouldn't give up his day job.

Although I wasn't a welder, I had learnt to weld in my apprenticeship and knew what a good weld should look like. Even cutting Karl some slack, his welding was still very poor. Karl just shrugged his shoulders but agreed with me. I had a go at it myself and, after messing about with the settings on the arc welder, started producing some decent-looking welds. The only bit of advice I could give Karl was to practise on some scrap metal first and get his technique right before starting on the window frames.

As I returned to the mast, I heard the loft door slam and a voice shout out, "Karl, you numpty, your weekend starts here."

Karl introduced me to 'Bowmer', saying, "Hey, Lynn. I would like you to meet my very best friend."

Bowmer was over six-foot tall and built like a very fit rugby player. He was wearing what looked like a very expensive suit; I thought he had just come from court or a funeral.

For the next half an hour, I listened to Karl and Bowmer hurling insults and abuse and generally being very obnoxious to each other. It was like being in a room with a pair of unruly two-year-olds throwing a tantrum over a favourite toy. If this was Karl's definition of best mate, it was a world apart from mine. I just didn't get it.

As I carried on working on the mast, I overheard Bowmer asking Karl what I was doing. Karl replied, "He's working on the mast I messed up earlier."

Bowmer laughed, saying, "That's standard for you. Deadloss is the name, bodging is your game."

Bowmer nearly wet himself with laughter when Karl told him he had promised to finish the mast and have it back up and in the customer's yacht the following afternoon.

"Typical of you, Deadloss. You have no chance."

From what I had learnt about Karl, 'Deadloss' was very apt. Karl was pretty unreliable. The sad part was he was a particularly good sailmaker but just useless at running a business.

Bowmer walked over to me and watched with interest as I worked on the mast.

"How come you know how to do all this tricky metalwork stuff?" he asked.

"It's easy, Bowmer," I said. "I'm a toolmaker by trade; I work with metal every day. If somebody has made something, I can usually remake it or fix it."

"What do you do for a living?" I asked him.

"I sit in an office all day," he replied.

That explains the suit, I thought.

"Well, I can see you're doing a really nice job on this mast—and thanks for helping Deadloss. He needs all the help he can get."

"It's no problem. It's just hard to concentrate with Karl trying to weld over there," I replied.

Bowmer wandered over to see what Deadloss was doing and started laughing at Karl's welding.

"That's the worst bit of welding I've ever seen in my life," he said. "I could do better."

Over the next few minutes, the two of them traded more insults, until finally Karl bit and shouted, "You bloody try it, Mister 'I-sit-behind-a-desk-all-day' pen pusher."

Bowmer started trying to weld. He seemed to struggle while wearing the welding helmet. He kept lifting it up and complaining he couldn't see properly. Suddenly, he stopped what he was doing and left the sail loft, only to return wearing a pair of sunglasses. Things were getting serious now; off came his suit jacket, and he began to weld. He called me over after a while to have a look at the welds, and I thought they looked pretty good.

"Bowmer, I think you are in the wrong trade. Welding is your calling," I said.

"You're right, Lynn," he said, laughing.

Karl agreed that his welds were good and was happy to let Bowmer carry on doing all the welding.

I heard Karl's Land Rover start up; he had disappeared for a while. Half an hour later, he came back carrying two slabs of warm beer. By this time, Bowmer had fully welded the first window frame, and it looked good.

Karl gave me a beer and I carried on with the mast. Bowmer and Karl were so engrossed in what they were doing that the slagging each other off stopped for a short while. They had a bit of an assembly line going. Karl would cut the steel and lay it out on the floor; Bowmer would tack and finish welding the windows.

After a few beers, Bowmer asked Karl, "How are you going to fit the steel guards to the window frame?"

Karl said, "I've hired a Hilti gun with extra powerful cartridges that can punch nails through steel. I'll go and get it from my office."

When Karl returned with the Hilti gun, I wandered over to have a look. This was a serious piece of kit.

Bowmer's eyes lit up when he saw the gun, and straight away, I could see he was desperate to play with it, getting really excited—just like I was when, as a kid, I was in a sweet shop for the first time.

Karl demonstrated just how powerful the Hilti gun was. He placed two pieces of scrap metal on the floor, both five millimetres thick, and fired a nail straight through both. Karl used the gun to nail in place the one finished welded frame.

Bowmer clearly needed to get out more; he was mesmerised by the gun and couldn't wait to play with it.

Bowmer's office background didn't give me any confidence in him playing with a Hilti gun. To make matters worse, he had already worked out how to release the safety guard. It went downhill from there rapidly.

Bowmer fired a nail across the loft. He had worked out that if he pushed the safety guard back and pulled the trigger, he could fire nails like bullets. He was ecstatic and shouted, "Look at this!" with a big grin on his face.

He fired another nail across the loft, sending Karl running for cover. The nail flew down the length of the sail loft and embedded itself in the far wall. I laughed and shook my head.

I tried to regain my composure and get back to work on the mast. I did find this hard, as Bowmer thought he was John Wayne, firing nails all around the loft.

"It's like working in Beirut in here!" I said, laughing. "Bowmer, you must have had a stressful week if this is how you let off steam."

"Lynn, I wonder if I can get one of these on the office stationery order," he said. "This is a great stress reliever."

After working late into the night, I finally got the mast finished, despite the dangerous working conditions. Karl was incredibly happy with the job and asked if I could give him a hand later that day to get the mast back in the yacht.

I happily agreed. As I left the sail loft, I could hear Karl shouting at Bowmer to put the gun down. I wondered if they would still be alive in the morning, especially if they kept drinking beer until there was none left.

Bowmer and Karl were complete opposites, which is why I think they got on so well. They were known for staying up all night drinking beer in the loft and talking all sorts of nonsense.

The next morning, Karl picked me up. I say morning—it was twelve o'clock by the time he arrived. Deadloss once more. We picked up the mast, carried it to the yacht and fitted it without any problems. It looked good, and the customer was delighted with Karl's efforts to get the mast built in double-quick time—if only he knew the full story. Back in the sail loft, I spent the rest of the day helping Karl finish the last of the welding and fitting the steel window frames and doors.

Karl was happy; his kettle was now safe from the kettle thieves.

"Fancy a pint?" he said.

As we walked to the yacht club, I asked Karl, "Where's Bowmer? You didn't kill him last night, did you?"

Karl just shrugged.

When we were standing by the bar with our first pint in hand, Bowmer walked in, still wearing his sunglasses.

"You okay, Bowmer?" I asked. "Your face is bright red—and why are you wearing your sunglasses in here? It's dark."

"I can't see," he said. "My eyes feel as if they have sand in them."

"What?"

The sunglasses then came off, revealing two white rings around his very red and sore looking eyes.

"Bowmer, you have arc eye, you idiot."

"Arc eye?"

"You got it from the welding. It's like sunburn."

"What, from not wearing the welding mask?"

"Yes, but don't worry—it will pass in two to three days. You'll just look like a giant panda for a while."

Karl said, "Bowmer, you should give up welding and stick to your desk job."

I could see Bowmer was annoyed. "Karl, once again, you've screwed my life up. I've got a one-to-one with my big boss on Monday, and I'll look like a giant panda. How was I supposed to know about arc eye, sitting behind my desk all day? You could have said something to warn me.

"Also, Karl, you owe me a new suit. I've trashed mine welding your bloody windows."

I was crying with laughter.

I spent the rest of the evening listening to these so-called best mates arguing, which was pretty funny. I knew they were the best of friends, but anybody else listening to them wouldn't have known it. They were acting like they hated each other.

The three of us soon became the best of friends. Most weekends, we met in the local pub for a few pints and attempted to chat up the local girls. Needless to say, we were never successful. This routine often got boring; Barry wasn't known for its nightlife or vibrant party scene.

There would often come a point in the evening when I would hear Bowmer or Karl say, "It's a lovely night for a sail.

Lynn, feel that breeze. Look—the sea is flat; you can see the moon and the stars. Let's go sailing."

Whenever we went sailing on a weekend, our aim was to get to Ilfracombe. We never made it. A few times I awoke as the sun rose over the horizon with my hand still on the tiller and Karl sitting on the opposite side of the cockpit with his hand on the tiller too. The gentle motion of the yacht, the salt air and warm breeze was fatal for sending us to sleep, leaving *Seefalke* to drift around in the middle of the Bristol Channel. This was poor seamanship, but I had some great nights. Some of my fondest memories are of waking up in the cockpit, looking forward to another glorious day sailing around the channel.

One weekend, I had promised to do some overtime, and to ensure I didn't get tangled up with Bowmer and Karl, I went to the Marine for a change. I'd narrowly escaped the night before, having seen them in the yacht club. I thought I'd be pushing my luck to go there two nights running. I instinctively knew that once the two of them got a few pints down, all I would get would be: "It's a lovely evening to go sailing, Lynn."

And I would be dull enough to go.

I walked into the pub only to find Bowmer at the bar, which was a surprise. The Marine wasn't his cup of tea; it was a rough dockworkers' pub.

"What are you doing in here, Bowmer?" I asked him. "You never drink in here; you always drink in the yacht club."

"What brings you up here, Lynn?"

"Me?"

"Yes."

"I'm in here trying to avoid you!"

"I know the feeling. I'm trying to avoid Karl. He's taking Liz to the yacht club for a meal, trying to make amends for last night."

"How is she? I haven't seen her in the yacht club for a while."

"Liz is fine, apart from being married to Karl."

"So, what happened last night?"

"I'll tell you once I've got you a pint."

Taking our pints to a table, Bowmer said, "You left the yacht club early last night?"

"Yes, I had work this morning, and wanted to have an early night."

"Wise move."

"Why was that?"

"Yes, well, err... I was hoping you were going for a sail last night, so I stopped by the sail loft to see what time the race started. Deadloss said the tides were all wrong, so I helped him with a sail for a few hours before going to the yacht club for a quiet pint."

"I hope you and Deadloss were finishing off my jib last night," I said.

"He hasn't even started it. His nickname isn't Deadloss for nothing."

"You're right there."

"So, you had a quiet night after I left?"

"Well, err, not quite."

I liked Bowmer's "not quite". It was one of his hallmarks.

"Is this why you're up here drinking, trying to avoid Liz?" I asked.

"Yes."

I knew from his sheepish look, I was going to get a story, a long story.

"Hang on, Bowmer, I'll get another round in before you start."

Returning from the bar, Bowmer started his story.

"Well, Lynn, after you left the club, Karl dragged me up here for a few more beers. Anyway, when we got here, it was dead, so we decided to go clubbing, but that was crap too. Karl then suggested that we go back to his house and get a fire going. It sounded like a good idea, even though it was quite late.

"When we got back to Karl's, I was surprised to see Liz still up. She'd been waiting for Karl to get in. As soon as she saw me, she gave Karl the 'I don't want Bowmer around' look. It's a look I'm getting used to seeing off Liz."

"You have that effect on most women, Bowmer."

"Ha. Funny. Anyway, Liz told Karl to get rid of me and to follow her up to bed. You know what Karl is like?"

"Yes?"

"Karl gave the 'Err, right, Liz. I'll be up in a minute, once Bowmer leaves and I've locked up.'"

"So, what happened?"

"Well, as soon as Liz left, Karl got a fire going and opened a bottle of whisky. We had a wee dram; we kept quiet, just chatting, threw some wood on the fire, had another wee dram. After an hour, the guitar came out. We threw more wood on the fire, had another wee dram and sang some sea shanties and put some more wood on the fire."

"Sounds like a good night to me," I said.

"It was. Anyway, I crashed out on the couch at about five a.m., by which time the room was roasting. The embers were still bright red, and I was trashed."

"Sounds about right for you and Karl," I said.

"It was. Err, until about seven-thirty this morning."

"Why? What happened?"

"Well, there was a loud banging on the front door. Liz got up and opened the door, and I could hear their next-door neighbour saying something, and Liz replying with, 'Oh no! Oh no!' I then heard Liz racing up the stairs before she started screaming and shouting at Karl, at which point, he came stumbling down the stairs. Liz then started laying into me. After getting me up, she marched the pair of us next door.

"'What are we doing in here?' I asked, still feeling very drunk.

"I was rubbing my eyes because at first nothing really made any sense. The only thing that did register was the acrid smell of burnt paper. It all looked quite normal at first. Well, apart from the paint on the wall being a bit black and the wallpaper hanging off. As my eyes got used to the light and I concentrated a bit more, I realised that the whole wall was black and burnt and probably shouldn't be. I remembered how big and hot the fire was that we'd had. It then clicked—it must have got hot enough to burn the wallpaper and paint off next door's wall. I knew we had overstepped the mark last night.

"Liz kept saying, 'Oh my God, oh my God. We're so sorry, we'll pay for the room to be repaired.'

"I found it hard not to laugh. I quickly made my escape before Liz kicked off again and blamed me for last night's fire."

Bowmer and I had a good laugh while he was telling his story. It was just typical of these so-called best mates; all the pair of them wanted to do was drink beer around an open fire and sing sea shanties, and most of all, go sailing. There's no harm in them, yet every time they'd get together, something would always go tits-up and pear-shaped. I could see then why they were such close friends.

"That sounds like a typical evening for the two of you," I said. "So, have you seen Karl today?"

"Yes. He was in the sail loft, working on a new mast that he'd been expecting to turn up this morning."

"What's the story, Bowmer?"

"Well, a young couple sailed into Barry last week and rafted up alongside another yacht for the night."

"So, what went wrong to get Karl involved?"

"Remember we had that big storm a week ago?"

"Yes?"

"Well, the two yachts got tangled up, and their yacht ended up with one of its spreaders pushed right through the mast, destroying it."

"New mast then. Sounds expensive?"

"It will be with Deadloss working on it."

"Well, he can't have messed it up yet. He hasn't asked for my help."

"He will," said Bowmer. "Mike, the owner of the yacht, would like to take his fiancée sailing tomorrow, and Deadloss had promised to finish the job by this evening."

"And has he?"

"No."

"That's a shame; the forecast is really good for tomorrow, apart from the light winds," I said.

I knew what would be coming next.

"Come on, Lynn, let's go for a sail. It's a great evening for a sail. There's nothing happening in this pub, and I'm not up for clubbing tonight."

"Sorry, Bowmer, I can't," I said. "I've promised to do some overtime tomorrow."

"Let's have one more pint and talk about it."

As Bowmer went to the bar, Karl walked in, followed by a couple of other people.

"Hi, Karl," I said. "What are you doing here?"

"I'm trying to avoid Bowmer after last night," he replied.

"Tough luck. Bowmer's at the bar," I said, laughing. "He told me you were going to take Liz to the yacht club for a meal. Apparently, you need to make amends after last night's fun and games?"

"Err, I will later. It's still early."

Karl then introduced me to Mike and his fiancée, who had followed him in.

I asked Karl if he'd finished Mike's mast.

"No," was the reply, followed by, "And, err, I can't finish it tomorrow. I need to order more fittings."

"That's a shame," I said. "It would be a nice day for a sail."

I got one of those rolling-eyes looks from Mike and his fiancée.

"What's your plan for tonight, Lynn?" said Karl.

"Well, Bowmer wants to go out for a sail after we finish the next pint. I can't see it happening; there's no wind, and I have work in the morning."

After we'd all had a few more rounds, there was no way I was going to drive to work the next morning, So I agreed with Bowmer to take *Seefalke* for a sail, with the caveat being there must be some wind in the harbour. Bowmer took this as a yes and started to wind Karl up, asking him over and over to come out sailing. Mike and his girlfriend listened to them in complete disbelief.

Karl kept on saying, "Err, no, I've promised Liz I'll be home early in order to take her out."

Bowmer kept on at Karl. "You can't finish Mike's mast in the morning, Deadloss; you might as well come sailing with us."

Finally, after a few more beers, Karl cracked.

"Come on then! Let's go for a sail," I said.

We all got up to leave the pub. Mike and his fiancée asked if they could come as well. I think they knew it would be the only sail for them that week, with Deadloss still working on their mast.

"No problem," I said. "Let's go!"

We walked down to the harbour. It was warm and there was a bright full moon, but no wind. Climbing into the dinghy, Karl rowed me and Mike's fiancée out to *Seefalke* and then went back for Mike and Bowmer.

With us all sitting in the cockpit, I said, "We have no chance of going sailing tonight; there's no wind."

Reluctantly, they all agreed: no wind, no sailing.

Karl said, "Lynn, go and put the kettle on and make us all a cup of coffee, and while you're below, can you pass your guitar out at the same time?"

While I was sitting below deck, waiting for a full kettle of water to boil, Karl was playing the guitar and singing "The Shoals of Herring" followed by "Leaving of Liverpool". To my surprise, Karl was playing and singing well; it was lovely to listen to.

Suddenly *Seefalke* rocked.

That's strange, I thought, jumping up and sticking my head out of the main hatch. I could see why the yacht was rocking; *Seefalke* was at the harbour entrance. Looking into the cockpit, Karl was still playing the guitar and singing, with his foot on the tiller. Bowmer, Karl's partner in crime, was sitting by the mast, sheeting in the now flying genoa.

"What are you two halfwits doing?" I said.

All I got out of the pair of them was an "err..." and a laugh.

Great, I thought. *There's no way back to the mooring now.* There wasn't enough wind to sail against the outgoing tide. Oh well, we were out for another night of drifting around the Bristol Channel.

Back below, I carried on making the coffee. While listening to the mainsail going up, I put a large measure of brandy in each mug before passing them around.

It turned out to be a lovely night. A nice breeze filled in, and *Seefalke* made good speed through the flat water. Above us was a beautiful full moon, and millions of stars shone brightly in the clear sky; the scene was magical. But even this caused Bowmer and Karl to argue about how many stars were up there. I was used to these two clowns going at each other like fed-up teenagers, but for Mike and his fiancée, this was a whole new experience. They both looked overwhelmed.

After an hour, I went below and put the kettle on for another round of coffee and brandy. Feeling hungry, I started to grill some cheese on toast. The smell of grilled cheese brought Mike's fiancée into the galley. We started to chat. She said she was in college studying social behaviour and psychology.

I started to laugh and said, "Well, you don't have to go far to study psychology around here."

We heard Bowmer and Karl kicking off again.

"Are they always like this?" Mike's fiancée asked.

"No, of course not—this is quiet for them. It's all part of their friendship," I said, laughing. "How did you end up in Barry with Karl working on your yacht?" I asked.

"We sailed from Penarth, planning to go around the Bristol Channel on a pre-wedding honeymoon," she said. "The weather forecast was not good, so we decided to stop in Barry for a few days. And basically, our mast got so badly damaged in the storm it had to be replaced. So, we were very unlucky losing the mast, and just to top it all, we had the misfortune of meeting Karl."

"Karl's got a good heart, but he's not very organised work-wise," I said.

"We have found that out."

"That's bad news about your mast. When are you two getting married?"

"The end of next month."

"That's good news. Are you excited?"

"Yes, it's all planned and paid for."

Bowmer came below for some cheese on toast, a chat and the warm.

Feeling tired, I decided to try and get some sleep, leaving the two halfwits in charge. I got into my sleeping bag and crawled into the quarter berth. I could clearly see and hear Mike's fiancée trying to get to know Bowmer. I think she was trying out her psychology knowledge on him. *Good luck*, I thought. Knowing Bowmer as I did, this conversation had the potential to go pear-shaped very quickly.

She started by asking him what he did for a living.

"I work in customer services, in charge of the whole department. So, I sit in an office behind a desk all day."

Well, this was met by a long, stunned silence. The poor girl could not get her head around this fact; I think she'd expected him to say he did something in the marine industry, like Karl.

After a while, I heard her slowly and quietly repeat "customer services manager".

Slowly, still shocked, she started talking again. "You deal with people every day?"

"Yes, loads. And face to face."

I saw her slowly mouth the words "face to face", not quite believing it. She composed herself, and said, "You must be good at what you do, being a customer services manager at such a young age?"

"I am," Bowmer said, with a big smile on his face.

Very modest, I thought

"So why are you so passionate about sailing?"

"Well, it gets me out of the office. You meet great people; I've made new friends from all over the world, all through sailing. Additionally, I've had some amazing experiences and some exhilarating sails that I will remember for the rest of my life, like tonight. You'll remember this sail, won't you?"

"So, are you saying that you would rather be out sailing than spending time with a girlfriend on a Saturday night?"

"Of course. As I said, some of the experiences I've had through sailing have been utterly amazing and many of them one-offs that I will never forget. It's not a fair comparison."

"Right, so sailing is better than having sex?"

"Well, let's put it like this—and maybe I haven't met the right girl?—but I can't say in years to come I will remember the sex I have had or even who it was with. What I do know is some of the sails I have had will stay with me forever. Sailing and racing yachts with some of your best friends in marginal conditions, pushing yachts to their limits, gives me an incredible buzz; it's both exhilarating and frightening, all at the same time. For me, these are incredible, special moments, and yes, in terms of relationships there has been nothing that compares to it yet."

"Right. So you really are saying that sailing is better than sex?"

"Err... I guess so," said Bowmer.

"Mike's just like you."

"What?" Bowmer said, looking a bit confused.

"He's just like you; he would rather go off sailing with his mates than shag me."

I could see she was getting herself really worked up.

I knew Bowmer had no idea where this conversation was going, but somehow, he had innocently stumbled and scored a direct hit on an existing problem in Mike and his fiancée's relationship. Which, for once, he had not intended and wasn't his fault. I knew I would have to deal with it.

Bowmer looked even more confused when she stormed off, back into the cockpit, where I could hear her laying into Mike.

"You're just like him down there, aren't you?"

"What?"

Poor Mike was very confused; he had no knowledge of the conversation that had just taken place down below.

"You would rather go sailing with your mates than stay in with me, wouldn't you?"

Karl came below, pretty damn quick.

"Bloody hell, Bowmer!" he said, startled. "What did you say to upset Mike's fiancée?"

"Nothing at all," said Bowmer.

"You must have said something. She's giving Mike some right shit out there."

From the quarter berth, I told Karl that Bowmer had told Mike's fiancée that sailing was better than sex.

"Bloody hell, Bowmer. Why did you have to tell her that?"

"Well, she started the conversation, and I wasn't going to lie, was I?"

I could not help but laugh.

Karl started kicking off at Bowmer, who for once hadn't done anything wrong. There was no chance of me getting any sleep with all this noise going on. Mike's fiancée came back below and looked Karl in the eye.

"You should be at home with Liz!" she said.

Well, that shut Karl up for a bit. I couldn't stop laughing— you couldn't write a book about it; this was turning into a situation from a comedy.

I stopped laughing when Mike's fiancée said, "I want to get off the yacht now!"

"What?"

I knew we were in the middle of the Bristol Channel, but where the closest point to go safely ashore was, I didn't have a clue. Mike's fiancée followed me up on deck. I tried to persuade her it would be better for her to stay on board and come back to Barry with us all.

"No, I want off, now," she said in a voice I could not argue with.

Digging a chart out and taking a fix, I found we were just off Foreland Point, heading into Lynmouth, which is a beautiful part of the North Devon coast, but not an easy place to get back to South Wales from on a Sunday.

"We can sail into the bay at Lynmouth," I said, pointing it out to her on the chart. "It should be light in an hour; we can drop you ashore there."

She happily agreed.

Anchoring in the bay, as the sun rose, we blew the dinghy up and Bowmer volunteered to row Mike's fiancée to the beach. Bowmer tried his best to explain that Lynmouth was in the middle of Exmoor and the chances of getting transport on a Sunday were pretty slim. More than likely, she would have to get a taxi to Barnstaple and then make several train connections to get back to Barry. The journey was certainly going to be both expensive and long. Bowmer even apologised and tried to backtrack on their conversation from earlier that morning. Mike's fiancée was having none of it—he'd made such a lasting impression on her already. To make a bad situation worse, Mike had decided to stay on board and return to Barry with us.

With Mike's ex-fiancée safely ashore, I cooked bacon and egg sandwiches for breakfast. It had been a long night. Before we had a chance to start our return trip back to Barry, the wind disappeared very quickly, and by midday, we were still anchored in Lynmouth Bay without a breath of wind. All we could do was enjoy the spectacular view. Bowmer and Mike were starting to panic about getting back to Barry and work in the morning. Looking out to sea, Bowmer could see a slight breeze coming across the water about two hundred yards away, but it didn't seem to be reaching us.

Desperate to get us out into the wind, Bowmer climbed back into the dinghy, tied a rope to the bow and tried to tow *Seefalke* out of the bay. Karl and I got the anchor up. For the next hour, we all sat on deck giving Bowmer more abuse.

"Come on, you old fart—only another mile to go! We can see wind on the water."

We were moving, but it was very, very slow going.

"Look, boys, it's not funny," Bowmer said. "I have important meetings to attend tomorrow."

Bowmer gave up rowing when we saw another yacht motor into the bay and drop anchor. He went over to enquire what their plans were and to see if there was any possibility of a lift. The yacht was a brand-new, thirty-eight-foot-long Westerly. There were two guys on board, who planned to have lunch before heading back to Swansea later that afternoon. They agreed to give Bowmer and Mike a lift once they had finished eating. We dropped anchor again and waited until the Swansea guys were ready to leave. About an hour later, they motored alongside, and the two rats jumped ship. Karl and I watched them motor out of the bay, heading towards Swansea.

Not too long after, the wind picked up, and Karl and I had a great sail back to Barry. As we sailed into the entrance of Barry Harbour, I could hear someone shouting in the distance.

"Roachy, you bastard, I hate you!"

I looked up to see where the shouting was coming from and saw Bowmer on the pier head. Karl and I laughed and waved. After we put *Seefalke* back on her mooring, we joined Bowmer in the yacht club.

I asked Bowmer how his trip went on the brand-new Westerly yacht. Over a couple of pints, Bowmer told us about his trip back.

"The guys on the yacht were useless," he said. "They did not have a clue about sailing.

"The yacht skipper tried to motor over the top of the Scarweather Sandbank at half tide. When I pointed out to them that they couldn't sail straight back to Swansea as there wouldn't be enough water on top of the sandbank and the trip would end in tears, the owner of the yacht said, 'What sandbank? It wasn't there on the way over to Lynmouth. Where did it come from?'

"After I pointed out the sandbank on the chart, I had to explain to him it was high water then. In the end, I took the helm and sailed the yacht back to Swansea to ensure the safety of all of us.

"I still hate you, Roachy."

"Why now, Bowmer?"

"Well, to top my weekend off, once we got back to Swansea, Mike and I legged it to the train station. We had a ten-minute wait for the Cardiff train. I then had a short wait in Cardiff for the Barry Island train, which was on time, and twenty minutes later, I was walking back to my car. I was convinced that I had smoked you, so you can just imagine my face when I saw you two clowns coming back into the harbour just as I was getting to my car. I hate the pair of you."

"Bowmer, you had no faith," I said. "We said the wind would fill in and that it was just a matter of waiting; it's not my fault you got all stressed and jumped ship the minute you could."

We had to laugh.

As Bowmer was leaving the club, I said, "Bowmer, you've surpassed yourself this weekend."

"Why is that?"

"Well, you nearly burned down a row of Grade Two listed houses, wound Liz up, you trashed Mike's relationship in one evening, and you nearly ended up on top of the Scarweather Sandbank."

"Yes—put like that, I've had a top weekend," Bowmer said, smiling. "It's the story of my life, Lynn."

"One day they'll make a film about our escapades, and no one will believe it," I said.

I had enjoyed every minute in Bowmer's company, and he was right: even if Mike's ex-fiancée didn't remember that night's sail, we definitely would.

A year later, Mike walked into Barry Yacht Club with another woman on his arm. He was looking for Bowmer.

"When you see Bowmer," he said, "please say thank you to him."

"For what?"

"I had a lot of issues with my relationship last year. He saved me a lot of money and hassle, and now I've found my soulmate. He did me a big favour. So please, I want to thank all of you, for that sail. I will remember that night for the rest of my life."

So will we, I thought.

Chapter 5
Dreams

Another friend of mine from Barry Yacht Club was John Hart, who, amongst a long list of other accolades, was a senior Royal Yachting Association (RYA) Examiner and Instructor. John was running a Yachtmaster Ocean Theory Course, which was aimed at sailors wanting to undertake long-distance trips, cross oceans or work as skippers in the superyacht industry. The course focused on celestial navigation: learning how to use a sextant to fix your position by measuring angles of the sun, moon and stars—the same astronavigation techniques that Captain Cook used nearly three hundred years ago. The course also covered preparing a vessel for a long-distance trip and learning about long-term weather predictions, including hurricane avoidance.

When John wasn't teaching or examining, he also delivered superyachts between the Med and the Caribbean, sometimes with his wife Maggs. John had recently delivered a hundred-and-twenty-foot-long yacht from the Med to English Harbour in Antigua. As part of the yacht club's winter programme, he had been asked to present a slideshow of his trip. On cold, wet winter evenings, talks like this were a welcome addition to the club's calendar, and this particular night was no exception. John's talk started with some photos of the yacht, which—by Barry standards—was colossal. In one photo, Maggs was standing with her back to the mast, with John saying, "You can see the width of the mast; it's wider than two Maggs."

At this point, a voice from the back of the yacht club said, "If Maggs stood sideways on, it would only be as wide as one Maggs."

Everyone in the yacht club burst out laughing. Maggs was a well-endowed lady.

I was very envious of John's photos from the Caribbean. He showed pictures of beautiful white sandy beaches and the glistening turquoise-blue sea, and everybody was walking around in T-shirts and shorts.

Listening to John's talk reminded me of a time when I'd been listening to the radio broadcasting live cricket from Antigua. I wondered again what it would be like to be sat in Antigua with the sun on my back, watching Brian Lara hit three hundred and seventy-five runs in the St John's recreation ground.

It didn't take long to convince myself that this was the life for me. Sun, sand and sea and being able to wear shorts and a T-shirt every day was a no brainer. It would be better than living in Ray Harris's boatyard.

If I could get a few things to fall into place, I could go and find that Caribbean sun.

I started to hatch my master plan of escaping Wales. Planning my trip was going to take some time, and so I set a goal of leaving in August the following year. The first goal I ticked off was successfully completing my astronavigation course. With my plan starting to come together and my dream becoming a reality, I now had plenty to occupy my time over the winter months.

My next task was to sort out a self-steering mechanism for the yacht, as it would be impossible to steer the yacht on my own for 24 hours each day. Self-steering was first used on model yachts before World War I. In 1950, the father of single-handed sailing, Lieutenant Colonel "Blondie" Hasler, developed the first practical self-steering gear, taking his idea from the model yachts. The problem I had was they were really expensive. The most popular system at the time was the Aries self-steering. I had been looking to buy a second hand one, but with no luck; they were well sought after and expensive.

Barry Yacht Club arranged a coach trip to the London Boat Show, and I booked myself a seat. I wanted to have a good look at all the self-steering systems to see if I could copy one at work. One system was made from stainless steel tubing, which was easy for me to copy. I had a chat with the rep and asked if their system would steer a forty-foot classic wooden yacht. He told me it would without any problem. I took a brochure and measurements, to see if it would fit *Seefalke*.

Before I left the show, I picked up a list of things that were vital to my trip, including almanacs and—as they were becoming affordable to the man in the street—my first GPS, which cost me two hundred pounds; it was on special offer at the show.

The self-steering system retailed for one thousand five hundred pounds, which was well out of my league. I knew then the only way for me to get a self-steering system to work on the yacht was to make one myself.

In work, there was stainless steel tubing, pipe-bending machines, plus lathes and milling machines, and I had a very good tig welder working with me. I spent hours each day throughout the winter slowly building the self-steering gear. I even cut all the gears required to make the mechanics work.

Once the steering system was bolted on the back of the yacht and all the fittings for the control lines were in place, I felt it was all coming together. Another big result.

As the weather started to warm up, I put *Seefalke* back on her mooring. At one evening race, Karl and Spud suggested I should have a small no.3 genoa, one that would fit between the mast and the forestay, then put two new inner genoa tracks in close to the mast. It would give me a better sailing performance to windward and make the yacht self-tacking. I wouldn't have to play around with the sheeting lines on each tack, which would be very handy for me if I wanted to sail into a small harbour or up a river. I made the inner genoa tracks as Karl suggested and helped Deadloss to make the no.3 sail I had ordered—it was the only way I was going to get it made.

Overall, the new sails and sail set-up were real winners, but the self-steering—who I had named George—was only working to a point. It wasn't reacting quickly enough, and consequently, the yacht was wandering too far off course before trying to correct itself. This was frustrating, as I couldn't work out what was causing this to happen. I decided to leave it and worry about it later.

Another piece fell into place: John Hart had just come back from another delivery to the Caribbean, and as luck would have it, he gave me all the charts he used on the trip, saving me a ton of money. All I had to do was rub out the pencil marks.

My goal was to sail across the Atlantic single-handed. To make this happen, I had to do a lot of planning. There were so many small details to work through, like getting all my inoculations to be able to travel in my new world. This was particularly important for the Caribbean and South America, where I would need a vaccination against Yellow Fever.

Another important job was to get my teeth checked. My NHS dentist was really good; once I told him what I was planning to do, he X-rayed my teeth, replaced several old fillings and gave my mouth a general spruce-up.

As I walked out of the dentist's, I bumped into Steve, the doctor from my diving club, who was taking a stroll in his lunch break. Steve asked when I was planning to leave, and did I have a decent first aid kit? I told him I had a homemade one. Steve asked if I had any drugs that would provide pain relief if I suffered a serious accident. I told him I didn't.

Steve said, "Right, follow me."

We walked back to his surgery, and after a quick chat in his office to confirm that I didn't have any allergies, he wrote out a handful of prescriptions.

"I have travelled a bit," he told me. "So I've given you the drugs I would take with me if I was brave enough to attempt your adventure."

Steve's last words to me were, "I haven't given you any drugs strong enough to knock you out, I hope."

With a fistful of prescriptions, I walked into the nearest chemist. The pharmacist straight away asked what I was planning to do. He was a bit surprised when I told him I was going to sail across the Atlantic on my own.

"Okay, that's fine; these drugs make sense now. It's going to take a while to get them all together—can you come back in half an hour?"

Bumping into Steve had been a real stroke of luck. When I came back, I was met by the pharmacist with a carrier bag full of prescription drugs.

"I've doubled the quantities of some of the drugs," he said. "Just to be on the safe side. Good luck on your trip, and I hope you never need to use any of these."

As he handed me the carrier bag, I asked, "How much do I owe you?"

"Nothing—you can have them for free. The government can afford it. One more thing, I think you should have one of these in your first aid kit."

The pharmacist handed me a small kit for teeth; I bought it and thanked him for all his advice. The last thing I needed was toothache, mid-Atlantic.

I thanked him again, saying I'd had a very lucky day.

I had been reading the transatlantic sailing guides and magazine articles on how to sail across the Atlantic. Basically, they all said the same thing:

Put enough food on board for a year's sailing.

Take the labels off the cans, number and varnish them.

I didn't know any different, so I did just that.

Aldi was expanding their supermarket network in the UK and had chosen to open a store in Bridgend. Their own brands were so cheap compared to Tesco and Sainsbury's. A tin of baked beans cost just nine pence. For the previous few weeks, I had been sampling their tin cans, trying to find out which ones I liked the most.

On my last big shop at the end of July, I bought:

24 tins of chicken curry

24 tins of beef curry

24 tins of chilli con carne

24 tins of baked beans

2 1kg tins of coffee

2 1kg tins of butter

2 1kg tins of cheese

Rice and pasta by the kilo.

I even bought a whole chicken in a tin. Last on my list was all the ingredients and equipment to make bread.

Fresh food I would buy just before I left.

One week on, and *Seefalke* was back in Ray Harris's yard. There were a few last-minute jobs to be done. One of them was to paint the yacht's underside. I managed to get hold of some commercial-grade antifoul from a friend of mine;

this was banned for use on domestic yachts. Antifoul is an inhibitor that prevents growth beneath the waterline and helps to protect against things like the teredo worm, which loves to make its home in wooden hulls. A lot of old antifouls had some pretty poisonous additives in them, like arsenic, etc. For this reason, new legislation banned the use of these paints for domestic and pleasure use.

A lot of yachts sitting in marinas don't get a lot of use, and so commercial-grade antifoul should not be used on them, as it was found to cause a build-up of toxins in marinas, which adversely impacts marine life and the environment. Antifoul sold for domestic use was widely considered to be less effective since the additives had been banned. *Seefalke* would be spending most of her life on the open water, and therefore, I thought it would be okay for me to use commercial-grade. Knowing that I would be gone for some time, I made sure I put plenty of coats on before I left Wales.

My next job was to find someone to go up the mast for me or alternatively, find someone to pull me up. I needed to fit a second block at the top of the mast to enable me to run a spare mainsail halyard in case the other failed. As I was walking around looking for Steve, my father turned up at the boatyard and agreed to go up the mast for me.

I strapped my father into my climbing harness and attached the mainsail halyard to it. I handed him a small tool kit and the spare block and halyard. Once he was ready and happy, I slowly pulled him up the mast using the mainsail winch.

The halyard I used to pull him up the mast started out as rope, as it was easy to handle, and then changed to wire after twenty feet. Once my father was fifteen feet off the deck, the rope part of the halyard ended and the wire part started to wrap itself around the winch, which was fine—or so I thought.

When my father was at the top of the mast, I wrapped the halyard around the two mast winches in a figure of eight. Feeling confident he was safe, I walked to the bow, holding the halyard in one hand. My father started to work on the mast. I asked him what the view was like. Before he had time to answer, he screamed and started to fall. Luckily for him and me, he had his legs and one arm wrapped around the mast, which he managed to grab hold of quickly. Thankfully, he only dropped three feet.

Looking back at the mast, I could see I had let the halyard in my hand go slack, allowing the wire to straighten and unwrap itself off the winches. Had he not held on, my father's next stop would have been the deck. Once I knew he was safe, I quickly moved back to the mast, pulled in the slack from around the winch and pulled my protesting father back to the top of the mast to finish the job. I learned some new swear words that morning.

When he left me, he got quite emotional. *Why?*

I didn't know it then, but this was the last time we would be together before he died.

With only a few days to go, I wanted to launch *Seefalke* for the final time. My grandmother, who was well into her eighties, wanted to come to Barry and see the yacht before I left. We made it a party day with food, beer, wine and soft drinks, to thank everybody who had helped me finally finish my restoration project. It had taken me over six years, and to mark this momentous occasion, I planned to break a bottle of bubbly on the bow for good luck.

While I was waiting for everybody to turn up, I was chatting to some friends, drinking a beer, when I heard my mother scream. Looking around, I could see my grandmother at the top of the ladder trying to climb aboard *Seefalke*. She was standing on one leg, trying to get the other leg over the guard wires. I had to quickly climb the ladder to support her. With a push and a shove, I managed to get her on deck and sit her down safely in the cockpit.

"I always knew you would go to sea one day," she said.

Bowmer turned up early in the afternoon and said he would not be around for my departure. He was taking part in the Teacher's Whisky Round Britain Race and would be joining the yacht the day I planned to leave. Bowmer wished me luck and told me to have a safe trip.

Just as he was leaving, he said, "Lynn, I bet you twenty quid you don't get past Lundy Island and you'll be back in Barry within the month."

Laughing, I accepted the bet. I thought it was good of Bowmer to make an effort to come and see me.

Finally, all my mates and friends had turned up, and Mum broke the bottle of champagne over the bow. Ray then lowered *Seefalke* into the water, with my grandmother sitting in the cockpit, waving to the crowd. Gran was complaining that the launch was too sedate; she'd been expecting *Seefalke* to be launched in the same fashion as a lifeboat. Once *Seefalke* was back on her mooring, I had to get Nan into a small rowing dinghy before we both could re-join the party.

The day before departure, my last job was to visit customs to sort out the necessary paperwork. The customs department was in the dock office, which is a very impressive Victorian building standing in a prominent position overlooking the dock, which it has done since 1898. I walked in and told the customs officer I was planning to sail to the West Indies. He told me that we were part of the EU, and therefore, I didn't need to complete any forms until I left European waters. He did give me some paperwork to show anybody with a vested interest that *Seefalke* had cleared Barry Harbour. Leaving European waters, if all went to plan, would happen in Las Palmas, Gran Canarias.

Walking out of the Dock Office, the only piece of advice the customs officer offered to me was: if I had any plans to sail to North Africa, I would be well advised to stop off in Marseille and buy myself an AK-47.

After leaving the customs house, I decided to walk back to the boatyard via Barry's main street to remind myself why I wanted to leave. It was midday, the sun was out and it was at least seventy degrees. All the older people I saw had big, heavy overcoats on. This was crazy; I was wearing a T-shirt, shorts and flip-flops. It was all wrong, and quite depressing. I couldn't work out why people in their early sixties were acting like eighty-year-olds. Seeing this gave me further conviction that I was doing the right thing; I had no desire to end up like these people in a few years' time.

My very last job was to go into Cardiff to see my grandmother. We chatted for half an hour. When I was about to leave, I was quite upset and started to cry.

"Don't cry," Nan said. "You will see me again. My father will look after you."

Back in Barry, Martin from Reading, one of my crew who was going to help me sail to Ireland, was waiting for me. My other crew member, Justin, was working and would join us in the morning.

Martin and Justin had kindly offered to help me sail the yacht to Cork. They were then going to catch the ferry back to Swansea, leaving me to carry on sailing south, if all went to plan.

After dropping Martin's gear aboard *Seefalke*, it was off to the yacht club for some food and a nice quiet pint in the company of my close mates.

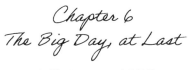

Chapter 6
The Big Day, at Last

15th August 1995

It took a few seconds to realise I was on the yacht, still dressed, all good news. I didn't remember getting back to the yacht the night before, or leaving the yacht club. Looking around, I could see Martin in the opposite bunk and an awful mess in the cabin: rice all over the floor, empty curry cans, plates, pans, bowls, spoons and forks all over the galley and chart table. In fact, the whole yacht was trashed.

Bloody hell.

"Martin, what happened here last night?"

"You cooked curry and rice for everybody."

"Did I?"

"Yes."

"Are you sure? I've only got three plates and three bowls."

"I know, I spent the night washing them. You filled them back up and passed them around again."

"I did? I can't remember."

"By the end of the night, you had the nickname of Jesus."

"You're joking?"

"No, I am not. It was like feeding the five thousand. It was good, though."

"What time did the party end?"

"About three."

"Great, I have had only five hours sleep."

"You had a lot more than that; you had passed out by one o'clock."

"It's no wonder I can't remember anything. Do you want coffee, Martin?"

"No, I'll have a tea, please."

While I waited for the kettle to boil, I thought about how Monday night was always a quiet night in the yacht club— I'd just wanted a pint with the boys. That idea had gone out the window; everybody I knew had turned up to buy me a farewell pint. I think the club gave me a fantastic send-off, despite remembering very little about it.

This was the first day of the rest of my life and the start of a huge adventure, the opportunity to realise my dream of leaving Wales. I was so excited and filled with trepidation, I had no idea where I would end up, and this was a really big day. My only regret was I was starting this adventure with a massive hangover and feeling like shit.

I knew Martin would be up to his old tricks, waiting until his tea got cold before drinking it. If I'd had any sense, I would have just poured cold water over a teabag. I handed Martin his tea, and with cups in hand, we made our way to the cockpit.

Looking around the deck, I said, "Bloody hell, Martin, what happened here? Look at all these bottles."

I was stunned. There were loads of bottles lying all around the yacht, including bottles of spirits, wine and beer, most of which were unopened.

"They're from the party last night," said Martin.

"I thought the party had finished at the yacht club? The last thing I remember was Howard, the Yacht Club Commodore, dancing on the coffee table."

"Lynn, you invited the whole yacht club back aboard for a party. You said the only rule was to bring a bottle."

"So how many came back?"

"Twenty?"

"And I cooked curry and rice for all of them?"

"Yup. You're lucky the yacht didn't sink."

"I can't remember any of that."

By ten o'clock, Martin and I had managed to get things shipshape. We tidied up the mess in the galley and on deck, and we got the sails hanked on, ready to go. The previous day's forecast proved to be spot on for a change: hot and sunny, with light winds from the south. High water was around eleven-thirty. In order to get the full benefit from the six hours of outgoing tide, we planned to leave an hour before high water.

Martin rowed the dinghy back to the yacht club, where, after I dumped all the empty bottles, I took a hot shower, singing "I'm Free" by *The Who*. After that, I felt a bit more human.

I had one more very important job to do. I ran up to the shop and bought one three-litre bottle of Inch's cider, to keep in the bilge until I got to my first port south, hopefully Lisbon.

Justin turned up, looking as fresh as a daisy. He had missed the party. Karl, Spud and Steve, my 'send-off" gang from last night, arrived looking red-eyed and very hungover. Looking at the state of my three friends made me feel a whole lot better. The last person to turn up was my mother. She wanted to say goodbye and wish me good luck. With everybody there, we made our way down the gangway adjacent to the old lifeboat slipway, where the yacht club's launch awaited us.

Karl told my mother to get in, too. She was a bit hesitant; I think Mum expected to wave goodbye to me from the harbour wall. With us all safely on board, we motored out and tied up alongside *Seefalke*, where Karl asked my mum if she wanted to go aboard. Mum was now kccn to see me off properly.

With Mum sitting safely in the cockpit, Karl untied the yacht club's launch and motored to the harbour entrance. Martin hoisted the mainsail; I cast off the stern line and sheeted the mainsail in. As *Seefalke* started to move forward, Justin pulled the bow mooring rope down the side of the yacht then cast it adrift. Once the stern was clear of the mooring, we were away.

I felt the yacht accelerate as the mainsail caught more wind, and we started to make good progress towards the harbour entrance. My new life and adventure had finally begun. When we were clear of the other yachts, and just as I was thinking of putting a tack in to head towards the harbour entrance, I heard my mum say, "Lynn?"

"Yes, Mum?"

"You're heading for the harbour wall?" She started to laugh. "There you are—off around the world, and your mum is still trying to tell you what to do."

We all laughed.

After a quick tack, we sailed out of the harbour. The boys in the club launch started cheering and firing off party-poppers and throwing toilet rolls about as makeshift streamers. Karl and the boys followed us for a mile before coming back alongside to pick up my mother.

After one last kiss, a hug and a wave from Mum, we got her safely back aboard the launch. One last cheer from the boys, and Karl turned the work boat around and headed back to the harbour. I started to cry.

"Don't cry, Lynn," Martin said. "You'll see your mum again."

"I know, but last week, Mum had my dog with her. When she left, my dog jumped up on top of the back seat and stared at me. I know he knows he won't see me again—he's too old. That's why I am crying."

As we sailed down the Bristol Channel, there wasn't a cloud in the sky, the sea was flat and *Seefalke* was sailing along beautifully in the light, southerly breeze. These were perfect conditions to be starting my trip. This was certainly shorts and T-shirt weather, although Justin and Martin didn't follow my lead. Instead, they decided to wear long-sleeve shirts, long trousers, big floppy hats, and factor fifty on every inch of exposed skin. I knew there was no point Martin exposing his skin to the sun; he would just burn, turn pink and then go back to white again. Justin was just as fair-skinned.

By 17:30, Lundy Island was in clear view, but the tide had turned, and with the light breeze, we were going to struggle against it. Progress for the next six hours was going to be slow. Despite this, it was going to be a lovely evening. I had the boys for company and some beers, so it wasn't all bad.

***

Wednesday 16th August

Another hot, sunny day. The wind had died away to nothing overnight, and so we had no option but to drift up and down with the tide, looking at Lundy. Oh, what fun it is, sailing a yacht without an engine.

***

Thursday 17th August

We all listened to the Radio 4 shipping forecast. It wasn't good: a high-pressure system was sitting right over Lundy Island and was expected to stay in place for the next week. After talking to the crew, I explained that high pressure often meant little or no wind, so sailing to Ireland would be out of the question. The idea of a few nights on Lundy was starting to look very attractive, so I suggested that we try and reach the south end of the island, where I knew there was a safe anchorage. Also, there was a great pub on the island, and on learning this, the boys took little persuading.

***

Friday 18th August

We spent the night drifting down the west side of Lundy, and by first light, we were off the southern tip. For the first time in two days, we had a light breeze, which allowed us to sail slowly into the anchorage, where luckily, we were able to pick up a mooring. Once safely tied up, Martin set to work on cooking up a full English for us. Glad to be moored up, full of food and very content, we decided to crash out for a few hours; we all needed to catch up on our sleep. Before going ashore, I snorkelled down the mooring chain to check that I hadn't done my usual trick of tying up to a lobster pot.

We were all excited; none of us had ever been on the island before, although Martin and I had sailed past it several times. Lundy is a Site of Special Scientific Interest, but more relevant to us, it is also home to the infamous Marisco Tavern. Apart from these two facts, we knew nothing about the island and were keen to explore.

With the dinghy blown up, we made our way to the beach. From the beach, there is a small road that clings to the cliff edge as it leads up the three-hundred feet to the top of the island. It was daunting enough walking up in daylight, and

I wasn't too keen on our chances of making our way down safely after a shed load of beer. One thing I did know: if we fell off these cliffs, our adventure would be over before it had begun.

Once on the top of Lundy, we had a quick look around. The island is only three miles long and just over half a mile wide; all we could see were two lighthouses, a church and a few farms. Most of the people we encountered were birdwatchers and conservationists, who seemed a serious lot, not our cup of tea really. Being boys on tour, what we needed more than anything was the pub and beer.

Shortly afterwards, it felt like we were in heaven; we were sitting outside the pub with our first pint of cider, enjoying a glorious, hot August day—what could be finer? After downing our first pints, we made short work of getting to know the barmaids. To my amazement, they seemed to take a shine to us. There was Suze, who emphasised that she was Suze with an "e" and not a "y". I'm not sure why she told us that, but it seemed very important to her. Martin really liked Suze-with-an-e and called her a "little doll". There was Charlotte, who Justin liked. Finally, there was Hazel, who I took a fancy to. Hazel was my age, my height, with long blonde hair; in fact, she was extremely attractive and was wearing a mini dress that left little to the imagination. All of us must have made an impression because at 3 p.m., when the pub shut for the afternoon, the girls wanted to know if we would be back that evening.

After an afternoon swim and some food on the yacht, we were back in the pub by 8 p.m., carrying on our conversations with the girls and drinking more beer.

One of the locals at the bar advised that the high-pressure system which had established itself over Lundy was forecast to stay for some time. The island was experiencing a drought, and the supply of drinking water was becoming a problem. It had got so bad drinking water was apparently being shipped from the mainland. One farmer said the army would be taking the cattle and sheep off the island, due to the lack of water.

When the bell rang for closing time, the girls invited us to stay on for a lock-in, which was a real result. There was little chance of us leaving the anchorage in the morning and so this was an ideal opportunity to get to know the girls.

Talking to Martin as we walked back down the dodgy road to the anchorage. It sounded to me like he'd got lucky and met a nymphomaniac who was mad for sex. Suze had told him that she had one boyfriend on the island and couldn't wait for another to arrive on the Ilfracombe ferry that was coming Monday. Justin and I had to laugh at Martin's luck.

***

Saturday 19th August

06:45

Martin and Justin were still asleep, and I was on deck with a coffee. There was a very light breeze, which I thought would build as the morning went on, and so I felt it was worth trying to leave. I hoisted the mainsail and cast off the mooring line, and slowly we started heading out to sea.

We had only gone a short distance when Martin came out on deck. As I looked over the bow, I could see a fin in the water.

"Hey, Martin, look at that."

The fin was coming straight towards us. We both expected the yacht to get hit by the fin; it was like something out of a *Jaws* film. Looking into the clear blue water, we could make out the shape of a basking shark. It was only about ten feet long, which was small for a basking shark. It must have been sleeping on the surface. We had crept up on it, and not realising we were there, the shark swam very slowly into us. This woke it up, and it quickly swam off with a big splash of its tail.

The noise of us jumping around on deck finally brought Justin out. Now that we were off the mooring, I started to worry. With no wind and the strong tide around Lundy, I had visions of us spending another two days drifting aimlessly around the approaches to the Bristol Channel. So, I asked Martin to dig out the long anchor warp and tie it together with all the sheets we had. I went below, changed into my Speedos, and picked up my fins.

"What are you doing?" Justin asked.

I ignored him. "Martin, please tie one end of the rope to the bow. Once it's secure, I'll swim back and fasten the other end to the mooring. All you have to do then is slowly pull on the rope to get her back to the mooring."

"But there are sharks in the water," Justin said.

I laughed and told Justin it was a basking shark, which feed on plankton and are harmless. I remarked that if I was really lucky, one might give me a kiss or, even better, a hickey.

"It's still a bloody big fish," said Justin.

"And a bloody big hickey," said Martin.

"Try explaining that one to Hazel!"

I started to swim to the mooring, but halfway there, the ropes came undone; I had forgotten that Martin had never been a boy scout. After a quick knot-tying lesson, we made it safely back to the mooring.

By lunchtime, we were back in the pub. The girls were pleased to see us, and after the pub closed for the afternoon, they met us on the beach for a swim. We had a great afternoon, swimming and getting to know each other better.

That evening in thc pub, all the talk from locals was the news that the army were coming in the morning to take the cattle and sheep off the island. All the farmers were talking about the best way to get their livestock safely down to the beach via the narrow, steep road.

We enjoyed a really good evening in the pub. Just before last orders, Hazel told us to stay where we were; there was going to be another lock-in. After a few more beers, we received some good night kisses before leaving the pub. In a good mood, we very gingerly made our way back down the cliff to the dinghy. As I sculled out to the yacht (sculling is using one oar to move the dinghy through the water), I noticed loads of phosphorescence in the water. There were tons of small, sparking dots lighting up the water, just like thousands of fireflies, flying together. It was a magical sight and confirmation of a thriving marine environment around the island.

Back aboard the yacht, we stripped off and went skinny dipping, jumping off the deck into the water. You honestly could not believe just how special the phosphorescence was. It was amazing; you hit the water and the light show around your old boy was unbelievable. We giggled like the drunken fools we were.

***

Sunday 20ᵗʰ August

I woke up to the sound of boat engines close to the yacht. Rushing on deck, I saw an army landing craft passing behind *Seefalke* to hit the beach. Today, all the cattle and sheep were to be taken off the island.

We spent the morning drinking coffee and watching the hive of activity on the beach. The best part of it was watching the sheepdogs driving the sheep and cattle down the cliff path and into the army landing craft. As one filled up, another one took its place. It was better than watching TV.

There was still no wind; the forecast for the next week was for the same weather. Martin and Justin decided it would be wise to catch the ferry to Ilfracombe the following day. It would take them most of a day to get back to Barry from there. As it was going to be our last day together, we spent it walking from one end of the island to the other, stopping to have a look at each lighthouse—via the pub of course. It was another beautiful day—sunny, hot, with no wind.

We spent the evening sitting outside the pub drinking on the lawn, even after our lock-in. It was so warm we stayed outside and drank, looking up at the stars. The girls were upset that my crew were leaving in the morning; we all got an extra kiss and a cuddle.

***

Monday 21st August

Despite drinking into the early hours, everyone was up early. It was going to be another hot, sunny morning with no wind. Martin and Justin had packed their rucksacks and were ready before we had breakfast. From the cockpit, we watched the Ilfracombe ferry tie up to the dock. Laughing and joking, I sculled the boys ashore, and we said our last goodbyes on the beach. I watched the boys walk over to the ferry, wondering when I would see them again.

I had only been back on the yacht half an hour when I heard shouting coming from the beach. Looking through the main hatch, I could see Martin and Justin trying to get my attention. I sculled back to the beach.

"What's the problem? Why aren't you on the ferry?"

"They won't sell us a ticket," they said.

"Why?"

"The guy on the ferry said we could only buy a ticket in Ilfracombe; he wouldn't let us on the ferry unless we had a ticket."

"That's bloody dull."

"Justin offered him a hundred quid if he let us on the ferry. The dull sod would not have it, telling us, 'It's not worth my job.'"

"It did not end well," said Justin.

"Why's that?"

"Well, Martin ended up calling the guy on the ferry an 'empty'. He was wrong: the guy was a real upside-down empty."

From the beach, the three of us watched the ferry leave the pier and Lundy without them.

I sculled them back to the yacht to drop their gear off. As I did, I asked, "What are you going to do now?"

"Find a phonebook," Justin said.

"Why?"

"Well, there must be a helicopter company around that we can use to get off the island."

This sounded like a good idea to me, but expensive.

"Maybe we could find a charter boat to come and pick us up," Martin said.

This sounded a better idea. Cheaper anyway.

"Or the wind may pick up, and we could sail back to Ilfracombe."

This was unlikely. The forecast was the same—high pressure over the island—and getting *Seefalke* into Ilfracombe would be difficult.

Back to the pub, over lunch, beer, and peanuts, we were all looking depressed. The girls were happy to see us, though.

Justin found a helicopter company. They wanted five hundred pounds to come out to Lundy and pick them up;

this would be their last resort. Martin had no luck finding a charter boat.

After another beer, I said, "We can do nothing about getting off the island today, so just forget about it, and let's go and have some fun with the girls after they finish at 3 p.m."

Justin and I had a lovely afternoon on the beach, swimming, snorkelling and relaxing with Charlotte and Hazel. Martin was fed up watching Suze with her latest boyfriend. Just to rub salt in the wound, Suze's new boyfriend had travelled over on the ferry Martin had wanted to leave on.

From the beach, looking out to sea, I saw a small yacht. We all watched the twenty-foot yacht motor into and anchor in the bay. There was a man and a young boy on board. Sculling over, I introduced myself to them.

John and his twelve-year-old son, Ben, had come from Swansea. They were only staying in Lundy for the night and planned to sail or motor back in the morning. I told John about my predicament and asked if he could do me a huge favour and take my crew back to Swansea with him in the morning. John happily agreed.

We were all a lot more relaxed that evening. Sitting on the pub lawn, the boys were happy, and the beer flowed.

Looking towards Ilfracombe, I pointed out another yacht coming into the bay. It looked like a modern yacht, around forty feet long.

John and Ben joined us. We had a very relaxed evening with them and arranged a time for me to drop my crew off in the morning. The pub bell rang for last orders, and it was Justin's round. He came back from the bar with a round of drinks and the biggest smile you've ever seen.

"Why are you smiling?" I asked.

"Well, I would like you to meet Andy."

Just behind Justin was a guy about forty years old.

"Andy is my next-door neighbour—he owns the yacht which has just anchored in the bay."

"You're joking?"

"Andy is taking *Mistress Ann* to Neyland tomorrow, where he's left his car. Martin and I can also have a lift back to Barry."

John and Ben could not believe our luck. Nor could I—this was brilliant news! Not only had the boys managed to get off the island, but they had sorted a lift all the way home too. All their travelling problems were now sorted. We celebrated their good fortune by making a toast to *Mistress Ann* with our last drinks of the night. Well, what we thought were the last. It turned out there was another lock-in. Again, we had another farewell party with the girls. I wonder if they thought we would ever leave Lundy. Hazel did start to call us the Groundhog Day Boys.

***

Tuesday 22nd August

After another late night, we were all up early. Martin and Justin were ready to leave; their rucksacks were still packed from yesterday. It was another nice, hot, sunny day with no sign of any wind. It didn't matter—the boys had a lift on a yacht with an engine.

With breakfast over, we loaded the dinghy, and I sculled them over to the *Mistress Ann*, telling Martin I would ring him from Dale when I finally got there. Watching them leave was quite sad; we'd had a great time, and I was now on my own. My next sail would be my first single-handed.

I watched the ferry come in with a new complement of tourists; the island was going to be busy for a few hours. Feeling bored, I went for a walk up the cliff path. I wanted to sit on the park bench at the top to enjoy the view over the anchorage. When I got to the bench, it was already occupied. There was an old man sitting there with his wife. She was holding his hand, and he had his eyes closed with a fantastic smile on his face, looking so peaceful. If he had been awake, I would have stopped and sat by them.

After a quick walk around the island, I went to the pub to see Hazel. She wasn't working that day and we had arranged to meet at the pub. I told Hazel about the old man I'd seen sleeping on the park bench and how happy and peaceful he'd looked.

"The old man you saw had suffered a heart attack," Hazel said. "He wasn't sleeping. A helicopter was on its way to take him off the island."

I thought to myself, there were worse places to die than looking at the fantastic view of *Seefalke* in the anchorage on such a beautiful day.

We spent the afternoon talking while we walked around the island before ending up back on the beach. I rowed Hazel out to the yacht to show her around. After we had a quick swim, I cooked some food, and relaxed and happy, we decided to make our way back to the pub. After two beers, I was feeling tired and was ready to go. I asked Hazel if she would like to stay the night with me on the yacht. She happily agreed, and in an instant, my tiredness disappeared.

Feeling very happy, we finished our drinks, and as we got up to leave, the pub door opened and in walked Ray Brown from Barry Yacht Club, followed by his wife and kids. I could not believe my luck—of all the people to see. I did try to leave with Hazel, but Ray insisted I introduce her to the family. Over a few beers, I told Ray about my story to date.

Leaving the pub a lot later with Hazel, I thought to myself, *I bet it will take Ray two nanoseconds to tell Bowmer and the boys in Barry Yacht Club about me and the barmaid on Lundy.*

Sculling back out to *Seefalke*, Hazel was surprised to see the phosphorescence in the water; she had never seen it before. I convinced her to go skinny dipping, and if I'd thought phosphorescence around my old boy was fun, the phosphorescence around Hazel's body was in a whole different league.

***

Wednesday 23rd August

It was no surprise to be waking to another beautiful day. What was a surprise was that for the first time in ages, there was actually some wind. There was a light breeze coming in from the south-east. I told Hazel we should take the opportunity to go for a sail. She was reluctant at first, but with a little persuasion, she agreed.

I gave Hazel a very quick lesson on how the tiller worked and what rope to pull once the mainsail was up. I also warned her not to stand up, because she could get hit by the boom. I pulled up the mainsail and let it flap in the breeze before I walked to the bow to drop the mooring line. The bow slowly started falling away, and as Hazel sheeted in the mainsail, we sailed out of the bay. I hoisted the genoa and sheeted it in. We had a lovely sail for an hour before the wind started to die.

I got Hazel to head back towards Lundy and the mooring. We enjoyed a really chilled sail back, running downwind, helped by the current for a change. Once we were back in the lee of the island, there was hardly any wind, so I dropped the genoa and picked up the boathook. *Seefalke* was three boat lengths downwind of the mooring buoy, so I told Hazel to push the helm down hard away from her and to head straight towards the mooring. We must have done something right; we stopped bang on the mooring buoy. I picked up the floating rope on my first attempt and made it fast on the anchor bollard. We were safely back on the mooring. I dropped the mainsail, and with the boom back in the gallows, we flaked the mainsail across the boom and secured it with some sail ties. We set about tidying up the rest of the yacht—I thought we made a great team.

The Radio 4 shipping forecast at 1355 hours advised of a big change in the weather. A cold front was expected in the next few hours. This was, however, going to be short-lived as the high-pressure system was expected to move back in later that week, I had no choice but to leave Lundy before I got stuck there for another week.

I took Hazel ashore, and we had a kiss and a cuddle before saying our goodbyes. We also swapped addresses, and I tried to persuade her to come sailing with me, but sadly to no avail. I thought about going to the pub for one last night, but with my sensible head on for a change, I managed to persuade myself that it was not a good idea.

Deciding to leave in the morning, I wanted the yacht prepared, ready to go. The dinghy was pulled on deck and deflated, and I tied it down to the cabin top. An hour was spent cleaning up the cabin by putting all my loose items away and stowing everything in its right place.

Being on Lundy for so long with Martin and Justin had seriously depleted my supplies of fresh food and water.

I needed to replace it before sailing south, so I got a chart out and decided to head for Dale. Although Dale was north-west of Lundy and the wrong direction for heading south, it was a place I knew well; it was easily accessible and a perfect destination for my first single-handed trip. There was the added benefit that I could restock my supplies in Haverfordwest, the main county town in West Wales. A further attraction was I knew the yacht club had good showers, and the Griffin pub was right next door.

The wind picked up as forecast in the early evening. Following my tea, it started to get quite rough in the anchorage. I had made the right choice not to go to the pub, and for once, I was going to start a trip without a hangover.

***

Thursday 24th August

I didn't sleep very well that night due to the motion of the yacht and awoke in time to listen to the 0555 hours shipping forecast. For sea area, Lundy, the forecast was: wind, north-west, force 4 increasing to 6 locally with some light misty rain, sea state moderate.

Great. There had been no wind for a week, and now I had wind forecast to come from where I wanted to go: Dale.

I knew that if I didn't take this opportunity, another high-pressure system was filling back in later that week and I would be stuck in Lundy once more. Spending more time with Hazel did seem really appealing, though.

As the wind had gone round to the north-west as predicted, the anchorage was in the lee of the island and conditions were much calmer. This was quite deceiving, as when I looked out to sea, I could see in the mist and rain and the white water on the horizon a sign of rougher conditions.

To get to Dale, I would need to tack quite a bit, so I planned to use my new no.3 genoa. I ran the sheets through the new genoa tracks and then back to the main cockpit winches. I pulled the genoa up, allowing it to flap in the breeze while I cast off the mooring line. Returning to the cockpit, I sheeted the genoa in and slowly sailed out of the anchorage. I was now on my first ever single-handed sailing trip.

Walking forward towards the mast, I untied the mainsail from the boom. I put the first reef in before hoisting the mainsail. I did all this while still in the lee of Lundy, which made everything really easy and well-controlled. I was quite pleased with how everything had gone so far.

Sailing in a northerly direction in the lee of Lundy was straightforward, but as I started to clear the top of the island, I could see a lot of rough-looking white water. There are very strong tides at either end of Lundy, and the white water was the start of some nasty-looking overfalls. It was at this point that I also got the full force of the wind, and it quickly became obvious to me that I had too much sail up.

With George steering, I first clipped myself onto the jackstay with the safety line from my Henri Lloyd foul-weather jacket. To reef the mainsail, I first had to let the mainsail out, leaving it to flap in the wind, which makes a horrible noise. I crawled up to the mast on my hands and knees, hanging onto my winch handle and making sure I kept my head well below the level of the swinging boom.

At the mast, I released the mainsail halyard and slowly lowered the boom into the gallows, which stopped it swinging around. I took three slides out of the mainsail track and pulled the mainsail down until I had the reefing cringle I wanted.

With the cringle over the hook on the boom, I was able to rehoist the mainsail before winching the clew down to the boom. Reefing the sail on my own with the yacht bouncing about, the sail flapping and the spray from the sea soaking me was exhausting.

After the mainsail was sheeted in, things settled down, and with the sail set, the boom stopped swinging around. I tied the reefed section of the sail to the boom.

The yacht was far more comfortable now, and I felt confident enough to put a tack in using my new sheeting system.

When the bow came through the wind, the genoa started to flap wildly. It got caught around the winch handle, which I had left in the mast winch. In horror, I watched the handle fly gracefully through the air and drop into the sea.

I had only been out at sea for an hour and already I had lost my prized winch handle. The one I had made out of the highest grade 316 stainless steel I could buy. Well, it taught me another valuable lesson: when working around the foredeck and mast, I was always going to make sure I left things secure from then on. I couldn't afford anything else to go swimming.

As I sailed along, my attention started to focus increasingly on George, who wasn't steering a very straight course. He kept steering up into the wind, resulting in the yacht luffing all the time. I added George to my list of things to sort out.

During the afternoon, the wind dropped to force 3 from the north. I shook the reefs out and changed up to a no.2 genoa. I was making good speed and sailing a course straight to Dale. I started to think that if these perfect conditions continued, I could be in Dale in time for last orders.

18:00
The wind dropped right off, and I was becalmed two nautical miles from Dale, at the entrance into Milford Haven.

19:30
The wind finally picked up enough for me to sail into Dale. After dropping the anchor and tidying up the yacht, the Griffin, my favourite pub was firmly in my sights. With a little glint in my eye, I blew up the dinghy and rowed ashore. I had to celebrate my first day of single-handed sailing with a pint or two. The trip had taken me most of the day, I had no calamities apart from my winch handle, and I got to Dale safely which was also good going; I was buzzing.

Sitting by the bar in the Griffin, I seemed to be a big hit with the barmaid—this was becoming a habit. I think it had something to do with my newfound sense of adventure and the glow I was giving off following my amazing day at sea. I enjoyed a really fun evening with plenty of banter. After three pints, I said goodnight to Kim, the barmaid.

She replied by asking, "Can I see you tomorrow?"

It would have been tempting to stay out longer, but I was tired and very content after my first day alone at sea.

***

Friday 25th August

I woke up to another beautiful, hot, sunny day, with no wind. I spent the morning on the yacht, working through my list of jobs. The two batteries had gone flat and needed to be charged, so I disconnected them and took them ashore in the dinghy.

My first stop was the Griffin, where I asked the bar manager if I could plug in my battery charger.

"Yes," was his answer. Great, my first job was sorted.

Needing a shower, I walked next door to the yacht club. Once I was spruced up, I went back to the pub for a pint.

I had a bit of luck—Kim told me it was her day off the following day. She was going into Haverfordwest and offered to give me a lift. I was sorted; I could do my laundry and pick up fresh food and other supplies for my trip south.

I got some change from behind the bar and gave Martin a phone call from the public phone box. He said the two of them had got back to Barry quickly. I thought they must be the luckiest hitchhikers around, getting from Lundy to Barry in one lift.

"Will you still be in Dale tomorrow?" he asked.

"Yes, I have a few more jobs to do, and there's hardly any wind forecast. The high-pressure system is still sitting over Wales."

"Good, I'll drive back down for the weekend. See you in the Griffin." Then he added, "There's one last thing—Hazel rang and asked if I had heard from you. She said to give her a ring on her home phone number."

"Thanks, Martin."

I called Hazel; she was happy to hear from me. She told me that she had been fired from the pub and had come looking for me on the Thursday morning. She had changed her mind and wanted to come sailing with me after all. Unfortunately, I had already left. Bloody great, just my luck: a pretty woman, who I liked, who wanted to come sailing with me—if only I had left an hour later!

I asked Hazel to come to Dale for the bank holiday weekend, with no luck. I didn't get it; she'd wanted to come sailing with me two days ago and now didn't want to make the effort to see me on the bank holiday. Totally confused by women again, I headed back to the pub. after a good chat with Kim and a couple of pints, I felt much better.

Kim was a pretty twenty-five-year-old. She was tall and thin with very short ginger hair and was quite boyish in her mannerisms. She told me she had lived in Dale all her life and felt quite trapped and wanted to escape. I told her about myself, my yacht, and my plans; she became very intrigued. She asked if I could show her around the yacht the next day. I was delighted. I hoped to show her my etching collection at the same time.

***

Saturday 26th August

This was laundry day. How exciting! Kim picked me up early in the morning and drove me into Haverfordwest, dropping me off at the laundrette. While I waited for my washing, I went shopping for the fresh supplies I needed, before returning to the laundrette to pick up my laundry. I was charged thirteen pounds, which seemed pretty steep to me, although I had no option but to pay it.

Kim picked me up and drove me back to Dale. I offered to buy her lunch to say thank you. We went to the Griffin; Kim found a table while I went to the bar to get drinks. While we were talking and having our food, a guy at the bar kept looking over and seemed to be giving me funny looks.

I asked Kim if she knew who the guy was. She told me it was her ex-boyfriend.

After we finished our meal, she said, "I better not go out to the yacht with you. Even though he's my ex, I don't want to upset him—we both live in this small village, and I have to deal with him most days."

I decided to leave Kim in the bar talking to her ex- and headed back to the yacht with my supplies. I figured that by the time I had put everything away, it would be time for

Martin to arrive. Once everything was stowed, I rowed back to the beach, where Martin was already waiting for me.

We headed to the Griffin, where I got a round in. We decided to sit on the wall to enjoy the evening sun and the view over the bay.

"Have you thought about sailing back to Ilfracombe and trying to get together with Hazel?" Martin asked.

"Yes," I said, "but a black cloud comes over me every time I think about it."

"What black cloud?"

"Well, over the last three months, I have had a fair bit of luck with the ladies—well, barmaids. There was Pam in Barry, Hazel on Lundy, and I'm now trying my best with the barmaid here, Kim. I think it's because I'm buzzing and have a sense of adventure about me, which I fear will go if I don't carry on with my plans.

"If I get together with Hazel and go back to Barry, I'm afraid I'll get stuck in the same rut and return to the very life I'm trying to leave behind. I feel that if I don't see my plan through, I will regret it for the rest of my life."

"I agree—you're doing well with the ladies—and I get why this trip is so important to you, but the prospect of a steady girlfriend isn't so bad. Most men have one. So why all these black thoughts?"

"It's Bowmer; he's giving me nightmares."

"Bowmer?"

"Yes, in my nightmare, I have this vision of walking into Barry Yacht Club on a Friday night and seeing Bowmer at the bar. He says to me, 'Hi, Lynn, fancy a beer?'

"And I say, 'Cheers, Bowmer.'

"He was convinced I'd only get as far as Lundy, and I can imagine him saying something like, 'How's the round-the-world sailor today? Remind me how far you got, then?'

"As he's passing me my pint, I say, 'Lundy, Bowmer.'

"That's my nightmare, my big black cloud. If I go back to Barry, I would face twenty years of abuse from Bowmer. He would be as tenacious and stubborn as a dog with a bone. He'd never give it up if I gave up now and returned to Barry."

"What a horrible thought," Martin said. "Twenty years, and the rest, you're right. I'd carry on sailing too if I were you, Lynn."

***

Sunday 27th August

Martin and I spent the next day doing the last jobs on the yacht. I checked and tightened the rigging and spent the afternoon sitting in the cockpit in the sun. Martin was covered in factor fifty, sewing up and repairing the sails. Karl had given me a complete sail repair kit, which made the job easy.

My final job, with help from Martin, was to get fresh water from the yacht club and check the long-range weather forecast. The high pressure was moving away for a few days bringing in some wind. The yacht was ready and so was I, and it was time for me to leave.

When I told Martin my plan to leave, he said, "Well, let's go and have a beer to celebrate."

Walking into the pub, I was greeted by Kim, who was serving behind the bar. She shone me a lovely smile and put two beautiful full pints in front of me. In an instant, I had two of my favourite things: a pretty girl smiling at me and a beer. I introduced Kim to Martin, and after a quick chat, I said I would speak to her later. Martin and I headed outside to sit on the wall; it was another stunning evening.

"Kim is very pretty," Martin said. "I think she fancies you."

"I know, but there's a problem. The ex-boyfriend."

"What's the problem?"

"I don't know."

Dale was a hive of activity. There were people walking around, enjoying the weather and watching the dinghies and windsurfers sailing in the bay. Sitting on the wall, Martin and I were enjoying the view.

Looking around, I could see Kim's ex- walking down the road towards the pub. I pointed him out to Martin. To my surprise, he walked towards me, stopped in front of me and said, "I see you're talking to Kim a lot. Do you like her?"

"Yes. I would like to get to know her better."

"Well, you can get to know her for as long as you want if you give me back the three thousand pounds I lent her."

"What?" I said, laughing.

Martin fell off the wall, he was laughing so much.

"Look, mate," I said, "whatever is going on between the two of you, I want none of it."

As he walked off, I helped Martin get back up. He was just crying with laughter.

"Boy, we don't half pick them," he said. "I try to pull a sex-mad woman on Lundy and all I get is a kiss and a cuddle, and you pick up a stunner here that comes with a three-thousand-pound price tag."

"You're right, Martin, we do pick them," I said, laughing.

***

Monday 28th August

I was up early and rowed Martin ashore. He needed to leave to get back to work, and I needed to leave to sail across the Atlantic.

As we said our farewells, Martin's last words were, "Once you cross the pond, let me know where you are, and I'll come and see you."

Before going back to the yacht, I needed to send my mother a postcard letting her know I'd left Dale. I couldn't ring her, as she was on holiday.

Checking the latest forecast, another Atlantic high was going to form over the country, bringing more hot weather and light winds from the south to south-west, which wasn't good for making my way down to Portugal.

Given that I had no engine, I decided to follow the advice given in the Admiralty Ocean Passage Guide. The first edition of the book was published in 1895, with routes for planning deep-sea voyages. It also provided information on the prevailing weather, currents, and even ice hazards. In the first part of the book, the information is tailored for modern shipping. The second part of the book provides details of the old routes that sailing ships used to sail around the world.

It was these sailing routes I planned to follow. Ships sailing from the Bristol Channel to the West Indies would head west until they hit thirteen degrees of longitude. At this point, they would change course and head south. This route enabled them to pick up favourable winds and the Equatorial current, which circulates clockwise around the North Atlantic.

Sailing on a yacht with no engine, single-handed, I had to take on board and follow the old sea captains' advice. The two advantages for me in following their advice were, first, I would be clear of the shipping lanes, and therefore, I would miss most of the ships heading into the English Channel, the busiest shipping channel in the world. Secondly, I would be sailing west of the continental shelf, meaning that if I got caught in a storm, I would be in deep water when crossing the Bay of Biscay.

This was my first long-distance, single-handed sailing trip. I was excited and nervous at the same time. I had a lot to learn, but all being well my next planned stop was Lisbon, Portugal. This was a trip of a thousand nautical miles. If I averaged a hundred nautical miles a day, the trip would take ten days, which was my goal.

Chapter 7
Leaving Wales

Tuesday 29th August 1995

07:00

My day of departure had finally arrived; I had one last cup of coffee in the cockpit while I went over my preparations, making sure I hadn't missed anything. I was as ready as I was ever going to be.

I hoisted the genoa, allowing it to flap gently in the breeze while I went forward and pulled the anchor back up on deck. Once that was secure, I returned to the cockpit, sheeted in the genoa, and sailed quietly out of Dale towards St Ann's Head. Once the yacht was settled, I gave the anchor a quick wash to remove the smelly mud before I stowed it below deck. Happy that the foredeck was clean, I turned the yacht into the wind, hoisted the mainsail and set a course to take me south of Ireland and out into the North Atlantic.

What a beautiful day for the start of my journey. The southerly breeze was slightly stronger than forecast but the sea was flat and it was lovely and warm. The barometer hand pointed at 1023mb and was rising slowly. The weather was forecast to remain settled until the high-pressure system over the UK moved on.

12:00

By midday, I had made good progress. I could see the Smalls lighthouse to the north of me. The Smalls were the last off-lying danger as I headed out into the Celtic Sea and the Atlantic beyond. To top my morning off, I watched a pod of dolphins swim around the yacht—a sign of good luck, I hoped.

On leaving Dale, I noticed that the yacht was taking on a small amount of water, which needed pumping out every couple of hours. This was something I needed to keep an eye on. I could see the water was coming in through gaps in the top planks, which had dried out in the hot weather. I was fairly sure that the planks would take up in a few days once they got wet. If my theory was wrong, it wasn't going to be much fun pumping the yacht out all the way to the Caribbean. To save the batteries, I planned to pump the water out by hand during the day and let the electric pump do the work overnight.

18:00. Pos. 51°10'N 005°42'W

I felt I had made decent progress for my first day. The boat speed had dropped slightly in the afternoon due to lighter winds, but overall, I covered 30NM, which I was happy with. As the last rays of sunshine disappeared beyond the horizon, I was treated to an amazing sunset.

My diet at sea was going to be pretty simple. I planned to eat all my fresh food first. For breakfast, bacon and eggs while they lasted, and a main meal of curry or chilli with rice for supper, followed by a black coffee with a small tot of brandy as a nightcap.

Due to the light winds and the lack of boat speed, George was struggling to hold a straight course, so I set the sails in a way that enabled *Seefalke* to steer herself, by letting the mainsail out, pulling the no. 2 genoa in tight and tying the tiller off into the centre of the yacht. I tried other ways to get her to move faster, but in the end, this sail set-up was the only way to keep *Seefalke* sailing on a reasonable course.

***

2nd day at sea
Wednesday 30th August

06:00

My first night sailing single-handed was uneventful. I did see a few trawlers dragging nets, all coming my way. To avoid the risk of collision, I changed course to head south for a few hours and stayed on deck to keep watch all night.

12:00. Pos. 51°04'N 007°20'W

From my evening fix at 1800 hours yesterday to noon, I logged 62NM over the ground, which for an eighteen-hour period wasn't particularly good. With the conditions settled as they were, I was happy just making some progress, sailing on a course of 220° magnetic.

18:00

I had a good second day; the weather was hot and sunny again. George was still struggling to steer the yacht in the light winds. I enjoyed curry and rice again for supper, followed by coffee with brandy.

The Atlantic Crossing Guide recommends a sleeping plan for single-handed sailors of a twenty-minute power nap at a time; this allows you to maintain a proper lookout. The theory being twenty minutes is long enough to get some rest but short enough to take evasive action if required.

Why only twenty minutes sleep at a time?

A ship can steam from below the horizon and be on top of you in twenty minutes.

***

3rd day at sea
Thursday 31st August

06:00

Last night, I'd tried sleeping at twenty minutes intervals for the first time. I had two alarm clocks set at twenty-minute intervals. I found I could wake up for the first two or three, but then for the rest of the night, I was just too tired. I slept through the alarm for four hours straight, which was not very clever. This was something that was going to require practise, or I'd have to try something different.

Only by chance did I wake up in time to catch the shipping forecast on my short-wave radio. The forecast confirmed there was high pressure still established to the east, and the barometer remained steady at 1025mb; I was still getting light, force 2 winds from the west.

12:00. Pos. 50°20'N 008°04'W
Logged 45NM in the last 24 hours.

The breeze was light all day, with nothing much to get excited about. George continued to struggle in the light conditions, which is a common problem for all self-steering gear. This meant I spent most of the day steering by hand, trying to make as much progress as I could. Although to be honest, I might as well have just left the yacht to her own devices, as progress was pretty slow. I was frustrated because I knew with just a bit more wind, *Seefalke* would have been sailing along nicely at six knots. I realised this was something I'd have to get used to and was all part of ocean sailing—but I did need George to perform better if I was going to follow my dream.

18:00
I changed my way of cooking my big evening meal. Instead of using one can, I'd use two tins of chilli or curry and boil a big pot of rice. My plan was to eat half the food one night and save the rest for the following evening. I stored the uneaten portion in the oven overnight. Doing the washing up and cooking every two days, placed less burden on my limited fresh water supply and cooking gas.

From the reading I had done on long-distance sailing, you are supposed to lose weight due to the motion of the yacht. However, so far, all I seemed to be doing was eating. Every morning I would wake up starving. After breakfast, the rest of the day was spent planning what to eat next. Based on how much I was eating, I couldn't see how I was going to lose weight.

***

4th day at sea
Friday 1st September

06:00
The wind was very light from the north-west and the sea had a small swell, knocking any wind I had out of the sails.

To stop the sails getting damaged and flogging themselves to death, I dropped them. On the plus side, at least I had a quiet night and got some sleep with no ships around. What I would do if I saw a ship, I didn't know; with no wind and no sails up, I was dead in the water, a sitting target.

For breakfast, I used the last of my bacon—no more English breakfast for me for a while.

Without any wind, there was not much to do, apart from keeping a lookout. I occupied my time by: reading my book, watching the dolphins, admiring the gannets and thinking about what I was going to eat.

12.00. Pos. 50°15'N 008°24'W
Logged 19NM in the last 24 hours.

I had expected my midday GPS position to be the same as yesterday's. To my surprise, I found I had moved 19NM south, even though I had basically been becalmed for the last 24 hours, which put *Seefalke* 145NM from Dale. The bad news was that the midday shipping forecast was predicting no change in the weather.

I had been using the GPS every six hours to plot my position on the chart. My course was all over the place. I had been chasing what little wind there was in an attempt to maintain boat speed, so progress was poor, but at least I was slowly moving closer to Lisbon. Given that I wasn't covering much ground and I was clear of the shipping lanes, I reduced my GPS fixes to one at noon each day to save the batteries. I would need the GPS a lot more when I got closer to land. From my last position fix, there was no land I could sail into within twenty-four hours.

I was keeping a ship's log, which recorded the weather, my compass course, boat speed and position, which I updated every six hours so that if my GPS packed up, I could still work out my position using 'dead reckoning'.

The barometer had started to fall, and late in the afternoon, the wind picked up to force 2/3 from the west. This enabled me to get full mainsails and no.2 genoa back up. To keep us moving, I had the yacht holding a course of 200° mag. After my evening meal, I played about with George and managed to get him working properly for the first time since leaving Dale.

***

5th day at sea
Saturday 2nd September

06:00

George's early evening performance was short-lived, and I ended up spending the night steering *Seefalke* by hand, under a big, bright full moon. I found it incredibly hard to stay awake; I kept falling asleep only to be woken up minutes later by the sound of the sails flapping. This was a long night and didn't do my beauty any good, and I didn't want a repeat performance. I needed to find a solution to fix George. So, I decided to spend some time watching what was happening so I could make some refinements in the hope I could get George working as he was designed to do.

I couldn't even cheer myself up with a bacon and egg sandwich for breakfast; I had used the last of my bacon and my bread. It was going to be porridge or cornflakes with my coffee in the mornings until I got the chance to bake some more bread. It wasn't all bad—I still had plenty of eggs.

Studying George, I could see that the vane was not staying in a vertical position. It was stopping either side, causing the servo pendulum rudder to be at an angle and the yacht to wander off course. Depending on which side the vane was on, the yacht would either round up into the wind and stall or she would bear away, leaving us sailing away from our course. To fix the problem, I added extra weight to the counterbalance. Following this, George's performance improved dramatically; the vane remained in the vertical position and the yacht was holding a much better course.

12:00. Pos. 49°26'N 008°50'W

Midday had become the highlight of the day. Marking my position on the chart and working out how far I had sailed in 24 hours was as exciting as it got on this part of the trip.

All my hard work from last night had been rewarded; I had covered 52NM and recorded my best noon-to-noon distance logged so far. George was working a lot better, holding a course to within five degrees. Maybe I needed to change its name to Bowmer—what a horrible thought! With the self-steering now working as it should, it was like having a second pair of hands or an extra crew. Life all of sudden had become so much easier.

18:00

The barometer and wind had stayed constant all day; the wind was still blowing force 4 westerly. My course was 220° magnetic, and George had the yacht sailing along very nicely.

My twenty-minute sleep pattern had not worked. I got so tired I slept right through both alarms. My new plan was to set my alarm clocks to go off every two hours. There wasn't much I could do about the twenty-minute-ship-over-the-horizon theory, but sleeping for two hours surely had to be better than sleeping for four?

After dark, I had a good look around the horizon to check for any ships. Thankfully, I couldn't see any. I went below and got my head down. When *Seefalke* was sailing on flat seas, there was no sound of water passing down the hull, and inside the cabin it was really quiet, making it very easy to fall asleep.

I had a dream, a very strange, vivid dream. Hazel the barmaid from Lundy was standing over me, shouting, "Lynn, Lynn, wake up! Lynn, please wake up!" All she had on was my Henri Lloyd waterproof jacket, which was undone, exposing her naked body—what an image.

Startled, I woke up. A sixth sense told me something was wrong, very wrong. Putting my jacket on, I glanced at my watch; I had only slept for twenty minutes. Sticking my head out of the hatch, I could see two ships. The first was on the bow, approximately two miles away, and the other ship was astern of the first. If I had not woken up, the second ship could have hit me.

I had met Clive, a retired ocean-going ship's captain, in Barry Yacht Club. He'd explained to me that on larger ships where the bridge is situated well aft, they can have a blind spot up to a quarter of a mile ahead of the bow. A little forty-foot wooden yacht could easily become matchwood if I didn't remain vigilant and keep clear. The last piece of advice Clive gave me was: if you see a ship and you have to alter course, make your course alterations bold, big, and early to show any stand-on vessels that you have spotted them and taken clear action to avoid the danger.

Therefore, my first cardinal rule of sailing became: if there was risk of danger to the yacht, it was my job to keep myself safe.

I quickly got myself on deck and changed course to sail parallel to the second ship. Once I had passed it, I returned to my original course. Sitting in the cockpit, I watched the ships sail into the night. I decided there and then that I either had a guardian angel or I was in touch with my sixth sense.

Once clear of danger, I went back to bed, hoping I would return to my dream about Hazel wearing my wet weather gear. Sadly, that didn't happen, but I had proved to myself that the twenty-minute-ship-over-the-horizon theory was right. I didn't see any more ships for the rest of the night and carried on with my two-hour sleep pattern.

***

6th day at sea
Sunday 3rd September

12:00. Pos. 48°10'N 010°00'W
Logged 90NM in the last 24 hours.

We had a good breeze the previous night, which carried on into the morning. I was really pleased with how well George was steering the yacht. His performance had vastly improved, and Georgie Boy was at his best when the yacht was sailing at around six knots. Anything more and he started to wander and deviate from the course.

From my midday fix, *Seefalke* was 280NM south-west of Dale, the barometer was steady at 1013mb and the yacht was maintaining a speed of five knots through the water. The wind remained force 4 coming from the west. I continued on a course of 220° mag.

18:00
What a great day. The weather was lovely and there was plenty of marine life around. I thought to myself that if the

weather and conditions carried on as they were, I'd be in Lisbon in no time.

With George working so well, my noon-to-noon run was steadily improving. I found the sailing quite boring; there was not a lot to do once the yacht and George were set up. The day consisted of scanning the horizon for ships, planning my meals, pumping the yacht out every so often and reading my book. I then repeated the same routine until it was time for bed. Then I would get up every two hours to check everything was as it should be.

***

7th day at sea
Monday 4th September

03:00
I was woken from my sleep by the sound of my sails flapping around. Back on deck, I soon found out I had no wind at all, but I'd been left becalmed with a small uncomfortable swell. With no other choice, I had to drop the sails to stop them getting damaged.

06:00
At first light, I had all the sails back up and the yacht moving again, back on course. While I was drinking my morning coffee, sitting in the cockpit, I had a strange thought. Was getting becalmed last night the calm before the storm?

12:00. Pos. 47°00'N 011°15'W
Logged 82NM in the last 24 hours.

This marked the end of my first week at sea. I was approximately 360NM south-west of Dale, sailing on a course of 220° mag. I was still enjoying the same steady wind, which had been blowing from the west for the last three days. The barometer had been slowly dropping from 1013mb all morning. The hand was now pointing to the word 'change' on the face of the barometer, meaning that more wind could be on its way, which gave me something to worry about after my strange thought this morning.

I decided to listen to the Radio 4 1201 hours shipping forecast. The synopsis wasn't great: a depression was tracking across the Atlantic, and the BBC was forecasting imminent gale force 8 winds for sea area Finisterre.

I was enjoying a nice sunny day with a good strong breeze; the only thing I could do was carry on sailing south as quickly as possible in the hope of missing the worst of the weather. My afternoon was spent making sure everything inside the yacht was put away in its proper place and anything that could break loose was tied down. I wanted to stop looking at the barometer, but I couldn't. It had dropped to 1003mb, with the hand pointing at 'rain'.

I could hear the voice of my astronavigation instructor, John Hart, in my head saying, "If the barometer drops three points in an hour, you are in for really bad weather."

18:00

Worrying about a storm was not a good idea; I had to deal with it. Looking out to the west, the sky was dark, but I started to see swells twenty feet high, a long way apart. I had an early tea and got my head down for a few hours before the fun started.

By ten o'clock, the wind had really picked up. The barometer was still dropping; it read a depressing 994mb and the hand pointed to the 'Y' in stormy. I knew the BBC forecast was going to be right. I could tell the warm front was approaching as it started to rain and the wind started to pick up veer (moving around in a clockwise direction). I went on deck and put two reefs in the mainsail and replaced the no.2 genoa with the storm jib.

***

8th day at sea
Tuesday 5th September

00:00

The wind was south-west force 7/8. Slowly, the yacht was beating to windward over the big swells. I kept an eye on George from the safety of the cabin steps, as there was a fair bit of white water rolling down the deck. George was managing to miss the biggest waves and seemed to steer the yacht over the crests pretty well. We would luff just as we hit the top of the wave and then we would fall away and sail down the back of the wave, before starting the cycle all over again. The yacht was comfortable, and watching how well George was coping with the conditions gave me a lot of confidence. I knew I could not have spent hours in those conditions steering the yacht by hand, and I'm pretty sure I would have done a far worse job.

I managed to get a few hours' sleep, safe in the knowledge that George was coping well with the extreme conditions. When I woke up and looked out of the main hatch, all I could see was white water, chaotic waves crashing into each other from every direction. There was nothing for me to do but carry on, trusting George. It was too dangerous to go on deck—it was underwater. All I did was periodically pump the bilge out and get some more rest.

06:00

At first light, the wind had moderated slightly to a force 6/7, with some shape back in the very large waves. What a way to end my first week at sea. The weather thankfully continued to improve throughout the morning. I had a clear blue sky, and it felt warm again, giving me something to smile about.

I had taken one reef out of the mainsail and put the no.2 genoa back up. The swell had dropped to about fifteen feet, and distance between the waves was getting longer, which was encouraging. The wind had dropped to force 5/6 westerly, making for much better sailing conditions. The barometer had been rising all morning and was at 1008mb, which gave me hope that I had seen the last of the bad weather. I was happy, the sun was out and I was sailing south, reaching across the face of the swells. Fantastic sailing.

12:00. Pos. 46°12'N 010°40'W

Logged 60NM in the last 24 hours.

After last night's gale I was still worried about the weather, so I made sure I picked up the 12:01 GMT Radio 4 shipping forecast. I was right on the edge of the long-wave radio signal range, five hundred miles south of the UK. All I heard, between the static *CRRR*, was "Severe gale—*CRRR*—force 10—*CRRR*—Sole, Plymouth, visibility poor, wind backing—*CRRR CRRR*—Sea areas Finisterre, Biscay, Trafalgar—*CRRR CRRR CRRR*—12. Hurricane Ir—*CRRR CRRR*—Imminent—*CRRR CRRR*."

My midday GPS fix put me in the middle of the Finisterre shipping forecast area. Where storm force 10 winds increasing to hurricane force 12 were expected imminently in the next six to twelve hours. Not good at all.

I had experienced bad weather the previous night and survived. At least I knew a bit about what to expect. But what scared me the most from listening to the weather forecast was I hadn't even known that the Beaufort scale went past force 8. To gain a bit more knowledge, I looked up the Beaufort scale description in my ocean passage planner book, and to be honest, I wished I hadn't.

Beaufort 8. Gale. Winds: 34 to 40 knots. Wave height: 18ft. Sea conditions: Large waves with foam blown off crests.

Beaufort 10. Storm. Wind: 48 to 55 knots. Wave height: 30ft. Sea conditions: Very high waves with overhanging crests.

Beaufort 12. Hurricane. Wind speed: 64 knots plus. Wave height: 46ft plus. Sea conditions: Giant waves, air full of foam and spray.

All I could do was pray that the forecast was wrong and watch the barometer for any indication that a storm was about to hit. The hand was pointing at 1008mb, and to my dismay, it had started to drop rapidly. I needed to prepare the yacht for another rough night at sea and get some hot food inside me while the going was good.

I debated whether to carry on sailing south in the hope of finding better weather or sail west to gain more sea room. I was approximately 180NM off the north coast of Spain, and only 60NM off the longitude of Cape Finisterre lighthouse. The one thing I knew I could not do was to sail east, onto a lee shore. Trying to find shelter in a harbour in a storm was out of the question.

All afternoon, I had been sailing south with the fresh south-easterly breeze, watching the swallows and the swifts flying east towards land. They'd known something bad was coming. My mood was further dampened by the fact the moon had a big ring of cloud around it: another indication that I was about to see some really bad weather.

The wind slowly started backing to the south-west and increasing in strength. The warm front was approaching. I knew the Radio 4 shipping forecast was pretty accurate, and the swifts weren't daft either: they knew something was afoot. I tried, but I couldn't pick up the 17:00 shipping forecast.

I put a third reef in the mainsail and changed the no.2 to my storm jib, as I didn't want to be messing around on the bow in the oncoming storm. After I set the sails and made sure George was happy, I went back below. I got all my anchor warp and spare rope and tied them together to use as a drogue, just in case I needed to slow the yacht down later.

Looking out to the west, I could see dense black clouds forming. There were periodic rumbles of thunder and huge forks of lightning. I could also see a lot of rain, and the swells were getting bigger as the wind speed increased.

The worst thing was looking at the barometer and watching the hand continue to drop towards the word 'stormy'. It had dropped ten points during the afternoon and still kept dropping. This was not good. I kept tapping the barometer with the back of my hand, in the hope this second-hand barometer I had bought at the Beaulieu yacht jumble was stuck and the hand would move back up. It didn't.

23:00

The wind had picked up to force 7/8. The barometer was down to 990mb; the hand was pointing to the 'm' in stormy—another eight points, not good. The waves were getting really big, forty or fifty feet in height, and the sets were getting a lot closer together!

***

9th day at sea
Wednesday 6th September

02:30

The waves were starting to break, and there was a lot of white water. The air was full of foam and spray, and as I sailed over the top of each wave, I got the full force of the howling wind. All I could see in this chaos was the next huge wall of water coming towards me. It's funny, even in these dangerous conditions, there was no point in being scared. I had to rely on fate, George and my workmanship in rebuilding the yacht. There was no way I could fight Mother Nature in her very angry mood.

The conditions were so dangerous I could no longer go on deck, as there was no deck to see. It was continuously underwater. I stayed in the cabin and relied on George, who, despite the conditions, seemed to be coping well.

I tried to get some sleep, but it was impossible with the sound of the waves crashing over the yacht and the wind screaming through the rigging. If that wasn't enough, there was also the crashing and banging of items in the cabin, not to mention the pots and pans clattering about in the cupboards. I had to hang on to my bunk to prevent myself from being thrown across the cabin with the rest of my things.

As difficult as this was. I had no option but to bide my time and ride out the storm. While pumping the yacht out every half hour.

06:00

At first light, I checked the barometer, and I wished I hadn't. The hand had passed the 's' in stormy and read 975mb. Checking back through the ship's logbook, the barometer pressure had dropped 33mb over the last 24 hours.

Outside, the wind was blowing harder and the waves looked a lot bigger. In fact, they were enormous—it was like looking up at a multi-storey building. I had at least one boat length of water stretching ahead of me when I looked up the wave and another behind to the trough.

Sitting on top of my cabin steps with my diving mask on was the only way I could see anything: there was so much foam and spray being blown around. All I could see were patches of broken white water.

Watching George steer the yacht in those conditions was amazing. How he did it, I don't know—which just confirmed to me that I had done a good job in designing and building the system. At the top of the wave, we got the full force of the storm; George would steer into the wind, luffing the yacht for a few seconds. As the wave passed under the yacht, the bow would fall off and we'd sail down the back of the wave into the next trough, where we would momentarily lose the wind. George would then start the whole process over again, hour after hour.

12:00

The wind had increased yet again, and by this stage, the waves were monstrous. *Seefalke* began to struggle to sail up the faces of them.

Several times, she would start up the wave and then stop before reaching the top. It was a horrible sensation when the yacht would slowly start to slide backwards.

My worry was the yacht would be pooped, meaning the bow would be pushed over the stern by the wall of water. Lucky for me, the stern dug into the face of the wave, stopping our backward slide, letting the wave pass, so *Seefalke* could sail over the crest and down its back.

Five times, *Seefalke* sailed up only to start sliding backwards down those huge waves. It was getting way too dangerous, and I had no option but to turn the yacht around— not an easy job, with plenty that could go wrong.

I knew sailing downwind with the mainsail still up would pose a number of problems: the yacht speed would massively increase, which I didn't want, and it would be all too easy for the yacht to gybe, which could damage the mast. With all my storm gear on and making sure I was clipped to the jackstay, I ventured on deck. After the first wave, I was drenched. Nevertheless, crawling to the mast, I waited for a lull in the trough and then dropped the mainsail as quickly as the conditions would permit. Once it was on the deck, I quickly lashed the sail to the boom.

To turn the yacht around safely, I needed to be in the trough of a wave. Ending up beam on, just below the crest of a breaking wave, with the full strength of the wind hitting *Seefalke* would be very dangerous. Luckily for me, I had no problem turning the yacht around.

With the wind now coming from behind, the yacht began surfing down the faces of the huge waves. The danger now was pitchpoling, which happens when the yacht races down the face of a wave, the bow digs in at the bottom of the trough and then the wall of water pushes the stern over the bow. Getting pitchpoled would be fatal.

Back in the cockpit, I set the storm jib up on the centre line of the yacht. By pulling both sheets in tight, I kept the yacht sailing downwind, and down the faces of those monstrous waves.

Getting the anchor warp and the other ropes that I had tied together earlier. I fastened the two ends to the main genoa winches before heaving the whole lot over the stern. I was amazed at how much drag all these warps created. They acted as a superb brake, slowing the yacht down to a safe speed. This was a major success, and I could start to relax a little bit.

My next problem was that I was sailing east towards the coast. I had a day's grace before I would run out of sea room and hit land.

Now that *Seefalke* was settled and more comfortable, I had time to look for something to eat that I didn't have to cook. I found a lump of cheese, a packet of peanuts and a Mars bar. I managed to make myself a coffee by hanging on to the kettle while the water boiled.

The yacht was leaking badly and pumping her out was an ongoing job. A small leak was not unusual, but the amount of water coming in had increased dramatically. There didn't seem to be any water coming from the bow or cabin, so the only place left to look for the leak was the counter—the very back of the yacht. There was only one way to check. With torch in hand, I crawled down the quarter berth, which was like a long, dark tunnel taking me under the cockpit. I started thinking to myself that if the yacht pitchpoled, I was definitely in the wrong place. Thankfully, I found the leak; the water was coming in through the rudder stern tube at the top where it joined the deck. Every time a wave hit the yacht's counter, water sprayed me like a shower. I was happy I had found the leak, but I couldn't fix it while the storm continued to rage.

For the last eight hours, I had been sailing in an easterly direction. I tried to get a GPS fix to check my position, without any luck. Maybe the waves were too big or the yacht was rolling around too much. Anyway, something was stopping my new six-satellite GPS from getting a signal, so I didn't have a clue where I was.

By my dead reckoning, I had sailed approximately 40NM during the previous eight hours, and I was concerned that if I went much further, I would start to sail into shallower water on the continental shelf. The barometer had started to rise again up to 990mb, and the waves weren't breaking quite so much, so I decided to alter course and start sailing south once more.

Back on deck, the wind was still blowing gale force. I pulled in the trailing warps before crawling to the mast to rehoist the mainsail. I managed to get part of the sail up, but for some reason, the sail jammed. I could not move it up or down; it was stuck. With the boom sitting in the gallows, all I could do was secure the loose sail as best I could with sail ties.

Sitting safely in the cockpit, I set the sails and George up so we could start heading south. My new course enabled me to sail diagonally across the waves, going over them at a thirty-degree angle, which was a lot more comfortable and safe. As we approached the top of the wave, the wind would increase and George would respond by luffing the yacht until she was over the crest, and then we would sail safely down the other side.

***

10th day at sea
Thursday 7th September

03:00

My batteries had gone flat. This was a nightmare—now I had no radio, cabin lights, automatic bilge pumps or navigation lights, leaving the yacht invisible to any shipping. Making this trip south harder still.

When I'd left Wales, the last thing on my mind was storms at sea. Now that I was in a big one, all I could do was deal with what was in front of me. To distract myself from thinking, I concentrated on pumping the yacht out every half hour, which was hard work and tiring, but essential, if I wanted to carry on following the dream.

06:00

Overall, the yacht coped well during the night despite the setbacks. In daylight, I could see what the mainsail had been catching on but decided to leave everything as it was until the weather improved. The barometer continued to move up, pointing to a better weather outlook. The waves were still big, though they were decreasing in size all the time, but the wind was still in the south-west and blowing hard. I had expected the wind to start dropping as my barometer rose, but it hadn't. I put this down to the fact that the barometer had been rising quickly, which was just as bad as falling quickly.

12:00. Pos. 44°08'N 009°46'W

My GPS came back to life for the first time in two days. Looking at my midday position plotted on the chart, I saw I had sailed 130NM south and 40NM east during the storm, putting me on the same latitude as the north coast of Spain and only 20NM off the longitude of Cape Finisterre. If the storm had lasted one more day, I would have been kissing the beaches of northern Spain, like all the other poor sailors who have died on this dangerous coastline. Frightened by that thought, I started working my way back out to sea, tacking into the still very large waves and against the wind to try to get back some of the sea room I had lost.

15:00

I fixed the problem with the mainsail track: a screw had worked itself loose in the sail track, preventing the sail from being hoisted. I tied myself to the mast using my safety line, and with me standing on the mast winches, hanging on with one hand, I managed to reach up and remove the offending screw, solving my problem.

I had been keeping an eye on the barometer; it was back to 1005mb and rising slowly, which was a good sign. As the weather improved, the wind started to drop. I managed to haul the mainsail back up, still with the third reef in. I needed to clean up the yacht and give myself a break before setting more sail. The last few days had been brutal. I was absolutely exhausted from the lack of sleep and the physical exertion of pumping the yacht out every half hour.

The weather got better by the hour until finally, I had blue, clear sky, and a warm afternoon sun on my back. Sitting in the cockpit, I wrote in my logbook that I had not seen a ship for days. As I did, *Seefalke* went over the top of a wave, and when I looked forward over the bow, I could see a supertanker two or three miles away. *Seefalke* went down into the next trough, and the ship disappeared from view. I expected to see another glimpse of the ship as we sailed over the next wave. To my surprise, the horizon was clear. I never caught sight of that ship again.

The yacht and I seemed very small in comparison to those still very large swells. It really was amazing to me how quickly I had got used to the Atlantic waves. All were far larger than anything I had ever encountered before, and I hoped I would never see weather like I had just experienced ever again. Sunny days and downwind trade-wind sailing were all I wanted from then on.

20:30

The wind was force 5 and dropping. So were the seas. The barometer read 1013mb and was rising. I was back to sailing with one reef in the mainsail and my no.2 genoa, on a course of 220° to 230° mag. The yacht was still leaking, and I continued to pump her out every two hours. Slowly, I got back into my normal routine at sea: curry and rice for tea, a tot of brandy in my last coffee for the night, and back to my sleep plan of setting the alarms to go off every two hours.

***

11th day at sea
Friday 8th September

06:00

I enjoyed a quiet night and was treated to a lovely sunrise. The barometer had steadied at 1018mb, and it turned into a glorious, hot, sunny day.

12:00. Pos. 42°55'N 011°05'W

Logged 92NM in the last 24 hours.

The weather had been improving all morning, leaving a flat sea and a stiff north-westerly wind. These were the sailing conditions I'd dreamt about before leaving Wales. Happy with the sea room I had gained in the last 24 hours, I set George up to take us south, down the coast of Portugal towards Lisbon.

22:00

Sitting in the cockpit, drinking my coffee, I watched the sun set. This was the perfect way to end a brilliant day. Sailing, wind and sea conditions were still the same and looked set for the night—what could be better?

***

12th day at sea
Saturday 9th September

06:00

I enjoyed a quiet night with very little to do. Twelve days ago, when I'd left Wales, my expectations of sailing across oceans had been filled with the thoughts of exciting experiences. All the books I had read talked about the sun and exciting trade-wind sailing. Finally, I was experiencing what I had dreamt about: fast, flat-water sailing.

12:00. Pos. 40°50'N 011°30'W

Logged 126NM in the last 24 hours.

Capo da Roca Lighthouse, the point that I would have to sail around that marks the way into Lisbon, was only 150NM away. For the first time in nearly two weeks, I started to get excited by the thought of getting back on dry land. I set George up to sail towards Lisbon, course 145° mag. Straight downwind sailing.

22:00

Another easy day with not a lot to do apart from eat, read my book and keep a lookout for any shipping traffic, which I expected to see soon as I got closer to the coast of Portugal.

***

13th day at sea
Sunday 10th September

06:00
More easy sailing all night, I was living my dream.

12:00. Pos. 39°18'N 010°34'W
Logged 101NM in the last 24 hours.

Early in the afternoon, I saw a yacht to starboard a mile or two ahead of me, sailing towards the coast. It was also around forty feet long. I counted four people on board; they looked like they too were having fun and enjoying the glorious sailing conditions. I kept a close eye on them, and as our courses converged, I could see they were all holding drinks. Only at the last minute did I realise they hadn't seen me. To avoid a collision, I was forced to tack at the last minute. I narrowly missed the other yacht. It was so close—there was less than ten feet in it as I ducked their stern. You should have seen the look of panic on their faces.

This was a wake-up call for me, another near-miss that was too close for comfort. I could have survived two big storms, only to be killed on a nice, sunny day in flat, calm conditions, by a yacht I had been closely watching. To be honest, I was quite annoyed with myself and felt a right prat. In the future, if there was a real risk of collision, I'd make sure I took responsibility to keep clear at the earliest opportunity. I had been doing this all the way down the coast with shipping and just needed to apply the same philosophy to everything else.

Shortly after my near miss, I saw a silver thing being dragged behind the yacht. It was the paddle of my self-steering gear. I was just glad it hadn't broken in the last storm—if it had, I doubt I would be sitting here writing this. I had to steer the yacht by hand until I reached Lisbon.

The last two days I had really easy sailing. I had hot sunny days with a good breeze. Looking at the barometer again, the pointer had moved slowly up and the days were getting hotter, meaning less wind coming my way.

22:00

I had a good breeze most of the day, but eventually, the wind dropped to a gentle, warm, force 2 breeze and the sea state was slight. I set the alarm for two hours and got my head down for a much-needed rest.

***

14th day at sea
Monday 11th September

I awoke to the sound of water sloshing around inside the yacht. The floorboards were floating in five inches of water. Half asleep, I immediately started to panic; I thought the yacht had sprung a more serious leak. When I checked my watch, it was 03:00, which explained why there was so much water. I had been asleep for five hours. Pumping the yacht out took me ages—it was a good job I woke up when I did.

Tired from pumping the water out, I planned to get back to sleep, but first, I wanted to check again for ships, so I stuck my head out of the hatch. I could not see any ships close by, although I could see a long line of lights in front of me off the port bow, which didn't make any sense to me at all.

Confused by all the lights, I turned the GPS on to get my position, which had *Seefalke* 20NM off the Capo da Roca Lighthouse. I could make out its light quite clearly—that light made sense. The other lights I had to study for ten minutes or so before I realised they belonged to a line of ships heading up and down the Portuguese coast. I could see at least forty to fifty of them; it was clear I was sailing into a very busy shipping lane. I couldn't afford to accidentally fall asleep at this critical time, so I perched myself on the top step of the companionway and filled myself full of coffee in order to stay awake and maintain a proper lookout.

06:00

Sailing into Lisbon meant crossing the shipping lanes. I sailed parallel to them until I could cross them at a ninety-degree angle to ensure that I crossed each lane in the shortest possible time. What had looked like a nice, long, straight line of ships last night was in fact scattered ships travelling in the same direction a mile apart, two or three abreast. I had never seen so many ships in one place and so close together before.

Sailing due east, I had to pick my way through the ships, altering course when necessary. I sailed around the sterns of the ships as close as I could in order to cross the bow of the next ship in the line at a safe distance. This was pretty nerve-racking, as the wind was light. It was times like this I wished I had more wind or an engine.

By mid-morning, I had managed to work my way through the shipping lanes.

12:00. Pos. 38°38'N 009°25'W
Logged 67NM in the last 24 hours.

Sailing past the town of Cascais, I finally saw the small number two channel buoy and the sandbank that protected the channel into Lisbon I had been looking for. As a precaution before I entered the channel, I set up my self-tacking jib system, as I had no idea how wide or busy the river would be. After a few practice tacks, I entered the channel. Following the instructions from my pilot book, I had to steer a magnetic course of 047°. The tide was against me; it was not going to be an easy sail in.

Sailing past Fort Bugio, I could make out the leading lights of Gibraltar and Estero. By keeping the leading lights in line, I stayed in the middle of the channel into the River Tagus. Passing the north channel, *Seefalke* started to surf down the waves leading into the river. This was fun sailing until the running back stay-wire got caught on the boom gallows. At the same moment, I accidentally gybed, and as the boom came across, it hit the runner with some force. The gallows got ripped off the yacht and flew into the water, leaving big screw holes in the cabin top—something else for me to fix.

As the river opened up in front of me, I could see a green buoy. Once I sailed past it, I had navigated all the dangers of the entrance and was safely in the river. I was a bit more relaxed now.

Next, I sailed past the fairy-tale Torre de Belem tower, the 16th-century fortification and gateway to Lisbon. However, while taking in the scenery, I wasn't paying attention and let go of the chart that I'd been holding on my lap. I watched it blow over the side. It was my only chart—I had to get it back. By gybing around, I finally manage to sail close enough to reach over the side and grab it. Luckily, charts float. You learn something new every day.

My pilot book referred to a free dock just after the Ponte de 25 Abril Bridge. I sailed up the river but couldn't find the dock. Getting tired, I turned *Seefalke* around and sailed back down the river. My self-tacking jib came in very handy and enabled me to tack back down quite easily. I noticed a lot of people were out sailing, enjoying the late afternoon sun.

I passed the Doka de Belem Marina just before the striking monument to Prince Henry the Navigator. I spotted that the marina had a pontoon with a hammerhead, which I felt I could sail onto. As I approached, I got the bow and stern lines ready and tied the fenders on. I sailed into the marina on my small headsail.

Another yacht was moored on the forward end of the hammerhead, with what looked like a very expensive self-steering gear on its stern. There wasn't much room astern of the yacht, so I let the jib flap and decided that it was safer to sail alongside the other yacht. Luckily for me, people came running down the pontoon, pointing to the rear end of the hammerhead. With four extra pairs of hands to stop me doing any damage to the yacht in front of me, I sailed onto the pontoon. My new friends said they had been watching me sail around from the yacht club. They'd realised I was single-handed and had come to give me a hand. Safely tied up to the dock, I thanked them for their help.

After I tidied up the yacht and put the sails away, I needed a beer—I deserved one after fourteen days of single-handed sailing, with a few storms thrown in for a good measure. I pulled out the three-litre bottle of Inch's cider from the bilge. Today was a good day to liberate it and celebrate my arrival in Lisbon.

Chapter 8
Carrying on South

The yacht in front of me was called *Kismet*. The crew turned up not long after I arrived, so I invited them aboard. We sat on deck sharing what was left of my bottle of cider. I had drunk half of it already, being pretty happy to be tied up next to dry land, talking to someone.

Kismet, which means 'fate' in Arabic, belonged to Dave and Siobhan from Wigan, who were taking the yacht down to Puerto de la Luz, Las Palmas de Gran Canarias, to join in the Atlantic Rally for Cruisers, more commonly known as the ARC. They would have headed south already had it not been for a yacht crashing into them and breaking a bracket on their pulpit, which needed straightening and rewelding.

Fate had brought us together. They were happy to be docked beside *Seefalke* and its drunk Welsh owner. My cider did not last long, so we moved over to *Kismet*. Dave had cold beer in his fridge—what a luxury. A fridge with cold beer. I was very happy; it was just what I needed. We spent the evening talking and drinking in the sun.

Siobhan asked if I was out sailing in the bad weather last week. I said I was.

"What was it like?" she asked.

"Bad. It was like being in a giant washing machine; I had never seen so much white water, or waves so big in my life."

"How big were they?"

"I wrote in my log 'waves over fifty feet in height'—that was my best guess. Big, huge, with broken white water on the crests. What was worse, I had no wind in the bottom of the troughs and howling wind on the crests."

It was only now that I got the full detail of the storm I had sailed through. David said he had been listening to the storm reports on his single-sideband radio. It was a hurricane named Iris, with winds recorded at one hundred and ten miles per hour; it was an incredibly deep depression of 957 millibars when it entered the English Channel. Most hurricanes weaken by the time they have tracked across the Atlantic, but not Iris. This storm had intensified so much it had closed all the commercial ports in Western Europe. It was reported that two yachts were missing, two cargo ships lost, and five people confirmed dead. This was all a bit too much to take in, very sobering. I had been extremely lucky.

Siobhan had offered to cook dinner for us all. I brought out the guitar, and Dave got out the wine. We had a good evening, but by seven o'clock, I crashed out, after setting my alarm to go off every two hours—I still had to pump the water out. Feeling very happy and safe for the first time in thirteen days—and very lucky—it took seconds for me to fall asleep.

***

Tuesday 12th September

I had my breakfast sitting in the cockpit, enjoying the start of what turned out to be a beautiful day. My first job was to make a list of all the repairs I needed to do.

Most of my clothes were wet and smelly and in desperate need of a wash. I shut the cockpit drains and filled the cockpit half full of fresh water from the dock. Using the soap powder that Siobhan gave me, I threw all my clothes into the cockpit and walked all over them as if I were treading on grapes to make wine. I opened the drains again to let the water out. With the washing done and rinsed off, I spread my clean clothes all over the yacht to dry. The yacht looked like a Chinese laundry; it hadn't taken me long to lower the tone of the neighbourhood. At least it didn't take long for my clothes to dry.

As Dave had been in the marina for over a week, he knew where all the important places were, like the bank, ATMs, public telephones, the yacht chandlery, supermarket and, most importantly, the garage down the road that sold cheap beer.

Armed with his local knowledge and guidance, I headed into Lisbon. First off, I took my batteries to a garage to get them recharged. Next, I went to the ATM to draw out some cash and then headed off to find the yacht chandlery to get some epoxy.

Back on the yacht, I tried to stop the leaks, with no luck; the water kept washing the glue away. I had to come up with a better plan. I put my snorkelling gear on and swam under and around the hull, but after a close look, I could not see any visible leaks.

Later that afternoon, I wandered up to the garage to buy some beer, replenish *Kismet*'s supply that I'd trashed the day before and pick up some change so I could call home. I had to check in with my mother, to let her know she still had a "sun" in her life.

Using the payphone, I rang home and got Mum to ring me back; it was cheaper than a reverse-charge phone call. Mum was happy to hear from me. She said she'd watched the news one evening and seen there had been a big storm in the Bay of Biscay.

"Lynn," she told me, "I found the Coastguard's number in the Yellow Pages and rang them. After a few rings, the phone was answered. So, I explained to the young-sounding Coastguard officer that I had a son sailing on a yacht in the Bay of Biscay.

"The Coastguard officer said, 'The name of the yacht, please?'

"So, I told him, '*Seefalke.*'

"He asked if you had a radio, and I said yes, so he said, 'Good, that makes it easy. Ring this number, and the operator will put a phone call through to him.'"

Mum was given a phone number to ring.

I explained to her that I only had a VHF radio, not a single-sideband radio, which ham radio operators use.

There's a scene in Tony Hancock's radio play *Radio Ham*, about a yacht sinking. It went something like this:

"My position is—*CRRR CRRR.*"

"Sorry, can you repeat that? I have dropped my pencil."

"I am sinking?"

"Hang on, I need to put money in the electricity meter."

I knew Mum had heard the radio play.

"So, Mum," I asked her, "what did you do?"

"I rang the number the Coastguard gave me. I talked to the operator, telling him the yacht's name. After waiting a few minutes, the operator said, 'Yes, we have his number' and gave it to me, saying just ring the number like you would for a normal phone call and you will be able to get straight through to him. Lynn, I didn't know you had a phone on the yacht?"

"I don't." I had to laugh; I had no idea where this conversation was going.

"I guessed that, because the next thing I did was I rang the number, and a German-sounding man answered.

"'Is this *Seefalke*?' I asked.

"'Ja, Mam,' he replied.

"'Is this the yacht *Seefalke*?'

"'Nein, nein. Dis is the Bundesmarine Frigate *Seefalke*.'

"'Oh, sorry, I have the wrong number,' I replied, so I hung up."

"Don't worry about it, Mum," I said. "I bet you gave him a laugh."

"It gets worse."

"How?"

"Well, I rechecked the number and rang it again. The same German voice said, 'Ello.'

"'Oh, hello. Err, it's me again—can you help me?'

"'Ja, Mam?'

"'My son is sailing his yacht in this storm Iris that is on the six o'clock news. Is there any chance you would see him?'

"'Vere is your son, Mam?'

"'He is in the Bay of Biscay.'

"'Vell, nein, Mam. Wir will not see your son as wir are in the Baltic Sea.'

"So, I hung up again."

"That's very funny, Mum," I told her. "Well, you tried."

"Lynn, one more thing before you hang up."

"What's that?"

"Bowmer rang me to ask if I knew where you were and asked if you are okay. He said he'd just finished sailing in the Teacher's Whisky Round Britain yacht race, which they helped win for Wales, and caught the tail end of Iris as they were sailing down the east coast. He knew that you must have been in the path of the storm and wanted to check if you had come out the other side okay. Bowmer said they had very rough conditions in the North Sea."

"Mum, tell Bowmer I'm fine and tell him it's cheered me up no end that he shared a bit of the same misery I did, the next time he calls."

I had to laugh—only a mum would try to phone you when you are at sea in a force 12 gale looking up at fifty-foot waves. What could she have done to help?

What I did learn was it must have been a big storm to hit the six o'clock news at home.

I had dinner on *Kismet*. We all had a good laugh when I told them about my mother's phone call—I put the accent on as well.

***

Wednesday 13ᵗʰ September

After my breakfast and a cup of coffee, my first job was to pick up my batteries. To stop them going flat again, I needed a bigger solar panel. I bit the bullet and went to the yacht chandlery to buy one. To my surprise, they didn't sell them. Instead, I had to phone and order one from the UK. I paid for it with my bank card and had it sent to the marina.

Walking back to the yacht, I stopped in the garage to pick up my recharged batteries. Whilst I was there, I picked up stamps and a couple of postcards. I sent one to my mother, the other to my last boss, saying:

For the next thirty years of my life, I am going to make every day long, hot and sunny. Please accept this postcard as notice of my resignation.

Lynn.

I hoped the card would bring a smile to his face and give him a laugh. Even though I must have been sacked a long time ago for being AWOL.

With the batteries reconnected and my automatic bilge pumps working again, I could leave the yacht unattended for longer and sleep without getting up every two hours. This was definitely progress.

I had to focus on finding a way to stop the leaks. Walking around town, it didn't take too long to find what I was looking for: a carpenter's shop. I asked if I could have a bag of sawdust. I was told, "Take all you want."

When I got back to the yacht, I put the sawdust in a plastic bag, which I poked holes in. Using my boathook, I pushed the plastic bag underwater all around the hull, shaking it hardest around the areas where I thought the leaks were. My cunning plan was to allow the fine sawdust to be drawn into the leaks by the force of the incoming water. After only a few minutes, most of my leaks had slowed down. When I swam under the hull, I could see where the sawdust had collected, so I rubbed more sawdust into the same areas. Finally, the leaks stopped altogether. Once the wood had time to dry out, I could fix the leaks from the inside, which would be a big relief.

After sorting my leaks out, I caught up with Dave, who was pretty fed up. He had just come back with his pulpit bracket that had been welded by the boatyard, having paid the equivalent of forty pounds for a simple weld. There was no way I could afford those prices—I'd need to find somewhere cheaper to get my own welding done.

I decided to go back to the carpenter's shop to pick up some more sawdust, which I thought would come in handy for the future. I also decided to take the broken paddle from my self-steering gear with me. On my way, I wanted to check out a factory I'd seen that had stainless steel furniture outside. As I approached, I was met by the manager, who spoke poor English but asked if he could help me. I managed to explain my situation using hand signals. After a bit of pointing at my paddle and interpretation between the two of us, I got him to understand that I needed some welding done. He said, "No problem, tomorrow."

I collected my sawdust before picking up some beers and ice on my way back to the marina.

I'd enjoyed another really good day. The evening was spent eating out for a change with the crew of *Kismet*. Life was starting to feel pretty good.

***

Thursday 14th September

I'd spent three days in the marina and hadn't got around to checking in, so after breakfast, I decided to pay a visit to the office. The marina manager spoke perfect English and straight away asked why I hadn't checked in. I explained that I had been carrying out repairs to the yacht following the storm and hadn't had the chance. I apologised and asked for his understanding. Once I explained, he was happy but also advised me to clear customs as they wouldn't be so understanding. He advised me to tell them that I had just arrived to avoid a hefty fine and a good telling off. Thanking the manager for his advice, I headed off with all my paperwork to find the Guardia Fiscal (immigration) and Alfandega (customs).

This proved to be a productive day. I got all of my administration sorted out and was up straight with the marina and customs. Walking back through town, I picked up my paddle for the self-steering which had been fully repaired. I asked the factory manager how much I owed him, and to my complete surprise, he said, in poor English, "No trouble, forget."

I was over the moon—a free repair on top of getting all my paperwork done, what a great day.

Once back aboard *Seefalke*, I found the wood around my leaks was dry enough for the epoxy to cure. Given that I was on a winning streak, I decided to epoxy the top and bottom joints of the stern tube, which I hoped would bring about a permanent end to my leaks.

After cleaning myself up, I met the guys on *Kismet* for my usual evening beer. I told Dave about the result I'd had with my self-steering paddle repair, but judging by the look on his face, I don't think he was too pleased.

This was my last night with *Kismet*, as Dave and Siobhan were leaving the next day for Porto Santo. To my surprise, they had gone to the trouble of getting their chart for Porto Santo and Madeira photocopied for me. I said I would catch them up as soon as I could and meet them there.

I had to look in my Atlantic Crossing Guide to find out where Porto Santo was.

***

Friday 15th September

I was on hand to cast off *Kismet*'s lines as she left the dock. I was sad to see them go; we had become good friends, and I was already keen to meet up with them again.

The marina manager delivered a letter to me while I was on deck enjoying my morning coffee. The letter advised that my solar panel was awaiting collection at the central post office. This was great news, as this was the only thing stopping me following *Kismet*. As soon as the marina manager gave me directions to the post office, I was off to collect my solar panel—I figured a couple of hours, and I'd be back on the yacht with the new panel fitted.

I found the post office without any problem, only to be told that my parcel was at another depot. After receiving another set of instructions, I was on my way. On arrival at the new address, I was told that this was the wrong place too. At this point, I started to think I was being seriously wound up. However, it turned out that there were three main post offices in Lisbon. I had to go to all three before I finally found my solar panel. After a long day walking around Lisbon, it was too late to fit the panel and all I wanted to do was drink a cold beer to calm down from a frustrating day.

***

Saturday 16th September

I spent the day running back and forth to the chandlery, picking up the electrical fittings I needed to get the two solar panels to charge the batteries.

At last, all my jobs were complete: the leaks and my self-steering were fixed. I just needed to pick up supplies, pay the marina and clear customs. I decided to leave the following day in order to catch up with *Kismet* in Porto Santo.

***

Sunday 17th September

Unfortunately, my departure plans had to be put on ice as both the marina and customs offices were closed. It just meant that I enjoyed a chilled day getting the yacht ready for sea.

***

Monday 18th September

06:00

After breakfast, I topped the tanks up with clean fresh water, paid my marina bill and cleared customs and immigration—even though Porto Santo is a Portuguese colony, I still needed to get my yacht papers stamped. Back on the dock, I turned *Seefalke* around so she was facing towards the marina entrance. I wanted to make sure I could sail out without any issues. As luck would have it, just as I was getting ready to leave, a yacht came in to pick up fuel. After a quick chat, they agreed to give me a tow out once they had refuelled.

The skipper said they'd be about an hour, which gave me time to get the sails ready. I had the main ready to go up in its sail track; the genoa was hanked on with the sheets sorted out and run back to the cockpit winches. Last but not least, I made sure the halyards weren't twisted. Once this was done, I studied the chart and planned my way back out of Lisbon.

Seefalke was ready to go back to sea, and I was left with time to have a coffee in the cockpit while going over everything in my head one last time.

The skipper of the yacht who'd agreed to give me a tow, walked over to tell me that he'd changed his mind and was going to stay overnight. Determined to leave, I rigged the mooring lines so they'd be easy to slip once I was ready to sail off the berth. I hoisted the no.2 genoa, leaving it to flap gently in the warm breeze, and gave the bow a push off before walking aft to slip the stern line. I trimmed the genoa, and as *Seefalke* gently picked up speed, I was able to steer clear of the berth. Once out through the marina entrance, I hoisted the main and started to sail down the river.

I enjoyed a lovely sail out of Lisbon. When I passed the impressive statue of Prince Henry the Navigator, I wondered if he would be looking after me and *Seefalke*.

Prince Henry was born in 1394 and was the fourth child of the Portuguese King John I; his mother was Philippa of Lancaster, the sister of King Henry IV of England. He is famous for the procuring and building of new cargo ships, designed using the caravel building method—'hull plank on top of hull plank'. These vessels used a Lateen sail—part of the sail in front of the mast—which enabled them to sail further and faster. They were also very manoeuvrable, with the ability to sail into the wind, making them independent of the prevailing wind, for the first time.

The new cargo ships enabled Prince Henry to develop Portuguese exploration and maritime trade with other continents and the islands of Western Africa. He is regarded as the initiator of what is known as the Age of Discovery.

The exploration of the Atlantic led to the discovery of easterly trade winds blowing close to the equator and the returning westerly winds in the mid-Atlantic. This knowledge opened the door for the voyage of Christopher Columbus to discover and return from the New World in 1492.

503 years later, in 1995, I was sailing on a caravel-built yacht without an engine, with a foresail in front of the mast, following the same route as Christopher Columbus. Hopefully to find a new world and life for myself.

I left Lisbon via the south channel, the same way I had sailed in. Sailing out through the narrow part of the channel with sandbanks either side, I heard a loud blast coming from a ship, which made me jump. Looking behind, I saw the bow of a huge cruise ship towering above me. How it sneaked up on me, I do not know. There was not much I could do—with no engine I had to carry on. I bet this looked funny: my small yacht sailing right under the bow of this huge liner, just like you see in cartoons.

I sailed straight on to get out of the way of the liner. It took me a good fifteen minutes before I passed the number two channel buoy. The ship altered course at the buoy and gave one more loud blast on the horn. I could see all the passengers on deck were waving at me. I waved back.

The liner quickly accelerated away, and I could see her stern starting to squat as she picked up speed. The liner must have been doing over twenty knots and seemed to slip through the water effortlessly. It was a really impressive sight to watch at very close quarters.

I set George up on a course to take me out of the bay. Having satisfied myself that there were no vessels around, I went below to make myself a quick sandwich and a cup of coffee.

With my coffee in hand, I climbed out of the main hatch only to find a small fishing boat at anchor abeam of *Seefalke*. The guy on board was happily waving at me; I waved back—it was all very pleasant. I then realised, as I looked at *Seefalke*'s wake, that somehow, she had sailed a perfect half-circle around the anchored boat. I could not believe it; the man in the fishing boat carried on waving at me happily, as if sailing around him had been planned. If George had maintained a straight course, we would have sliced the little boat in two. I think the fisherman would still have been waving, albeit in distress. I don't know if it was George or somebody else, but someone was certainly looking after me—perhaps it was Prince Henry?

18:00

I had enjoyed a good day. I sailed out of the bay, passing Cascais, and picked up a north-westerly wind and found a southerly current. My course was 240° mag, which would take me out of the bay into the Atlantic. For tea, I enjoyed fried egg and cheese sandwiches, with a coffee and a tot of good Portuguese brandy. I was straight back into my life at sea.

***

2nd day at sea
Tuesday 19th September

06:00

I was up most of the night, keeping a close eye on a number of ships and small fishing boats. The morning turned into a lovely sunny day, with a fresh breeze and a calm sea. And I had the bonus of having George working well again.

12:00. Pos. 37°43'N 011°21'W

Logged 110NM in the last 24 hours.

Another day with perfect sailing conditions, moving effortlessly along. All I had to do was keep a lookout for ships, pump the yacht out, read my book and decide what culinary delight to have for tea.

***

3rd day at sea
Wednesday 20th September

06:00

I awoke at first light, and while I was chilling out in the cockpit with my coffee, I was treated to an amazing sunrise, which signalled the start of another perfect day at sea. As the sun rose higher in the morning sky, *Seefalke* slipped along in the stiff breeze and flat sea. This was the sort of ocean sailing I had always imagined.

12:00. Pos. 36°13'N 013°47'W

Logged 148NM in the last 24 hours.

I had my best noon-to-noon run, since leaving Wales, and from my position on the chart, I had already sailed over halfway to Porto Santo. I was starting to enjoy the trip after another effortless day of reading and keeping watch on deck.

21:00

I lost George; the weld broke again on the paddle shaft. So much for my free weld. No doubt Dave from *Kismet* would be happy when I told him.

***

4th day at sea
Thursday 21st September

12:00. Pos. 35°04'N 015°26'W
Logged 105NM in the last 24 hours.

Another good 24-hour run, even without George. Last night, I set the yacht up to sail herself. With the prevailing north wind and flat sea, keeping *Seefalke* on a broad reach had been easy and very comfortable sailing.

18:00
Seefalke was becalmed, and there was not much for me to do other than drink my coffee and watch another brilliant sunset.

***

5th day at sea
Friday 22nd September

06:00
With the early hours came more wind, and I enjoyed a lovely sail under a star-filled sky and warm breeze. The morning brought another idyllic day, although the barometer had dropped slightly, signposting a possible change in the weather.

12:00. Pos. 33°59'N 016°00'W
Logged 70NM in the last 24 hours.

The weather did start to change, with a more overcast sky, a choppier sea and, interestingly, a drop in wind. With the confused sea and reduced wind, I could not get the yacht to steer herself, and so I spent the afternoon keeping her on track.

18:00
The wind died away to nothing, leaving me becalmed with an uncomfortable swell, so I took the sails down to stop them shaking themselves to bits.

22:30

After my nightcap, I tried to get some sleep, but with the yacht wallowing and the halyards clanking against the mast, this wasn't easy. I went up on deck and tied the halyards to the jackstays to keep them away from the mast. I thought I would have peace at last; however, as soon as I returned to my bunk, something was rolling around and making an irritating noise. I couldn't believe it. The yacht would roll one way and I would hear a ding, then she'd roll back the other way and there'd be another ding. This was so annoying; I couldn't get back to sleep. In fact, I stayed up most of the night trying to find the offending item but to no avail. I wrapped T-shirts around my cups and plates and stuffed toilet roll around my pots and pans, all of which helped—but I still hadn't isolated the rattle. This was getting seriously annoying.

Finally, I found a single torch battery rolling around behind a drawer and managed to get a few hours' sleep.

***

6th day at sea
Saturday 23rd September

06:00

After breakfast, I found that my batteries had gone flat—probably caused by me having all the cabin lights on, looking for that sodding battery. This was bad news, as it left me without a radio, navigation lights and no automatic bilge pump again. I should have bought two even bigger solar panels and bigger batteries.

As the morning sun rose, the wind picked up to a force 3 north-easterly. The yacht was sailing along beautifully under a full mainsail and no.2 genoa.

12:00. Pos. 33°15'N 016°00'W

Logged 44NM in the last 24 hours.

My noon fix had me only 20NM north-east of Porto Santo; I saw the outline of the island in the distance. That afternoon, the wind went light again, and I was back on the helm, steering by hand in an attempt to keep the yacht moving in the fickle breeze.

Progress was painfully slow. The island was tantalisingly close, and I wanted to be sat at anchor with a cool beer in my hand.

18:00

I was becalmed 10NM north of Porto Santo. I realised I wasn't going to get in that evening, so I took the sails down to make the yacht comfortable so I could make up for my lost sleep last night.

***

7th day at sea
Sunday 24th September

06:00

After a very good night's sleep, I awoke early to the sight of the beautiful, lush, green, tropical island of Porto Santo. Excited by having a steady breeze, I reset the sails and set a course towards the island.

08:00

Sailing past the small island of Porto de Cima with its distinctive lighthouse, I could see yachts at anchor in a small bay, marking the entrance to the harbour with its marina inside.

11:00

I anchored outside the harbour wall with thirty other yachts. There were yachts from Sweden, Norway, UK, Germany, America and Canada, but what really cheered me up was the sight of the Welsh flag flying from the stern of one. As I looked at all the different yachts, I suddenly had a sense of belonging.

The marina was full of cruising yachts; this little island was buzzing with activity. I was keen to explore and wasted no time in blowing up the dinghy and rowing into the marina. It didn't take me too long to find Dave and Siobhan sitting in the cockpit of *Kismet* and soon the beers came out and we started swapping our passage stories.

They'd experienced conditions similar to me; the only difference was they were able to motor when their boat speed dropped off and got to Porto Santo a lot quicker.

***

Monday 25th September

After a leisurely breakfast, first on my to-do list was to clear customs and immigration. There was another mountain of paperwork to go through; each form I had to fill out three times I was convinced no one would ever look at ever again. As soon as my yacht papers were stamped, I headed off to take a closer look at Porto Santo. The island was beautiful, and the locals were incredibly friendly. For a small place, it had great amenities; I even found a DIY store that seemed to sell everything. The only thing missing was a boatyard where I could get my self-steering repaired again.

Porto Santo is the first stopping-off place for yachts planning to cross the Atlantic. The yachts slowly migrate south through the autumn, waiting for the hurricane season to end before starting their passages. As part of the ongoing tradition, yacht crews paint flags and murals on the harbour wall with names and messages of luck to signify their safe passage and good wishes to future crews embarking on the same endeavour.

This was the start of the partying too. Although I didn't know it at the time, I would see some of these yachts repeatedly over the coming few months. The owners of the other Welsh yacht turned out to be two friends from Swansea who were doing the ARC rally. It was great to buddy up with some fellow Welshmen and socialise with kindred spirits.

I made some good friends in Porto Santo, and I certainly had a good time exploring the beautiful island with Dave and Siobhan. After two weeks of sightseeing and partying, it was time to carry on sailing south.

***

Tuesday 10th October

08:30

After a good English breakfast, I went to clear customs, only to be told there was no need for any further paperwork as I was heading for Madeira, which is part of the same group of Portuguese islands. All I needed to do was sign in again on arrival.

Sailing out of the anchorage with just the no.2 genoa up, I followed behind five other yachts. After I got the mainsail up, I thought it would be fun to see if I could catch them before I got to Funchal.

It was a hot, sunny day with not a cloud in the sky, and a prevailing force 4 breeze was blowing from the north-west.

12:00

The yacht was sailing beautifully along. I had caught and overtaken most of the other yachts. There was one wooden fifty-footer in front of me, we were both reaching, and it became clear that this had turned into a race between the two of us. I could see the crew looking up at the sails and trimming them, trying to squeeze every last ounce of speed out of their yacht. I was doing the same. Trying to helm and trim the sails at the same time was hard work but thoroughly enjoyable.

15:00

The wind had shifted more to the west, which meant I was now sailing hard on the wind. *Seefalke* was at her fastest point of sail. After three hard hours, I finally caught and overtook the other yacht and slowly pulled away.

17:00

By the time I reached Pta do Garajau, I was a mile ahead of the other yacht. Sailing towards the amazing Cristo Rei statue, I started to think about how I could slow the yacht down enough to sail into the harbour safely. Under the statue, the wind stopped, just like a fan had been switched off. The sails went from being full to hanging like bags of rags. Slowly, the yachts I had overtaken earlier caught up and then sailed into the same dead air. One by one, they started their engines and left me behind.

It took me another two hours of hard work before I finally sailed into Funchal and anchored. Oh, what fun it is to sail a yacht with no engine.

Looking around Funchal Marina, I saw a big sign saying, 'Madeira Engineering', which was great news—I could now get my self-steering fixed.

***

Wednesday 11th October

Up early, after breakfast, I was off to clear in again. First stop was the Capitanian-de-Porto (port captain), followed by Guardia Fiscal (immigration) and Alfandega (customs), then on to Policia Maritima (maritime police). I would need to replicate all this when it came time to leave. I was still wondering what happened to all the paperwork they kept stamping in triplicate.

After filling in a few more trees, I decided to have a wander around town with what little of the day was left. No surprise, I ended up back at the marina bar, which overlooked the myriad yachts that were moored up. The majority of berths were taken up with cruising yachts planning to do the ARC, which included my friends on *Kismet*. There were additional yachts taking part in a French single-handed yacht race from Madeira to Barbados. All told, there were a lot of yachts packed into the tiny marina.

One thing you couldn't miss were the posters everywhere requesting information about a missing yacht that had left Ireland around the same time I had sailed out of Dale. The yacht had a young couple on board who hadn't arrived in Madeira as expected. All I could think of was they had been caught in Storm Iris. The missing yacht was a stark reminder of what can go wrong. Drinking my beer, I thanked my lucky stars that I had weathered the same storm.

***

Thursday 12th October

I paid a visit to Madeira Engineering to try and get the design fault in George fixed. I wanted to machine a piece of metal, to prevent the blade from breaking again.

I met the engineering manager, who spoke good English. I explained what I needed to be machined and gave him a drawing I had made, but unfortunately, he didn't understand what I wanted. To try and solve the problem, I explained that I was a toolmaker by trade.

To my surprise, he said, "So, you can use a lathe?"

"Yes," I said. "I've been using them all my working life."

"Okay, follow me."

I was taken to the machine shop. There were four men working on lathes. The manager went up to one of them, then turned back to me and said, "Here, you can use this one."

The lathe was a Triumph 2000, which I had worked on all through my apprenticeship. The lathe operator stepped back and pointed to the lathe. I hadn't expected the guy to let me use it, but sure enough, he was happy for me to jump on. I stuck my lump of metal in the chuck, had a quick look at the tool bit, checked the tool was centred using a rule, and finally I checked the speed and feed, which were all good.

It was at this point that the lathe operator who had been fussing around me realised I knew what I was doing. I started to machine the part, the swath coming off looking perfect—a nice silver colour. After a few minutes, I was left alone; the lathe operator wandered off. Half an hour later, I was all done.

With the new part made, I fitted the two parts together. I asked the manager if I could get the parts welded, and he kindly took me to the welding shop. The parts were TIG welded together, leaving me just a small weld to clean up on the lathe. Job done.

I went back to the office to ask the manager how much I owed.

He said, "If you come and work for me, the job is free."

The lathe operator had been well impressed with my skill on the lathe and had provided a glowing reference to the manager, who was desperate to take me on. It was a tempting offer—Madeira was a lovely place, and everyone seemed really friendly. But if I stopped there, I had this nagging doubt that I wouldn't get to fully experience what the future had in store for me. After a minute or two's consideration, I politely declined.

I paid the bill, which came to less than fifteen pounds. I was one very happy camper, confident that I had fixed George once and for all.

Madeira is a lovely island with great walks and views. It's also an island steeped in history; it's a shame that the harbour couldn't live up to the rest of it. After a week in this very busy, uncomfortable anchorage, I'd had enough.

Kismet was leaving to carry on sailing south, and I decided to follow suit. Our plan was to sail to Selvagens Grande, one of a small group of islands between Madeira and the Canary Islands. This was a nature reserve, uninhabited apart from the conservation wardens who looked after it.

***

Tuesday 19th October

My morning was spent walking to customs, immigration, the port captain and, finally, Policia Maritima. With all my paperwork in order, I picked up some fresh supplies, meaning I was clear and ready to leave.

Before *Kismet* left, Dave and I had one last look at the chart and pilot book on Selvagens Grande, although there was not much information. The islands are hard to spot from a distance due to their flat nature and they are poorly lit at night, but there is a fair-weather anchorage on the south side of the island.

As I helped *Kismet* off the dock, the last thing Dave said to me was, "Leave your radio on channel sixteen, I will let you know what the islands are like when we get there."

15:00
Before I left, I sat in the cockpit drinking a cup of coffee, just spending ten minutes relaxing, and thinking over whether I'd got everything I needed for my trip south. Happy that I was ready, I started preparing the yacht for sea.

There was a light wind blowing directly into the anchorage, meaning that I would need to tack my way out of the bay.

With the mainsail pulled up, I let it flap while I went to the bow to haul up the anchor. I soon realised that the anchor was stuck. I went back to the helm and sheeted in the main and sailed over the anchor to break it free. Once I had broken the anchor out, I let the yacht come up head to wind before going back to the bow to haul the anchor aboard. Shortly afterwards, I heard a cheer, and when I looked around, I could see *Overlord*, a stunning, blue, hundred-square-meter. She was another Windfall yacht. The crew were clapping and cheering at my seamanship—at least, that's what I told myself!

Once I cleared the harbour, I stowed the anchor, cleaned the mud off the deck, got the no.2 genoa up and set George to steer a course of 140° mag. There was a lovely force 4 northerly blowing. This meant I was in for some lovely downwind sailing all the way to the Canaries. George seemed to be performing well following his repair, but just when I thought I could relax, a bloody great big tuna fish jumped out of the water less than ten feet from the yacht. While it was an amazing sight, it would have made a right mess of the yacht if it had landed in the cockpit.

That night there was a decent moon and a star-filled sky. It was beautiful, and if that wasn't magical enough, the phosphorescence in *Seefalke*'s wake was mesmerising. I often thought how good it would be if you could bottle the stuff. You would make a fortune. Not that I had any direct experience, but I reckoned looking at phosphorescence was better than taking any mind-bending drugs, and it was free.

***

2nd day at sea
Wednesday 20th October

12:00. Pos. 31°36'N 015°27'W

Logged 95NM in the last 21 hours.

After my midday fix, I had changed course to sail towards Selvagens Grande when to my surprise my VHF radio burst into life. I had forgotten it was on. Dave on *Kismet* called to say they would not be stopping on the island and he advised me to do the same—motoring into the anchorage looked tricky. They were going to carry on and go to Santa Cruz in Tenerife.

20:00

The weather wasn't so good. It had become overcast and the sea was quite choppy. It was early evening when Selvagens Grande first came into view. As the pilot book had said, it was difficult to spot due to its low-lying nature and there were no lights. Dave's advice turned out to be spot on, and I, too, decided to carry on to Tenerife.

***

3rd day at sea
Thursday 21st October

06:00

The wind dropped off in the early hours, and it poured with rain, making the visibility poor. I was pleased I had made the decision to carry on and give Selvagens Grande a wide berth. I spent the night sitting on top of the cabin steps keeping watch; there were a few ships around but nothing to worry about.

As morning broke, it was still overcast. The wind was all over the place, and the wind speed was up and down every five minutes, which made sailing very frustrating.

12:00. Pos. 30°05'N 015°55'W

Logged 95NM in the last 24 hours.

From my midday fix, I was 85NM north of Tenerife. The sun finally came out to grace me with its presence, and a nice northerly breeze filled in. I would have enjoyed a lovely downwind sail had it not been for the swell left over from earlier. I put a preventer on to stop the boom from swinging back and forth across the deck. Sailing downwind was not George's best direction—a common problem that plagues most self-steering systems.

***

4th day at sea
Friday 22nd October

05:00

I had stayed up all night, sitting on my top step; I was too close to land to risk falling asleep. My GPS position fix put me due east of Santa Cruz. With a very good breeze blowing between the islands, I didn't want to stop. I decided to carry on sailing down the east coast of Tenerife and head for Los Cristianos on the south-west corner of the island instead.

A good breeze carried me until I was south of Pta de la Rasca, right at the bottom end of Tenerife, where I lost the wind. The sails hung limply, and the sea was like glass. It was baking hot. Thankfully, I was entertained by a small pod of pilot whales swimming around the yacht, which was great to see.

14:00

I finally wrote off the prospect of doing any sailing for the rest of the day, as there wasn't a breath of wind. Before leaving Wales, I'd made a bracket for attaching my two-horse outboard to the stern quarter of the yacht. That afternoon seemed like the perfect opportunity to try it. The bracket worked a treat, and the outboard pushed *Seefalke* along at two knots, which was pretty good. I left the main up to help catch any breeze, and very slowly, I motor-sailed through the flat, calm water, towards the port of Los Cristianos.

Approaching the harbour in the middle of the main channel, I heard a loud ship's horn. Astern of me was a large ferry, which nearly ran me down. I don't think the captain was overly chuffed that I was taking up the channel, but there was nothing much I could do. He had to wait until I'd covered the last few hundred yards into the harbour.

Once in the outer harbour, I stopped the outboard and dropped the anchor in the perfect spot between two French yachts. Just as the anchor bit, a large gust of wind came from nowhere, the mainsail powered up and the yacht started sailing over the anchor.

The anchor dug in, and *Seefalke* started to sail around in a circle. I ran to the mast to drop the mainsail, but it was stuck. For a good five minutes, I tried to get the sail down while *Seefalke* kept on doing laps around the anchor.

You should have seen the look on the French crews' faces as I got closer and closer to them with every lap; it was a picture. When the gust subsided, I finally got the mainsail down, by which time the two French yachts had moved.

I put two anchors down, as the harbour was a bit exposed to a southerly wind and was full of yachts. My pilot book also said that the holding wasn't particularly good. I had two CQR (Coastal Quick Release) anchors out. On my thirty-five-pound anchor, I had attached a hundred feet of half-inch chain, while my smaller twenty-five-pound anchor had fifty feet of chain and then anchor warp. I snorkelled down to check the two anchors and set them in properly. Everything looked fine. I was anchored in twelve feet of water on a sandy bottom.

With *Seefalke* safely at anchor and tidied up, I filled in my logbook. I had sailed over 1900NM since leaving Barry, endured some pretty bad weather and overcome every challenge thrown at me so far. For someone who'd had no single-handed sailing experience before leaving Wales, this was a pretty good achievement. I felt pretty chuffed with myself, and to celebrate, I went ashore, found a pub and enjoyed a cold happy-hour beer.

Sitting outside the bar in the sun, watching the world go by, it soon became apparent that Los Cristianos was the party capital of Tenerife, with lots of bars, nightclubs and restaurants. Most of the tourists were English and German. It reminded me a lot of Barry Island or Blackpool; the only difference was it was hot, and the beer was cheap.

***

Saturday 23rd October

I found the harbour master's office, and all my paperwork was stamped in five minutes, which was really easy and a lovely surprise. I spent the day finding out where the banks and supermarkets were—and more importantly, which bar sold the cheapest beer.

On my second night lying at anchor, a strong southerly wind blew straight through the harbour entrance, and with it came a nasty swell. The following morning, after a very uncomfortable night, I went to check the anchors. The breeze had dropped, and the conditions were much improved. However, the warp from my second anchor was lying over the bow roller with no weight on it. When I recovered the rope, it became clear from the frayed end that the rope had parted. I had no option but to get my snorkel and fins on and take a closer look at what had happened during the night.

On diving down, I found both anchors had wrapped themselves around a rock. The warp must have chafed on the rock and consequently parted. I'd got lucky—if I had anchored with one anchor, using only anchor warp, *Seefalke* would have been on the beach. I could have very easily lost the yacht.

It served as a big wake-up call. I had a spare anchor chain and immediately realised that it was doing no good sitting in the yacht. From that moment forward, I made sure that both anchors went down with chain on them and no warp.

A couple of days later, I was sat in my favourite bar having a quiet beer when Dave and Siobhan from *Kismet* walked in. This was a lovely surprise, as I hadn't expected to see them again until I got to Las Palmas.

After bidding them good afternoon, I asked, "What are you doing here? When did you get in?"

"In that southerly blow we had the other night, a lot of yachts got damaged in the Santa Cruz anchorage as the harbour was packed with yachts," Dave said. "We got lucky and escaped any damage. So, we decided to find somewhere quieter to stay before we join up with the ARC again."

"We only got here an hour ago," said Siobhan.

"Well, it's great to see the two of you," I said. "So, how did you find me so quick?"

"That was easy," Dave said. "We passed *Seefalke* on our way in, so when we came ashore to see the harbour master, we asked him which bar sold the cheapest beer, and he led us straight here."

"You are not hard to find, Lynn," said Siobhan.

***

Saturday 30th October

Kismet was planning to sail to La Gomera before finally sailing up to Las Palmas to join the ARC. I followed them. Dave gave me another photocopied chart; we still had time to kill before we tried to cross the pond.

I sailed from Los Cristianos to La Gomera at night— that was when the wind always picked up. I sailed into San Sebastián de La Gomera, anchor ready on deck. The wind was blowing hard straight into the harbour.

I left the mainsail up on the basis that if I had any problems, I could quickly tack back out of the harbour. As I approached the anchorage, I brought *Seefalke* about and came up head to wind, making sure that the main was fully eased. After dropping both anchors, I went back to the mast to drop the sail. Once again, the mainsail jammed in the track and wouldn't come down. Although the yacht was tacking back and forth, she remained head to wind this time.

There were some nervous-looking yacht crews watching me struggle to get the sail down. After an embarrassing ten minutes or so, I finally managed it. By the time everything was sorted, I had dropped back to within a few feet of the other yachts. I quickly pulled in some of the chain, pulling myself forward and clear of them.

Getting the mainsail down was becoming a real pain, making a mockery of my much-improved boat-handling skills. I had to go up the mast to find out what was going on. Dave kindly agreed to help and pulled me up the mast. I finally found the problem: a few screws had worked themselves loose halfway up the mainsail track. All I had to do was remove the screws, repair the holes with wooden dowels, and refasten the screws. This proved to be a nice, easy, cheap fix. I hoped this would cure the problem once and for all.

La Gomera is a beautiful volcanic island, 1500 metres high. The central mountains catch the moisture from the prevailing trade winds, giving the top of the island its jungle climate, in contrast to the warmer, sun-baked cliffs of the coast. The island became a UNESCO World Heritage Site in 1986.

The crew from *Kismet* and I went to the tourist information office to enquire about things we could do while staying there.

The young guide looked at the three of us and said, "You look fit; there is only one walk for you." He pointed to a map. "Catch the number thirteen bus to the top of the island, then hike down this trail. There is a bus stop at the bottom, where you can catch a bus back to town."

What a great hike it turned out to be. The vegetation kept changing as we made our way down the mountain until we were walking in banana groves. At one point we followed a stream until it just seemed to disappear. It wasn't until we were nearly down the mountain and looking back up at where we had come from that we realised the stream had disappeared over a cliff edge and had turned into a high, very impressive waterfall.

What the young guide didn't tell us was that there was a fantastic bar waiting for us at the end of our walk. We couldn't help but call in for a round of cool beers, which topped off a perfect day.

Given the beauty of the island, we decided to do a few more hikes, which all turned out to be equally good. This was a fantastic way to explore the island, not to mention sample more of the local beer.

The next day, it was back to the information centre to go on the whistling tour to learn about the islanders' unique way of communicating over long distances. The whistling speech, called Silbo Gomero, can be heard two miles away. The whistled language is indigenous to the island and has been around since Roman times. It was adopted by the Spanish settlers in the 16th century. When this means of communication was threatened with extinction in the 21st century, the local government required all children to learn it in school. What a great day out we all had.

Kismet only stayed in La Gomera for three days before leaving for Las Palmas and the ARC rally. They had to be in Gran Canaria two weeks before the start of the rally in order to register and have their yacht checked. The ARC was leaving on 19th November, close to the end of the Atlantic hurricane season.

I left for Las Palmas two days later to find out what the ARC was all about.

***

Monday 6th November

I predicted that the sail from San Sebastián to Las Palmas would be challenging, as I expected adverse currents and headwinds the whole trip. Although the route was twenty miles longer, I decided to sail around the top of Tenerife to pick up more favourable winds. I was concerned that if I sailed the more direct route around the bottom of the island, I would be battling headwinds the whole way.

I had a good sail up to Punta de Teno before the breeze died during the early part of the evening.

***

Tuesday 7th November

06:00

My progress on leaving La Gomera was painfully slow. I had little wind and spent the night trying to claw my way off a lee shore, which wasn't much fun. I had spent hours on the helm and all I had to show for my efforts was 18NM.

12:00

The only positive I could take from the morning had been another glorious, hot, sunny day, which was great for topping up my tan.

16:00

I was becalmed off the west coast of Tenerife and very close to the shore—I could see the surf breaking over rocks. I dug the anchor out and stowed it on deck in case I needed it in a hurry. In an attempt to drum up some wind, I started whistling my little heart out. This was something the old-timers used to do to summon the wind gods. It seemed to work, as shortly afterwards a breeze filled in from the south-west and I was able to steer a course of 060° mag, taking me away from the coast.

***

Wednesday 8th November

06:00

Once again, I spent the night perched on the top step of my companionway; I wasn't comfortable sleeping when sailing so close to a lee shore. At first light, I passed the group of islands off the north-east corner of Tenerife, El Roque de Fuera being the most northerly. Once clear of Tenerife, I was able to free off and start reaching towards Las Palmas.

My gamble to sail the extra distance and go north of Tenerife had paid off, and with more wind, my boat speed had increased to seven knots. George was steering a straight course, and everything was looking good.

The Canaries are lovely islands, but sailing around them with little wind, on a yacht with no engine, had proved really challenging.

12:00

George had managed 42NM in just six hours. *Why do I bother to steer?*

19:30

I was only 5NM from the harbour of Puerto de la Luz, Las Palmas, but it was already too late to enter before it got dark. I decided to play it safe and dropped the genoa before sailing slowly east on the mainsail to gain a bit more sea room.

***

Thursday 9th November

06:00

There was little wind throughout the night. I saw a few ships and only had time to grab a few twenty-minute power naps. After my breakfast, a big rain squall came through, and the wind picked up dramatically, leaving me to put an urgent reef in the mainsail. Then, as quick as it came, the squall passed and I was left becalmed.

After drifting around for a couple of hours, the wind finally picked up and, true to form, was coming straight out of the harbour. I had no option but to tack back and forth all the way into the anchorage.

10:00

I managed to find a spot to anchor in amongst what seemed like thousands of other yachts. Because of this, I had to anchor a long way out. I went ashore to see my friends at customs and immigration, where to my surprise, I was told my ship's papers and my passport would be held until I left the island.

I asked why, and the very polite customs officer explained that the Canaries are technically a province of Spain and are not part of the EU, which I did not know—every day's a school day. The officer confirmed that my papers would be safely returned to me on my departure.

Las Palmas was well catered for in terms of amenities. There were banks, supermarkets, boatyards and a very large, safe marina. The ARC would start from here in a week or so, and there was an air of excitement and a vibrant scene around the waterfront and marina. What made it for me was walking around looking at the yachts and talking to their crews. It was really cool.

I met up with most of the yachts I had been sailing south with since leaving Lisbon, and I caught up with the guys from *Kismet*. They were hidden among all the other yachts. I was pleased to have found them, and once again enjoyed their company and a few beers. *Kismet* had been in Las Palmas a week and had been through the registration process and safety checks. They were fully compliant and authorised to join the rally.

I couldn't enter the rally for a number of reasons. First off, they don't allow single-handed sailors. You also had to carry an SSB radio, life raft and Emergency Position Indicating Radio Beacon (EPIRB).

All of these rules probably should have told me something. I did have an EPIRB and a life raft—the Tinker Tramp dinghy

143

I used to row ashore. I didn't have an SSB radio as they were big, very expensive, and used a lot of battery power.

The last thing stopping me from joining the ARC was the considerable entry fee, so it was a nonstarter for me. It was still fun being in Las Palmas, watching everybody getting ready to leave.

Some of the single-handed sailors looking to join the ARC put 'crew required' signs up, and some of the girls looking for yachts to crew on put their own signs up.

The best sign I saw was:

My name is Helga. I am a tall, blonde, 24-year-old Swedish girl, with some sailing experience. I can cook and will be happy to take any position under the captain and can orgasm in four languages.

People came from all over the world to look for a trip across the pond. Most of them got lucky and found a place. I wanted to sail across on my own, although I was really tempted to take a very attractive twenty-five-year-old, tall, skinny Norwegian girl called Annika with me. If I'd had the time to get to know her better or could have had a week doing some sailing with her then I might have been swayed. But taking a chance on someone I didn't know and spending thirty days stuck with them on a small yacht could have been a recipe for disaster.

In the end, Annika found a place on another yacht and that solved my problem.

I got to know most of the people looking for places on yachts. Basically, they were all broke and, like me, couldn't afford to drink in the bars, where the price of the beer seemed to jump up every hour. To solve this problem, a group of us threw money in a kitty and bought twenty-four-can slabs of beer from the bar, at the wholesale price. We shared the cans amongst the group, which worked well, although the beer was warm, so we called our little group the Warm Piss Club!

The ARC was leaving on the 19th of November, heading for St Lucia. I didn't fancy sailing with a thousand yachts around me, so I planned to leave on the 22nd and go to Barbados. I figured this would be enough of a gap to prevent me from sailing into the fleet.

The big day arrived, and I helped *Kismet* leave the dock. Wishing them good luck, I wondered if I would see them again on the other side of the pond.

It was impressive to see the start of the ARC. There were a thousand yachts sailing south at the same time; it was like the start of the Round the Isle of Wight race, which I had seen on TV. Annika waved to me from the deck of a yacht as it passed. She was wearing a very small bikini, and I was starting to regret my decision. I thought to myself, *Roachy, you are a dull bastard sometimes.*

After the ARC left, Las Palmas was like a ghost town, with only a few single-handed sailors left. I completed all my last-minute jobs and stocked up with fresh food, which included: eggs, potatoes, bread, cheese, flour, yeast, apples, oranges and water. I cleared customs and was handed my ship's papers and passport as promised, meaning I was free to leave.

I rang my mother to tell her I was starting my Atlantic crossing. Mum wished me luck; I told her to book a flight to Barbados for some time after Christmas so she could have a holiday and celebrate my crossing.

Chapter 9
Crossing the Pond

Wednesday 22nd November 1995

After breakfast and a quick coffee, I went ashore to get the latest weather update from the harbour master. A low-pressure system was tracking over the island, meaning I would have a northerly wind as it passed, which was just what I needed to start my trip.

I was really excited and itching to get going. The dinghy was rolled up and tied to the cabin top, all my food stowed away, the water tanks full and the sails ready to be hoisted. I had the North Atlantic Ocean chart on the chart table with my intended route set out. This just left me to sit in the cockpit and go through my routine of having a coffee while making sure I hadn't missed anything before getting the anchor up and setting sail.

I based my passage plan on averaging one hundred nautical miles a day, which wasn't very ambitious but was realistic, based on the sailing I had done since leaving Wales. If I could maintain this daily average, I would be sitting in a bar in Barbados in approximately 27 days, just in time for Christmas. I had enough food and plenty of water to live well for a month and a half.

I had to ration my limited water supply, to only half a gallon a day. It had to go a long way to cover all my needs. These included brushing my teeth; making coffee; fresh water for drinking, cooking, rinsing rice and washing myself. I used seawater for everything else, such as washing my dishes, though I rinsed them with fresh water. If I did run low, I planned to catch rainwater, just like in the old days.

This was another reason I hadn't asked Annika to join me; I couldn't see her washing her long, blonde hair in anything less than half a gallon of fresh water.

I had a slight breeze on leaving the anchorage, but not a huge amount. I had a full mainsail up and my no.2 genoa.

Only 2700NM to Barbados. I'd left Wales in August, which seemed a lifetime ago. I had already learnt a lot in four months and gained precious experience that would serve me well on the next leg of my trip and the realising of my dream.

I felt all sorts of emotions as I embarked on this stage of my voyage. To my knowledge, no Windfall yacht had ever crossed the Atlantic, let alone single-handed, and I was about to become the first person to try.

12:00. Pos. 28°17'N 016°09'W
Logged 11NM.

The wind had picked up as forecast to a force 4 from the north-east, and with it came a large swell. George was coping well, even though we were running downwind with a big following sea. I had to put a preventer on the boom to stop it swinging around dangerously above my head.

I spent a great afternoon sitting by the mast looking at the bow as we sailed over the swells in front of us. The yacht would surf down the faces of the swells, and just at the point when I expected the bow to bury itself in the back of the swell in front and drench me, the toe rail would draw level with the water and stop, then the bow would rise and we'd sail over the top of the next swell. This motion repeated itself endlessly, and although each time I was convinced that the bow would disappear under a wave, it never happened. The surprising thing to me was no water came on deck either.

South of Gran Canaria, my plan was to change course and head for the position 20°00'N 25°00'W, following the old sea captains' advice. In my Admiralty ocean passages book, the old sailing ships would head for that position. It was at that point they would expect to pick up the favourable trade winds. Then they would either sail west until they hit the islands of the Caribbean or south if they were sailing down to South America.

Early that evening, the wind increased, bringing bigger swells with it. To make the yacht more comfortable, I pulled the mainsheet in tight, holding the mainsail in the centre of the yacht. I went to the mast and dropped the main, which to my delight came down quickly and easily. What wasn't so pleasing was that the sail must have got caught up on a top spreader, as it brought the port top spreader down with it. It was too late in the evening to do anything about fixing the problem, so I set George up to carry on sailing downwind, but with just the no.2 genoa up. I planned to tackle the repair in the morning when I hoped the conditions would be more settled.

***

2nd day at sea
Thursday 23rd November

06:00

In the daylight, I could see the extent of the damage. The port top spreader had snapped clean off. Luckily for me, the intermediate rigging was supporting the mast at this point. I thanked my lucky stars that I had made and brought a spare set of spreaders for the trip. Had it not been for the small issue of climbing two-thirds of the way up the mast, this would have been quite a straightforward fix. As it was, there was still a good swell running and the yacht was rolling around a lot. I had no option but to wait for more favourable weather conditions.

I weighed up my limited options. I didn't want to sail back to Gran Canaria against the prevailing wind and current with a reduced sail set-up; it would be very hard work. The same was true if I headed for Los Cristianos. The only two viable options were to carry on and head south towards the Cape Verde Islands or simply wait until the sea calmed down, making it safer for me to climb the mast. As I had only been at sea for a day, I didn't really want to turn back. There was no danger of me losing the mast; so, I decided to carry on sailing south.

12:00. Pos. 26°32'N 015°55'W
Logged 105NM in the last 24 hours.

This was a good 24-hour run, considering I only had the no.2 up. I think I must have had a favourable current with me as well. The weather had been steadily improving all morning, so I put the mainsail up with the third reef in it. This brought the head of the sail down below the broken spreader, meaning that there was no additional stress on the mast. I was also sailing on a starboard tack, which meant the good spreaders were on the windward side and taking all the loadings. George was holding a course of 200° mag. Once this was all sorted, there wasn't much to do, other than keep a lookout, read my book and think about what to have for tea. The options were curry or chilli with rice—how lucky was I?

18:00
On my second night at sea, I was already back in the rhythm of sailing, with my nightcap of coffee with a tot of good Spanish brandy. For some reason, I had the theme from *M*A*S*H* in my head. Strange!

***

3rd day at sea
Friday 24th November

06:00
The course, wind, and sea state remained the same as the day before. There was no need for me to get involved or adjust George in any way.

12:00. Pos. 24°35'N 017°05'W
Logged 133NM in the last 24 hours.

A good noon-to-noon run, considering I was underpowered and still sailing with a broken spreader. Given that things were pretty settled, I decided to start reading a new book. When I first left Wales, my grandmother gave me a book as a present, and her last words to me before leaving were: "Do not open this present until you are sailing across the Atlantic."

Well, I decided that now was a good time to find out what my grandmother had bought me. I couldn't believe it; she had only gone and got me *Moby Dick* by Herman Melville. Bloody great—thanks, Nan. I don't think it was the best book to be reading at sea, even if I was a long way south of Newfoundland! If the prospect of being sunk by Moby Dick wasn't bad enough, I still had the theme from *M*A*S*H* going around and around in my head. Sinking ships, "Suicide is painless"... This wasn't good. Maybe someone was trying to tell me something?

***

4ᵗʰ day at sea
Saturday 25ᵗʰ November

06:00

Conditions remained pretty constant; I hadn't touched George in the previous 24 hours. At first light, I saw my first ship of the crossing (*Allegra*) and called her up on the VHF. I wanted an up-to-date weather forecast. *Allegra* advised that high pressure was moving in, bringing lighter winds and calmer conditions, which was great news, as I would have a chance of climbing up the mast and fixing the spreader. It wasn't all good news, though—the radio operator also said that there was a yacht missing from the ARC. I told them I hadn't seen any other yachts since leaving the Canaries. The ship thanked me for the information before disappearing over the horizon.

12:00. Pos. 22°38'N 018°00'W

Logged 127NM in the last 24 hours.

In order to protect the mast, for the last four days, I had been sailing a more southerly course on starboard tack, down the coast of North Africa. I was well off my intended course and started wondering if there was a suitable port I could sail into. Given how close I was to the coast, this felt like a safer option than trying to repair the mast at sea. Sadly, I had no charts for the west coast of Africa, and there was no information in my Atlantic Crossing Guide either. This was hardly surprising, as I was supposed to be heading west towards the Caribbean.

***

5th day at sea
Sunday 26th November

06:00

For breakfast I had my last bacon and egg sandwich, finishing the bread and bacon. I still had eggs for a further two weeks, so long as I remembered to turn them twice a week, but it was going to be porridge and cornflakes for breakfast from now on. I just needed to keep reminding myself that cornflakes with powdered milk was the "breakfast of champions".

12:00. Pos. 20°44'N 019°00'W

Logged 126NM in the last 24 hours.

I had not touched the helm or changed course since the top spreader broke. For the last five days, I had been sailing downwind with a strong prevailing northerly and was now 340NM off course. For the first time since leaving Gran Canaria, the wind and seas had calmed down. I altered course to a bearing of 260° mag in order to start making progress towards Barbados.

I spent the day reading *Moby Dick* and topping up my tan. Thankfully, the theme tune from *M*A*S*H* was no longer going around my head. Lucky me.

***

6th day at sea
Monday 27th November

06:00

After my morning coffee, during my usual walk around the deck to check the rigging and throw the dead flying fish back into the water, I found a nut. Finding anything metal on the deck is a worry, as it means it has worked lose from some part of the yacht. Looking up the mast, I could see one of the bolts that fastened the lower portside spreader to the mast was missing its nut and the whole assembly was loose. This left me with no other option: I had to resolve these issues quickly, otherwise, there was a real risk of me losing the mast.

12:00. Pos. 20°08'N0 20°44'W
Logged 104NM in the last 24 hours.

I attempted to climb the mast for the first time, without success. The yacht was rolling around too much, flinging me about and smashing me into the mast. It was simply too dangerous, and I had to abort the mission. I desperately needed the wind and sea to abate before I could try again. From my midday position, I was close to Porto Grande, São Vicente in the Cape Verdi Islands, so another option was to pull in there and repair the mast in the safety of a harbour.

I started to reflect on how easy this job would have been if I had another pair of hands. All of a sudden, half a gallon of water a day for Annika to wash her hair seemed a small price to pay in return for her winching me up the mast.

***

7ᵗʰ day at sea
Tuesday 28ᵗʰ November

06:00
To my delight, the sea had flattened right off and there was only a very light north-easterly breeze. There was just enough wind to keep the sails full, and I spent the morning trying to devise a suitable method for climbing the mast safely. On the occasions I had gone rock climbing with Deadloss, we sometimes used Prusik knots, which are very simple yet effective knots that can be used for scaling sheer rock faces. Two of these tied to a climbing rope allow you to support your body weight by placing your feet in loops. The beauty of these knots is that when there is weight on them, they lock, and without any weight on them, you can easily slide them up or down the rope. This allows you to ascend or descend the rope in a controlled fashion.

Using my sail ties, I made three rope loops, one for each foot and one to attach to my climbing harness. By wrapping the rope loops three times around the genoa halyard, I tried to pull myself up the mast. It worked, but it was very hard work and slow. Each time the yacht rolled, I swung away from the mast, which was pretty scary. When the yacht rolled back the other way, I would crash into the mast, leaving me battered and bruised.

In the end, I used one rope loop. With the Prusik knot for safety on the genoa halyard, I put my foot between the mast and the mainsail, and I used the mainsail slides as a ladder. After two steps, I would hang on to the mast with one arm and slide my Prusik knot up the halyard. This worked and was a lot quicker, but still very tiring.

Now that I had worked out a system for getting up and down the mast, I needed to work out the best way to replace the broken spreaders. My first job was to loosen all the rigging apart from the lower shrouds.

12:00. Pos. 19°20'N 021°54'W
Logged 81NM in the last 24 hours.

Once I had climbed up to the lower spreader, I noticed a crack in the end of it. I'd have to replace it first. I unbolted it and climbed back down to pick up the spare. With the lower spreader back in place and the intermediate rigging retightened, I climbed up to the top spreaders, removing the broken portside spreader and the starboard spreader to use as a pattern.

All was going to plan until on my way down, I heard a splash. My tool bag had split open, and all my tools in the bag had gone over the side—what an absolute nightmare.

After consoling myself and picking up my spare set of tools, I went back up the mast, only for my watch strap to get caught on something and then break. As I tried to grab at it, I nearly fell myself. I watched in horror as the watch landed on the coach roof. It bounced a couple of times before landing on the deck, and fortunately, it stopped next to the toe rail. I was incredibly lucky.

I spent most of the afternoon shaping the old lower spreader into a new top spreader, all by hand. It was quite a satisfying job and very time-consuming. I was pleased to have a break from climbing the mast and the ensuing bruises

153

on my arms and legs. I had already climbed the mast five times and was absolutely exhausted.

Having completed my woodworking task, I climbed the mast once more to finish the job. Just as I got everything completed, I took a quick look at the horizon, only to see a huge supertanker on my port side. The vessel was only a couple of miles away and was something I definitely didn't want to see while stuck up a mast. Luckily, the tanker was on a parallel course, and there was enough sea room for it to clear me at a safe distance.

As I started to relax, I was treated to the sight of a giant manta ray gliding through the water just off the starboard side of the yacht. I watched it for a couple of minutes in awe. This beautiful creature just seemed to cut through the water without any effort.

20:00

It took me all day to replace the spreaders and to retighten the rig. I had to climb the mast twice more to make sure the spreaders were straight. Once I was sure everything was as it should be, I clamped them in place and wrapped tape around the ends to prevent the mainsail from chafing on them.

For the first time in a week, I was sailing with a full main and no.2 genoa. My course was west; the boat speed was back up to six knots. I felt fully rewarded for the marathon job on the mast. I was feeling pretty proud and chuffed with myself for what I had accomplished. Despite being covered in bruises and exhausted, I could sleep easy in the knowledge that the mast was secure, and I could now get back on track.

***

8th day at sea
Wednesday 29th November

06:00

Something very strange happened to me in the night. All I know is I could see myself lying on my bunk. I tried to wake myself up, but I couldn't. This very strange experience only ended when I woke to the sound of sails flapping. I'm not sure whether it was some form of out-of-body experience caused by physical exhaustion from the exertion of the day, or if, in fact, it was just a dream.

The morning turned into another hot, sunny day. The north-easterly prevailing wind and a flat sea were helping my progress no end. *Seefalke* was powered up, and I was feeling pretty good about life, as I was sailing back on course towards Barbados.

12:00. Pos. 19°03'N 023°15'W
Logged 77NM in the last 24 hours. Course west.

This wasn't a bad 24-hour run, considering all the trials and tribulations of the day before.

I was truly back in the rhythm of long-distance sailing again. At first light, I would make myself a coffee, take it into the cockpit and watch the sun rise. This was followed by a walk around the deck looking for anything out of place, like screws, nuts, flying fish. Some days I'd find screws and wonder where they had come from. I'd thoroughly check the mast, rigging and sails, and once this was done, I'd make sure George was working properly and keeping *Seefalke* on the correct course. After this, there wasn't a lot else to do except decide what meals I was going to have. The rest of my time was spent reading, trying to get a midday fix using my sextant (which I found very hard and was not very successful at), playing the guitar or listening to the BBC World Service on my shortwave radio.

After my evening nightcap, I would watch the sun set, before getting ready to hit my bunk. I would have one last look around before setting my alarm clock to wake me up in two hours' time. When the alarm went off, I'd get up for a quick look around, check the yacht was still on course and then pump her out. If everything was okay, I would go back to sleep for another two hours.

Sometimes, if it was quiet, I wouldn't even get out of bed to check the yacht's course. I would just look out of the main hatch at the North Star. If it was in the right place, I'd know I was on course and go back to sleep.

***

9th day at sea
Thursday 30th November

06:00

I slept well during the night, apart from having nightmares about whales sinking ships. *Moby Dick* was definitely not on my top ten best books to read while sailing across the pond single-handed. Nan would have a lot to answer for the next time I saw her.

12:00. Pos. 19°00'N 025°00'W

Logged 100NM in the last 24 hours.

From my midday fix, I had reached the position where the old sailing ships picked up easterly trade winds. It had taken me nine days to get to this position, and Murphy's Law had struck. Instead of enjoying a lovely easterly breeze, I was experiencing a light westerly headwind. So much for following the old-timers.

***

10th day at sea
Friday 1st December

06:00

I didn't have a very good night. There'd been a lot of rain squalls about, and the weather that morning wasn't much better. The sky was dark and overcast and I was still sailing against a headwind.

12:00. Pos. 19°00'N 25°45'W

Logged 42NM in the last 24 hours. Wind light.

A long and frustrating day. The wind kept oscillating; one minute it was blowing hard and the next I'd find myself becalmed. Looking on the bright side, I only had two thousand nautical miles left before reaching Barbados.

22:00

The wind had died completely, leaving a bloody horrible swell. Everything was rolling around, crashing and banging.

To stop the sails getting damaged, I took them down, which brought some peace and quiet.

I came up with a plan for getting a better night's sleep, and that was to place a cushion on the cabin sole and wedge myself between the two berths.

***

11th day at sea
Saturday 2nd December

06:00

The squally weather from yesterday had thankfully gone, but the swells remained. At least the sun was out and I was sailing, although the wind couldn't really make up its mind. I steered the yacht for a while, reading my book at the same time.

12:00. Pos. 18°39'N 026°05'W

Logged 28NM in the last 24 hours.

Becalmed, no wind.

From my midday fix, I was 90NM north of the Cape Verdes. The GPS was showing that with the westerly set in the current, I was slowly moving away from the islands. This was good news, and to celebrate this small victory, I spent the afternoon making bread. You cannot beat the smell of fresh bread. While the oven was on, to make full use of the gas, I baked potatoes at the same time.

Early evening, the wind picked up from the east. Force 4. Course 240° mag.

***

12th day at sea
Sunday 3rd December

06:00

The wind that filled in during the night carried through into the morning, and I was starting to feel optimistic that I was finally picking up the easterly trades. George was steering a reasonable course although wandering a bit. Self-steering systems are not good at sailing downwind, and to try and help him, I altered course in order to keep the genoa full and not lose the wind behind the mainsail.

12:00. Pos. 17°30'N 027°20'W
Logged 100NM in the last 24 hours.

By lunchtime, the easterly trades had become more established and I was enjoying a good force 4/5 breeze and maintaining a course of 240° mag. *Seefalke* was being picked up by the following swells and propelled forwards; she was revelling in the conditions. I had good hull speed, and Barbados was getting closer.

***

13th day at sea
Monday 4th December

06:00
The wind kept blowing all night, same conditions as yesterday. George had everything under control.

12:00. Pos. 16°28'N 029°45'W
Logged 152NM in the last 24 hours.

My best noon-to-noon run so far. Moving well with big following seas, I saw a ship on the horizon. I called it up on the VHF and asked for a weather forecast for the next couple of days. I was told the conditions would remain unchanged, which was great news. I was about to end my conversation when the radio operator asked me if I had a GPS.

"Yes," I replied.

"Can you pass your position to us?"

"Yes, why?"

"We are a Russian cargo ship, and we don't have GPS on board."

They must have been having better luck with their sextant than I was. I had to laugh.

***

14th day at sea
Tuesday 5th December

06:00

I had good wind all night and George had everything under control. I saw a masthead light on another yacht at 0400 hours; however, there was no sign of it at first light. I even tried to call it up on the radio, but with no luck.

12:00. Pos. 15°22'N 032°00'W

Logged 145NM in the last 24 hours.

I was enjoying another lovely day, and we were eating up the miles. To celebrate two weeks at sea, I baked some more bread. Things didn't get much better than this.

Although, that was until I was digging around in the lockers under my berth, looking for something for tea, when I found a whole chicken in a can, which I could not remember buying. I had baked chicken with baked potato and fresh bread—what an absolute winner. As I mentioned before, you're supposed to lose weight sailing long-distance due to the constant motion of the yacht. Not me. With the amount of food I kept eating, there was no risk of that happening.

21:00

The barometer had dropped, and there seemed to be a big change in the weather coming. There were squalls with a lot of big, black clouds around. It got quite wild, with a lot of spray and white water being blown over the deck. To make the yacht comfortable, I changed the foresail to the smaller no.3 genoa and put the third reef into the main.

***

15th day at sea
Wednesday 6th December

02:00

When I checked George, I noticed that one of the lines to the tiller had snapped. This was something I'd need to fix in the morning when the weather calmed down. To get through the rest of the night, I tied the tiller up on the centre line and got the yacht set up to steer herself.

06:00

The squally, stormy weather I had experienced during the night had gone, leaving a nasty swell. I took a reef out of the mainsail and reset the no.2 genoa to keep the boat speed up, helping *Seefalke* to push through.

Fixing George was easy, and as the weather improved, he had us back on course, trade-wind sailing on another overcast morning. Definitely not sun-bathing weather, and not what I had expected.

12:00. Pos. 14°10'N 033°55'W

Logged 117NM in the last 24 hours.

After I plotted my midday fix, I was nearly on the same latitude as Barbados. All I had to do now was keep sailing west.

My late-night tot of brandy in my coffee had come to an end with the last of the brandy. No more nightcaps for me. I was going to miss my little bit of self-indulgence each night.

***

16th day at sea
Thursday 7th December

06:00

The weather conditions had been constant for the last 24 hours, and George had everything covered.

12:00. Pos. 13°25'N 035°50'W

Logged 140NM in the last 24 hours.

The weather had changed again. The wind was very variable in speed and direction. The swell was very confused and seemed to be coming from different directions; this made things very uncomfortable. This definitely wasn't in the brochure, nor consistent with what I had read about trade-wind sailing.

160

For something to do, I put a message in the empty brandy bottle and dropped it over the side. I wondered if it would ever be found.

***

17th day at sea
Friday 8th December

06:00

A northerly wind set in early the previous evening and stayed throughout the night. George had us sailing on a reach, which meant fast sailing, and the best news of all was we were still heading due west.

12:00. Pos. 13°23'N 038°15'W

Logged 141NM in the last 24 hours.

Another 140-plus nautical mile day, sailing in the right direction. We were making good progress and only had 1250NM to go.

***

18th day at sea
Saturday 9th December

06:00

It had been a dark, stormy night, with a lot of rain and a horrible swell. I'd stayed below deck, leaving George to get on with it while I got some sleep.

I used the last of my eggs that morning, which was the end of my fried egg sandwiches for breakfast. From now on, it was back to cornflakes with powdered milk, or porridge again.

12:00. Pos. 13°35'N 040°13'W

Logged 115NM in the last 24 hours. Course west.

I had a shower on deck, in the cold rain. It was bloody horrible.

***

19th day at sea
Sunday 10th December

12:00. Pos. 13°37'N 042°11'W
Logged 115NM in the last 24 hours. Course west.

I shook the reef out of the mainsail and was back to a full main and no.2 genoa. With only a thousand nautical miles to go, I was looking forward to spending Christmas in Barbados.

***

20th day at sea
Monday 11th December

06:00
The wind had been fickle all night. Consequently, I spent most of the night becalmed. I woke up to another cloudy, grey overcast morning with big, black rainclouds. Not exactly the weather I had expected this far south.

12:00. Pos. 13°38'N 043°21'W
Logged only 68NM in the last 24 hours.

One of George's steering lines had broken again, and to fix it this time meant leaning over the back of the yacht to rethread the line. For my own safety, I clipped myself onto the jackstay while hanging over the stern.

With George fixed, he was back steering the yacht, which left me to ponder a question I had been asking myself for a while. A question that single-handed sailors should have an answer to: How do you get yourself back aboard if you fall over the side?

I was clipped on to the jackstay, so I thought it would be an idea to find out. I was about to step off the deck when thankfully I came to my senses and realised what an idiotic idea this was. Instead, I grabbed the self-steering and swung myself around the back of it.

Straight away, I knew something was wrong. The safety harness didn't get caught up in the steering gear as I expected it to. When I checked, I had stupidly clipped both ends of my harness onto the yacht—I wasn't attached. Jumping off would have been a super dull thing to have done. I got a cold shiver just thinking about what it would have been like to watch my yacht sail away. I could have paid the ultimate price, just for wanting to know how hard it was to get back aboard. I couldn't believe how stupid I am at times and was extremely relieved that I hadn't gone through with my experiment. I had been incredibly lucky to avoid being shortlisted for a Darwin Award.

I did hear a story of a single-handed French sailor who fell off his yacht and watched in horror as it sailed away. Miraculously, the wind started to change and in the end, went around in a full circle. The self-steering followed the wind, and the yacht ended up sailing close enough to the yachtsman for him to climb back on board. I hope he bought a lottery ticket when he finally got back ashore.

Somehow, I don't think I would have been that lucky.

14:00

There was a change in the weather; the wind increased to force 4 from the north-east. The clouds had lifted, leaving a glorious, hot, sunny afternoon.

***

21st day at sea
Tuesday 12th December

06:00

The wind was constant all night, and I didn't have much to do other than sleep and pump the yacht out.

12:00. Pos. 14°17'N 045°30'W

Logged 130NM in the last 24 hours. Course 290° mag.

I had an eye on the barometer. It had been dropping slowly all morning, and if that wasn't worrying enough, my main water tank was empty. The only fresh water I had left was in my two five-gallon water containers.

21:00

The wind had been building all evening and had increased to force 5/6 from the north. I put a reef in the main, and the yacht felt all the better for it. I was sailing a course of 280° mag.

***

22ⁿᵈ day at sea
Wednesday 13ᵗʰ December

06:00

Walking around the deck, doing my usual morning checks, I noticed a large shape under the yacht. It was big, with a lot of white dots. A whale shark—the largest fish in the sea, growing up to fifty feet in length. Luckily, they're harmless, and although this was a big one, it posed no threat.

12:00. Pos. 14°37'N 047°48'W

Logged 135NM in the last 24 hours.

All morning, the swell had been getting bigger from a north-easterly direction, while the trades were still blowing from the east. Although the waves were twenty feet high, this was a long, rolling swell, which made for some exhilarating sailing. It was a great day to be on the water.

***

23rd day at sea
Thursday 14th December

06:00

I had a relatively uneventful night until, while on deck checking for any shipping in my vicinity, I was hit in the side of the head by a flying fish. This was totally unexpected and gave me quite a fright, and boy, did it hurt. Once I had recovered my senses, I threw the poor fish back in and watched it swim away.

12:00. Pos. 14°56'N 049°45'W
Logged 115NM in the last 24 hours.

From my midday position, I was only 580NM from Barbados, or five days at my present speed. I changed course in order to sail towards the north end of the island. I was still sailing in a lovely force 4 easterly breeze on a heading of 260° mag.

All the way across, I had been trying to master the use of my sextant, but I was finding it very difficult. A lot of the morning weather leading up to midday had been overcast, making a noon fix impossible. Only twice did I manage to take a sun sight over the three weeks I had been at sea. Without my GPS, I would have been totally reliant on my sextant for taking sights and working out my position. Based on my very mediocre performance to date, I think I would have been buggered.

I would have had to use old, traditional techniques, relying on a dead reckoning position, taken from the ship's log, yacht speed, compass course, magnetic variation and compass deviation. Corrections for variation and deviation would have to be added or subtracted from the true course to arrive at the compass course I wanted to sail, making navigating at sea difficult. I was really happy I could rely on my GPS.

One good thing about being out in the middle of the Atlantic was that I knew where I was not, and that was close to land. In simple terms, if I carried on sailing west, I knew I would hit land at some point. Had I been stuck without a GPS, I would still have hit land; it would have just been a mystery where.

***

24th day at sea
Friday 15th December

06:00
Another easy night. I didn't even get out of my bunk to check my course, just had a look out through the main hatch for the North Star. The good breeze stayed all night and looked to be set in for the day.

12:00. Pos. 14°16'N 051°50'W
Logged 128NM in the last 24 hours.

Trade-wind sailing at last, on a hot, sunny day. Days like these were what I had dreamt about. Finally, I was following my dream.

***

25th day at sea
Saturday 16th December

06:00
It turned out to be a beautiful day. I had a good breeze from the east, made only better by a lovely flat sea. There was a pod of dolphins swimming around and playing under the bow, which was great to watch. This was more like what I'd expected trade-wind sailing to be all about. *Seefalke* was sailing at six knots towards Barbados.

12:00. Pos. 14°00'N 054°28'W
Logged 155NM in the last 24 hours.

My best 24-hour noon-to-noon run logged so far. I must have been getting closer to land; there were a lot more seabirds flying around the yacht. One landed on the deck, where it sat for an hour before flying on.

***

26th day at sea
Sunday 17th December

06:00
I woke up to find the weather conditions unchanged from the previous 24 hours.

12:00. Pos. 13°55'N 056°48'W
Logged 136NM in the last 24 hours. Course 260°.

I was nearly there. I was starting to pick up Barbados radio on medium wave; all they were playing were Christmas carols.

My sixth sense told me I had company, and sure enough, when I looked out, I could see another yacht on the horizon. It was the first I'd seen since leaving Las Palmas, and I was keen to keep an eye on it.

As our paths started to converge, I could see that it was a sixty-foot Swan. They had no sails up and were motoring. The yacht came close enough for the crew to wave. I waved back, and one crew member shouted across, "We're in a rush; we've run out of beer!"

"Don't drink it all!" I shouted back. "Save some for me!"

***

27th day at sea
Monday 18th December

06:00
I had the same weather conditions again, very easy trade-wind sailing. A joy.

12:00. Pos. 13°30'N 058°28'W
Logged 100NM in the last 24 hours.

From my midday fix, I was only 64NM east of Barbados. I had read in my cruising guide that I would be able to see Barbados from forty nautical miles away. The highest point of the island is over one thousand feet.

Excited by the thought of seeing land, I was on deck reading my book. I kept looking forward, and finally, around three o'clock, in front of me I saw the island of Barbados.

With land in sight, I started to ask myself: do I really want to stop sailing and deal with people again? I was really getting used to my rhythm of life. Faced with the prospect of having to get fenders and anchors out and go through the pain of dealing with customs and immigration all over again, I suddenly felt like carrying on sailing. I had become that comfortable at sea.

***

28th day at sea
Tuesday 19th December

06:00

Being close to land again meant I had been on deck keeping a lookout all night. I saw a few local fishing boats, and one huge cruise liner lit up like a Christmas tree.

I'd sailed past Harrison Point at the north end of the island earlier, then followed the coast down to Bridgetown. Sailing in the lee of the island was hard work. With little wind, it took me most of the morning to sail to Bridgetown.

My cruising guide informed me that all yachts had to clear in with customs at Deep Water Harbour, which I wasn't too happy about. So, I called Barbados Coastguard, via the VHF radio. I tried to explain that my yacht had no engine and asked if I could sail straight into Carlisle Bay, the main anchorage for Bridgetown, which would be easier for me to do than sail into a harbour I knew nothing about.

The answer was, "No, man. You have to come into the deep-water harbour first to clear customs and immigration. We will send a Coastguard boat out to guide you in."

I had no idea what to expect in the harbour. While waiting for the Coastguard, I dropped the genoa, got the anchor on deck, dug out my fenders and found my mooring lines. I even got a bowline ready in anticipation of my tow into the harbour.

When the Coastguard boat turned up, I was told to follow them. Sailing downwind into the harbour was not much fun. I expected to see a dock for yachts to tie up at, but there was nothing. No Pontoon, no dock—all I saw was a rough stone dock wall.

The Coastguards were not much help. They made me sail to within fifty feet of the dock before coming alongside to help manoeuvre the yacht onto the harbour wall.

I knew I should have carried on sailing!

After dropping the mainsail, I got the fenders tied on the starboard side. I had to tie up the yacht onto chains hanging off the dock wall next to a ladder. How I was going to sail off the dock wall, I had no idea.

Standing on dry land for the first time in a month was all a bit strange. Everything kept wobbling back and forth. But by the time I had walked into customs and immigration, I had gotten used to it again. Once my papers from my last port had been checked and I'd paid the clearance charges, I was free to leave the harbour.

Why customs made me sail into the harbour and then didn't come out to check the yacht out, I did not know.

I was trying to work out how to get out of the harbour when another yacht motored in. I let it tie up alongside while the crew went to deal with customs. They gave me a tow out of the harbour and into Carlisle Bay, where I anchored *Seefalke* right off a beach bar called the Boatyard. My cruising guide informed me that the Boatyard was the only place in Barbados I needed to know about.

Sitting in the cockpit, drinking a coffee, I reflected on my trip across the pond. Since leaving Wales, I had sailed approximately five thousand nautical miles. I'd expected my sail across to be hot and sunny, leaving me to work on my tan. It was nothing like that at all; it had been overcast a great deal of the time.

I saw hardly any sea life, only one manta ray, one whale shark, some dolphins, one big tuna, and flying fish, most of which ended up dead on *Seefalke*'s deck. There wasn't even much birdlife until I got close to land. As regards marine traffic, I only saw three ships and a yacht the whole crossing. That said, I'd seen plenty of water—well, the top of it. I was incredibly proud of my achievement.

For safety, I dropped my second anchor and dived into the warm, clear, blue water I had dreamt about, to check that both anchors were dug in properly. Satisfied that all was well, I gave myself a saltwater wash. After a quick freshwater rinse, I looked for some clean clothes so I could get ashore and start to explore.

From the Boatyard, it was only a short walk into Bridgetown, where I could get to the bank and the supermarket. The Boatyard had showers and laundry facilities on site, and you could buy cooking gas and top up with fresh water.

Best of all, they sold ice-cool beer. I ordered my first beer for nearly a month, and the barman gave me two. I had hit the jackpot—it was happy hour.

I had a good first evening, leaning on the bar, looking out at *Seefalke* anchored in Carlisle Bay. A proper shower and doing my laundry were going to have to wait until the morning.

***

Monday 20th December

Well, I was like a dog with two dicks. I had enjoyed a great first night ashore—or at least, I think I did. I must confess, I cannot remember getting back to the yacht and I awoke with an almighty hangover. Monday's special at the Boatyard involved paying twenty US dollars and then enjoying free drinks all night. I could see another hangover coming.

After breakfast, I was back to the Boatyard for a shower and to do my laundry. I refilled my water tanks while I waited for my laundry to dry.

Once I'd sorted out the yacht, I went for a wander around Bridgetown and took the opportunity to call home and tell Mum she still had a "Sun". I also sent a postcard to the boys in Barry Yacht Club. First off, I asked Bowmer to send me the twenty quid he'd bet me—I had got a lot further than Lundy Island. I must admit, I was pretty chuffed at winning the bet, and even though Bowmer would be gutted, deep down, I knew the boys would be full of admiration and happy for me.

On my way back to the Boatyard, I found a big supermarket, which really surprised me. I'd thought the shops would be more basic. Prior to leaving, I had read all the books on Atlantic sailing, which included tips on the right foods to take for long-haul sailing and how to stock up for a whole year. There were even tips for preserving eggs by varnishing them! I'd been left with the distinct impression that the Caribbean was made up of a bunch of primitive islands where you would starve if you didn't go properly prepared. Nothing could have been further from the truth; Barbados had everything I needed and more.

The first thing I saw in the supermarket was "I CAN'T BELIEVE IT'S NOT BUTTER" on the shelves.

Why I'd packed a year's supply of food on board, slowing the yacht down, when everything I needed was on the island,

I don't know. I would be eating the tin food stored on *Seefalke* for the next year. The only items I found hard to find were the UK brands we take for granted—Mars bars, HP sauce, etc.

What makes cruising life so good is meeting new people who have shared the same experience. Over Christmas and the New Year, different cruising yachts came into Barbados and anchored in the bay. Each yacht brought another excuse for a party with new friends. I was loving this lifestyle, which made all the struggles of getting there totally worthwhile.

I heard plenty of war stories during happy hour in the Boatyard. Here are a few I would like to share with you.

I heard this first story after telling folks about my drama of climbing the mast to fix the top spreader:

A few years ago, an old couple were sailing across the Atlantic when they discovered there was a problem with the rigging at the top of the mast. Luckily, the mast had steps, making it fairly easy for the husband to climb it. At the top, he tied himself on for safety. While working on the mast, he suffered a massive heart attack and died. The poor wife couldn't get him down and had no option but to sail to Barbados. It took her five days with her dead husband still hanging from the top of the mast.

Not a nice story. I am glad I hadn't suffered the same fate when I'd fixed my mast. *Seefalke* and George would have carried on regardless.

I got this second story from a Canadian family sailing on a catamaran. I first met them in Lisbon:

Halfway across the Atlantic, the husband was looking out of a porthole and could see fins. He shouted, "Dolphins!" and the family all rushed on deck. They soon realised the fins were huge and belonged to a big pod of killer whales. They watched in horror as the whales tacked in the wake of the yacht and accelerated towards them. Just a few metres away, some of the whales dived under the yacht, and others did a belly roll, showing their white undersides before too disappearing beneath the boat.

This game went on for about two hours before the killer whales finally swam away. You can imagine how relieved the family were; they'd had visions of the whales trying to sink them, just like in Moby Dick *or the true story of the Bayles*

171

family (117 Days Adrift). Thinking themselves lucky, they breathed a big sigh of relief, only to find half an hour later, one of their rudders fell off. Luckily, the catamaran had two rudders, so after jury-rigging their broken rudder, they were able to sail safely into Barbados.

My last story is about a family sailing across the Atlantic on a twenty-nine-foot yacht:

On a calm, hot day, the family were enjoying perfect sailing conditions. The father was in the cockpit reading his book when he noticed a fin in the boat's wake, just breaking the surface of the water. Thinking it was a dolphin, he called to his wife and daughter—just like with the other family. They climbed into the cockpit, excited to see the dolphins. However, it soon became apparent that the fin belonged to a big shark.

Slowly, the fin got closer until it was swimming alongside them. It was then that they realised the shark was a great white and longer than their yacht. Everybody on board watched as it dived and disappeared, only to resurface in the wake of the yacht again. It slowly tacked back and forth across the wake, slowly getting closer and closer to the yacht.

This time, as the great white shark passed, it lifted its massive head out of the water and looked straight into the cockpit with one very big, cold, black eye. The family told me the shark seemed to smile at them. Never had they felt or seen anything so evil in their lives. When the shark finally disappeared again, it was even more frightening for them wondering where it was. Was it under the yacht, stalking them?

It took them a few days to recover from this experience, and they had nightmares for weeks afterwards.

I spent six weeks in Barbados and had a really good time, meeting up with the pond yachties, watching and waiting for new yachts to come in. *Kismet* turned up. They had sailed from St Lucia back out to Barbados; they had a tough sail against the wind and current. We all had a good time catching up and swapping our sailing stories over a few beers.

My mother came out to visit me for a stay on the yacht. She had a great holiday, made even more special by members of the Hash House Harriers, a worldwide running club I met in the Boatyard. They were a great bunch of guys who took us all over the island and in doing so made Mum's holiday one to remember.

Barbados was a beautiful island, but they didn't seem to have much call for a toolmaker, and with no marinas or boatyards, finding work there was going to prove difficult. After my long summer, my vacation was over. It was now time to go and find some work.

Chapter 10
Barbados to Antigua

Wednesday 7th February 1996

An ex-pat friend told me his brother Steve, a carpenter by trade, was working in St Lucia and looking for another pair of hands. Knowing that it was going to be difficult to pick up work in Barbados, I decided to head for St Lucia and look him up.

Once I had the yacht ready to go back to sea, I walked to the customs and immigration office to get my yacht papers and passport stamped, which saved me the hassle of trying to sail back into the harbour. With everything sorted, I was free to leave. I stopped on the way back to pick up fresh food and a few other bits and pieces I thought would be handy for the trip.

Back on the yacht, I rolled my dinghy up and tied it to the cabin top, pulled up the anchor and set sail for St Lucia. I expected the 100NM trip to take around twenty-four hours. With the prevailing wind and current, it only took me fourteen to get to the northern end of the island, but by then it was too dark to enter the lagoon. I decided to spend the night out at sea and then head in early the next morning. By 10 a.m., I was safely anchored in the bay, outside Rodney Bay Lagoon.

***

Thursday 8th February

As I rowed ashore, I noticed *Whitt Merrel* in the anchorage, a yacht I had first seen in Porto Santo. The crew were a father

174

and son from Belgium who had sailed across the pond with the ARC. As I rowed past, the son was on the bow, pulling up the anchor.

I shouted over to the father, "Nice anchor windlass you have there!"

"Yes, it's very good—I made it twenty-four years ago!" he said, laughing. "If you'd like to come aboard, we can motor over to *Seefalke* and tow you into the lagoon."

St Lucia was a beautiful island, but there wasn't much happening there workwise. I met with Steve, who told me I would have a much better chance of finding work in Antigua. He said there was a much bigger yacht-based industry there. Steve told me to look up a company called Woodstock and ask for Andrew; he was always looking for skilled people with boat building experience.

***

Tuesday 13th February

After spending only five days in St Lucia, I cleared customs and immigration and left the harbour, sailing downwind through the narrow channel and out into Rodney Bay. Once clear of St Lucia, I headed north, passing to the west in the lee of Martinique, Dominica and Guadeloupe. It was a shame not to stop off at all these beautiful islands. I hoped, with some money in my pocket, I would be able to visit them at a later date.

Antigua is approximately two hundred nautical miles up the island chain. So, by my reckoning, with *Seefalke* sailing with the prevailing easterly trade wind on a reach, I'd be there in a day and a half.

***

Friday 16th February

My sail to Antigua was hugely frustrating. I had little wind for virtually the whole trip and spent the night becalmed in the lee of Guadeloupe. Altogether, it took me twice as long as it should have. I finally arrived off the entrance of English

Harbour as the sun was setting for the night, so I had no choice but to stay up and sail around in circles and wait for a new morning to arrive.

In daylight, the entrance to the harbour was easy to spot. There are pillar-like formations that look as though they've been carved into the cliffs on the starboard side of the entrance as you sail in. These rock formations are aptly named the Pillars of Hercules. Once I had these in my sights, entering the harbour was straightforward.

My struggle to get to Antigua was well worth it. Sailing into English Harbour is one of those moments you never forget. It is one of the most iconic harbours in the world. This natural harbour is steeped in history and was made famous by Admiral Lord Nelson, who commanded the British fleet during the late 18th century.

Sailing in, I saw the influence the British Navy had had on the harbour. I passed the fort on Charlotte Point and another fort, Berkeley Point, at the entrance to the harbour. Both would have been heavily fortified, and it was easy to imagine the English firing canons from the ramparts. Safely, I sailed into Freeman's Bay, where I anchored close to the beach.

English Harbour was full of yachts. It seemed like there were hundreds of them moored all around. After blowing up my dinghy, I went ashore at Nelson's Dockyard itself. Straight away, I knew I had made the right decision to sail to Antigua and look for work. There were big expensive motorboats and superyachts moored stern-to around the perimeter of the old stone quay. I couldn't help but take a good look at the millions of pounds' worth of boats that were moored before me.

After I paid a quick visit to the museum, I found out that Nelson's Dockyard is a heritage site and the only working Georgian dockyard in the world. Walking around the restored buildings was incredible, and I could almost picture what life in the eighteen-hundreds would have been like. The dockyard looks like something out of a pirate film set, and you cannot help imagining what it would have been like in Nelson's day. Thankfully for us all, the dockyard was restored in the 1950s after sixty years of hurricanes and neglect had taken their toll following the British departure from the island in 1889.

I was so engrossed looking around I nearly forgot I had come ashore to check in.

I found the customs and immigration office housed in a shed that was the original rope store from the time of Nelson. It was in these sheds that I first met John, a very large immigration officer. It did not take too long to realise that John was not too happy with his lot, so I nicknamed him Unhappy John.

John handed me the forms I needed to fill in, which were becoming very familiar. I was starting to suffer from déjà vu every time they were put in front of me; it felt like Groundhog Day. The questions relating to the yacht's name, last port of call, date of arrival, duration of stay and my rank within the yacht complement were standard across every form I'd filled in.

I got to the place on the form where it asked for my rank, and I wrote *captin*. John was watching me as I filled it in.

"That's wrong," he said.

"What's wrong?" I asked.

"Captin."

I said, "I am the captain?"

"No," said John. "It's wrong."

"Okay?" I said. "If you say it's wrong."

I crossed out *captin* and wrote *owner* instead.

"That's still wrong," said John.

"But I am the owner," I replied in a raised voice.

"Give me the form," said John, expressionless.

I passed the form over. John crossed out *owner* and wrote in *captain*. I had spelt captain wrong!

I learnt later on from another ex-pat that the way to keep Unhappy John sweet was to talk about Manchester United; he was a massive fan. At the time, this should have been an easy conversation, as they were on track to win the League and the FA Cup. Sadly, I never caught John in a good enough mood to risk having a conversation about Man U.

Having navigated customs and immigration, my next port of call was the National Parks office to obtain a cruising permit. After a long day of form filling, my documents were in order and I was free to have a good look around.

Rowing around English Harbour, I realised that with its long, narrow inlet, sheltered on both sides by high ground, it was a very sheltered natural harbour, ideal for sitting out the oncoming hurricane season. Finally, I found a quiet and safe place to anchor, and with the help of a superyacht's rib, I moved *Seefalke* into Ordnance Bay opposite Clarence House. I spent what was left of the day exploring English and Falmouth Harbour in search of Woodstock Boat Building, but to no luck. On the plus side, I did find the Galley Bar and the Mad Mongoose for happy hour. Little did I know that these bars were soon to become a regular part of my life.

The next morning, I got up early, and once again went in search of Woodstock. I walked all over the place but I couldn't find their workshop. So, looking for help, I walked into a big green tin shed with a sign over the door saying 'Seagull Services'. There was a man sitting by the door drinking a bottle of Guinness, so I asked him where I could find Woodstock.

"Why? What's up?" said the guy.

"I'm looking for work."

"What do you do?" he replied.

"I'm a toolmaker by trade."

"Come into my office," he said.

The guy introduced himself as Piggy and pointed to his business partner, Flemming, who was playing solitaire on the office computer.

Both partners welcomed me into Seagull Services. I had a job, starting the next day.

That was the start of my career in Antigua. I had been on the island for less than two days and I had already picked up a job in Falmouth Harbour—what a result! After all those years of being out of work in Wales, I'd arrived on a little island in the Caribbean and found work straight away. This completely validated my decision to jump in my yacht and do something constructive, and it also made me realise how hard it had been trying to find toolmaking work in the UK.

When I'd left Barry, I had one of the biggest yachts in the harbour; however, moored in English Harbour, *Seefalke* paled into insignificance. My pride and joy was tiny in comparison to the majority of the yachts there and in neighbouring Falmouth Harbour. It didn't take me long to realise that Antigua is a yachting mecca, a millionaire's playground.

Even for me, it was hard to take it all in. Owners would board their yachts via helicopter, landing on the superyacht's helipad. And if that wasn't enough, their ribs and launches alone were bigger than *Seefalke*.

Antigua plays an important role in the Caribbean and Mediterranean charter boat circuit. These luxurious sail- and motorboats spend the winter months in the Caribbean and then leave before the hurricane season to spend the summer in other parts of the world. Very wealthy people are willing to spend tens of thousands per week to enjoy a no-expense-spared holiday on a luxury yacht in these idyllic Caribbean islands.

Most of the marine-based businesses around Falmouth Harbour were owned by ex-pats. There were quite a number of us. It didn't take me long to find my feet, settle into a routine and get used to my new life in this tropical paradise. Each morning started with a row ashore before walking through Nelson's Dockyard on my way to work. For lunch, Katie, a local girl who had a wooden food shack opposite Seagull Services, would cook me a huge plate of chicken and rice. I think she felt sorry for me and thought I was malnourished. Following lunch, I'd go back to work until about four and then wander over to the Mad Mongoose bar for happy hour.

If I didn't leave after happy hour, I usually got stuck in a bar for the night. There was usually a brief interlude for tea, where I normally called into a local food shack called Grace Before Meals. My last stop of the evening was the Galley Bar in the Dockyard, where I would have one final beer before rowing back to the yacht. It won't come as any great surprise, but most mornings I woke up feeling like shit.

I enjoyed the ex-pat experience, having a happy-hour beer after work. It was a very chilled way to meet up with friends as the sun set on balmy, still evenings in the Caribbean.

In any event, I had a lot of catching up to do. When I turned up for work at 8 a.m., Piggy would already have an opened bottle of Guinness on his desk.

Piggy was one of life's true characters, and one of my fondest memories of him was when I was sitting in the office one morning and he was standing just outside the main entrance, having an argument with the woman who owned the refrigeration business next door. The argument had been going on for a good five minutes when I heard her say, "And Piggy, look at me when I am talking to you."

"I am?" he said.

I noticed Piggy had been nodding his head a lot—I'd thought he'd been saying yes.

"Piggy, stop looking at my tits."

I heard Piggy moan and say, "It's the only place I want to look. I've made my choice."

The poor woman stormed off; Piggy won that battle. I had to laugh—looking at her tits would have been my choice too.

One morning, Piggy asked me if I was going to enter the Antigua Classic Yacht Regatta this year. I soon learnt that the regatta was world-famous and held in April each year, the start of a two-week sailing festival followed by Antigua Race Week. Piggy said this was the highlight of Antigua's sailing calendar and marked the end of the charter boat season in the Caribbean.

I was keen to enter the regatta if I could find a crew. I got in touch with my mates back home, to see if anyone wanted to come out. I was delighted when Martin from Reading and Bowmer agreed to come out.

Before I'd left Wales, Bowmer would tell me—on average at least once a week—that he had been to Antigua in 1991 to race on a Swan during Race Week. So, he knew what to expect. He'd also sailed *Seefalke* quite a bit before I left Wales and was a really good sailor who knew his way around the yacht.

Martin would be good at keeping us entertained and doing the cooking on board. I also knew that the two guys would get on well together, as we had all sailed together in the past.

I was really excited about racing the yacht on this world stage. I had never raced her against other classic yachts before, but with a good crew, we had a chance of doing well. I also wanted to remind Bowmer that he owed me twenty quid for sailing past Lundy Island, which he'd conveniently forgotten to send to me.

Martin from Reading flew straight out from the UK and arrived eight hours later. I was able to pick him up, as I had the use of the work pickup truck.

Martin walked out of customs covered in sweat, complaining about the heat. After I passed him a beer, he told me Bowmer was on a standby ticket with American Airlines and planned to make his own way to English Harbour after he arrived.

The next evening, Martin and I were relaxing in the Mad Mongoose with happy-hour beers in hand, when Bowmer finally stepped out of a taxi. After he had a few rum and Cokes, we got the long story of his standby flight. He had flown via New York and San Juan in Puerto Rico before arriving in Antigua on the last flight of the day, having missed the connection in San Juan and ending up having to stay the night—a thirty-hour trip in all. On reflection, I think he wished he'd paid the four hundred pounds and flown straight out to Antigua.

After we dropped Bowmer's gear off on the yacht, we moved *Seefalke* onto the dock so we could enjoy the festivities without having to row back out into English Harbour each night. With the yacht safely tied up and to celebrate the start of their holiday, I took the boys up to Shirley Heights.

Shirley Heights provides spectacular views over English and Falmouth Harbour. If you ever look at a holiday brochure for Antigua, you will definitely see a picture taken from Shirley Heights; it's a view I never got tired of. We drank rum punch and partied to the live pan band while watching the sun set. It was a brilliant night and a perfect start to the boys' holiday. With a few drinks inside us, Bowmer and I were winding up Martin something rotten. He took it in good spirits, and it wasn't long before he was dishing it out as good as he was getting. We were all getting on really well, and we were starting to bond as a team.

The first few days of their holiday were spent getting *Seefalke* ready to race, although we usually finished up relaxing on Pigeon Beach and going for a swim. One afternoon, after we had sailed *Seefalke* to Falmouth Harbour Marina, ready for the first race, Bowmer and I were in the water and Martin was lying in the shade of a tree, covered from head to toe in factor-fifty sun cream. Martin does not tan; he goes a nice pink colour, then turns white again. We were just coming out of the water when a beautiful girl walking past Martin stopped, looked down at him and said, "You are the whitest person I have ever seen in my life."

Bowmer and I cracked up laughing.

"Even complete strangers are abusing me!" said Martin.

"Come on, Martin," I said. "I'll buy you a beer to cheer you up."

The three of us wandered along the beach to Bumkin's Beach Bar. There we ordered a beer and burger. Martin started talking to two girls who were enjoying the second week of their holiday. They were from New York, and straight away I could tell that Martin fancied Victoria, a curvaceous, plus-sized lady. Her friend, Gillian Ryan, was a very petite, attractive, dark-haired lady who I immediately took a shine to. Bowmer didn't fancy either of them, which was typical— I'm convinced he preferred looking at yachts.

The rest of the afternoon was spent trying to chat up the two girls. We were getting on well and arranged to meet them that evening in the Copper and Lumber Store, as it was two-for-one night. Two rum punches for the price of one— this could be fatal if you didn't pace yourself. Excited at the prospect of a date, we arrived early and sank a few rums to loosen up a bit.

The Copper and Lumber Store was a very impressive, fully restored building, but it had low ceilings and small windows, so it was quite dark inside. So, I can be excused for having a vacant expression on my face when a lady came up to me and started talking to me as if we had met before. I was a bit confused, scratching my head, wondering who this young lady was, when she said, "You don't recognise me, do you?"

Suddenly it clicked—it was Gillian. I saw Bowmer laughing at me, giving me the dickhead sign.

The next morning, I was up early, waiting for the kettle to boil. Looking around, I saw Bowmer's feet sticking out of his quarter berth, but there was no sign of Martin. Coffee in hand, I made my way on deck to watch the marina come to life, with the yacht crews getting ready for the first race. Bowmer joined me in the cockpit.

Smiling, he asked, "Get anywhere last night?"

"With who?"

"That bird you were chasing—the one who told you she was Meg Ryan's sister? You know, from the film *When Harry Met Sally.*"

"Has Meg Ryan got a sister? Anyway, no I didn't."

"Lynn, I need to give you some advice."

"Bowmer, I've seen the effect you have on women—you are not best qualified to hand advice out. Ask Karl. Or Mike and his ex-fiancée."

"Yeah, but he did thank me later."

"True, but it's going to be a sad day when I listen to your advice on how to pull a girl."

"This advice will definitely help you."

"Okay, what is it?"

"Well, for a start, it's always a bonus if you can remember what your date looks like when she first turns up."

"I agree—yes, it would have made a better impression," I said, laughing. "I'm sticking to beer from now on; you can keep the rum punch."

"What happened to Martin?" Bowmer asked.

"The last thing I can remember him saying was he was taking Victoria skinny-dipping, down on Pigeon Beach."

We were still debating the outcome of Martin's endeavours when he came walking down the dock, smiling like the cat that had just got the cream.

"Have a nice swim?" I asked.

Before Martin could answer, Bowmer said, with a big smirk on his face, "You haven't been panic-shagging already, have you? It's not even the end of our first week."

"I don't know what you mean."

"Well, you've obviously gone low early to avoid disappointment."

"Bowmer, you're a tosser."

I was crying with laughter.

Martin was still standing on the dock when he pulled out of his pocket a small pair of black frilly knickers. "Look and weep," he said victoriously.

"I didn't know there was a joke shop on the island," I said.

"What do you mean?" said Martin, scratching his head.

Again, Bowmer jumped in. "Which washing line did you nick those from?"

"What are you two on about?"

"Victoria would never get those on—they're way too small," we both said, smiling.

"Ha ha, very funny. You two can bugger off right now," said Martin, laughing.

***

First Race
Course: The Butterfly
Start time: 10:30

Race day was finally upon us, and despite all the initial banter, there was an air of trepidation on board *Seefalke*. We were about to take part in one of the premier classic yacht regattas in the world. The courses set by the race committee differed each day to test the yachts and their crews to the full. We were in Vintage Class B and sailing the Butterfly course. While our class wasn't very big, we were up against some stiff competition, and *Seefalke* did not have the best setup for racing. Her sails were tired after all the sailing I had done getting to Antigua, and despite Bowmer's best efforts, I refused to leave all my worldly possessions on the dock just to save a bit of weight.

The entrants in our class were as follows:

Seefalke. A 50 sqm, 41.6ft-long Abeking & Rasmussen sloop built in 1936.

Flicka. A 45ft Alfred Westmacott ketch built in 1945.

Dione. A 52ft William Fife sloop built in 1912.

Misha. A 32ft cutter built in 1939.

In line with the sailing instructions, we had a white class pennant flying from the port spreader and a small pair of black frilly knickers flying from the starboard spreaders as our battle flag.

We got off to a good start, and the conditions were ideal for *Seefalke*—a light breeze and flat sea. The slightly larger yacht *Flicka* was the fastest in our class, but despite being quicker, she wasn't making ground on us. We enjoyed a great tussle with *Dione*, who was also a faster yacht. We swapped places with her a number of times as we sailed around the course.

To be honest, the racing was secondary to just watching the spectacle; there were many glorious yachts sailing in the regatta. I had seen some of them on the covers of *Classic Boat* and *Yachting World* magazines.

We were the third across the line in our class, but Bowmer thought we had done well on handicap. This made for a great first day of racing; however, we would have to wait for the results to be published before we could work out our 'corrected' position. This is managed by the race committee and involves applying a correction factor (handicap) to the time taken to sail the course. This converts your actual time to an elapsed time. The handicap system is used to smooth out differences in speeds, which allows yachts of different shapes and sizes to race together in the same class.

Once we were back on the dock, I went ashore and bought a crate of beer and some ice to celebrate. We spent the afternoon drinking beer and chilling on the dock. There was a lot to take in, and I couldn't quite believe we had just competed in the Antigua Classics.

Later on, we made our way to the yacht club for the posting of the results. There was an air of excitement as crews and owners waited anxiously for the race officer to come out of the sailing office holding the results. The results were delayed, which presented a further opportunity to drink more beer. Finally, the wait was over, and the race officer came out clutching the results. As soon as these were posted, there was a mad rush as crews raced over to find out how they had got on.

The Result of the First Race
Course: The Butterfly
Vintage Class B
1st *Seefalke*
2nd *Dione*
3rd *Flicka*
4th *Misha*

We had done it; we had won our first race in our class. I don't know what had gotten into Bowmer, but he seemed intent on making sure the whole of Antigua Yacht Club knew about our victory. I'm not sure whether it was down to too much sun, rum, beer, or all of the above, but he was being a total pain in the arse. There were plenty of very wealthy yacht owners in our midst who had spent fortunes on their pristine yachts. What they didn't need was Bowmer trying to rub their noses in it and spoiling their otherwise lovely evening. I could see that this was going to end in tears, and sure enough, it wasn't long before the commodore politely asked us to leave before Bowmer upset the entire yacht club.

You can take the man out of Barry, but you can't take Barry out of the man. Bowmer was living proof of this, although he was certainly keeping us fully entertained. What a laugh.

I did get Bowmer to apologise to the commodore before we left. Following our departure from the club, we lost no time in carrying on our celebrations in the Mad Mongoose, where we met the two girls from New York.

The next morning, I woke up without a hangover, which was incredibly rare. I was enjoying a coffee and watching the world go by when Bowmer came out to join me.

"What happened to you last night, Roachy?"

"I crashed out early after getting nowhere with Gilly. What about you?"

"I ended up clubbing in Abracadabra's."

"That sounds like a great night."

"Yeah, it was okay. I got talking to this girl who seemed pretty keen."

"Well, what's wrong? You don't sound very enthusiastic," I said. "So, what happened then?"

"Nothing."

"Why not?"

"I couldn't be bothered. I think she was staying ashore somewhere, and I had visions of oversleeping and not getting back here in time to go sailing. So, when I was drinking my last beer, I looked at the girl, then thought about *Seefalke* and said to myself I'd rather be on the yacht in the morning. So, I made some excuse and left her at the bar."

"Never mind, Bowmer. Here comes Martin—you can get some top tips off him on the best ways to approach panic-shagging."

Martin walked down the dock and stopped at the back of the yacht.

Bowmer looked at him and said, "You ever thought about entering the Olympics? You could be on for a gold medal with all the late-night swimming you're doing lately."

I chipped in. "Well, he can't train in the day; he would burn his arse."

"You two can sod right off," Martin said with a big smile on his face.

***

Second Race
Course: Old Road
Start time: 10:30

Conditions were once again perfect, and after another good start, for the majority of the race, we held our own against *Dione* and *Flicka* and were destroying them on handicap. However, just as we rounded the fourth mark, the breeze dropped and we fell into a hole. *Dione* and *Flicka* were just far enough ahead to carry the last of the breeze to the finish. Due to the lack of wind, the organisers thankfully shortened the course.

Just after *Seefalke* crossed the finish line, the committee boat called us up to say that we had crossed the line from the wrong direction. Bowmer was furious and adamant that we had crossed the line from the direction of the last mark, which was the correct way. Despite his protests, if we wanted a finish time, we'd need to sail through the line from the opposite direction, which we did.

Having received a hooter to confirm we had finished, we headed back to the dock. The whole way in, we had to endure Bowmer, who was still going on about the race officials. It took a lot of beers before his mood improved. He was still grumpy as we made our way to the yacht club.

Later that evening, we were surprised at the results:

The Result of the Second Race
Course: Old Roads
Vintage Class B

1st *Flicka*
2nd *Seefalke*
3rd *Dione*
4th *Misha*

Considering the drop in wind and our cock-up at the finish, we had done really well. With a first and second under our belts, we were in a very strong position. This called for another celebration—though Bowmer was banned from speaking to anyone in the yacht club unless they spoke to him first.

Having studied the results, Bowmer deduced that the final race was going to be a two-yacht affair. *Flicka* and *Seefalke* were the only yachts that could win our class; we had a first and second, and *Flicka* had a first and third. Even if *Dione* and *Misha* finished first and second, neither yacht could win the overall prize.

We left the yacht club before there was risk of any further upset and carried on partying in the Mad Mongoose. Bowmer spent most of the evening explaining his master plan for beating *Flicka* in the final race and lifting the class trophy. In simple terms, we needed to cover *Flicka*'s every move and get them to sail in our dirty air for as long as possible. 'Dirty air' is a term for turbulence that comes off the sails and can massively affect your boat speed if you sit in it for any length of time.

***

The Third Race
Course: The Cannon
Start time: 10:30

It was another beautiful, hot, sunny Caribbean day. The easterly trade wind was quite brisk and there was more sea running, which favoured the heavier boats. However, we were going to stick to Bowmer's plan and try and sail *Flicka* out of the race.

We had an excellent start and were in front of *Flicka* and *Dione*. This was where we needed to be in order to sit on

Flicka and dictate the race. Bowmer was happy with our early progress and was smiling, which was very out of character— so much so, that Martin joked that his big open mouth was slowing us down.

On our second leg of the course, we were approaching the windward mark when we realised the buoy had broken free. The race mark was just flipping over in the breeze. Technically, if you don't go around a mark in the course, you can be disqualified, and there was too much at stake for us to risk anything. Bowmer wanted us to carry on, so we decided to chase the buoy. *Flicka* was close behind us, but looking back, *Dione* had already turned and altered course, heading for the next mark. A number of other yachts followed suit. *Flicka* stayed with us for another few minutes, before finally turning. It was at this point that we made the decision to follow *Flicka*, which we did all the way to the finishing line.

As we crossed the finish line, the helmsman on *Flicka* raised his sailing cap and gave us a polite nod. His gesture and acknowledgement really cheered us up and showed us what a good job we had done during the regatta.

After the race, we sailed back into English Harbour and tied up just outside the Galley Bar. We celebrated the last race with a few beers before walking over to the yacht club to get the results. This time as we walked in, we were all given name tags with our yacht name on them. I think the idea was it would help people to talk and be more open with each other.

I found a table in the corner out of the way in the hope of keeping Bowmer quiet. My plan was working well while we drank a few beers and waited for the results to be posted, until Kenny Coombs, the regatta chairman, came over to talk to the three of us.

"Hey, lads. You did well today."

"What do you mean?" I asked Kenny.

"Well, the owner of *Flicka* flew in some hotshot American Olympic sailor to helm the yacht in today's race."

Bowmer said, "Are you serious?"

"Yeah," Kenny said. "I think he was on the helm on an America's Cup yacht too."

"They flew him in for one race," I said in disbelief.

We had to laugh.

"Yes, and unofficially, you Welsh boys beat him."

Kenny had a good laugh when I told him I had flown Bowmer in from the States too. Although, I'm pretty sure Mr Hotshot didn't come via San Juan on a twenty-dollar standby ticket.

We were all still laughing when the results came out.

The Result of the Third Race
Course: The Cannon
Vintage Class B
1ˢᵗ *Dione*
2ⁿᵈ *Seefalke*
3ʳᵈ *Flicka*
4ᵗʰ *Misha*

We had won our class, Vintage B.

Bowmer had the biggest smile on his face I have ever seen; I think he was quietly chuffed with our success.

My plan was still working until Bowmer found a magic marker and crossed out his name on his tag and wrote on it instead: "I stuffed Mr Olympic Hotshot."

It was not too long before he managed to upset a lot of rich people. I had to get him out of the yacht club before we had a repeat of the other night's performance. So, we drank up and went off to the Mongoose to carry on the party.

***

I have lots of fond memories of the 1996 Regatta. The Olympic hotshot tipping his cap to us as we crossed the finishing line on the last day was the best. It was amazing how things changed on the back of that regatta. In a short space of time, I went from being just another ex-pat staying on a yacht to someone who was widely recognised and heralded for winning his class at the Classics.

What is lovely about the Antigua Classics is that you get to see some of the largest, fastest and finest classic yachts in the world being raced in a very sportsmanlike and gentlemanly way. It was also lovely to have been able to sail *Seefalke* with the guys and have the opportunity to spend some quality time with them and just catch up. I felt pretty good about life post the regatta.

At the official prize-giving a few days later, I was presented with a superb cut-glass wine decanter for winning our class. I felt immensely proud, and there was a huge cheer as I went up to collect the trophy from all the other competitors. Everyone seemed genuinely pleased for me. This was a great night.

After the classics, there was a week of partying before the start of Antigua Race Week. First was the Mount Gay Rum party. These were prevalent at regattas around the world. It was an opportunity to pick up a coveted Mount Gay Rum hat and T-shirt, which were highly collectable and sought after. Oh yes, and there was the small matter of free rum all night, too. I must say the rum certainly helped people get into the party spirit and participate in the beach games, including a tug-of-war. We all enjoyed a great night on Galleon Beach and spirits were high.

Later the same week we attended the Antigua Rum party, which was another opportunity to consume copious amounts of free rum, get another hat and party hard, this time on Pigeon Beach. It seemed that the same people were all destined for another hangover and sleep deprivation, although no one seemed to care. With a lazy day to follow, there was plenty of time to recover before the next party.

We had hit the party scene pretty hard for a fortnight, and so, by the time the boys needed to fly back to the UK, we were all partied out. We all needed to detox and take things a little slower.

The guys flew home on the first day of Race Week, taking my glass wine decanter back to Ogmore for my mum to look after. I rang Bowmer a few weeks later and asked him how his long trip home via San Juan and New York went; I just knew there was going to be another tale of woe. It turned out that the connection from San Juan to JFK had been delayed, meaning Bowmer missed the connecting flight back to Heathrow. The staff at JFK wouldn't allow him to stay in the airport overnight, and so he'd needed to find somewhere else to stay. I asked him what he ended up doing and he said:

"When I got to New York, it was nearly midnight, so I decided to call Martin's bird Victoria, who gave me her phone number before she left Antigua. She told me to give her a call if I was ever in New York, so I did."

"I bet that was a short conversation?" I said.

"Yeah, pretty much. She was in bed and answered the phone half asleep. I reminded her of our conversation and asked her if she fancied picking me up and taking me back to her place. She was having none of it. Before I had a chance to say anything else, she hung up."

I couldn't help but laugh. Bowmer's trip home took thirty hours, and after paying for a night in a hotel, all told, he saved about sixty pounds on the cost of a direct return flight. He did, however, confirm that Mum was well, and the decanter had made it back safely, which was a relief. I thanked Bowmer for his efforts and said I looked forward to seeing him in a year's time.

Race Week is the end of the sailing season in Antigua, and shortly afterwards, there is a max exodus. It's both difficult and very expensive to get insurance for yachts during the hurricane season, so vessels either head north to America, south to Trinidad or Venezuela, or across the pond to start the summer circuit in the Med. All of a sudden, Antigua was like a ghost town with all the marine-related businesses closing for the summer, together with the bars and restaurants. I was amazed at how quickly the complexion of the island changed.

There was no point staying in Antigua, so I headed south, cruising around the bottom part of the Caribbean. First, I went to Dominica, before calling into Grenada and finally on to Trinidad. I sailed back to Antigua in late autumn to start back at Seagull Services in time for the winter season.

Christmas was soon upon us, which was always a nice time in English Harbour. All the expatriates, yacht crews and locals got together for Christmas Day. A longboat was filled with ice to chill the champagne and beer. Music was provided by a local live band, the weather was great, and there was a real party atmosphere, with people wearing fancy-dress costumes and having fun. Lots of the guys brought their dogs, and we all enjoyed a really chilled afternoon. The festivities finished around four o'clock, leaving people free to do their own thing in the evening.

Jenny Gordon, who owned the yacht next to mine in Ordnance Bay, invited all the single-handed sailors for Christmas dinner at the house she was looking after. This was a lovely way to finish off our Christmas Day celebrations.

New Year's Eve was another party. I must have had a good night, because I woke up on the yacht, unable to remember how I got back. Feeling like shit, I walked down to Pigeon Beach for a swim. I was up to my neck in water, when a friend of mine, Tin-Tin, walked down the beach, carrying a six-pack of beer.

He threw me one, saying, "Lynn, you look like shit. Drink this, it's the hair of the dog."

1997 started as 1996 ended: with a beer. That year, I entered the Classics again. Martin came over to crew for me, but Bowmer was in the middle of buying a house and changing area with his job, so he couldn't make it. Instead, Little Wayne, my Kiwi friend, was mad keen to crew for me. Wayne was the engineer on a superyacht. I first met him when I was doing some work onboard; he was a great guy with an infectious laugh. Not too much happened in the races to remember—all our adventures were in the bars or leaving parties.

One of the evenings, I walked into Last Lemming restaurant, and standing by the bar was James, the skipper of the superyacht *Adela*, another yacht I had worked on. Next to him was a person I recognised, but I couldn't put a name to their face. James introduced me to Dennis Conner, who was sailing on *Adela* that week. The name and face clicked. Dennis Conner was the most famous sailor in the world; he was the America's Cup skipper, who'd lost the America Cup for the first time to the Australian syndicate headed up by Alan Bond.

James asked if I'd like a beer.

"Ask a silly question?" I replied.

Conner said, "I'll get them."

My claim to fame is that Dennis Conner bought me a beer. I tried to talk to him about sailing in the regatta without much luck, so I thanked him and walked away with the beer he bought me.

We did have a good sail in the third race—the Cannon. As soon as we tied the yacht up on the dock, outside the Galley

Bar in English Harbour, the party started. My crew were still buzzing and talking about the race when I saw my friend Jane Coombs walking down the dock. I invited her on board for a beer.

"Well, Lynn, you did well today," she said.

"Why's that, Jane?" I asked.

"Well, you came sixth overall in the entire fleet."

After downing a few more beers in the Galley Bar, I started thinking about our sixth place and wondered how well we could do with a decent set of sails and a full complement of experienced sailors. I'd finished two Classics using a set of knackered old sails that had been cut down. The mainsail was five feet too short on the foot, and I only had a no.2 genoa, which was too small for lighter conditions. The sails were second hand when I got them and since then had seen plenty of miles. They were ready for the bin.

We had quite a party that day, lots of crews hopping from yacht to yacht talking about the regatta and the yachts they had raced against. At one point in the afternoon, I must have had twenty people on *Seefalke*; I thought she was going to sink.

The afternoon session carried on into the evening with another party, this time at the Last Lemming. Martin and Wayne disappeared early on—they were chasing a couple of girls. I was out of it, so I decided to slip away back to the yacht and crash out, without the embarrassment of being dubbed a lightweight.

When I got up the next day, Martin was still absent, which left me thinking he had scored after all. I made a coffee and sat in the cockpit watching the world go by. I was suddenly disturbed by Dave, off *Polaris*, one of our neighbours.

"Morning, Lynn," he said. "Your crew must have had a good night?"

"Why is that?"

Dave pointed to a body in his cockpit.

"One of yours?" he questioned.

Martin was asleep in the cockpit, covered in mud and blood. He soon woke up.

"What happened, Martin?" I asked.

"All I remember is chasing a girl called Big Debbie. We ended up in the Mad Mongoose, where somehow, I lost her. It was pretty late, I was completely smashed and a bit fed up, so I decided to come back to the yacht. After that, I have no idea what happened, only that I ended up lying on the ground, covered in blood in the pouring rain."

"So, why did you sleep in the cockpit of *Polaris*?"

"I don't know."

Dave laughed, saying, "No harm done."

The classic yacht regatta was over for another year and our free berth had come to an end, so we moved *Seefalke* back to her mooring in Ordnance Bay. To get back and forth to the yacht, I was lucky enough to borrow a dinghy from Jenny Gordon.

As in previous years, there were a series of rum parties leading up to and during Race Week. One of the highlights was the Antigua Rum party on Pigeon Beach. By eight o'clock, I was out of it; I had drunk more than my fill. I made my way back to my bunk, leaving Martin and Wayne to carry on partying.

The next morning, Wayne was nowhere to be seen, but to my surprise, Martin had made it back aboard.

"How come you're back?" I asked him. "I thought you were going to stay with Big Debbie?"

"That was my plan, but Big Debbie had other ideas. Wayne got lucky; he wandered off with a German girl."

Sitting in the cockpit, I saw only my dinghy tied up to the stern.

I asked Martin, "How did you get back last night?"

"You had taken your dinghy and I couldn't find Jenny's—it wasn't where we left it—so I wandered around until I found the one on the little beach outside the Admiral's Inn."

Pointing to the stern, Martin said, "I paddled that white piece of shit back using a piece of driftwood I found."

I couldn't see another dinghy on the stern, but I did see another painter, so I got up to have a look. Under the water, I could just make out a white dinghy.

"So, Martin, you used that dinghy? It floated long enough for you to get back here?" I said. "Getting back to the yacht was a piece of cake, then?"

"Hardly, I got halfway back when a bloody great dinghy motored past, leaving a huge wake, which swamped the dinghy and sent me swimming at the same time."

Laughing, I said, "Oh, so you swam back?"

"No, I swam to the bow of the nearest yacht, where I managed to bail the water out of that piece of shit I was in. It took half an hour of bailing before I could get back in it. Just as I started paddling again, the same bloody dinghy went tearing past for a second time, and before I know it, I'm back in the drink. Fortunately, people in another dinghy saw me fall in and came to my rescue. They dragged me out of the water and towed the sinker back to *Seefalke* and dropped me aboard."

"An interesting night you had," I said, laughing.

The final big party of the week was the Mount Gay Rum party at Galleon Beach. There were hundreds of people wanting to get their free hats, T-shirts and Mount Gay. I was standing at the bar next to a little American guy when suddenly there was a shout from one of the bar staff.

"One minute to go! Free rum in one minute!"

We all started to count down the seconds. Ten, nine, eight—then a big shout of "Free rum!"

The little American guy said to the barman, "Could I have a beer, please?"

With a look of disbelief on his face, the barman said, "Sorry, mate, we're only serving rum."

I woke up relieved to find myself back on the yacht. How I got back, I've no idea. I couldn't believe that Martin had made it back too.

Sitting in the cockpit, I asked him, "Did you have a good night last night?"

"Yes, we ended up in the Mad Mongoose again, chasing two sisters, until Wayne passed out. I managed to drag him back through the dockyard to the dinghy."

"Well done," I said. "So, no issues like the other night?"

Martin said, "Not exactly."

"Why?"

"Wayne and I were smashed, but I got him into the dinghy and rowed back to the yacht. Wayne started to climb aboard, took two steps, tripped, and fell head-first straight into the water. It took me five minutes to get him out, by which time we were laughing like fools. I'm surprised we didn't wake you up. As soon as I got him back on deck, he took two steps and walked straight off the deck and ended up back in the water. I went through the whole rigmarole again, and the dozy idiot did exactly the same thing for the third time. I got him back out of the water; this time he fell fast asleep and I couldn't wake him. I was fed up, so I left him to sleep in the dinghy."

"What a pair of plonkers you are," I said. "So, where's Wayne now?"

"I left him in the dinghy."

"What, tied up to the stern?"

"Yes."

"Martin, the only thing I can see tied to the stern is one of Jenny's dog leads."

"What? I must have tied up the lead instead of the painter."

"We had better go and find him."

It didn't take too long to find Wayne; he was still fast asleep in the dinghy, drifting out of English Harbour.

After Race Week, there was the usual exodus of yachts, and soon English Harbour was a ghost town again. Luckily, Seagull Services had picked up a big refit on a yacht called *Hide and Skip*, which kept me employed through the summer months. I had lots of fun during that summer, despite most of the bars being shut.

There was one particularly nice summer's day, with a clear blue sky and very little wind. I walked a friend's Labrador called Koby to Fort Barclay at the entrance to English Harbour. While I was sat on one of the fort's stone walls, a French yacht slowly motored in, towing a dinghy on a long painter. The skipper motored around until he found a suitable place to anchor. Then the guy ran quickly to the bow and dropped the anchor. After checking everything was okay, he made his way back to the cockpit and stopped the engine. The owner then spent five minutes sat there, making sure the anchor wasn't dragging. Once he was happy, he went below to presumably put the kettle on. Five minutes later he stuck his head out of the main hatch to check his position. Once satisfied that the yacht hadn't moved, he went below again. Ten minutes later, he returned to the cockpit with a mug in his hand. All of a sudden, he started to panic as he realised his yacht had started drifting out to sea. He ran to the bow to check the anchor, which was sitting in his dinghy, which had been under the bow when he originally dropped it. I could see him having a good laugh to himself once he realised what had happened. He did, however, have a good look around in the hope that no one had watched him make his mistake. It was at this point that I started clapping, and in response, the guy gave me a very graceful bow.

That evening, I was in the Galley Bar for happy hour, telling Andy from Sun Yacht Charter the story.

He said, "I have a better one than that. Last week we chartered a yacht to a couple for their holiday. I went out with them for a couple of hours to make sure they knew what they were doing. Once I was happy, I got them to drop me back on the dock. I didn't think any more about them until they arrived back on the dock two days later."

"So, what happened?"

"Well, I asked them what was wrong, and they said that they had run out of anchors and had to come back because we had only given them two. I explained that they were supposed to recover the anchors and not just abandon them on the seabed."

"You're joking?" I said, laughing. "Hey, disposable anchors might catch on."

Andy didn't seem very impressed with my suggestion.

1997 ended with some sad news: one of Jenny's dogs had been poisoned and killed. Regrettably, it was quite a common occurrence in Antigua. On one night alone, forty-nine dogs were poisoned. Antigua was not all paradise in the sun.

I helped Jenny bury the dog at sea. The poor thing had a 5hp Seagull outboard motor strapped to its back to help it sink.

Chapter 11
Nineteen Ninety-Eight

My New Year's resolution was to get new sails for the yacht and invite Bowmer and the boys from Barry to come out and have another good go at the classic yacht regatta. I wanted Karl to make the sails and figured that if I could get him to come out, he would do a really good job of them. Using the work phone, I rang Karl and told him I wanted two new sails made: a mainsail and a 150% genoa. Karl said it wouldn't be a problem; he said he would fax over a form for me to complete with the measurements he needed in order to make the sails. Once I'd sent it back to him, Karl said he'd get cracking straight away. First resolution achieved already. Great.

To my surprise, Karl faxed me the form within an hour of me ringing him. That was definitely out of character for him; in fact, I hadn't even known that he had a fax machine. I thought he must be finally getting his act together.

Karl's form had a picture of a yacht on it, illustrating the measurements that I needed to take. He needed to know things like the length of the mast, boom, forestay, etc. To provide accurate measurements, I needed to borrow a long tape measure, so on my way back from work, I called into Antigua Sails and borrowed one from my mate Tin-Tin. Once the form was filled in, I faxed it back to Karl, and to my total amazement, I had a quote within a week.

Happy with the price, I rang Karl and was met with more surprises. Karl now had a credit card machine, so I paid for the sails upfront. The only thing I did point out to Karl was that I was outside the UK, and there was no need for me to pay any VAT. I can still remember his words like it was yesterday.

"No problem, Lynn. I have a good friend in the yacht club who is head of customs and excise in Cardiff; I'll make sure you get the VAT back."

I was reassured by this and knew Karl would make an excellent job of the sails. I really hoped he would come out and sail in the regatta with me. Despite all the banter and mickey-taking, Karl was a good friend.

My new mainsail and a no.1 genoa were sorted. Next, I needed a decent crew. I rang Martin from Reading, but he couldn't make it. Mind you, that probably wasn't a bad thing after his exploits last year. He was lucky not to have killed himself.

I rang Bowmer and told him there were strong rumours flying around Antigua Yacht Club that two J-Class yachts were going to race in the Classics. If the rumours were true, this would be the first time that two "Jays" had raced against each other since the 1930s.

As soon as I told him that, he was in. I also gave him the news that I had ordered a new mainsail and no.1 genoa.

Bowmer was even more excited and asked, "Great—who from? North, McWilliams or Antigua Sails?"

I replied, "Karl."

"YOU DICKHEAD!" he shouted.

"Why?"

"I can't believe you ordered them from Karl. He's still a nightmare and you'll be lucky to ever see them—you know how unreliable he is."

"I know all that," I said, "But he's our closest friend. I'm hoping we can get him over here and sail with us, which will motivate him to get the sails made in plenty of time."

"Okay, Lynn, I understand that, but he's called Deadloss for a reason. He's useless, and if he didn't work for himself, he would be totally unemployable."

I knew Bowmer was talking sense. Although Karl was an excellent sailmaker, he was easily distracted and completely clueless at running a business. He was always leaving things to the last minute and being very relaxed about issuing invoices and collecting outstanding money. The business was a financial trainwreck.

"Sorry, Bowmer, Karl is good at making sails. He's my mate, too. I've placed the order and I've paid for them. You will need to keep on top of Karl for me—and one more thing: he has three months to make them."

"What?! That's never enough time for Deadloss."

"I'll leave you to find a crew. Get the best—we have two J-Class yachts to beat," I said jokingly.

"Roachy, if we beat the Jays, I will eat my socks."

"That's a bit extreme, Bowmer. You might catch some disease unknown to man."

A week later, I was in work when Bowmer phoned.

"I've put a crew together. They're all mad for it."

"Great—who?"

"Foxy, Wattsy, Spud and me."

"Who?"

Bowmer repeated, "Foxy—Mike Fox—he's built like a brick outhouse and will be great on the rail if it gets rough. He's massive."

"Well done, Bowmer," I said. "If it's the Mike I'm thinking about, he's the one that drives very expensive, fast cars and with even more expensive women with him all the time."

"You got him," said Bowmer. "Next, I found Ian Watts—Wattsy—you know, the tall, skinny one from the yacht club. He's like a stick insect; he will be great on the foredeck. We don't want much weight up there."

"I know Wattsy well. He's a great lad, and likes chasing women, so he should do well over here during the regatta season."

"And then there's Hugh Davies—Spud—who you know. He's cleaned up this year in the local racing and is working for Deadloss, so he'll have a vested interest in getting the sails made."

"Well done, Bowmer, that's great. How did you come up with the guys?"

"I chose them for the following reasons. One: they're all pissheads. Two: they love to party. Three: they're all very good sailors. And four: most importantly, they're the only guys who are up for it and can get the time off work in April."

"Brilliant, what about Deadloss?"

"No, he's skint, and Liz has put her foot down," Bowmer replied.

"That's a shame; I really wanted Karl to come. See you soon, Bowmer," I said and hung up the phone.

Not a bad crew, I thought. Bowmer had come good. The guys were all experienced sailors, and Bowmer hadn't long taken part in a Five Nations challenge racing around the UK in one-design boats. He was mate on one of the two Welsh boats that went on to win the event. With our class win in 1996 and finishing 6th overall in '97, I felt confident that we could do some real damage in the forthcoming regatta. The only guy I didn't know very well was Foxy, who did most of his sailing out of Cardiff. However, Bowmer had vouched for him, so that was good enough for me, and in any event, I knew they'd all be an absolute scream to be around for two weeks.

With everything falling into place, I had three months to get *Seefalke* ready to race, which was bags of time.

Chapter 12
My Story

With the crew and sails sorted out, life in Antigua carried on as normal. The big event in February of that year was a total solar eclipse. Antigua turned out to be one of the top places to witness this rare occurrence. English Harbour was full of charter yachts coming in to enjoy the event. On the day, I worked until midday then made my way back to the yacht to enjoy the eclipse. It was a lovely hot, sunny day, with a clear, blue sky and absolutely no wind. The conditions were perfect for watching the eclipse.

As I had a free afternoon, I started working on *Seefalke*'s brightwork and sanded her toe rails ready for varnish. The best way to do this was from my dinghy, starting at the stern and working my way around the yacht. This was a really chilled way to spend the afternoon.

While I worked on the varnish, a French charter yacht came in and anchored just in front of me. I didn't really pay much attention, not until one of the crew, an old guy, stripped down to his birthday suit and started taking a shower on the aft bathing platform. *Disgusting*, I thought. Why take a shower on the back of the yacht, when there would be two or three showers on a yacht that size? Oh well, that's the French for you.

I noticed the rest of the crew; there were two old couples and one very pretty young woman about twenty years of age. One by one, the oldies stripped off and took showers on the back of the yacht. Praying that the young, attractive girl would follow suit, I very quickly moved my dinghy to the bow and started sanding the toe rail there, meaning I was only thirty feet away from the French yacht.

My timing was perfect. I got to the bow just as the young lady who looked like a supermodel started to take off her bikini in preparation for her shower. I was sat there open-mouthed—I couldn't believe my luck—when suddenly, out of nowhere, a solitary gust of wind caught *Seefalke* and spun her round a hundred and eighty degrees. I was now facing completely the wrong way, with no view. It probably served me right for perving in the first place. Someone upstairs has got a sense of humour. I did see the funny side, and it made me laugh.

The eclipse was great; I watched it through a welding glass filter. It lasted for less than ten minutes, but in that time, it got darker, flowers closed and all the nocturnal bugs came out. The colour of everything changed, which was just fantastic, and the temperature dropped. I was impressed and felt lucky to have been in such a prime location to watch the whole thing.

A few days later, as I walked to the Galley Bar after work for a happy-hour beer, I overheard a group of American tourists outside Nelson's Dockyard. By the entrance to the dockyard were two huge anchors and huge chain links from Nelson's day. These were huge lumps of iron that would have taken the whole crew turning massive capstans to haul them up to the bow of one of Nelson's ships.

I heard one American lady talking to her husband say, "Gee, honey, are those anchors made of wood?"

I had to laugh; I don't think floating anchors will ever catch on.

Getting back to my new sails—I had been ringing Karl once a month to check on his progress. Each time I spoke to him, he said it's all in hand and I don't need to worry.

I thought everything was sorted until, in work one day, three weeks before the boys were due to fly out, I received a phone call from Spud. He wanted to know the LP (luff perpendicular) length for the genoa.

"Why do you want to know the LP, Spud?" I asked. "Karl said the sails were already made?"

"Karl has only just ordered the material," Spud said. "Don't worry—I'll make sure your sails are made, even if I have to make them myself."

Spud was excited about coming over and sailing in the regatta. He said all the UK yachting magazines had big articles on the two J-Class yachts racing for the first time in sixty years.

After work I had to go and find Tin-Tin from Antigua Sails to get him to explain the LP measurement and to borrow his long tape measure again. Fortunately, Tin-Tin agreed to come and give me a hand: on the proviso, I bought him a Red Stripe beer. Deal done. I rang Spud to pass on the measurement he wanted.

I rang Bowmer two weeks before the crew were due to come out. After a general chat, he asked about *Seefalke* and asked if I'd raced her this year.

"Yes," I said. "I entered the annual Green Island Race."

"How did you get on?"

"We won," I said.

"Cool."

"Well, not really."

"Why?"

"Well, there were only two entries and the other yacht T-boned the committee boat at the start."

"What? He hit it?"

"Yes—lucky it was only one guy in an inflatable dinghy."

Bowmer said, "That was a short race, then?"

"Yes," I said, laughing. "All I had to do was cross the start line, a forty-two-foot race."

"So is *Seefalke* ready to race, then?" asked Bowmer.

"Yes, she's out of the water getting her bottom scrubbed and antifouled and is looking good," I said. "Has Karl made the sails yet?"

"According to Spud, not yet, although the cloth has arrived and they will take about a week to make. I'll try and get Spud started on them for you."

"Thanks, Bowmer, that'll be great. Anyway, I'll see you in two weeks. Getting excited?"

"Too right, I can't wait. It's been a long year already, and I'm really looking forward to two weeks in the Caribbean sun."

What I had forgotten to mention to Bowmer was that I had taken *Seefalke* out of the water at Antigua Slipway and dropped the rudder out to inspect the rudder stock. It was a good job I had, as there wasn't much of it left.

Teredo navalis worms, otherwise known as naval shipworms, had eaten their way deep into the stock. This was a major issue, and I talked with Andrew from Woodstock as to how I could repair this in time for the regatta. We both agreed I needed a new rudder, and as this was a specialist job, Andrew said he would make it and promised to get it done in time. I was seriously relieved, one big weight off my mind.

I put *Seefalke* back into the water. I couldn't leave her on the hard for very long; Antigua's heat would soon dry the planks out and the hull would quickly open up. I put her back on the mooring with only two weeks before the first race and a week before the boys were due to arrive.

I had a yacht with no rudder. Great.

Less than two weeks before the regatta, I rang Karl.

He said, "I have some good news: the number one genoa is finished."

"Well done, Karl, that's great," I said. "What about the mainsail?"

"I haven't started the mainsail yet because the cloth hasn't arrived."

"What? Spud said the cloth came in last week?"

"It did, but I had to use it to make another sail I promised to make for someone else who placed the order two months ago."

"Bloody great. Thanks, Karl."

"Your material is due in today. Don't worry—Spud will bring the sails with him when he arrives in Antigua."

"I bloody hope so."

Feeling angry and let down, I hung up. Bowmer was right: Deadloss was useless and unemployable.

Andrew from Woodstock was giving me the same runaround with the rudder as Karl was with the sails.

In a similar conversation, he said, "Your rudder will be finished before the thirteenth."

"Bloody great, Andrew. What month?"

"April, I promise."

I had to hope that the two of them pulled through, otherwise I wouldn't have a yacht for the boys to sail on. If *Seefalke* wasn't fit to race, I was in for a shedload of grief from Bowmer. It didn't bear thinking about—another nightmare. I'd get abuse from him for the rest of my life.

How could getting three things made—two sails and a rudder—be so stressful?

Chapter 13
Bowmer's Story

The highlight of the weekend was the phone call from Lynn letting me know he had ordered sails from Karl and asking if I could find a crew to race in that year's classic yacht regatta. I was keen and well up for it. I could see why Lynn was using the sails as a carrot to get Karl to Antigua, but he must have forgotten what Deadloss was like during the three years he had been away. If he'd had any sense, he would have got Antigua Sails to make them.

Lynn asked me to keep an eye on Karl, so periodically I stopped off after work at Karl's sail loft. I called in one evening and Karl and Spud were still hard at it, which made a nice change.

"Alright, Bowmer, what's happening?" Karl asked.

"Two things, Karl. I've had a phone call from Lynn asking me to sort out a crew for the Antigua Classic Regatta and to check that you've got your act together and are making his new sails."

"Don't worry, Bowmer—it's all in hand. Lynn has paid me, and I've ordered the material."

"Good. *Seefalke* with new sails will be a rocket ship, and we need them if we're going to do well in the regatta. Anyway, are you pair of numpties coming?"

"I'm skint, and Liz would have a fit if I went," Karl said. "She thinks I'd stay there and she'd never see me again."

"Well, Karl, you really would be doing Liz a favour. I'm surprised she hasn't bought you a ticket already and packed your bags. You should really think about joining us."

"Bowmer, you are a tosser."

Spud said, "I'm well up for it. I bet Wattsy will be too."

"Good, who else can we get to come? Have a think, Spud, and I'll get my secretary working on the flights tomorrow."

I was sad Karl couldn't come as the banter would have been immense, although, with Spud and Wattsy coming we had the makings of a good holiday and a decent crew for the racing.

***

March 1998

We didn't have long to go, and we were all getting excited. Wattsy had roped in Mike Fox, who would be good on the yacht, the flights were booked and paid for, and we had been buying stuff for the trip. Spud and Wattsy were proud owners of new passports, and I had been getting stuck into Karl about his apathy in relation to Lynn's sails.

On another futile trip to the loft, I asked him how the sails were coming along.

"Don't worry, Bowmer," he told me. "They're in production."

This was a standard phrase of Karl's when nothing had been started.

"I heard you say that last month and the month before," I said.

"They will be ready—stop panicking!"

"I heard you say that last month too."

***

5th April

With only a week before we were due to fly out to Antigua, I was back in Karl's loft.

"Karl, have you made the sails?"

"I will. I will. I just need to order the cloth."

"Order the cloth?! You told me you already had the cloth?"

"I used it on another order that was two months overdue. The guy threatened to kneecap me if I didn't make his sail."

That's not a bad idea, I thought. It seemed to be the only way to get Deadloss to make the sails.

"So, you used Lynn's sail material. You're a tosser!"

"Don't worry, Bowmer. I've ordered more—it's due in today."

"I can't believe this. You've had months to make Lynn's sails. If these aren't ready by Sunday morning, you're in deep shit."

"It's all in hand, don't worry."

***

8th April

There were only four days before we were due to fly out. I phoned Karl from the office.

"Alright, what's happening?" I asked. "Please tell me you've made Lynn's sails."

"Good news, Bowmer: the cloth came in earlier."

"What do you mean the cloth came in earlier?"

"The cloth is here, and Spud will start on them once I find the sail dimensions Lynn faxed to me back in January."

"I don't believe you, Karl. Put Spud on the phone?" I was tamping. While this was totally consistent for Karl, I couldn't believe he'd screw up this badly on Lynn's sails.

"He can't speak to you," Karl said. "He's too busy looking for the fax."

"Deadloss."

"Calm down! Bowmer, the way you're going, you'll have a heart attack."

"Calm down?! Karl, you've got four bloody days to make a genoa and a mainsail."

"Look, who's running this sail-making business?"

"Clearly, it's not you!" I shouted down the phone.

"It's all in hand. I've just found the fax. They will be made well before you leave on Sunday."

***

Friday 10th April

I woke up early feeling really happy and got up straight away. I was looking forward to a stress-free time away from work. Only eight hours of work to go—yippee! I had been dreaming of seeing Lynn and sailing on his beautiful old classic yacht with new sails and having a laugh with my mates. I always found the build-up to sailing events exciting and was looking forward to seeing Wattsy and Spud in the pub later that day to talk about our trip.

As I walked out my front door to go to work, the phone rang. It was Spud on the line.

"Hiya. Get your arse down here as soon as you finish work; we're going to be having a late one."

"What? We're going to the Park"—a famous pub in Barry—"later."

"We ain't," said Spud, cutting me off mid-sentence. "We need to get Lynn's sails made."

"The lying tosser! He said you had been working on them already!"

"I can't believe you fell for that one, Bowmer. You know what he's like."

I have never been a violent person, but at that moment in time, I could see why the threat of kneecapping the bastard was the only way to get the sails made.

"We haven't got time to argue. Come down and help us," urged Spud, cutting off my increasingly offensive expletives.

My last day in work should have been spent dreaming about sun, sea and rum. Instead, I spent it thinking of my best mate, that useless bastard Karl Deadloss for a very good reason.

Leaving work after a very long, busy and stressful day, I headed over to Karl's excuse for a business. With a deep breath, I opened the door and went in. I opened up with a barrage of abuse and called Karl every last derogatory name I could think of. I can't remember ever being more upset. Karl had done some pretty dumb things in the past, but this far outweighed his previous faux pas.

Everything I said, Karl had heard before, and from the look on his face, the abuse went straight over his head. So, I gave up and said, "Right, Deadloss, what's my first job?"

"You can start by getting the cloth off the shelf and finding a ball of string so we can mark the shape out on the floor."

"What, you haven't even started them yet? You total tosser."

"Right, you two, stop slagging each other out and let's get on with it," said Spud.

Spud was right. Karl and I set to work. I'm not sure how it would've seemed to outsiders looking in, but we actually worked really well as a team. It didn't take long before the shape was marked out on the floor and we were cutting cloth and sticking the seams together ready for sewing. We worked all night in the loft, and by 6 a.m. the following morning, we had built the no.1 genoa. We'd gone through coffee like no tomorrow, while Spud got his caffeine fix from numerous cans of Red Bull.

With another long day and night ahead, we decided to go to the Bridge Café for a full hit. The Bridge Café was an institution. You went to the counter and paid before entering the kitchen to place your order with the two sisters who did all the cooking. Breakfast always took ages to come as it was all cooked to order, which left plenty of time to go next door and get the *Daily Star* and *The Sun* to read some mindless drivel.

When we got back to the loft, Wattsy joined us for round two: making a top-drawer mainsail in under 24 hours. We laid the measurements out on the floor, cut the cloth and taped it together ready for Spud to sew it. While that was happening, we cut the reinforcing patches for the reefing points, head, tack and clew. Karl got on with making the bolt rope to go on the luff, and we set the hydraulic press up ready to press the cringles for the three corners, the reefing pendants and the eyes for the sliders that would go up the mast.

By 6 p.m., most of the sewing was completed and we had the makings of a mainsail. We decided to take a break to get a takeaway and go home to pack our gear for the trip. Before heading back to the loft, I put my bag by the front door, ready for the following day when Foxy would be picking me up at 5 a.m.

It had just gone midnight when we finally finished the sails and placed them in their bags. We got Foxy to call down and put the sails straight in his car to save time later that morning. To thank Karl, Spud and Wattsy, I called Red Dragon Radio and got them to play a dedication—"More Than a Feeling" by *Boston*. I thought the title of the song was quite apt.

I was ecstatic in the knowledge that the sails were finished; I couldn't quite believe that we had built two sails in 36 hours. I'd had every expectation of turning up in Antigua with no sails and being greeted by a very disappointed Lynn. Now the holiday could start.

Despite it being late, I was determined to go to Friars, a nightclub just down the road from Karl's loft. Friars had a licence until three in the morning, which was plenty of time to get a load of rum and cokes down me—I wanted to get into the Caribbean mood.

Just as I was waving goodbye to Karl, he said, "I need one more favour, Bowmer."

"What now?"

"Can you take these forms to the VAT office in Gatwick? If you don't, Lynn won't get the VAT back."

"You're having a laugh."

"No, I've spoken to Corinne Hobbs"—head of custom and excise in Cardiff—"and that's what you need to do. He said to mention his name, and everything will be sorted."

I must have been tired, to actually believe him.

Spud decided to go home, so I gave him the forms for safe-keeping, while Foxy dropped Wattsy and me off at Friars.

As I left Karl's sail loft, I told Spud to make sure he got me up at five. I knew with a good drink inside me and being ridiculously tired, I was going to struggle.

***

Saturday 11ᵗʰ April

Getting home was a blur. I decided to go to bed fully dressed so that I was ready for my early morning start. I'd only have to put my shoes on and lock the front door as I bailed out onto the street. I fell asleep on top of the duvet, and it didn't seem five minutes before I awoke abruptly to loud banging on my upstairs bedroom window. I pulled the curtain back to find Wattsy the other side of the glass shouting at me. I remember being quite perplexed as to how he was managing to fly.

"Get up, you tosser!" he shouted as I lay back on the bed.

All of a sudden, I remembered today was the start of our big adventure. With that, I stumbled down the stairs, put my shoes on, grabbed my bag, and locked the front door as I ventured onto the street. My early morning get-out-of-bed plan had worked a treat.

"How the bloody hell did you get ready so quick? You were in the bedroom sparked out a minute ago," said Wattsy, looking very confused.

Just as confused, I asked him, "How did you manage to fly up to my bedroom window?"

"I didn't fly, you knob. I had to stand on Spud's shoulders and then pull myself up to your window ledge. Come on, let's go!"

Foxy drove us all to Gatwick. It was a bit of a squeeze with the four of us, our luggage and two big sail bags. I took the opportunity to catch up on some much-needed sleep, which made the four-hour journey go really quickly. As we entered the terminal, it felt like my holiday had well and truly started, and boy, I needed it after all the stress of getting the sails made.

Being quite early on a Sunday morning, the airport wasn't too busy, and we got to the check-in desk pretty quickly. Not long afterwards, our bags had been weighed and checked in, save the blooming sails which had to go to a different part of the airport. Spud and I went to find the correct drop-off point while Foxy and Wattsy went off to have a drink in the departure lounge.

After everything else, I couldn't believe that I had got stitched up with having to sort the VAT out. That should have been done well before getting to the airport. After a few wrong turns and asking several airport staff for directions, we ended up in a narrow corridor with a window and door at the far end with 'Customs and Excise' written above the window. There was no one around, so I knocked on the glass several times before a middle-aged guy appeared. He just stared at us, and it was quite clear that we were disturbing his otherwise peaceful morning. I just knew that this was not going to be a masterclass in customer service.

With a sigh, he opened the window. "Yeah?"

This guy had the personality of a brick, but knowing that I needed to get these forms agreed, I smiled, and hoped that would promote some friendly rapport. Despite my best endeavours, the guy just stood there. After a long, awkward silence, I decided to speak.

"Right, well, my name is Bowmer, and I am trying to get some VAT back. We are taking some sails to Antigua."

"Give me your forms."

"Our friend Corinne Hobbs told us you could help us with the forms."

"Corinne who? I've never heard of him."

"Corinne is the head of VAT in South Wales?"

"Yeah, and?" he said, holding his hand out. "Where are your forms?"

I passed them over to him.

After a quick look at the forms, he passed them back to me, saying, "These forms are blank."

"What!?"

"You will have to fill them in."

At this point, I was ready to explode. I was tired, hungover and this bloody nightmare just kept going. Here I was, stuck in some never-to-be-seen-again corridor with a job's worth and blank VAT forms that Karl had stitched me up with. Had Karl been within ten feet of me at that moment, I would have knocked him into next week.

I knew damn well that I wouldn't be able to fill the forms in correctly, so I said to the guy, "Okay. Is there any chance that you could help me fill these in please?" I stood there smiling.

"One minute," the guy said with a big sigh and walked off.

He returned with a three-hundred-page book and thrust it into my hand.

"What's this?"

"A book on completing VAT forms."

"Look, mate, I can't read this. I have a flight to catch in a few hours."

The guy then sniffed and shrugged his shoulders. I recognised this as the universal sign for "I couldn't give a shit".

Feeling really annoyed, I closed my eyes and rubbed them to compose myself. I needed to keep my cool.

"Surely it's not that hard for you to help me fill these forms in," I said. "If you can help me, it will be really appreciated."

"I've just given you the book—what more do you want?"

I decided that there was no point in arguing any further and filled the damn forms in to the best of my ability, with help from Spud. I did have to ask for a pen, which upset the VAT officer further. We managed to fill in most of the form, but then it came to specifying the cost of the sails.

Spud didn't know what Karl had charged Lynn, so I had no option but to ring Deadloss. First, I had to go and find a payphone. I tried a few times with no luck, so I kept trying until eventually, Liz came to the phone.

"Hi Liz," I said in a quiet, friendly tone. "It's Bowmer."

"What do you want this time in the morning?"

"Sorry to call so early, but I need to speak to Karl. We're at Gatwick Airport and I'm going to miss a flight in a minute. Is he there? Any chance I can speak to him?" I said with a big sigh.

In the background, I heard Karl say, "If that's Bowmer, tell him to bugger off."

"I heard that," I said. "Look, Liz, this is really important. Please put him on."

"What do you want?" said Karl.

"Right, I'm in Gatwick at the VAT office, and I need some details to fill in the empty VAT forms you gave me."

"You mean I forgot to fill them in?"

"Yes, you know you did."

"Sorry, Bowmer," said Karl, laughing.

"Look, Karl, shut up, stop laughing and just answer these questions. How much did you charge Lynn for the sails including the VAT?"

"I don't know. Lynn paid for them months ago," was Karl's reply

I almost had an aneurysm. I knew Karl was inept, but I couldn't believe he didn't know a simple detail like the price. I really didn't know how he functioned in life.

"What do you mean? Surely you know how much you charged?"

"The paperwork is in the loft. I really don't know."

"Great! Just bloody great!"

Spud started to laugh.

"Look, Karl, I'm not kidding about. Please tell me the price?"

"Just make it up."

Hearing this, Spud was creased up in fits of laughter.

"Make it up?! You can't say that! I'm standing outside the VAT office."

"Er, just put about er... Er... Three hundred and eighty pounds."

"Really, Karl? We're just going to guess?"

"Yeah, three hundred and eighty pounds should do it."

"Karl, it's just taken the three of us over thirty hours each to make these sodding sails. That's more than ninety hours of labour, plus materials. If you charge three hundred and eighty pounds, that means you're working for under five pounds an hour!" I shouted down the phone.

"Yes, Bowmer, put down three hundred and eighty pounds."

I looked at Spud, who was still laughing.

"Fine! I'll put three hundred and eighty pounds."

I put the phone down on Karl and wandered back to the VAT office to carry on filling in the form. On the next line, I had to work out the VAT at seventeen-and-a-half percent. This should have been easy for me, but my brain was shredded. Looking around and pressing my nose to the glass slider window, I could see a calculator on the desk on the other side.

"Excuse me," I said. "Can I use your calculator?"

"No."

"Please, I can see your calculator right there. Can I just borrow it for a second? I promise to give it back."

With a huff, he skulked off to get the calculator.

I looked at the rest of the form, and it was straightforward. The only other thing I didn't know was Karl's VAT registration number. The only way I could find that out was to ring Deadloss again. I composed myself as I walked back to the payphone.

"Hi Liz, it's Bowmer again."

"I'll get him."

"Wait... I'm actually better off speaking to you, Liz."

"Why?"

"I just need the VAT registration number. Karl won't know it."

After a pause of a few seconds, she came back and reeled off the number. It was nice to be finally getting somewhere without having to shout, swear or ask a million questions.

The form was three pages in total. I looked over it a few times. I then asked Spud to check it. We then knocked on the glass again to get the VAT guy's attention.

"Yeah?"

"I've filled it in."

"Fine," he said.

"Please can you just have a look at it?"

"Why?"

"Just, please, I'm not sure if I've filled it in correctly."

"It should be fine."

"Just take a look, mate, and we'll be on our way."

With a roll of the eyes and another sullen sigh, he held the form out in front of him for less than ten seconds.

"Yeah, it's all good."

He picked up a rubber stamp, stamped each page and handed me back the last page as a copy, which I folded up and shoved into my trouser pocket.

"Brilliant! Thanks, mate."

Spud and I ran back down the corridor into the departure lounge just in time to hear the final call for our flight!

I don't remember much about the flight at all, apart from the boys being super excited. What I do remember is the amazing feeling as I stepped off the plane. I was now away from the stress of the work. I didn't have to think about Deadloss and the mess with the sails. I could also put behind me the stress of the VAT guy. *Relaxation, sailing, drinking and nice weather, here we come,* I thought.

Antigua airport is small and pretty busy. We arrived at about 3 p.m. local time. There seemed to be a lot of other people arriving to take part in the forthcoming regatta. I had first visited Antigua in 1991 to race on board a Swan 59, and again two years ago to race with Lynn, so I knew my way around the airport and led the guys to passport control, visualising my first glimpse of Falmouth Harbour, followed by a cold beer, an hour from now. My holiday would be in full swing.

When we got to customs, we walked through the "nothing to declare" gate. This was an anxious moment. Although we had the paperwork for the sails, we didn't look like your average holiday-makers carrying them through. Sure enough, there was a customs guy waiting for Spud and me on the other side.

"They're a nice pair of matching bags you have there. What's in them?

"Sails," we answered together.

"You here for the regatta?"

"Yes."

"Sir, are they your sails?"

"No."

"Do you mind if we ask a few questions about them?"

"No problem, sir."

"Follow me, please."

Off we trudged behind the customs officer. I couldn't believe this—when was my nightmare going to end? Why were customs getting so arsey over the sails? Maybe it was a random check? These sails were proving to be the bane of my life. I was going to make damn sure that Lynn knew the full extent of the trouble I had gone to in delivering the blasted things to him. In my mind, I had racked up a stack of beer that he was going to owe me.

In a hot interview room, I was asked again by the customs officers what our business in Antigua was. I told him we were on holiday from the UK, taking part in the Classics.

"Who are the sails for?"

"We are taking them to Antigua Yacht Club, where they are being collected for a yacht. Spud made the sails and has been asked to hand them over to the commodore."

"So, Spud, what is your involvement with these sails?" asked the fed-up looking customs officer.

"Well, I work for a large sail-making company in Wales. My boss knew I was sailing in the regatta and asked me to bring them out and hand them over to the commodore of the yacht club," said Spud, sweating.

The customs officer kept repeating the same questions over and over about who the sails were for. Spud kept to his story. When one officer said they wouldn't let us have them, I made a comment about them only being sails and I didn't see what the problem was.

Tired of going round in circles, the customs officers asked us if we could show them the sails. Spud and I unpacked them and spread them out on the floor.

One of the officers said, "These look very nice."

Spud beamed. "Yes, I helped to make them."

"Expensive then?"

"Not really," said Spud. "My company only charged three hundred and eighty pounds for them. Bowmer has the VAT receipt."

I quickly dug out the rolled-up VAT return form I had stuffed in my pocket at Gatwick. After I straightened it out, I handed it over to the customs officer. He had a look of disbelief on his face when he saw the total price.

"That's only five hundred US dollars," he said, not quite believing it. "Well, sir, you will have to pay duty on these very nice sails. Fifty US dollars."

I quickly handed over the fifty bucks. Now we were free to leave. Both Spud and I were desperate to pack the sails up and get out of there. We didn't want to give them any more opportunities for more questions or to change their minds. When we stepped outside, the temperature rose dramatically. In the bright light, I put my sunglasses on and looked around for the other three. It didn't take long. I spotted Lynn's suntanned face with three beers in his hand.

"Where have you two been?" he said, passing a beer to Spud and me.

"Don't you start!"

"You've been ages. Your beer is warm."

"I know! We've had the pleasure of dealing with the very nice customs officials who have been quizzing us about your bloody sails. I didn't want to draw attention to the fact that they are for you, in case this caused you any immigration issues."

"They're finished then?"

"Yes, we finished the bloody things at one o'clock this morning."

"Great—we might be able to go racing after all. Why didn't you want to say the sails were for me?"

"In case you have outstayed your welcome and become an illegal alien."

"I'm fine, Bowmer, I have a work permit. How much was the duty on them?"

"Fifty dollars."

"That's cheap, I expected a lot more than that."

"You can thank Deadloss and the VAT man for that."

Lynn took out a big wad of US dollars and handed me the fifty.

"How much you got there?" I asked.

"Six hundred US."

"That's about three hundred and sixty quid?"

"Yes—I expected to spend this lot on the duty!"

"I spent hours stressing in that VAT office trying to save you seventy pounds, and Deadloss because of his incompetence has saved you just over three hundred quid. I hate the two of you."

Lynn started to laugh, and I started swearing profusely at him.

"Calm down, Bowmer, and drink your beer—you're two behind us already," he said. "The way you are carrying on, you're going to have a heart attack, and that would spoil your holiday."

"That's what Karl said!"

"How is Karl?"

"Don't talk to me about that tosser either! What did you mean by 'might' be able to go racing?" I asked.

"I'll tell you later; it's all sorted."

"You're starting to sound like Deadloss, Lynn."

Spud and I followed Lynn, who was proudly carrying the sails. As we walked into the car park, I saw Jenny Gordon, a friend of Lynn's who I had met two years ago on my last trip. Jenny was sitting in the driving seat of a beaten-up old pickup truck with her two big golden retrievers beside her. We threw our gear into the back and climbed in. Foxy and Wattsy looked very relaxed. They had their sunglasses on and were laid out in the hot sun, beaming. Even Spud was smiling when he got in. I started to complain as I climbed into the back of the rusty pickup. This was typical of Lynn, turning up in a wreck. Why couldn't he have arranged a nice car or a taxi?

The best road in Antigua was the one inside the airport perimeter. Once outside, Antigua was the pothole capital of the planet. It was the roughest ride I've ever had, only made bearable by the fact that Lynn got Jenny to stop off at a petrol station to buy more beers. We all had a good crack on the trip back to English Harbour, and I finally started to feel like I was on holiday.

Above Falmouth Harbour is a vantage point at Fry's Hill, where we stopped so the boys could get their first taste of the scene they would soon be part of. Stretched out before us was the harbour, full of yachts. Millions and millions of pounds' worth of yachts. It was a beautiful sight. It's one of those views you never forget. I had been building this moment up for the guys, and they weren't disappointed when we stopped to take in the vista.

I felt at home as we pulled up in English Harbour. We had finally arrived, intact and with the sails, and I could finally relax and start enjoying my holiday. First on the agenda was to get drunk on whatever alcohol was available. Jenny parked outside an old powder magazine, where we unloaded our gear and walked down to an old dock. Looking out into the bay, I could see my home for the next two weeks.

Seefalke looked quite tidy from the shore. Lynn said he had taken her out to antifoul her and repaint the top sides.

Necking another beer, I felt relaxed for the first time in weeks. I watched as Lynn blew up the dinghy.

"What's wrong with the dinghy, Lynn?" I asked.

"It's just a small leak."

"Why haven't you fixed it?"

"I haven't had time; I've been too busy working. It's not a problem."

"It will be at midnight after we've had a skinful."

"I've thought of that problem, Bowmer," said Lynn. "Our first job before Jenny comes back to take us to Shirley Heights is to moor *Seefalke*, stern-to, onto the dock."

With the dinghy pumped up, Lynn rowed us out to the yacht one by one. My beaming smile was soon wiped off as I climbed on board. The yacht was a far cry from the beautiful yacht I had sailed on two years earlier. It looked like a sun-bleached wreck.

"What have you done, Lynn?"

"What do you mean?"

"The yacht's in a right state. When was the last time it moved?" I uttered.

"Last week when I antifouled it. Why?"

"It's a complete mess."

"We won the last race we entered."

"That short race you told me about?"

"Well, yes?"

"When was the last time it was varnished?"

"Errr... Two years ago, I think," he said. "Don't worry, Bowmer. I spent all morning cleaning down below."

I couldn't believe the condition of the yacht. It looked like it hadn't been moved in a year. Inside was a disgrace too; Lynn had been living on it for years, and it was certainly starting to show. To get the yacht to a standard where we could sleep on it would take several hours of cleaning.

In simple terms, the yacht was hanging. It was like entering a bachelor pad owned by a complete slob. I was disappointed that Lynn hadn't made more of an effort to get things sorted ahead of us arriving. We had a lot of work ahead of us to get the yacht looking her best again.

One of the highlights of the regatta was the concours d'elegance, where the yachts got to take part in a parade, showcasing the matching outfits of the crews and competing for the coveted trophy for the best-turned-out yacht. Despite some of the yachts being seventy to eighty years of age, most of them looked brand new. Based on *Seefalke*'s current appearance there was only one award she would be getting, and that was Shed of the Regatta.

Despite my critical comments, the yacht was very much as I expected. Lynn had been living aboard for the past three years, and housekeeping wasn't one of his strengths or top priorities. I'd expected that we'd need to do some work ahead of the racing; I just hadn't bargained for quite so much. So much for my quiet, relaxing holiday. Still, we had a few days, and with five of us on it, washing the yacht and getting the varnish up to scratch wouldn't take long.

One by one, we went below deck to pick our bunks. I decided to sleep in one of the two-quarter berths. This was a favourite trick of mine. By sleeping in a quarter berth, you couldn't get crushed by some drunken oaf falling on you in the early hours of the morning. The ones on Lynn's yacht were narrow but with enough room for me to crawl in. I just needed to remember not to lift my head too high in the mornings, otherwise I'd either hit the deck beams or slice my head open on the main fixing bolts for the cockpit winches—they had sharp edges where Lynn had cut them off.

Wattsy and Spud claimed the berths in the main cabin, leaving Lynn in the forepeak. Foxy decided to sleep on deck under the stars; he was too big to get into the other quarter berth. Lynn said it was a great option as it hardly ever rained at that time of the year and when it did, it was very short-lived.

Foxy made me laugh with the comment that Lynn's yacht was "beyond basic, but great". He was right, it was basic. There was no shower, the toilet was based on the 'bucket and chuck it' concept, and there was no hot running water for washing. Foxy was definitely being polite or just had rose-tinted glasses on; there was nothing great about the living quarters on board *Seefalke*. I often wished Lynn had gone on an interior design course when he originally rebuilt the yacht. Saying that, the restoration work he had done was brilliant. He'd proved that by getting himself to Antigua in the first place.

Sitting on the deck, I put on my hat and sunglasses and lathered on my factor-fifty sunblock. I reached into the cooler for a beer and watched Lynn unpack the sails. I had actually done it. My job was over, my mission to make and deliver the genoa and mainsail now complete. I was on holiday.

Then Lynn said, "Where are the sail track slides?"

"What do you mean?"

"There are no sail track slides on the sail."

"Deadloss, you tosser!" I shouted.

"Don't worry, Bowmer—we can take them off the old sails," said Spud.

"Another job for us to do?"

Lynn said, "I bet there are no hanks on the genoa either."

He was right.

"Bloody great. More work," I said. "I am supposed to be on holiday."

"Don't worry about it tonight. It's another one to add to the list of jobs I'll hand out in the morning," said Lynn, who seemed very chilled about it all. "There are five of us and we have a week, so there's no need to panic."

I wasn't surprised there was something wrong with the sails. Deadloss very rarely got everything right first time. I had lost count of how many times he'd put the wrong-sized luff rope in a sail or forgotten to add the camber lines or mixed the sail numbers up.

It didn't take me long to realise that there was no tiller, and worse still, there was a hole in the deck where the rudder stock should have been. This rather important part of the yacht was missing, and all of a sudden, my stomach started to churn.

"Lynn, when you said we might be able to go racing, did that comment have anything to do with the rudder?"

"Oh yeah, I was going to tell you about that," Lynn said very sheepishly. "Errr... Well, I need a new one. But don't worry, it's on order."

"Lynn, I have heard that for the last four months from Karl, and now you're sounding just like him. A rudder is quite an important piece of kit to have on a yacht," I said sarcastically. "What happened to it?"

"Well, a few weeks ago, I took the yacht out of the water to antifoul it."

"Yes?"

"I decided to take the rudder off to check it, at the same time."

"Right. You actually did that?"

"Yes. Anyway, after looking at the rudder stock, I could see it had been eaten by worms. When I tried to pick it up to put it in the work's truck, it broke in half."

"What?"

"Yeah, the guys in Woodstock said it had been eaten by teredo navalis worms."

"I don't care what the bloody worms were called, Lynn! How are you going to fix it?"

"Don't worry, Bowmer; the boys at Woodstock are making a new rudder, and they've promised that I will have it before the regatta begins. To keep you happy, I'll take you to Woodstock tomorrow."

Our first job was to moor *Seefalke* stern-to onto the powder magazine dock. Negating the need to use Lynn's dodgy dinghy late at night was the only saving grace of this trip so far.

That night, I could have done with going to bed or lying in one spot and drinking myself into a stupor. However, Lynn had arranged with Jenny to pick us up and take us up to the lookout at Shirley Heights before she went off to work at "The Inn". As we were going out, we all got dressed up, wearing nice white shirts and dark trousers. Lynn didn't bother; he was very casual. I don't think he owned a pair of trousers or a shirt.

Jenny came back with the pickup truck. Instead of taking us directly up to Shirley Heights, Lynn got her to drop us all off at the bottom of a cliff, where a sign pointed up to Shirley Heights.

"We're not going up there, are we, Lynn?" I asked.

"Yes, Bowmer. It'll save us twenty dollars each on the entrance fee, and it's only a short ten-minute walk at the most, with some great views of the harbour."

"You tosser!"

"What's wrong, Bowmer?" Lynn said, laughing,

"I wouldn't have come if I knew we were going to walk up to Shirley Heights."

"It's a good party up there!"

"I know, I've been here before, but to make us walk up the side of a sodding cliff is out of order as it's about one o'clock back home, we've had no kip and we've got our best clobber on."

"You are in training, Bowmer. Drinking training."

That's the one thing we didn't need training in, I thought to myself.

I had been telling the boys about the Shirley Heights experience for months. It took half an hour to walk up there, through a woody, rocky path. We gave Lynn a hard time until we started to hear the music and smell the BBQ. Despite being dressed up in our finery, we looked a right mess by the time we arrived at the top. We were hot and sweaty and covered in dust. Lynn looked the same as when he'd started.

The view over English and Falmouth Harbour didn't disappoint. We could see *Seefalke* on the dock below. Our spirits were lifted when we drank our first rum punch and enjoyed the carnival atmosphere. As the sun went down, there was music in the form of a calypso pan band. It was fun watching the other tourists dancing. We all got drunk and had a good time. Now it felt like a boys' jolly!

***

Monday 13th April
Five days before the first race

In the morning, Lynn woke us all up. After a coffee and a sandwich for breakfast, Lynn delegated our jobs for the day. Wattsy was going to do the electrics on the yacht; none of the lights or the VHF worked. Foxy was given cleaning and varnishing duty. Spud, Lynn and I were going to work on the mainsail. We spread the sail out on the grass outside the powder magazine, and with a cooler full of cold beer and water—I don't know who drank the water—the three of us started to work on the new main. The first job was to cut the slides off Lynn's old mainsail and sew them one by one onto the luff of the new one. Luckily, when Lynn first left Wales, Deadloss had given him a sail repair kit, so we had all the tools to fix the sail. For once, Karl had done something right.

By early afternoon, the sail was ready to go back on the yacht, and there was an air of anticipation as it was bent onto the mast track and the foot slid along the boom. With all the boys looking on, Lynn winched the mainsail up the mast.

It did not fit.

The head of the sail was at the top of the mast; the boom was still sitting on top of the coach roof. The sail was too long.

We all moaned, "Karl, you tosser."

Spud said he could alter the length of the sail by cutting the top (head) off and reshaping it. This was a big job. Spud explained that he would have to cut the pressed eye out and unstitch the webbings to release the headboard, unstitch all the reinforcing panels so he could reuse them, cut the sail to the right length and then sew it back together. This was easily an eight-to-ten-hour job and would be impossible without the use of a sail loft.

Luckily, the sail loft was only two hundred yards away, and Lynn called in a massive favour from his friend Tin-Tin, who was too busy to do the job himself but gave us access to the loft floor and his sewing machines. The only proviso was that we needed to work around Tin-Tin's busy schedule, and all for the princely sum of a case of Red Stripe and some ice. Without Tin-Tin's kindness and support, we would have been completely snookered. As it was, we had everything we needed to get the alterations done and still be in a position to race.

Lynn ran off to get the beer while Spud and I spent the rest of the day going through the laborious process of carefully unpicking all the stitching in the head of Lynn's new sail. I felt pretty upset. Karl had once again got my stress levels to boiling point. After Lynn dropped the beers off, he left us to carry on with the mainsail while he sewed the piston hanks onto the luff of the new genoa in case Deadloss had messed that up too.

We left the sail loft at eight o'clock that night to meet the boys for food and some beers in the Mad Mongoose. We gave Lynn the good news that we had successfully unpicked the head, cut the sail to the correct length and reshaped it. All that was left to do was for Spud to sew it back together in the morning.

There was further good news when Lynn confirmed that the genoa was a perfect fit and shape.

***

Tuesday 14th April
Four days to the first race

We were up early again, and after a strong black coffee and a sandwich, Lynn allocated the jobs for day two. Wattsy was to carry on with the electrics, Foxy needed to get another coat of varnish on, and Spud already knew what his priorities were.

Leaving the boys to get on with their jobs, Lynn and I went off to Woodstock. It was a nice morning with a lovely fresh breeze. We walked past all the big charter yachts, and I was feeling pretty buoyed by the sight of all the beautiful yachts and charter boats.

As we strolled along, I said to Lynn, "Given that Spud will have the mainsail finished later today, and assuming you have a plan for getting the rudder back in the yacht, we should think about going for a shake-down sail tomorrow."

"Sounds like a plan, Bowmer."

When we got to the wooden shack that was Woodstock, Lynn introduced me to Andrew, the owner, and then to Andrew's business partner, "Doggy Dipshit". Apparently, he was in a punk rock band and had changed his name by deed poll. I had to seriously question some of Lynn's new friends, but then, thinking about it, he was also best mates with myself and Deadloss, so who was I to judge? Anyway, they seemed like nice guys, so all was good with the world.

"Where's the rudder then, Andrew?" asked Lynn.

"Over there."

"Where?"

"There, near the lathe. Sprout is working on it."

We both walked over to where Sprout was working. I could see the old rudder broken in two, propped up against the lathe.

"Morning, Sprout," Lynn called.

"Hi, Lynn," he said. "Before you say anything, I haven't got any further with your rudder, I've been getting pulled off onto other jobs."

"Sprout, you've had this rudder for two weeks. The first race is on Saturday!"

"I know—I'm really sorry!"

"Well, what you've done so far does look really good." Turning to me, Lynn said, "What do you think, Bowmer?"

For the first time in my life, I was struggling to get my words out. My blood pressure was through the roof.

"That's... That's not a rudder. It's just a big lump of wood, Lynn."

"Bowmer, you need to chill. Have a bit of faith. It's all been glued and bolted together; the rudder stock has been nicely shaped. All we have to do is shape and profile the blade and it will be finished."

"Lynn, a properly shaped rudder is critical to the performance of the yacht, and there's no shape in that at all."

"Well, it won't take us long to put that right."

I couldn't believe it! I was looking at a piece of greenheart eleven feet long and about six inches in diameter, which was bolted to an oblong piece of mahogany four inches thick, nearly six feet long and thirty inches wide. It had no shape to it at all. There again, I did think the prospect of Lynn sourcing a readymade rudder for a fifty-square-metre yacht built in 1936 was pretty slim.

I was totally underwhelmed and could see that we had another mountain to climb and not much time to climb it in. My early-morning euphoria had quickly turned to disappointment and despair. I had spent all my money getting out to Antigua to go sailing, endured months of being fobbed off by Karl about the bloody sails and the VAT, and now this. I felt physically sick; I had conned the boys into coming out to race, and we were now faced with the prospect of watching the regatta from the beach, which wasn't going to sit well with them. I could see myself getting seriously filled in.

After an awkward silence, I blurted out, "Bloody great."

I wasn't happy at all, and what made matters worse, Lynn seemed so relaxed.

Sprout then said, "I can only spend half an hour on it today. Let me get the jigsaw and cut the shape at the back of the rudder for you."

"Thanks, Sprout," replied Lynn.

I protested again. "It's going to take hours to shape this lump of wood into a rudder, Lynn, and that's before we paint it and get it back in the yacht."

"Yeah, I can't see you boys racing this year," agreed Sprout.

"Terrific," I muttered.

"It will be fine, Bowmer," Lynn said, putting a reassuring arm on my shoulder. "There's two of us and we have time."

Sprout cut the back of the rudder to shape, and Lynn thanked him again.

"No problem, boys," he said. "And good luck. Help yourself to my tools."

"Cheers, Sprout," said Lynn.

I couldn't believe Lynn; he didn't seem to have a care in the world. By this point, you could have peeled me off the ceiling. I was absolutely bouncing. I just kept thinking about all the time I had spent on the sails, the cost of the flight and now the seemingly impossible task of shaping, painting and reinstalling Lynn's rudder. There just didn't seem to be enough time to get all this done.

I was at a real low ebb. If one more thing had gone wrong at that moment in time, I think I might have lost it. I couldn't help but have another rant at Lynn.

"Roachy, you have totally conned us. You got us out here on the pretence that the yacht was ready to race. Instead, it's a complete shambles. There's more chance of me walking on water than us turning this block of wood into something that resembles a rudder. Trust me, we're going to be watching the regatta from the beach. I can't believe this is happening."

"What's your problem, Bowmer? Stop moaning and give me a hand. Let's get the rudder on its edge so I can mark out the lines for us to work to."

Lynn went into Sprout's toolbox and found a pencil, a tape measure and a square. With me holding the rudder up, blade pointing upwards. Lynn told me to hold the tape measure close to the rudder stock, while at the same time he ran the tape measure along the radius of the blade to the bottom pintle. Lynn then halved this measurement, which gave him the centre line of the blade. A line was drawn across the edge at that point using a pencil and square. After a quick check and measurement of the old rudder we were using as our pattern, Lynn then marked a small line three quarters of an inch either side of the centre line.

He then found a long strip of thin wood with one straight edge. I held that end on the rudder stock while Lynn gently bent the strip to the pencil marks he had marked either side of the centre line. This produced a uniform curve that he could then run a pencil along to transfer the shape onto the block of wood. We repeated this four times until we had marked out the profile we needed on both sides of the rudder.

"So, what do you think, Bowmer?"

"Well... Errrr..."

Sprout had used the old rudder as the pattern, and this was what we were copying. Looking at the lines Lynn had marked on the rudder, it looked pretty good. Actually, it looked like a direct copy to me.

"Roach, where did you learn to do this type of stuff?" I asked.

Lynn just said, "That's the hard part done. Now we needed to turn this big block of mahogany into a perfectly elliptical, aerodynamic shape, just like the pattern."

For me, this was going to be a big ask and a long day, and if we messed this up, there were no second chances. I must admit I was pretty nervous, but Lynn, without a care in the world, reassured me by saying, "Look, Bowmer, we just need to keep checking the shape against the old rudder. What could be simpler?"

The Germans had done a decent job of building the original rudder, as I knew from sailing on *Seefalke* before. The water flowed effortlessly over it. If we ended up with an exact copy, we would be in a good place. A bit happier with this thought in my head, we set to work on shaping the rudder to the lines marked on the wood. Most of my time was spent shaping this huge block of wood that Lynn thought was going to look like a rudder blade. I was using a hand plane, and very soon my soft office hands were covered in blisters. The more I moaned about my hands, the more Lynn wound me up. Every time my plane blade became blunt, I gave it to Lynn to resharpen. He proved to be a master at that.

At around five o'clock, Woodstock closed for the night. Doggy came over to check our progress and seemed pretty impressed with our efforts.

"The rudder is looking good, boys," he said.

We walked back to the yacht feeling a lot more confident that we would get the rudder finished in time. On our arrival, there was more good news: Spud had finished the repair on the mainsail and was about to pull it up the mast. Once it was up, we could see that it fitted beautifully, and the shape looked great too. Thankfully, there were no creases radiating out from any of the corners. Fair play, the guys had all worked really hard. Foxy had finished the sanding and had two coats of varnish on it. Lynn was happy and told him the brightwork looked really good. Wattsy had managed to get all of the electrics working, meaning that we now had a radio and lights.

After a long hard day for all of us, we walked over to the Mad Mongoose for food and beer, and we enjoyed a good night out. I told the boys about the block of wood we had transformed into something resembling a rudder. They just rolled around laughing. I'm sure they thought I was winding them up.

***

Wednesday 15th April
Three days to the first race

Lynn outlined the tasks for day three of our mission. Foxy, Wattsy and Spud were to carry on with the varnishing, including a light rub-down between coats, and Lynn and I were back to Woodstock.

On first inspection, we were pleased with yesterday's efforts on the rudder. Our block of wood was well on its way to looking like a rudder from a 1936 classic yacht. We had invested a lot of time and effort into shaping it and I just hoped we had got the profile correct. Feeling confident that we were on the right track, we continued to work on it all morning, until we needed a break and some food.

By lunchtime, we were on the home straight, and we aimed to have the rudder ready for a coat of primer by late afternoon. Lynn agreed to take me to "Katie's" a local tin shack that did great food. Lynn ordered us a couple of beers and sat down, while I asked Katie for a menu.

She just laughed. "It's chicken with rice or rice with chicken. Which do you want?" she asked.

Before I had a chance to answer, she shouted, "Who's your friend, Lynn?"

"This is Bowmer, one of my crew."

"He's cute."

I quickly sat down next to Lynn, who was just laughing at me.

"I bet you've never been called cute before, Bowmer."

I have to say, Katie was certainly a force to be reckoned with. She was a very big girl, who I think had been overdoing the chicken and rice and the gym.

Lynn didn't need much ammunition and promptly started taking the mick out of me. "Have a crack at it, Bowmer—she might put a smile on your face."

Sitting in Katie's, looking across the marina, I quickly changed the subject by asking Lynn, "How are we going to get this rudder back on the yacht?"

"At this moment in time, I do not know. I haven't worked that one out yet."

"Bloody great." I sighed.

"Let's get another beer," said Lynn. "We'll sort it out somehow."

As we left, Katie shouted across to me, "If you're back tomorrow, Bowmer, I'll cook you a Johnny cake."

"That's too good an offer to miss!" Lynn said. "Katie makes the best Johnny cakes around."

After lunch, we were back hard at it.

At three-thirty, Lynn said, "I'm going to knock it on the head for the day."

"Okay. Why?"

"I need to get the yacht registered for the regatta by five o'clock, otherwise we won't be able to race."

"I thought you said you had already entered the regatta."

"I have to register and pay the hundred-dollar entry fee. I wasn't going to waste money if I didn't think we had a chance of getting the rudder back into the yacht. I'll see you in the yacht club later. I need to go back to the yacht to change and pick up the regatta entry form."

The new rudder was taking shape, but to finally finish it and get it into the yacht by the following evening was still a big ask. After another long day, I decided that it was time for a beer, so I packed up and headed over to the yacht club.

I was sat by the bar when Lynn walked in.

"Hi, Lynn," I said. "I thought you were going back to the yacht to change?"

"I did."

"Are you sure?"

"Yes, why?"

"Well, those clothes look like the ones you were working in earlier."

"Bowmer, you're not my mother."

I was starting to think that Lynn only owned one pair of shorts, a T-shirt and flip flops!

After a bit more mickey-taking, Lynn introduced me to Piggy, the regatta chairman. Piggy was also Lynn's boss and a friend. He was well versed in all of our pre-race issues.

"Lynn, is that yacht of yours ready to race yet?" he asked.

"No. But it should be by tomorrow night with some luck. We're still working on the rudder."

"Will you make it?"

"I don't know, Piggy," Lynn said. "But we're gonna give it our best shot."

"Well, at least you're entered now, which is one less thing to worry about. Good luck with getting the rudder finished, and enjoy the regatta."

Our race entry was now official. Five smelly Welshmen were raring to go. All we needed now was a half-decent yacht to race on.

***

Thursday 16th April
Two days before the first race

We were up early again. Lynn gave Foxy, Spud, and Wattsy the task of stripping the yacht to make it as light as possible. Lynn told them to take everything off that wasn't required for racing. The self-steering, toilet, old sails, tools, workmate—the whole nine yards. He said he would borrow his work's truck to pick the gear up later. Lynn and I were back to Woodstock for the final assault on the rudder.

By lunchtime, the rudder was nearly finished, and so it was back to Katie's for lunch and a couple of beers. I was feeling a lot happier. Remembering my conversation with Katie from the day before, I went straight to the counter and ordered chicken, rice and one of her famous Johnny cakes.

As we sat eating, I looked out over Falmouth Harbour and was quite envious of all the yachts that were out sailing.

I couldn't help thinking that we should be doing the same. The old adage that "Perfect Preparation Prevents Poor Performance" certainly didn't form part of our mantra.

Talking of poor performance, I wasn't even getting to enjoy the parties. I was too bloody tired every night. Undertaking eight hours of manual labour in sweltering heat was a far cry from my day job, sat in a nice, air-conditioned office, typing away on a computer. By the time I'd had tea and a few beers, I was ready to collapse in my bunk. I should have stayed at home and given Ray Harris and Karl a week of my time, free of charge.

It was mid-afternoon when we finally got the rudder finished. We were both incredibly chuffed with the end result and spent a long time admiring the fruits of our labour. It was a lovingly crafted rudder, a beautiful piece of work. It seemed a great shame that the thing would spend its life under the yacht where no one would see it or appreciate the full beauty of our handiwork.

All I had left to do while Lynn went to get the truck and the guys was to give the rudder two quick coats of primer and a layer of antifouling.

Lynn seemed to take ages coming back with the boys, which for once, I didn't mind too much as it gave the primer time to go off.

"Where have you been?" I asked.

"We've been moving all the gear off *Seefalke* into the storeroom at Seagull Services. So much weight has been taken off the yacht—we can now see three inches of antifoul above the old waterline. The boys have been working really hard. And what have you been doing, Bowmer?"

"I've managed to get two coats of primer on and I'm now carefully applying the antifoul, making sure the brush strokes run horizontally across the rudder. I want to ensure that we optimise the smooth flow of water across the blade."

Lynn grabbed a brush to help me get the job finished. I was horrified when I took a closer look at his work. Lynn had just slapped the paint on. The brushstrokes went in all directions. All my effort had gone to waste; there were lumps and bumps everywhere.

"I hate you, Roachy!"

"I know, Bowmer, but we haven't got the time to do a good job. We have to get the rudder back in the yacht as soon as possible in case it doesn't fit and we need to make changes."

"I know, but can't we let the antifoul dry first?"

"No. It will be dark in an hour."

"I still hate you. Look at my side! It's perfect."

It took all of us to lift the rudder onto the truck. It was pretty heavy, and awkward to handle too. The antifouling was still soft, and we ended up with paint all over us as we manhandled the rudder into the truck. As we were leaving Woodstock, I heard this really high-pitched noise coming from one of the sheds.

"That sounds like an electric planer," I said to Lynn.

"It is."

Bloody great, I thought, after my many hours of manual work, with the blisters to show for it. I had to let it go, otherwise my head would have exploded.

With the three boys holding the rudder in the back of the truck, I asked Lynn how we were going to get the rudder back in the yacht. I still didn't have a clue how Lynn was planning to make it happen, given the yacht was still in the water.

Lynn seemed pretty relaxed and not worried about it at all. Every time I probed him for information, all I got back was, "Don't worry, Bowmer. I have a plan."

I was starting to get worried. The rudder stock only needed to be a fraction too thick or the blade slightly too long and all my efforts would have been in vain. The prospect of watching the regatta from the beach didn't bear thinking about, and I was praying that the rudder would go back in the yacht without a hitch.

Once we got back to the dock, Lynn finally explained the plan. First, we needed to move *Seefalke* back to her mooring, where there was deeper water. The plan was to then float the rudder out to the yacht, before threading a sail tie down through the rudder tube. Once this was showing out the bottom of the yacht, Lynn would swim down and attach the sail tie to the top of the rudder stock. It was then down to Lynn to locate the rudder stock in the bottom of the rudder tube. The final part of the exercise would be to haul on the sail tie until the top of the rudder stock popped out of the stern deck.

After explaining the above, Lynn asked, "What do you think of the plan then, boys?"

There was an uneasy silence. Everyone was thinking the same as me: Lynn had totally lost the plot. How on earth was he going to force a large buoyant chunk of wood under the yacht and then effectively stand it on end in order for us to pull the stock up through the bottom of the yacht? This plan had disaster written all over it, and I could feel a knot in my stomach. Lynn would need to hold his breath while working with tools and in restricted visibility. And even if we succeeded in getting the rudder back in the yacht, there was still the small matter of securing a bracket to ensure that the rudder couldn't fall off.

Despite the odds, this was our only viable option, and reluctantly, we all agreed Lynn's way was the only way.

"Okay, let's go before it gets dark," he said.

We dropped the rudder into the water and attached it via a rope to *Seefalke*'s stern. Foxy quickly let the stern lines go as Wattsy pulled on the bowline that was attached to the mooring. Slowly, she was pulled away from the dock and back into the middle of the bay, onto her mooring. I got the longest sail tie I could find, and using a winch handle for weight, I lowered the sail tie down through the rudder tube. Lynn, with his snorkelling gear on, dived down and retrieved the sail tie from under the yacht. After removing the winch handle, he secured the sail tie through the eye in the top of the rudder stock.

We watched as Lynn lined up the rudder stock with the bottom of the rudder tube. This was the moment of truth. Was the rudder going to fit through the bottom of the yacht? Lynn gave us the signal that he was going to make the rudder sink, and after thirty seconds, we were to start hauling on the sail tie. None of us thought that this had a cat in hell's chance of working. However, after thirty seconds, we slowly pulled on the sail tie as agreed. To our absolute amazement, a few seconds later, the rudder stock appeared out of the top of the rudder tube. We were all ecstatic!

Lynn surfaced to the sight of us dancing around the cockpit, but before we could get too carried away, Lynn needed us to haul the stock up as high as possible so he could locate the rudder onto its pintle. It wasn't long before the rudder was fitted perfectly.

Lynn then shouted from the water, "Stick the tiller on and tell me how it feels, Bowmer?"

"It's a little stiff but feels okay," I shouted back.

"Shall we leave it? Or do you want me to try and adjust it?"

"No, leave it," I said. "We don't have a lot of time."

"Okay, Bowmer, I think you're right. It should wear itself in."

We then passed Lynn some threaded bar, together with two nuts and the corresponding washers. The threaded bar was needed to fasten a bracket to the back of the keel. In order to do this, Lynn also needed a torch, hammer, and a couple of spanners. We watched Lynn as he worked underwater until finally, he climbed back into the dinghy after goodness knows how many dives.

"So, does it look good, Lynn?" asked Foxy.

"It's all done, bolted up. The rudder looks like a perfect fit to me," he said with a very big smile on his face.

By the time he finally got out of the water, it was a completely dark Thursday evening. We were all buzzing from the sheer relief of finally getting the yacht ready to race. The achievement of building and then fitting the bastard rudder was amazing, I now felt that all the hours of planing and sanding had been worth it. I did, however, give Lynn a load of abuse and called him a tosser for all the grief and aggro he had put us through over the previous five days.

As he climbed back on board, he asked what time it was.

"Why?" I asked.

"I've got the skippers' briefing to go to."

"Well, you better get your skates on. It starts in ten minutes."

Lynn got changed pretty damn quick. Mind you, he only had two items of clothing to put on. Wattsy kindly agreed to row us both ashore. As we stepped out of the dinghy, Lynn asked Wattsy if he and the others could moor *Seefalke* back on the dock. Then, once that was done, they were to meet us in the Last Lemming for the welcome party.

We had all worked incredibly hard on the yacht since arriving, and that Thursday evening felt like the first time we could properly let our hair down and relax. All of *Seefalke*'s topsides had been rubbed down and varnished half a dozen times, and the hull had been touched up where the paint had been scuffed. She looked like a new yacht. Additionally, the mainsail had been unpicked, recut and sewn back together; the yacht had been rewired. and we had built and installed a new rudder. Then there was the small detail of completely stripping the yacht of all Lynn's stuff, which had taken the boys a day in itself. We had done all we could to get the yacht ready, which just left us with the difficult task of drinking beer all night.

The following day was effectively a free day, as all we had to do was sail the yacht around to Falmouth Harbour, where it would be moored for the duration of the racing.

We were finally ready!

***

Friday 17th April
One day to the first race

As soon as we awoke, Lynn was on our case. He couldn't find his coffee cup.

"What do you want your coffee cup for?" Spud asked.

"For a cup of coffee?"

"Your coffee cup will be as much use as an ashtray on a motorbike," Spud said.

"What do you mean?"

"We have no gas, or water."

"What?"

"Yeah, we took it all off to make the yacht lighter."

Lynn wasn't at all impressed. "Bloody great, I can't even get a cup of coffee on my own yacht. Sorry, boys—I need a coffee in the morning."

After a lot of negotiation, it was agreed that the gas bottle, cups, spoons, coffee and water container could come back aboard. Lynn agreed to leave them on the dock each morning before heading out to the start line. Spud and I were happy with this arrangement.

Once finalised, Lynn took us ashore for a big fry-up to thank us for all our efforts. After breakfast, we were strolling back to the yacht when Lynn started shaking his head and said something about his sixth sense.

I asked him what was up, and he said, "My sixth sense is telling me that I'm going to meet Elizabeth Meyers."

"Who?"

"Elizabeth Meyers—the owner of the J-Class *Endeavour* and that huge support boat *Bystander*. She's one of New York's richest woman A-listers."

"What does she look like?"

"I haven't got a clue."

"Do you trust and really believe your sixth sense?" I asked.

"Oh, yes. It hasn't let me down, my sixth sense. It got me here in one piece, didn't it?"

"Well, surprisingly, yes."

"Trust me, I'm going to have Elizabeth Meyers sat in the cockpit of my yacht before the racing is over."

"Have you been smoking something? Why in heaven's name would one of the richest women in the world want to sit in your cockpit, speaking to us bunch of numpties?"

"I'm telling you, Bowmer, it's going to happen."

"You really have lost the plot this time. If that lady steps one foot on your yacht, I will eat my rancid trainers."

"You had better start cleaning them, then, and get yourself a knife and fork."

Back on the yacht, Lynn said, "Come on, boys, we have to get this yacht around to Falmouth Harbour. We have a free berth on the dock as we are now part of the regatta."

I took the helm while the boys untied the yacht and got the mainsail up, and slowly we headed out to sea in the light breeze. It was a stunning day for a sail. I will never forget that morning, tacking out through the anchored yachts. *Seefalke* felt alive and responsive. Straight away, I could tell we had transformed the old girl.

All the boys had a beer in their hands. Lynn was relaxed, as if we hadn't done anything special. I got my pipe out and had a puff; this was a moment to savour.

On the way to Falmouth, we put the no.1 genoa up for the first time. The sail looked amazing; the shape was spot on. Deadloss had got something right, for a change. The only problem was we couldn't adjust the genoa cars. They were seized solid, which was a pain, as we couldn't control the shape of the leach.

I thought Spud was about to give Lynn some abuse about the lack of maintenance, but to my surprise, he said, "Roachy, what makes you so special?"

"What do you mean, Spud?"

"Well, for one, none of us would have had the guts to sail single-handed across the Atlantic, and when there's a problem like the sail that didn't fit, or the rudder, and now these bloody genoa cars won't move, you just act as if you don't have a care in the world. So, what makes you special?"

Well, this conversation got my interest.

"I'm not special, but I do attract interesting people around me—like you lot, for one," Lynn said. "Really, I just think differently to the rest of you. Because the car won't move, you're thinking we won't trim the sails properly, the yacht will sail slower, and we will lose the race. So, your thought process is leading you into a spiral of depression, taking you down. Am I right, Spud?"

"Well, yes."

"Spud, think of it this way, if you start a yacht race and you are one hundred yards away from the start line as the gun goes off, all the way throughout the race you'll be thinking about the shit start you had."

"Special One—you are right about that," said Spud.

"But if you're a yard off the start line when the gun goes off, you'll be thinking what a brilliant start you had. And for the rest of the race, you will think, 'I have a very good chance at doing really well.' So, you have given yourself a positive, uplifting mindset."

"It's that thought process that makes you different to the rest of us?"

"Well, when I see that seized block you are kicking, I think: 'Ten minutes with some WD40 and a hammer and a pair of pliers, I'll get them working.' I had the same positive thoughts when I sailed across the pond. If I had a problem, I knew I had the ability to solve and fix it."

"That's interesting," I said.

"As for the sail and rudder, I knew you as part of our team, Spud, you would fix the mainsail, Wattsy the electrics. Both jobs are your trades. Leaving Bowmer and me to work on and finish the rudder, and Foxy has done a brilliant job on the brightwork. And to top it all off, Foxy is in the insurance trade, which I will need if Bowmer messes up when he tries to get the yacht onto the dock," Lynn said with a laugh. "Apart from that, my sixth sense didn't warn me about the sail, or the rudder, or missing this regatta, and I had you lot to do the work."

I had to laugh at Roachy's belief and total trust in this special sense of his. Still laughing, I said, "Special One, tell Spud about Elizabeth Meyers and our bet."

Spud said, "Elizabeth who? Tell me over a beer later—we need to get this yacht sailing faster. When was the last time you moved these bloody cars, Special One?"

"Ha ha, very funny," Lynn said.

"You moved them last, Spud, in 1993."

Great, just great. More sodding work.

Spud said to Lynn, "We need to find a way to flatten the leach on the mainsail to give us more power on the downwind legs. The boom is too low to the deck to rig an effective kicking strap, so we need to rig a vang that will give us a direct downward pull from the boom to the toe rail. We can use the vang to flatten the leach when the mainsail is eased."

I explained to Lynn that it was important to get the leach as flat as possible for the downwind legs; this was something we had used to good effect in the past. Lynn found an old piece of rope, wrapped it around the boom, and using a cleat, we experimented on the lead and different anchor points on the deck. This downward sheeting of the boom made a big difference to the boat speed, which I could feel through the helm. Having proved the concept, though, this meant more work once we got into Falmouth marina.

Sailing up the channel into Falmouth Harbour, we dropped the genoa and carried on sailing on just the mainsail. As we approached the marina, we were met by Sprout from Woodstock, who was driving a large inflatable rib.

"Hi, boys. I never expected to see you here today. You must have finished the rudder and fitted it?" he said in amazement.

"Neither did I, I must admit," I said. "I didn't think we would make it when I first saw that big lump of wood."

"Bowmer, your problem is you don't have any faith," said Lynn, laughing.

Sprout knew we had no engine and offered to tow us into our allotted place in the marina. Feeling confident, I said we would sail in. Sprout told us to head for a very small space between two Bristol Channel pilot cutters.

Sailing into the marina, we could see the dock was full of classic yachts and one mistake on our part could end in lots of tears. True to form, there was a sizeable audience forming as crews from the other yachts watched in anticipation of a calamity. Entering the berth was tricky because we were sailing downwind and needed to turn the yacht around in order to kill our speed and to moor the stern to the dock.

Just as we neared the dock, I spun the yacht around and sat head to wind until *Seefalke* lost all her way. Wattsy dropped the anchor. Spud wanted to leave it behind to save weight, but the race rules said we had to have one on board.

I got my well-oiled crew to force the mainsail out against the wind. Wattsy controlled the anchor chain as we sailed backwards into our allotted berth. I didn't tell Lynn that I had not done this manoeuvre before on a 41.6-foot long nine-ton yacht. Thankfully, it worked a treat. Lynn and Spud passed the stern lines over to the two yachts either side of us. As Foxy dropped the mainsail, we stopped perfectly alongside *Marguerite T*, a Bristol Channel pilot cutter. We received a rapturous round of applause from the spectators. We'd managed to sail in and tie up without putting a mark on anyone's yacht or upsetting anyone—another first.

Safely tied up—and right outside the yacht club, which would be the centre of all the parties—it was now game on. It was good to be feeling part of the regatta at last.

Lynn and Spud went off to the yacht chandlery to look for some pad-eyes. Wattsy took some money out of our yacht kitty to get a crate of beer and some ice, leaving Foxy and me to have a really good look at the beautifully restored *Marguerite T*. We soon found out she was owned by two guys, Scrimshaw and John Steel, from Covey Island Boatwork, based in Nova Scotia in Canada. The cutter had just been rebuilt, and this was her debut regatta. She looked absolutely stunning.

It was Scrimshaw, aptly named due to the fact that he carved ivory for a living, who we met first. We got chatting to him, and straight away, Scrim recognised our Welsh accents. He asked if we knew Barry, as the yacht used to work out of the harbour there. I straight away confirmed that there was a picture of *Marguerite T* hanging on the wall in Barry Yacht Club, which blew Scrimshaw's mind. We hadn't told him that we were from Barry or that we were well versed in the history and traditions of the iconic pilot cutters. This whole chance meeting got even more bizarre when Foxy stuck his head out of the hatch of the pilot cutter and announced that there was a picture of Barry Harbour hanging in the companionway. What were the chances of us bumping into some guy who owned a pilot cutter from Barry in the middle of the Caribbean? Straight away, we formed a real bond with our neighbours, and we knew then that this was going to turn into a really special trip.

Our other neighbour was also a pilot cutter, but a very modern fibreglass copy, owned by a Swiss couple sailing with their two daughters. They had entered the regatta sailing in the Spirit of Tradition Class, a class for modern yachts built to look like old traditional yachts. We gave them the nickname of Swiss Family Robinson.

Lynn and Spud returned from the yacht chandlery with some pad-eyes for the deck and some bolts. We managed to borrow a drill and drill bits from the Swiss family, together with an electric extension lead, which we were able to plug into their generator. It didn't take long to drill and bolt the pad-eyes to the deck, which meant we could now rig our vang for the downwind legs. The only downside was that I now had a further four bolts sticking through the deck above my berth to bash my head on.

That was a relatively quick job, but then it took us over an hour to free up the genoa cars, with the use of WD40. We got there in the end, and finally, all the jobs were complete. All that was left was for us to admire our surroundings, look at the other yachts, relax and enjoy a few cold beers, which Wattsy had bought for us.

After an hour of just chilling, we decided it would be nice to go for a swim and grab a beer before the party at the Last Lemming. We walked to Windward Beach carrying a cooler full of beer. Windward Beach was only a short way from the marina, and as we walked across the golden sand, we were treated to the most amazing sight. There was a myriad of classic yachts of all shapes and sizes sailing just off the beach. There was nothing better than sitting on this sun-drenched beach, drinking beer and looking at some of the prettiest yachts on the planet. This was a magical afternoon; we were all so happy to just be there and take part, not to mention sinking a few beers at the same time.

While we were sat there, a guy carrying a load of expensive-looking camera equipment walked over to us. He asked if we could look after it while he went for a swim, which we happily agreed to.

Following his swim, he walked back to where we were sitting and started to dry himself off while looking at us inquisitively.

"Thanks, guys, for looking after my camera."

"No problems, mate," said Foxy.

"So, what brings you guys to Antigua?"

"We are here for the regatta," Foxy proudly announced.

"You lot are in the regatta?" he asked.

"Yup."

"Shouldn't you guys be out practising, then?"

"We have done our practice—all three miles of it!" Foxy joked.

"That's enough?" The guy laughed while watching us drink beer.

Foxy said, "Fancy a beer?"

"Sure, why not?" he said. "So, who do you think you will win?"

"Us, of course!" laughed Foxy.

Each one of us nodded and cheered while clinking our bottles of beer together.

"Good luck to you, boys. Where are you from?"

"Wales."

"And the name of your yacht?"

"*Seefalke*!" we all shouted proudly.

"I will keep an eye out for you. Good luck against the J-Class yachts."

I think he wanted to laugh at our ludicrous prediction but wasn't sure whether we were being serious or not. We had made our statement of intent with straight faces, but I think he had some idea we were pulling his leg, although at that stage he couldn't suss us out.

"Well, I'm Michael Kahn," he said. "I'm one of the photographers covering the race. I will look out for you guys tomorrow."

"You will see us at the front of the fleet—we are here to win!" shouted Foxy as Michael started walking away.

We were just having a laugh and joke—we didn't seriously believe that we could win the regatta outright. After all, we had only finished bolting the yacht back together a few hours earlier. Our goal was to do as well as we could, but not at the expense of enjoying ourselves and getting wrecked every night.

The world's press had their eyes on the J-Class yachts. This was the first time two Jays had raced against each other in sixty years. There was huge excitement surrounding this event, making the 1998 Classics a regatta that would go down in yachting history.

Endeavour and *Velsheda* had both gone through multimillion-dollar restorations, and to see these 130-foot-long thoroughbreds in real life was simply unreal. Both yachts were full of rock stars (slang for well-known professional sailors), including some guys I knew from the UK and North Sails. There were upwards of twenty guys on both yachts, and they looked tiny against the sheer scale of these leviathans. The rigs alone seemed to touch the sky.

These immaculately turned-out yachts and their no-expense-spared crews were a far cry from us bunch of tramps living on a cramped yacht with no washing facilities. Spud had taken the water tank off the yacht to save weight. Even basic hygiene tasks like taking a shower and brushing our teeth had to be carried out on the dock using a hosepipe. All the time we had spent sticking *Seefalke* back together, these guys had been out practising and working the yachts up ready for the regatta. On reflection, our preparation had been pretty poor and we definitely didn't deserve to do very well.

We stopped for a burger, fries and a beer before we returned to the harbour to wander around the Yacht Club

Marina and look at all the other yachts. Being yacht mad, this was a dream for the boys. For Lynn and me, it wasn't such an attraction—we had done the regatta before—but we still loved looking at the shinier, bigger yachts. The Jays were really impressive, one-hundred-and-thirty-feet long, with one-hundred-and-sixty-foot carbon fibre masts in them. One winch on a J-Class was worth more than my house, and there were at least twenty of them along the deck.

"Look at that, guys," Foxy said, pointing at *Velsheda*.

"What?"

"The way they're marching off the sails."

I looked over and could see the crew all in matching uniforms, marching in military precision, taking the sails off to the sail loft. It was a sight to behold. I wondered what they thought of us drinking our beers and staring at them. They definitely wouldn't have considered us to be a honed race crew, that's for sure.

Spud suggested that we should get a matching uniform as well, so we all headed to the open market in Nelson's Dockyard and bought some beige cotton trousers and tops. These were a world away from the pressed white uniforms that the professionals had, but they were comfortable, and at least we were all wearing the same kit. We now looked more like a team and were in keeping with the other crews taking part.

As a crew, we walked to the Last Lemming for that night's party.

As we walked in, Lynn said, "I'll be back in a minute; I'm just going upstairs to the yacht club."

"Why?" I asked.

"I want to see what handicap they've given us."

"Okay. I'll get a beer in for you and meet you outside on the lawn."

Well, Lynn came back with the biggest smile on his face I had ever seen.

"What happened to you?" I asked. "Did you get laid up there or something?"

"No, not quite. Better than that."

"Come on."

"Well, Bowmer, in ninety-six and seven, *Seefalke*'s handicap was nine hundred and fourteen."

"Yeah?"

"Well, they reckon my handicap has been too low for the last two regattas and they have put it up to nine hundred and twenty-four, which is total charity. With new sails, a new rudder, clean bottom, and you bunch of halfwits, we ought to do pretty well, when you think we won our class in ninety-six and finished sixth in fleet in one race with old, worn-out sails I had used to cross the pond. So we must be able to do better than that this year."

"You are joking, Roachy. We have a better handicap?"

"Yes, Bowmer, so we have a chance to win our class and maybe spoil the J-Class party."

"Have you been on the rum, Roachy? You've lost the plot again?"

"No, Bowmer—I'm telling you we have a real chance here. I hope you're ready to get those trainers in that big mouth of yours?"

"I'd rather lose the regatta."

"No, you wouldn't."

Lynn had disappeared by eight. Pissed, he'd crashed and burned yet again. His last words as he staggered out of the pub were: "Take it easy tonight, boys. We have a race to win tomorrow."

Smiling, we all said, "We'll drink to that."

Chapter 14
The Regatta

Saturday 18th April

I was up early with no hangover—strange! Looking around the yacht, I saw Bowmer was fast asleep with his feet hanging out of the quarter berth, shoes still on. Spud was snoring away; Wattsy was nowhere to be seen. On deck, I found Foxy passed out and fast asleep.

It was another beautiful Caribbean day. The marina was quiet, and this was a great time of the day to do some reflecting before the rest of the dock started stirring. After my early-morning swim on Pigeon Beach, I stopped at the marina shop to pick up sandwiches, water and ice for the cooler. On my return to the yacht, the crew were up, but looking far from their best, I dished out the sandwiches and water for their breakfast, which was met with mixed reactions.

While I waited for the kettle to boil to make all of us a coffee, I asked what time they had got back to the yacht.

Foxy said, "Around two, I think."

"Where's Wattsy?" I asked.

"He pulled this really good-looking woman last night and was last seen walking to Pigeon Beach for a swim."

Back on deck, I could see Wattsy walking down the dock. Before he got back on the yacht, Bowmer asked, "Who was the woman you were with last night, Wattsy?"

"Why do you want to know?"

"Well, with that tight red dress she had on, she reminded me of that famous film actress I had a crush on."

"You're right—she was stunning. But which actress are you talking about, Bowmer?"

"Marilyn Monroe?" I suggested.

"No, it's not her," said Bowmer.

Foxy offered Raquel Welch, or Brigitte Bardot.

"No, it's not those two either."

"I've got it," said Spud. "The only actress I can remember in a tight red dress is Jessica Rabbit."

"That's her, I think."

"Bowmer, Jessica Rabbit is a cartoon character; she's not a real woman," Spud said. "I always thought you were weird; I know why now."

"It can't be her then," said Bowmer.

"Who then?" we all asked.

"I don't know—all I remember is she wore a red dress."

None of us knew another actress in a red dress, but Wattsy's girlfriend had picked up the nickname of Jessica Rabbit.

Wattsy said, "No wonder you haven't pulled yet, Bowmer. You're looking for the wrong sort of woman."

"You're right, Wattsy. After drinking all day in the hot sun, by the end of the night, everybody looks like cartoon characters to me."

We all had a good laugh at Bowmer.

I asked Wattsy who the girl actually was.

"Well, Lynn, she's French, her name is Stephanie, and Bowmer has got one thing right about her."

"What's that?" asked Bowmer.

"Rabbit," said Wattsy.

My last job before leaving the dock was to go to the yacht club and get a weather forecast. I left Spud in charge of getting all the gear off the yacht. The suitcases, gas bottle, kettle, cups and even the cushions were all left in a pile on the dock.

We sailed off the dock at 08:30; I didn't want to get caught up in the rush to leave the marina. Given that we had no engine, leaving first made sailing out to the course a lot less stressful. Wattsy got the genoa up, and with Bowmer on the helm, we slowly made our way out into the channel. I told the boys that the forecast was good, with a light easterly trade wind expected all day, with around ten to twelve knots of breeze. Light winds together with flat seas made the sailing conditions perfect for *Seefalke*.

Just as we got the mainsail up, a dolphin surfaced alongside the yacht, which is considered by many to be a sign of good luck.

"Look, boys—a dolphin," said Foxy. "That's so cool."

"Hopefully, that's a good omen," I said, smiling.

As we sailed towards the starting area off Windward Beach, the dolphin continued to swim alongside us, playing effortlessly in the bow wave of *Seefalke*. I don't know what it is about dolphins, but there is something truly magical about the way they seem to dance with the yacht. It doesn't matter how many times I witness their presence, it's a sight that brings me joy every time.

As we entered the starting area, the only thing left to do was to change into our matching beige crew gear. By 10 a.m. the stage was set. We were looking cool, the weather was great and *Seefalke* felt alive. Our uniforms were right for the period when the yacht was built in 1936; our appearance was going to really set off any photos that got taken of us sailing the course.

The Classic Class A, the smaller, working yachts, were the first class to start at 10:15, which made for an amazing sight from our vantage point on *Seefalke*.

***

First Race
Course: The Butterfly
Start time: 10:30

There were two classes starting at the same time: Vintage Class B and Vintage Class A. We were in Vintage Class B, which was all yachts under forty-five feet in length, while Vintage Class A was everything over forty-five feet.

Once the Classic Class yachts cleared the line, we were in race mode. Bowmer took the helm. Although I had thought of asking Spud, who was the better race yacht helm, Bowmer had more experience on the helm of *Seefalke* with a hangover.

My job was taking care of the genoa trimming. Foxy was on the mainsheet, with Wattsy on the bow, keeping an eye on other yachts and calling the distance to the line. Once the race started, Wattsy would move back to the mast and call out to me how to best trim the genoa and would help the sail around the mast every time we had to tack the yacht.

Finally, Spud would sit behind Bowmer and focus purely on tactics. *Seefalke* was a simple yacht to sail, and it was going to be our decision-making around the course that would really make the difference between doing well and being down the pan.

Spud's strategy was to keep the yacht trimmed for optimum speed at all times, stay out of trouble on the start and sail the shortest possible distance between marks while maintaining 'clean air'. Common sense really.

Spud worked out that the committee-boat end of the line was favoured to start from.

At 10:20, the ten-minute gun was fired. This was the start of our sequence, and so we started timing our runs to the line and checking the wind direction to ensure the committee boat remained the favoured end. Spud wanted us to start as close to the spectators and committee boat as possible to gain maximum advantage. However, this was a risky manoeuvre, as the other yachts could push us away from the start line. To pull this off, our timing needed to be perfect; we had to approach the line with the yacht fully powered up to ensure we hit the line with maximum speed yet without being early.

With three minutes to go, Spud called for the yacht to be brought head to wind. With the sails gently flapping in the light breeze, the yacht finally stopped moving. We knew from our timed runs that from our current position, it would take a minute to hit the line at full speed. So far, everything was going to plan.

As we counted down the final minutes, I had a good look at the rest of the yachts in our start. They were all beautiful classic yachts. To my surprise, they were all holding well back from the line. It soon became apparent that the owners of those gorgeous yachts weren't keen to mix it up and risk a collision that would certainly result in damage. We were on our own.

I could hear the excitement of the spectators as we approached the line, and the clicking of SLR cameras as photos were taken from the spectator boats. I could see Flemming on the stern of the committee boat; it looked like he had been tasked with firing the start gun. Foxy saw Mike Kahn in the middle of the crowded press boat and gave him a wave.

One minute and forty-five seconds before the start, Spud said, "Come on—power her up, boys."

"No, it's too early," I said. "Trust me, I know the yacht."

"Okay, Lynn."

The last thing I wanted was for us to be over the line early and pick up a five-minute time penalty, which would have killed off any hope of doing well in the regatta.

Seventy-five seconds to the start.

Spud said, "Power up, boys."

I thought it was still too early, but very reluctantly, I agreed with Spud.

I said, "Okay, let's go."

Wattsy was on the bow, calling boat lengths and the time to the start gun. I was still nervous about getting the genoa in quickly; I knew how fast we could get up to hull speed. Bowmer was reluctant to get us heading straight for the start line. Spud was shouting at all of us to power the yacht up.

We were going to be early.

Wattsy said, "Twenty seconds, four boat lengths, boys."

"We're too close," I said.

Bowmer was still trying to sail down the start line. Spud was shouting at him, "Bowmer, hold your course! Lynn, get that bloody genoa in! Foxy, power the mainsail up now!"

Wattsy shouted, "Ten seconds!"

I was looking at the committee boat and the line to the buoy, thinking we must be over, when Wattsy shouted again.

"Two, one, we are going over the—"

Bang! The cannon was fired; we were off and racing.

I watched Flemming, my boss, jump in the air, shouting, "WHAT A BRILLIANT START!"

From the spectator's boat, I could hear the clicking of cameras, followed by clapping and cheering.

We crossed the line with inches to spare and fully powered up. Spud had the biggest grin of all of us. When I turned around, the other yachts in our start were still approaching the line; they were a long way behind us already.

After our brilliant start, we got to work on trimming the sails and talking about our tactics as we headed for the first mark. Wattsy was calling the gusts, allowing me to trim the genoa accordingly. Meanwhile, Bowmer was constantly talking to Spud and Foxy about weather helm—the tendency of a sailing vessel to turn towards the source of the wind, creating an unbalanced helm that requires pulling the tiller to windward. The more weather helm we had, the harder Bowmer had to pull on the tiller, slowing the yacht down.

Sail trim and a well-balanced yacht are key for boat speed, and Bowmer was on our case every few seconds to trim the sails. All I heard, from the start of the race all the way around the course until we crossed the finish line, was "Roachy, pull in the genoa two inches," and seconds later, "Ease the genoa out by three inches." Wattsy was on my case as well, calling genoa trim endlessly.

It didn't take us very long to sail past the yachts in the Classic Class A start. By the first mark, we were out on our own. Our mark rounding was tight, and all told, we sailed a flawless race.

Although we had the perfect start to our campaign, the best part of the day was taking in the atmosphere and looking at all the stunning yachts. The real highlight was watching the two J-Class yachts duel for the first time in sixty years. These yachts were absolutely huge; the loads on everything were immense. From all across the racecourse, you could hear the unmistakable sound of sheet winches every time the sheets were eased.

We crossed the finishing line to the sound of a cannon being fired, confirming that we were first yacht home in our class. There were loads of shouts and screams coming from the spectator boats, and Bowmer stated that there was nothing better than the sweet smell of gun smoke when crossing the line at a regatta.

Once we were safely away from the line, we dropped the genoa and hung around to watch the J-Class yachts cross the line, which was a truly amazing sight.

Not too long after, *Liberty*, a big schooner crossed the line. She was in our start, but not in our class. Bowmer said, "We will have to watch her."

For a bunch of scruffy Welshmen sailing a rebuilt yacht, we'd had a pretty decent first day. Spud was confident that we had cleaned up. Being the first yacht to finish in our start and class, and also the first yacht to cross the finish line, we would most probably be first overall in the fleet.

"In yacht racing terms," Spud said, "we've racked up three 'bullets'," meaning we were first yacht to cross the start and finish lines in this race.

The dock was empty as we sailed back in under mainsail; the majority of yachts were still out racing. Two boat lengths from the dock, Bowmer spun *Seefalke* into the wind, Foxy dropped the anchor over the bow, and Spud and Wattsy backed the mainsail. We slowly reversed *Seefalke* towards the dock. I threw the stern line to the waiting crowd, who made it fast on the dock. Once the mainsail was dropped and flaked over the boom, Foxy tensioned the anchor warp to hold us off the dock. *Seefalke* was all tied up by early afternoon— not bad going, considering we started the race at 10:30.

Shortly after tying up, we gave the Swiss replica Bristol pilot cutter a hand to moor alongside us. We hadn't finished getting the lines on when their daughters passed across a cold beer to each of us; this was a great way to start our celebration. The Swiss family were really impressed by our sailing performance today and said we had done really well to beat the J-Class yachts home. Although they'd started later than us, the father said he'd still expected them to have beaten us home given the differences in handicap. We were chuffed with the Swiss family's comments, which brought huge smiles to all our faces. We couldn't wait to find out the results later at the yacht club.

I went and bought a case of beer to carry on the party. Sitting on the deck, reflecting on the day's events and enjoying the sun, what could be better? A minute didn't seem to pass before another person came up to congratulate us; we were certainly getting a taste for our newfound fame. People were even leaving crates of beer on the aft end of the yacht, in recognition of our success. At one point, I counted five cases.

These were very greatly received and shared with all who came aboard for a chat.

Bowmer, being the eternal cynic, told us to be careful. The cases of beer were an attempt to nobble us ahead of the following day's race.

"What planet are you on, Bowmer?" I said. "We are quite capable of nobbling ourselves; we don't need outside help."

Despite all the local well-wishing, we had definitely caused an upset with the yachting press. Having a bunch of blokes from Wales upstage the Jays wasn't the news they were looking for. The whole build-up to the 1998 regatta had been about the debate as to which J-Class would ultimately lift the overall regatta trophy.

Spud and I decided we needed food before we headed to the yacht club to get the results. Foxy left us as he wanted to walk around the dock first, saying he would meet up with us later.

Stepping off the yacht, I saw a very attractive girl wandering down the dock towards us. She stopped to talk to Spud.

Bowmer, sitting in the cockpit, saw her and said, "Wattsy, Jessica Rabbit is here for you."

Spud and I started laughing.

Wattsy had to apologise for the rude comment, but after he explained to her that Bowmer thought she look like a film actress, she said, "Mr Bowmer, thank you for the compliment. You can call me Stephanie." She had a soft sexy French accent.

As Stephanie turned to walk down the dock with Wattsy, she gave Spud and me a wink.

We started to follow when I heard, "Roachy, can you pass me the hosepipe? I need a cold shower before I join you in the Mongoose."

When I reached the yacht club lawn, I looked back and Bowmer was standing on deck, holding the hosepipe over his head, still wearing his shoes.

We had beer while we waited for him to join us in the Mad Mongoose. When he saw that our beers were empty, he went straight to the bar and ordered three more and three bowls of chips, which we all enjoyed.

"I'm still hungry," Bowmer said when we were done. "I can eat all that again."

We all agreed: "Go on, Bowmer, go and order the same again."

Five minutes later, Bowmer was still at the bar but now shouting.

I went over to find out what was happening. "What's the problem, Bowmer?"

"This numpty behind the bar is the problem—listen to this." He turned to the barman. "Please can I have three beers and three bowls of chips?"

The barman replied, "You've already had them."

Bowmer said, "I know I have had them, but I would like to have three more, please?"

"But you've already had them."

This time, Bowmer started to throw his toys out of the pram. "What planet are you on? All I'm trying to do is order the same again. How hard is it to get three beers and three bowls of chips around here?"

"You have already had them."

I had to step in and place the order before Bowmer lost his cool.

The party that night was on Pigeon Beach, but first, we had to go to the yacht club. The results were being posted at 5 p.m., and we wanted to find out how we had done at the earliest opportunity. To our dismay, the results were delayed for an hour, and while this was an agonising wait, it did mean we had time for some more beer, so it wasn't all bad.

Foxy and Michael Kahn wandered into the yacht club and came over to meet with us.

"I thought you were winding me up when you said you were here to win," Mike said. "After watching that start, you guys really are rock stars, aren't you? Man, I haven't seen a yacht sailed like that in years."

"We told you we are here to win!" we all said, laughing.

"I believe you now—that start was inch-perfect. As the gun went, your bow crossed the line; Dennis Conner doesn't get them any better than that. It was awesome to watch. So how many of you are pros?"

"We all are. Well, when it comes to drinking, that is."

We continued to wind up Mike, who hung on our every word.

"Come on, boys—let me buy you all a beer," he said.

Piggy, who was the chair of the race committee that year, finally posted the results. We all rushed to the results board to learn the long-awaited outcome of our first race.

The Result of the First Race
Course: The Butterfly
Position in Fleet
1st *Seefalke*. Vintage B.
2nd *Endeavour*. Spirit of Tradition.
3rd *Velsheda*. Spirit of Tradition.

What a way to kick things off. With a clean sweep, it really was time to party—we were all ecstatic. To celebrate, we went straight back upstairs to the yacht club bar, which was now starting to fill up with the good and the great. Everyone was smartly dressed, and it didn't take much to work out that we were amongst yachting royalty. However, that didn't deter us from being loud, which started to attract a number of stares and comments. Flemming, commodore of the club that year, politely suggested that we leave before he started receiving complaints about us.

As we were walking out, Piggy said, "Well done, boys—you beat all the yachts in the regatta today, including the Spirit of Tradition Class. They race for their own prize and they can't win the Classic Yacht Regatta outright. Go and enjoy the party on Pigeon Beach, have some fun and stay off the rum."

"No chance of that," said Bowmer.

Spud asked Piggy if he could use his phone.

"Yes, no problem," Piggy said. "But keep it short."

Spud wanted to call Karl to let him know how we had done. I dialled the international code and handed the phone to Spud as Karl picked up the phone.

Spud said, "Hi, Karl, guess what? – Bullet, bullet, bullet." And hung up the phone.

"Was that short enough, Piggy?" he asked.

"Yes," he said, "Brilliant."

When we finally walked over to Pigeon Beach, the party was in full swing, and there were people everywhere. We found Foxy still talking to Mike Kahn. They were sharing a bottle of rum with only one can of Coke in the sand between them. We went over and joined them.

I asked if they had enough Coke. Foxy said, "If anything, my drink is a bit weak," and took the opportunity to put more rum in his glass.

Wattsy turned up with Jessica Rabbit. He looked happy, so I think he had been having some fun.

Prior to the regatta, I had been working on a yacht called *Air Flow*, a big American charter yacht. There were two stewardesses on board, and I fancied one of them. Her name was Penny; she was tall and skinny, with long, flowing, sun-bleached, curly blonde hair—my type. I really fancied her, and I had been taking her out on and off for a short while. Sadly, our meeting up was restricted to when she could get time off in between charters.

Penny saw me sitting on the beach and came over to congratulate us on our win.

Sitting on Pigeon Beach, chatting to a very attractive lady and drinking beers with my sailing buddies put a huge smile on my face. Life couldn't get much better. I felt like I had finally arrived and made a mark in this big world.

My feeling of success, however, was short-lived. By 8 p.m., I had crashed and burned once more and made my way back to the yacht, leaving the boys to carry on partying.

***

Second Race
Course: Old Road
Start time: 10:30

I was up early the next day and was really excited about our second day of racing. Looking around the yacht, the boys had all made it back after the party, although they were still dead to the world. Sitting in the cockpit with my morning coffee, I caught sight of Penny, who climbed aboard and joined me for a chat before we walked over to Pigeon Beach for an early-morning swim.

On my way back, I stopped to pick up sandwiches, water and ice for the cooler. Everyone was still fast asleep when I got back aboard, so I decided to boil the kettle and make another coffee, which was enough to wake Bowmer. To my dismay, he was still fully dressed from last night, and he clambered out of his bunk and went to sit in the cockpit without saying a word. I passed him a hot cup of black coffee to try and bring him round. For once, Bowmer didn't say a lot, which left me to carry on chilling as I drank my coffee and watched the marina slowly come to life. Gradually, more and more people emerged and started preparing the yachts for another day of racing.

I saw Stephanie walking purposely along the dock and pointed her out to Bowmer.

"She doesn't look very happy," he said. "Look at the scowl on that beautiful face."

"Wattsy is down below," I said. "Maybe he did a runner last night."

Bowmer shouted into the cabin, "Wattsy, that Stephanie is inbound!"

She stopped on the dock right in front of us, just as Wattsy poked his head up through the main hatch. He looked a right mess.

"Wattsy, where did you go to last night? Have you got the twenty dollars you owe me?"

Quick as a flash, Bowmer said, "You didn't have to pay for a bonk last night, did you?"

We were both crying with laughter. I spat my mouthful of coffee all over the side deck and nearly choked.

Wattsy tried to protest his innocence to Bowmer. "I only borrowed the money, you tosser."

"Yeah, right, Wattsy."

From the dock, Stephanie said, "Mr Bowmer, you are so rude, but I like big, strong men—older men, like you. It is a shame I have to leave today."

Bowmer started to shift around a lot when Stephanie said, "Of course, Wattsy did not pay for a 'bonk', as you call it. He had it for free. Twice."

No wonder he did a runner after two rounds with Jessica Rabbit. He looked to be in a right state—a third one might have killed him.

As Wattsy walked Stephanie to the waiting taxi, I stepped onto the dock, and Bowmer said, "Roachy..."

"Yes," I said. "I'll pass you the hosepipe."

I wandered up to the yacht club to get the weather forecast. Conditions were the same as yesterday: flat seas and light easterly trades, perfect for *Seefalke*.

Walking back to the yacht, I bumped into Penny and grabbed the opportunity to have another chat. I was seriously besotted with her. Not only was she gorgeous, but she had a fantastic personality to match her looks.

"Lynn, will you be at the party in the Last Lemming tonight?" she asked

"I can't see why not."

"Great, I'll meet you there."

As she started walking off, she said, "I'm watching the racing on *Air Flow* today; I hope you stuff the fleet again."

All the gear was stripped off the yacht prior to leaving the dock at 08:30. Once again, we left the berth early and headed out to the race area under just the mainsail. This allowed us to chill and get in the zone, ready for the race.

"Lynn, what are you smiling about?" Bowmer asked.

"Oh, nothing. It's just, I've got a date with Penny tonight."

Bowmer started to laugh. "Dream on. I think you have as much chance of getting into Penny's knickers as I have of farting the alphabet."

"Bowmer, you were farting the alphabet last night—I know; I had to listen to it," said Spud, laughing.

"I have a chance then?" I said.

We had a good start again, but not quite as good as the day before. The rest of the yachts started a lot closer to us, but despite this, we were still the first yacht to cross the line out of the two classes.

The big American schooner *Liberty*, who'd won her class in 1996, was in our fleet. We had a close race with her. The light airs gave us an overall advantage, although she was able to carry a lot more sail downwind, meaning that she passed us a couple of times, which was a brilliant sight.

The best moment of the day came on the last windward leg. We had just tacked, and Wattsy and I were sitting on the windward rail when Spud shouted, "Hey, boys, look forward!"

Moments later, the bow of *Velsheda* passed about sixty feet away. Suddenly, everything seemed to go dark as the yacht crossed our path. It's not until you have the privilege of seeing one of these things up close that you appreciate their sheer size and majesty. The yacht was doing probably ten or twelve knots upwind, and the spray coming off the leeward bow was unreal. The mast and sails seemed to touch the sky. What an amazing sight!

Velsheda's one-hundred-and-thirty-foot-long hull only took a few seconds to pass in front of us.

She did cause us one big problem. Sailing through the huge wake coming off her stern shook all the wind out of our sails and stopped us dead in the water. Luckily, it only took us a few seconds to recover and get *Seefalke* back up to hull speed.

Crossing the finishing line, we got another canon with *Liberty* close on our heels. We had raced really well again with no mistakes, first in our class, and beating all the other classic yachts in our start again.

We were slowly making our way to the dock when the Swiss Family Robinson offered to tow us in. As we tied up alongside, the two daughters handed over the beers. It was as if they instinctively knew we needed a drink. What a great way to get towed into the marina and back onto the dock.

It was only 2 p.m., and I wandered up to the store for a case of beer and ice, so we'd have something to drink as we watched the fleet come in. A lot of people came on board and said well done. Again, more beer was dropped off on the back of the yacht, which again, we gratefully accepted and drank.

At 5 p.m., we went to the yacht club to get the results, but again, they were delayed for over an hour, which left us with no option but to drink more beer. Finally, Piggy posted the results.

The Result of the Second Race
Course: Old Road
Position in Fleet
1st *Velsheda*. Spirit of Tradition.
2nd *Seefalke*. Vintage B.
3rd *Endeavour*. Spirit of Tradition.

Another good result! We left the yacht club before we got too loud, although we didn't have far to walk as the party was downstairs at the Last Lemming, underneath the yacht club. The bar was buzzing; all of the yacht crews were there enjoying a drink and swapping their war stories from the second day of racing. Wattsy was looking longingly into the eyes of his new girlfriend. Foxy was engrossed in conversation with his newfound buddy, Mike. Spud and Bowmer were chatting to two attractive women. Just as I was starting to feel lost, in walked Penny, who was looking stunning.

With beers in hand, Penny and I wandered outside and sat on the yacht club lawn, gazing out across Falmouth Harbour and looking at the beautiful classic yachts. I was hoping to see the green flash as the sun dipped below the horizon, a sign that you are in love.

I think Penny could sense I wanted our friendship to be something more, but before I had a chance to say something, she said, "Lynn, I like you a lot, but I can't go out with you."

"Why?" I asked

"Err... well... I'm comfort shagging the skipper of *Air Flow*."

Bloody great, I thought. *Why can't you have comfort shagged me?*

After our awkward conversation, Penny left.

I wasn't in a very good mood at all.

I returned to the bar and bumped straight into Bowmer.

"What's wrong?" he asked. "You look really pissed off."

"Penny!"

"I told you you had no chance. What happened?"

"Penny said she can't go out with me because she's comfort shagging the skipper of *Air Flow*."

Bowmer just cracked up. "That's just priceless—it could only happen to you," he said, as he nearly choked on his mouthful of beer. When he finally stopped laughing, he said, "Why can't she comfort shag the both of you?"

"I don't know, Bowmer. I don't understand women. I had the same problem last month with another girl. I was in the Mad Mongoose talking to her when she said, 'I can't go out with you because you like me too much.' How does that work?"

"How the hell do I know? But you sure do pick them."

I had a few more beers with the boys before I'd finally had enough beer for one day. Feeling fed up, I left the boys to party and headed back to the yacht.

***

Monday 20th April

After my early-morning swim from Pigeon Beach, I went and sat in the cockpit and enjoyed a coffee, watching the world go by. My early night had done me good.

Looking over to the Bristol pilot cutter *Marguerite T*, I saw Scrimshaw stepping on deck, also with a cup of coffee in hand.

"Morning, Scrim."

"Good morning, Lynn. How are you feeling?"

"Good. Why do you ask?"

"Well, you lot seemed to have a good night."

"What do you mean?" I looked at him slightly confused.

"Well, Lynn, last night I was sat in your cockpit with Wattsy, Foxy and that photographer, Mike. They were drinking rum with only one can of Coke between the three of them."

"That's no surprise," I said. "What time was this?"

"Around midnight."

"I had passed out below deck by then."

"Ah! I wondered where you were, at the time."

"So, I missed the fun. That's good," I said with some relief.

"Well, not really."

Oh no, I thought. "Why?"

"As we were sat here, I saw a very elegant lady walking down the dock. She looked like she was off one of the big classics. She was casually dressed but looked really sophisticated in a pair of checked shorts and an expensive-looking polo shirt. She looked as though she had enjoyed a great evening somewhere. To be honest, I didn't pay much attention to her until—"

"It sounds to me you showed her plenty of attention."

"Well, not really. It's what happened next that made me remember her. She was walking past when I heard Mike Kahn say, 'Look—it's Elizabeth Meyers.'"

"Then Wattsy said, 'Who?'"

"Mike said to Wattsy, 'She's one of New York's wealthiest ladies and has spent millions of dollars restoring *Endeavour*, and Wattsy, she's also the owner of *Bystander* the big motor boat at the end of the dock.'"

"All of a sudden, I was very interested in her. *Seefalke* was in its usual state—you had clothes drying all down the side of it, and the cockpit was full of empty rum and beer bottles.

"Mike started waving, and she waved back. Elizabeth walked nearer to *Seefalke* and called out, 'Do you mind if I come aboard?'

"Wattsy said again, 'Sod off, Mike. You're pulling my plonker.'

"'It's Elizabeth Meyers,' Mike said. 'I'm telling you, Wattsy. I'm a friend of hers, and don't be so rude.' He started slowly slapping Wattsy across the face, three or four times, each time saying. 'Wattsy, she is the owner of *Endeavour*. That is Elizabeth Meyers.'

"'Sod off, Mike,' Wattsy said."

"You're joking, Scrim," I said.

"No, Lynn, and the night got better."

"What happened next?"

"Well, Foxy staggered to the stern of the yacht and helped Elizabeth on board, apologising for Wattsy's uncouth behaviour. At the same time, he introduced himself and handed her a bottle of Red Stripe."

Bloody great, I thought. Foxy was supposed to be the sophisticated one amongst us.

"Lynn, it was surreal. Elizabeth Meyers, the millionaire owner of *Endeavour*, was sat in your cockpit drinking beer with your drunken crew.

"She had a little look around the deck and the mess.

"'Looks like you boys are having a good party?' she said to Foxy.

"Foxy politely said, 'We're really enjoying the Regatta.'

"Then I heard Elizabeth say, 'Where is the yacht owner? Can I talk to him?'

"'Yes, I'll get him for you now,' said Foxy excitedly.

"Foxy went below to find you, and I could hear him shouting 'Lynn! Lynn! Lynn, Elizabeth Meyers is in the cockpit and wants to speak to you.'

"I was shocked when I heard you say, 'Tell her to fuck off and come back tomorrow.'

"Foxy returned to the cockpit, telling Liz that you were too busy to see her. Obviously, she'd overheard, what you said, and said, 'Yes, well, I got that, Foxy.'

"A few minutes later, you surface from below, sit in the cockpit, grab a beer and start having a sensible conversation with her. Wattsy left after a while, saying he was going to look for a new bunny girl, which didn't make any sense to me.

"Mike and Foxy then left to find some more rum. I returned to my yacht and sat in the cockpit, leaving you to carry on your chat with Liz. The daft thing was, you actually seemed to be having a really good time—you were coherent and talking; the pair of you were laughing and joking. You were getting on so well you started to even call her Lizzy. It was totally surreal, at one point I thought you'd scored."

"Does the story end there?" I said, hoping.

"No, there's more. Bowmer and Spud then came walking down the dock. Bowmer shouts over to you, 'Bloody hell, Roachy, you don't mess around. Penny only dumped you two hours ago—who's the new chick?'

"And you said, 'The lady you just called a chick is Miss Elizabeth Meyers, Bowmer.'

"'Fuck off, Roachy,' he said.

"'She is, Bowmer,' you said.

"'Err...' he said. 'Oh, sorry, Miss Meyers.'"

Scrim said, "It did make me laugh when Lizzy said to Bowmer, 'I've only been on this yacht for an hour, and I've been told to fuck off four times and now I have been called a chick.'

"'Err, sorry,' said Bowmer.

"Spud apologised for Bowmer's bad language and introduced himself. Foxy and Mike came back with another bottle of rum and another can of Coke. She then says to you, 'You guys are partying like there is no race to win tomorrow. You Welsh boys are wild.'

"After a couple of hours, the party broke up. Not long after, Mike left, and his parting words were, 'Guys, you're hitting it a bit hard tonight?'

"'We've done this every night since we arrived in Antigua,' said Foxy.

"'Yes, but you need to win the regatta tomorrow,' said Mike. 'Don't mess it up now.'

"'So?' said Bowmer bluntly.

"'Well, you'll be upset if you don't do well tomorrow because of a hangover.'

"'I'll tell you what will really make me upset, is not having another beer,' said Bowmer.

"When Bowmer said that, you all cheered. Mike just shook his head at you lot and laughed. He left then and walked Lizzy, as you called her, down the dock to *Bystander*."

I couldn't believe what I was hearing, but—knowing myself—it was probably true.

"You're joking, aren't you, Scrim?"

"No, mate, it's all true. There's no way I could have made that story up."

I was totally shocked by what Scrimshaw had told me—I couldn't remember anything about last night—but decided to let it go as I was sure Scrim was winding me up.

One thing I did know: the yacht was trashed. There were beer cans and empty bottles of rum everywhere—not too many Coke cans though. Spud was up early and gave me a hand to clean up. Wattsy was nowhere to be seen, and I figured he had stayed out all night partying. All I could see of Bowmer were his rotten feet sticking out of the quarter berth. Every time I asked him to get up, he just groaned and hurled abuse, blaming me for his hangover. Foxy was in a right mess too. He had spent most of the morning feeding the fish and was so rough he decided not to race. The weather report from the yacht club confirmed that the wind was expected to drop later in the day, so leaving Foxy's fifteen stone of relaxed muscle on the dock was not a bad idea.

I was putting the sandwiches and water on the yacht when Wattsy turned up, looking like the cat that had found the cream. Bowmer finally started to stir. It was time to leave the dock and go racing with my well-oiled crew.

"Come on, boys—let's go," I said.

Spud said, "So, Lynn, aren't you going to wait for that girl you were chatting up last night?"

"What girl?"

"The one you picked up in the Mad Mongoose?"

"When did I go to the Mad Mongoose?"

"We both went down there for a quiet beer after Penny told you she was comfort shagging her skipper."

I looked at Bowmer. "I asked you not to repeat our conversation."

"I didn't—I only told everybody once," said Bowmer.

"Bloody great. Thanks, Bowmer. Come on—let's go and get off this dock before I hear any more stories that will give me nightmares."

We were taking our lines off the Swiss Family Robinson yacht when Mike Kahn climbed aboard *Marguerite T.* To say he wasn't looking his best was an understatement. He did manage to groan "good luck" to us and asked to try and sail close by if we saw him on the racecourse so he could get some shots of us. As a final comment, he joked that we should sign a sponsorship deal with a beer company. We all laughed, and I yelled back, "That's a great idea, but could they afford it?"

We sailed off the dock under full main and made our way out of the harbour. Unlike the previous two days, there was no talking about tactics or our approach to the race; we knew what we needed to do. Everyone understood their role in making a dream a reality.

Despite his huge hangover, Bowmer was on form again.

"Hey, Wattsy, what happened to you last night?" he asked.

"I found a new girlfriend, a Swedish masseuse. She's good at it too—I found out down on the beach."

"Great, I've been here a week and I haven't come close to meeting a woman," Bowmer said. "Roachy, I hate you."

"Why now, Bowmer? It's not my fault if you only get hot under the collar for cartoon women."

"It's because you get us so bloody drunk."

"I'm not pouring rum down your throat, Bowmer. You need to take a leaf out of my book and have an early night once in a while."

"What, like the one you had last night?"

"Okay, last night was an exception."

"Yeah, right, Roachy."

As we slowly sailed down the channel towards the start line, Bowmer lit his pipe. It somehow seemed to suit him. He was hungover, relaxed and happy.

"Lynn?" he asked. "Can you remember anything from last night?"

"No, not one thing after I left the yacht club," I said.

"Really? That was early."

"Yes."

The sad thing was that the boys' version of what happened last night matched Scrim's, which wasn't good. They all took great delight in winding me up. They made out that the only reason Lizzy had come on board was to make me an offer for *Seefalke* so she could put it in a glass cabinet in the hallway of one of her houses as an ornament.

"Well, my sixth sense was right, Bowmer," I said. "I did meet Elizabeth Meyers. You had better get yourself a knife and fork because you're going to be having BBQ trainers for tea."

"It doesn't count. You don't remember meeting or seeing Miss M."

"What's that got to do with it? I told you I would meet her, and I have."

"Nope, you have to remember meeting her. Which, thankfully, you don't."

***

Third Race
Course: The Cannon
Start time: 10:30

This was a really lovely race, a very simple course—basically sailing on a reach out to sea for six nautical miles, and back twice. While this was not a particularly tactical course, it was a great opportunity to see all the yachts as they sailed out and back. This was a real spectacle and made for some fantastic photo opportunities.

The downside for us was that *Seefalke* had a short waterline length, and further offshore we expected the conditions to get choppier, which wasn't great for *Seefalke*, who was at her best sailing upwind in flat water.

Spud's plan for today's race was to stay out of trouble in clean air and avoid larger, faster yachts sailing above us—

in sailing terms, getting rolled. The last thing we needed to happen was to sail in another yacht's dirty air coming off their sails. That would absolutely kill our boat speed. We needed to keep *Seefalke* sailing in flat water throughout the whole race, if we could.

With *Seefalke* heading towards the start line, we eased the sheets to slow her down. All was going to plan, and we had our favourite place by the committee boat again.

Wattsy said, "We are ten boat lengths from the start line."

Spud said, "Two minutes."

The sails flapped in the gentle breeze, and the yacht was almost stopped in the water. We just needed to maintain and protect our position before we could begin our timed run to the start line.

Liberty, the big schooner, started to sail above us, blocking our wind. *Flicka* and *Dione*, two yachts in our class, who we had not seen in the first two races, were now quite close to us, but behind and below us.

Spud was on it and keeping close tabs on our position. "If we don't move now, our plan is going to go tits up, boys. Get those bloody sails in now. Let's get the yacht powered up, or we will be buggered."

We sheeted the sails in and started to power the yacht up. Wattsy continued to call the line and told us we were on it. Spud started shouting at Bowmer to bear away and sail down the line. From my position, I could see *Dione* and *Flicka* heading straight towards us. To me, it looked like they were trying to push us over.

Spud was still shouting at Bowmer to hold his course.

Dione and *Flicka* were bearing down on us, quickly getting closer and closer. I could see Bowmer trying to steer away from them; still, Spud shouted at Bowmer, "Hold your course!"

I was thinking this could be a very expensive mess in a few more seconds.

Spud shouted, "Ten sec to the start—go for it, Bowmer!"

I winched in the genoa as fast as I could. Spud trimmed the mainsail.

Wattsy said, "We are going ov—"

I never heard the rest. The gun went, and we were out in front again—first over the line in our start and class, with clean air and flat sea. Fair play to Spud, he knew how to read the start and had the balls to fight for those all-important inches that could make the difference between winning and losing.

Once we all settled down and had stopped shouting at each other, Bowmer flicked a switch and was back on his A-game, telling us all how to trim the sails by the feel from the tiller. A quick look around at the yachts behind us, I could see no protest flags flying, and there was no call for us on the VHF radio from the committee boat. Our start was good. It wasn't pretty and was very scary, but still, we had a very good outcome.

Liberty was the closest yacht to us, behind and to windward. *Dione* and *Flicka* were also behind but to leeward of us, locked in their own private yacht race. By the time we were halfway down the first leg, we had caught up with the yachts from the first start. They were bunched into two groups, about a quarter of a mile apart. Spud told Bowmer to steer towards the leeward group, and we trimmed the sails to suit. Once behind the last yacht, we altered course and sailed between the two groups, which allowed us to maintain clean air.

Before *Liberty* could follow us through the gap, the yachts closed right up. *Liberty* was stuck in the middle, with dirty air coming off the surrounding yachts, which really slowed her down. This allowed us to pull clear of the chasing fleet.

Halfway up the third leg, we watched *Velsheda* coming up behind us. She was on her own—I did not see *Endeavour*. I did wonder if Lizzy had a hangover after last night's party with us Welsh boys.

A J-Class yacht bearing down on you with such pace was a really impressive and unforgettable sight. Bowmer and Spud were surprised when *Velsheda* caught the last yacht on our leg of the race and rolled them instead of doing the gentlemanly thing of dropping below them. Being the fastest yacht in the fleet, it just powered over the top, stopping the other yacht dead with all the dirty air coming off her huge sails. *Velsheda*'s next victim saw this and started hardening up to try and sail above *Velsheda* to protect her wind. We could hear the strain of *Velsheda*'s genoa sheets as she did the same. The noise coming from the sheet winches could be heard for miles away. Very quickly, *Velsheda* rolled that yacht.

Liberty went hard on the wind to try and stop the same thing happening, with no luck. We were next, so we tried the same but with the same outcome: *Velsheda* devoured us in about ten seconds flat.

Spud said, "Let's carry on sailing to windward until we are above and out of *Velsheda*'s dirty air." Which we did.

To be honest, what *Velsheda* did was completely unnecessary and arrogant. With her speed and power, she could have easily sailed through the lee of all the smaller yachts who, like us, were competing for trophies. *Velsheda* had nothing to prove. The whole fleet had done the same thing, going hard on the wind, which had been completely futile.

The big downside of getting rolled was we had to sail in the disturbed air coming off *Velsheda*'s sails. Trying to sail through her wake was bad enough—it was like hitting a standing wave. In our case, it nearly stopped us dead.

We rounded the last mark and started to weave our way through the oncoming yachts, trying to maintain clean air and stay out of the chop created by their wake. All we had to do now was keep out of trouble.

As we headed for the finish, we sailed past the *Marguerite T* with Mike on board. We all gave him a wave as he started taking photos of us looking cool in our smart crew uniforms.

Liberty slowly caught us. She was flying her big downwind sail between her masts, which she had used to good effect in overtaking us on the downwind legs in race two. Spud told us to harden up to make her sail below us, which she did.

Wattsy, sitting on the rail, looking forward, shouted out that *Liberty* had stopped. She had no wind and sailed into a hole. Spud and Bowmer were on the case straight away, looking at the water for signs of breeze and any opportunity to sail around the dead spot.

Spud said, "Bowmer, I can see breeze about a quarter of a mile to starboard of *Liberty*. Get the sails in, boys, so we can harden up and get into that breeze."

As we sailed over the top of *Liberty*, three yachts tried to sail over us. Each time, we hardened up to protect our clean air and got the attacking yachts to sail below us. The only one that gave us trouble was *Winsome*, a fibreglass ketch in the Spirit of Tradition class. Bowmer refused to be rolled, despite all of us shouting at him not to sail off into oblivion.

He shouted back, "I'm not going to let that plastic piece of shit sail over the top of us."

We trimmed the sails to go hard on the wind again.

Finally, *Winsome* dropped below us, which put a big smile on Bowmer's face—a very rare sight.

As I looked back down the fleet, *Dione* was a lot closer to us than she had been in previous races and was doing well until she sailed into the same hole as *Liberty*. Two miles from the finish, there were only three yachts in front of us.

Bowmer asked, "Spud, what do you want us to do here?"

Spud said, "Stay well above them and sail over the top. I reckon we will pass them pretty quickly."

After we sailed over the last yacht, we eased the sheets and reached to the finish. We went over the line to the sound of the cannon and the sweet smell of gun smoke. We had once again beaten all the other classic yachts in our start and finished first in our class, collecting another bullet.

Following the final race, we qualified for a free berth in Nelson's Dockyard. As we headed back to English Harbour, we saw Sprout in his rib, just outside the harbour entrance.

"How did you get on?" he asked.

"Very good, after a couple of tense moments at the start," I told him.

"The rudder stayed on, then?"

"It did. Thanks for your help," said Bowmer.

Sprout said, "Given that the Parade of Sail is taking place later and the harbour will be heaving, would you like me to tow you to your berth once you have done your sail by?"

"That would be great," I replied. "Thank you."

Sprout towed us in and put us on a berth outside the Galley Bar. Wattsy dropped the anchor, Foxy was on the dock ready to take our stern line, and with five cold beers waiting for us, we were like a well-oiled machine. Once *Seefalke* was safely moored stern to, we flaked the mainsail over the boom, put the sail cover on and gave the yacht a quick washdown. She looked lovely. I had a real sense of pride at what we had achieved over the past eight days—what a story for all of us to tell the grandkids.

Foxy said he'd met a guy with a big camera and followed him up to the old fort overlooking Windward Beach. He said he'd got a great view of the race and thought we had smashed it.

We knew it was going to be a long day, so we had some food in the Galley Bar. While we were waiting for our burger and fries to turn up, the crew from *Liberty* came over and had a beer with us and politely asked if we could turn the yacht around. We asked why, and their reply made us laugh. They said all they had seen for the last three days was the stern of *Seefalke*, and they were sick of the sight of it.

We helped *Marguerite T* to moor up alongside us. Mike had taken some great photos of us all, which he promised to send on. We had one quick job to do before the party started, and that was to retrieve all the stuff we'd left on the yacht club dock in Falmouth Harbour.

We partied for the remainder of the afternoon, talking to the other crews. Everybody who came on board brought a bottle or case of something, none of which was water.

Still dressed in our crew uniforms, we walked over to the yacht club, to get the results of race three. The results were delayed again for nearly two hours, so we just sat there, quietly behaving ourselves for a change. Mike Kahn joined us and bought us a beer. He kept saying that the world's yachting press wanted a J-Class yacht to win the regatta.

Finally, Piggy posted the results.

The Result of the Third Race
Course: The Cannon
Position in Fleet
1st *Mariella*. Classic Class A
2nd *Cintra*. Classic Class B
3rd *Seefalke*. Vintage Class B

We knew we had done well and won our class but didn't know where we had placed in the overall regatta results; those results weren't posted.

To celebrate, we had a few more beers, getting louder, happier and quite pissed. I know we upset a few people, because not long after the results were posted, Flemming chucked us out of the yacht club. It seemed funny—at the start of our first race, he'd been leaping in the air and swearing in praise for us, and now, after we'd done so well in the regatta, he was throwing us out.

Leaving the yacht club, we went downstairs to the Last Lemming. From there, we had a few more beers in the Mad Mongoose, and our last stop was the party at the Copper and Lumber Store. It was an amazing night, from the little I remember.

Chapter 15
The Prize-Giving Party

Tuesday 21st April

My brain was bouncing around like a ball in a pinball machine. I kept wondering if this was to be the day I would have my fifteen minutes of fame. After a quick cup of coffee, I walked over to Pigeon Beach. Every hundred yards, I bumped into somebody I knew, and everyone wanted to chat about our amazing success. The one question they all asked was: had we won the overall regatta? I kept replying that I didn't know and couldn't wait to find out.

I managed to get to Pigeon Beach and had my swim. On my walk back to English Harbour, I was stopped by more friends who had the same question, to which I gave the same answer. I finally got back to the dockyard at eleven. The guys had surfaced and asked me what I'd been doing all morning. I explained that every man and his dog had stopped to speak to me, and all they'd wanted to know was whether we'd won the regatta outright.

We knew it was going to be another marathon day of partying, so we went to Limey's, a local café above the Copper and Lumber Store, for breakfast. There were great views looking over the dock and out towards the entrance of the harbour. Limey's speciality was their full English breakfast with black pudding and Johnny cakes. I ordered in five.

We were sitting at a table in the long, narrow room when the crew of *Liberty* walked in. They looked just as rough as we did. The guys sat at a table on the other side of the room but slightly behind us. Once they realised we were sat in front of them, they cracked the same joke about having spent all week behind us. We all had a good laugh.

Talking to the crew, they were convinced that we had won the regatta and were all rooting for us which was great. They said it was really nice to see a yacht sailed properly, going in tight to the marks and using the right tactics. Those accolades put a smile on all our faces.

After breakfast we all split up and did our own thing, agreeing to meet up later at the first party of the day: the Heritage Festival, at the Admiral's Inn.

I decided to wander back to *Seefalke* for an hour. Spud joined me. Walking past the Galley Bar, I saw that Piggy and members of the yacht club race committee were sitting by the bar drinking a beer. Piggy called us over.

"Would you boys like a beer?" he asked.

Of course, we accepted.

Piggy said, "You've caused some trouble in the yacht club."

"Why's that, Piggy?" I asked. "Is it because you had to throw us out again last night?"

"No, that's not the issue. All the world's yachting press are here, wanting a J-Class yacht to win the regatta, and you lot of scruffy Welsh boys have driven a coach and horses through their little party."

"I don't get it?"

"With your first, second and third in fleet, you have beaten every other yacht in the regatta. Lynn, the Spirit of Tradition Class yachts have their own race within the regatta—they're the fastest yachts and are bound to win, with their carbon fibre masts, 3DL sails and professional crew all bankrolled by multimillion-dollar owners. If a J-Class yacht wins, the yacht club and the world's press are happy campers."

"Sorry, Piggy, I still don't get what you are on about. We sailed well and very professionally. *Velsheda* sailed over the top of every yacht in the fleet in the last race—that's not cricket, and it cost them."

"I know, Lynn. Still, in all my years of being on the regatta committee, no other yacht has beaten the yachts in the Spirits of Tradition Class. I don't think it will ever happen again. I still don't know the final outcome of the discussion yet, but suffice to say, you've caused a real headache. There's a final meeting with the sponsors at two to decide the final outcome. Whatever happens, I'll see you at the prize-giving party tonight."

"Okay. Thanks for keeping me informed, Piggy, and for being on our side."

"I'm not on your side, Lynn; it's just we shouldn't change the rules because we do not like the result."

Leaving Piggy in the Galley Bar with another beer in his hand, I asked Spud if he fancied a coffee. It was going to be another long day of drinking.

We walked over to the Copper and Lumber Store and sat in one of their booths. The place was dead.

"Well, Spud, what do you think about Piggy's comments just now?" I asked.

"Well, as far as Piggy is concerned, we've won the regatta, but we still don't know, do we?"

We were the only two in the Copper and Lumber, and it was fifteen minutes before we saw a waitress. We finally managed to order two coffees.

The waitress looked at us and said, "I will have to go and make it?"

"Yes, that sounds like a great idea."

We both had a laugh at the Antiguans—they have such a laid-back approach to life. While we waited for our coffees to turn up, my sixth sense started to warn me about something.

Finally, our coffee arrived, and we were still deep in conversation when a couple walked past us.

Spud said, "Hi."

The lady said, "Spud, what's the coffee like?"

"It's okay," he said. "But if you want quick service, you had better buy the place."

The lady laughed.

"Who was that, Spud?"

I don't know why I bothered to ask. My sense had already told me the answer.

"Elizabeth Meyers," said Spud

"Oh," I said, looking confused.

"Roachy, you cannot remember a thing about the other night, can you?"

"No."

"Roachy, what are you like? What are you like?"

We joined the boys at the Heritage Festival. It was a great afternoon—all the ladies were dressed up in Victorian clothing; there were tea and cake stalls, bookstalls and art stalls, and Scrim was selling his bone carvings. Penny was also there, teaching decorative rope work. It was a nice, chilled afternoon. Even Wattsy got involved in the gig racing with his new girlfriend.

I was quite happy sitting on the grass, drinking a beer and talking to the boys. Mike Kahn joined us, and we were all having a good time watching the fun, until Jenny Gordon said to me, "What are you going to wear to the prize-giving party tonight? It's quite a posh affair, and it starts in two hours."

For the rest of my crew, a white shirt and a tidy pair of trousers was not a problem, but for me, it was a huge one. I didn't own a shirt, and I hadn't worn a pair of trousers in years.

The only problem the boys had was they all wanted to iron their clothes and have a hot shower. Thankfully, Mike came to their rescue, on the proviso that he became our official photographer at the prize-giving. We all laughed at his request until we realised he was being serious. We happily agreed.

Jenny agreed to sort me out and find me some decent clothes to wear. I arranged to meet her at Temo Sports, where I was a member. Half an hour later, I was sitting by the bar with a beer, and Jenny walked in with a white shirt, a pair of black trousers and a pair of really nice black shoes.

"Lynn, try these on," she said. "They should fit you, as you're about the same size as Paul."

"Paul who?"

"Don't worry about that; just try it all on."

After a hot shower and a shave, I tried on my new clothes.

As I walked out of the changing room, Jenny said, "Don't you clean up well, Cinders? I've never seen you in tidy clothes before. Come on, let's go and get your prizes.

"Just one thing, Cinders—don't go partying with those shoes and trousers on after the award ceremony finishes, okay?"

"What about the shirt?"

"That's mine; it's no problem. It's just the trousers and shoes—I've got to get them back before Paul misses them."

"Yes, Jenny, no problem."

The award ceremony was at the Admiral's Inn and was a very posh and glitzy affair; with everyone attending in smart attire. The place was filled with photographers, sailors, millionaires... and then there was us. We found a table to sit at, and shortly afterwards, the ceremony started. Piggy was the host; he started calling out the awards. It was slightly embarrassing as time after time I was called to the stage.

"Best Elapsed Time for Vintage Yacht goes to *Seefalke!*"

"Best Local Classic goes to *Seefalke!*"

"First Yacht in Vintage Class B: *Seefalke!*"

Our table was full of glassware, wine decanters and a bottle of champagne, which we opened and drank straight away.

As more and more prizes were awarded, you could sense the tension building. We were getting closer to the announcement everyone was waiting for: the overall regatta winner. Finally, the time came, and after a big build-up, Piggy announced the third place in fleet. It wasn't us. We didn't take second prize either, and we were all convinced that we were going to end up with nothing. We thought the regatta sponsors had won and a J-Class yacht would win overall.

Finally, Piggy called out, "First in fleet and overall winner of this year's regatta, receiving the Wayfarer Marine Trophy...

"*SEEFALKE!*"

At that moment, I was genuinely dumbstruck and so were the boys. We didn't move for a few seconds; I don't think we believed what had just happened. Piggy called *Seefalke* again, and this time, we all piled onto the stage and I did a giant leap into the air.

Kenny Coombs handed me the Wayfarer Marine Trophy—a silver plate, which I could keep. It came as a complete surprise to me. I was also personally awarded the overall first prize of a very expensive Rolex watch.

We were asked to pose for a picture. We declined, saying that we couldn't pose for any pictures until our official photographer, Michael Kahn, had taken our picture first.

Once Mike was done with us and the other photographers had finished taking theirs, we were interviewed by the world's press. It was funny, as when I was asked where I had learnt to sail, the first thing that came out of my mouth was, "Roath Park Lake."

It was a small lake in Cardiff, where you can hire rowing boats and sail model yachts. The boys cracked up.

As we left the stage, I heard Piggy say, "The Welsh cannot play rugby, but these boys can certainly sail."

People kept coming up and congratulating us. This felt strange; at the start of the regatta, we'd been kind of ignored. We had just entered the regatta for fun. We were known as the five smelly Welsh men who had a good time partying and drinking too much. We had been thrown out of the yacht club for being a little bit loud, and because we wound a few rich people up.

Now, all of a sudden, we were revered by everyone at the prize-giving. As a crew, us Welsh boys had sailed to the best of our ability and won.

Funny world.

Bowmer gave us all a speech. He said to the boys this was a once in a lifetime experience. A win by a small yacht would not be easily repeated. He bet that next year the committee would make absolutely sure the bigger, wealthier and sponsored yachts would win. The odds would get stacked against a bunch of numpties like us who were there to have some fun and sail well. The funny thing was he sounded like Winston Churchill.

I kept my word to Jenny. I went and changed, and hid the Rolex in a safe place, before going out to the live blues concert and party. I borrowed a pair of jeans off Wattsy. I knew we would all end up in a nightclub and have a very late night.

Chapter 16
The End of the Holiday

Wednesday 22nd April

What time I got back after the prize-giving, I have no idea. It was a long day drinking in the sun and partying all night. I remember waking up with an almighty hangover and feeling like death. As I sat in the cockpit with my first coffee of the day, I watched as the Galley Bar opened, thinking, *That's what I need: a good breakfast with the hair of the dog.* I walked the twenty feet to the Galley Bar, and slowly, one by one, the rest of the crew got up and joined me.

In the Galley Bar, we all had our fifteen minutes of fame. I gave an interview with a German yachting magazine. Mike the photographer joined us for breakfast and took some more photos of us all. Then, thankfully, the regatta was over for another year.

The UK yachting press were not interested in talking to us, and the local press were the same—all had expected a J-Class yacht to win. What made it worse for Bowmer was he knew the UK yachting magazine reporters from his win on the Teacher's Round Britain Race.

We had to get the yacht back onto her mooring; the regatta was over and so there was no more free berthing. With Foxy on the bow pulling up the anchor, Bowmer, in the dinghy with a line to the bow, towed *Seefalke* through the anchorage back to the small dock by the old powder magazine in Ordnance Bay.

The party that afternoon was down Pigeon Beach, an English Harbour Rum party. As we walked over to the beach, I popped into the yacht club to have a final look at the results of the last race, also the overall results of the regatta.

It was interesting: *Seefalke* beat *Velsheda* by two minutes on corrected time. If *Velsheda* had done the gentlemanly thing and not sailed over the top of every yacht in the last race, with each yacht pushing her to windward, she would have been a lot quicker, making up the two minutes and winning the regatta. Moral of this story: always be a gentleman in sport. Play fair, just like the crew of *Liberty* had said to us.

On the beach, the party was in full swing. After a few beers, we started to join in the fun events. We entered the tug–of–war and were pitted against *Velsheda*. Us five against five of their crew. Foxy was the anchor, and the rest of us just stood, looking at the opposition. This wasn't going to be a fair fight. We were five slightly drunk and unfit Welshman against five completely sober, very fit professional sailors twice our size.

Well, as you could have guessed, they trashed us and pulled us over the line and dragged us quite a bit more too— maybe trying to get their own back.

We were happy enough. Now we were out of the competition, we could carry on drinking, which we would've done anyway. I always tried to look on the bright side of things.

Jenny watched us lose in the tug-of-war. When we were pulled over the line, she heard Foxy shout, "Ow!"

"You okay?" she asked.

Foxy said, "I cut my foot on something, it's only a graze."

"Was it that?" said Jenny, pointing at some sort of root in the sand.

"Yeah, I think so."

"That's a root of a Manchineel tree," said Jenny, "and it's very poisonous. If that was the root that cut your foot, you'll need to go to hospital now. Come on, Foxy—let's go."

She was right. The next time I saw Foxy, his leg had swollen up to three times its normal size. It was a right mess. Foxy was quite upset—not because of the pain or the size of his leg, but because the antibiotics were going to prevent him drinking rum at the upcoming Mount Gay rum party on Galleon Beach, the biggest party of the week.

A regatta wasn't a regatta without a Mount Gay rum party. It also marked the start of Antigua Race Week. We were all looking forward to it and had put some hard training in over the last ten days. To keep Foxy happy, Jenny gave him a lift to the beach, and to make him feel better, we promised to get him a coveted cap.

We all managed to get one of the limited Mount Gay hats. It was no ordinary hat; it was to be treasured and worn with pride at other sailing regattas.

After drinking free rum all afternoon in the hot sun, we were all in a right mess, apart from Foxy. Our day ended in the Mad Mongoose. I cannot remember getting back to the yacht, but I know for me it was early.

After the Mount Gay rum party, there would be another rum party, on another beach. To tell the truth, we were all partied out after two weeks of drinking. Thursday was spent wandering around the docks in Falmouth Harbour looking at the millions and millions of pounds of racing yachts. A few asked if we would crew for them; one owner offered to charter a yacht for us to race. In the end, the boys decided they'd had two brilliant weeks in Antigua, had won more than they ever expected, but combined with the hassle of changing their flights home, another week of sailing and partying would be too much. We decided to decline the offer.

Friday was the boys' final full day in Antigua. They wanted to have one last sail on *Seefalke* and asked me to show them a bit more of the island. The only part they'd seen so far were the bars and beaches around English and Falmouth Harbour.

Jenny Gordon suggested we sail down the coast to Green Island; she could drive up to Harmony Hall with Foxy to meet us. From there, they could catch the ferry over to the island. We decided it would be a great place to chill out and have a BBQ on the beach. This was a plan; I gave Jenny some money for food, beer, and ice.

All last year, I had been working with Kenny Coombs, and he had been pestering me for a sail on *Seefalke*. Kenny and his wife Jane joined us. Including Wattsy's latest girlfriend, we had a full crew on board.

We sailed off the mooring on the mainsail. Bowmer was on the helm, happily puffing away on his pipe. Once clear of the anchorage and as we approached the entrance to English Harbour, we pulled up the no.1 genoa.

It was a beautiful day; the sun was out and there wasn't a cloud in the sky. There was a hot trade blowing from the east, and although we had to beat upwind, Green Island was only eight miles east of English Harbour. We had a brilliant sail to windward, and every now and then the spray would cool us all down. You couldn't have asked for a more perfect day for a leisurely sail along the coast. *Seefalke* was well over-pressed for the conditions, but we didn't mind. She pushed her way through the big, clear, blue seas, and despite the spray, we were all laughing, having fun and enjoying the sail.

The entrance to Green Island was a small, narrow cut, with rocks on one side and a sandbank on the other. Once through the cut and into the lee of the island, we entered a large, sheltered bay. *Seefalke* loved those conditions: a good breeze, flat water allowing her to sail at full speed, with the leeward toe rail underwater. Kenny took the helm and had a grin from ear to ear.

We anchored off the beach. Jenny and Foxy were already on the island. The only other yacht in the anchorage was *Air Flow*, the yacht Penny was working on. Great. Kenny blew the dinghy up and took Jane ashore. The rest of us dived off the yacht and swam in the warm, clear water to the beach. We had a great day swimming, snorkelling and drinking beer. With BBQ chicken and sausages, it was a great way to round off the trip. Even Bowmer took his shoes off, for what seemed like the first time in nearly a fortnight.

As I sat on the beach, I watched Spud walking out of the water towards me.

"I don't believe you, Roachy. I snorkelled under *Seefalke*, and what do I see? A bolt sticking out of the hull a foot long."

"I know," I said.

"We had to drag that through the water when we were racing. How the hell did we win? Why didn't you cut it off?"

"No time," I said. "It was dark by the time I got that bolt to fit. With everything else going on, I forgot about it. Doesn't matter, we won."

Bowmer snorkelled around the yacht, and when he got back to the beach, he said, "You *are* special—only you would leave a bolt that long sticking out of the hull and still win the regatta. The other handicap was the antifoul on your side of the rudder. Roachy, it's awful."

We left Green Island sailing on the no.1 genoa only. We were all chilled and looking forward to a gentle downwind sail back. As we cleared the back of the island, sailing into the cut between the rocks and the sandbank, the genoa halyard snapped, and the sail fell to the deck.

"Get the mainsail up!" Spud shouted.

Working like the well-oiled team we had become, we had the mainsail up in seconds, keeping *Seefalke* underway.

Kenny was impressed by the yacht, but more impressed by the crew. We had an easy downwind sail back to English Harbour. By the time we got back to the mooring, it was dark. That evening we all went to the Mad Mongoose for our last meal together.

The boys caught a taxi to the airport on Sunday, taking all the decanters back with them, plus the silver plate. Bowmer wore the Rolex, as I couldn't afford the duty on it. Everything was going back home to my mother.

On our last sail together, Bowmer told me the rudder was feeling very stiff. I had very little work after Race Week, so I took the yacht out of the water and dropped the rudder to check it. I'm glad I did because I found a split in the rudder stock. I had Woodstock repair the rudder again. At the same time, I put a one-foot-long copper sheath around the bottom of the rudder stock to give me a bit more protection against teredo navalis worms.

I antifouled the yacht again, spending time to do a good job this time, and replaced the bolt I should have cut off before the first race. Bowmer and the boys would have been proud of me.

Chapter 17
Leaving Antigua

Tuesday 26th May 1998

After three years in Antigua, it was time for me to set sail again before I got myself into another rut. I had a thirst for more adventure and wanted to get away ahead of the forthcoming North Atlantic hurricane season. I decided to sail south, open-minded as to where I would end up.

My electronics on the yacht had piled up over the years, and they all needed replacing. St Martin, the half French, half Dutch island, was the place to go for tax-free electronics, so that was my first port of call before starting my journey south. The passage from Antigua to St Martin was quick, and I arrived off Pittsburgh Harbour very early in the morning. From past experience, I knew there were many unlit boats and buoys around—Pittsburgh was one harbour I didn't want to sail into at night. So, I waited for first light. I wasn't a huge fan of the harbour. Every time I went there it was busy, and the harbour was exposed, making the anchorage very uncomfortable in any swell.

My first job ashore was to have breakfast. I found a nice café overlooking the harbour, with an English breakfast on the menu. Fed, I headed for customs and immigration to check in. After three years in Antigua, all my yacht papers were out of date. This was another good reason to go to St Martin: they were very relaxed about paperwork, as long as you paid.

I used my week there to buy a new pair of binoculars, two new VHF radios—one being a rechargeable handheld radio—a new up-to-date GPS and another fifty-five-watt solar panel, which I fitted.

Before leaving St Martin, I stocked up with fresh food and refilled the water tank. After a busy day, I stopped in the local bar for a happy-hour beer, where I bumped into a girl I knew from Antigua. Erica was the chef on a yacht I had done some repairs on.

In the middle of Antigua Race Week, there was a lay day with a range of fun activities including: swimming, drinking and tug-of-war competitions that the yacht crew participated in. The final comp was a wet T-shirt contest. Erica had won when her T-shirt came off. I remembered Erica for two other reasons: she was bright and very bubbly.

Erica wanted to go to Barbados to catch a flight home and asked if she could come sailing with me as I was heading south. *Why not?* I thought. Erica was fun to be around, and it would be nice to have some company for a change.

On 3rd June, after clearing customs with all new-legal paperwork, we left St Martin.

We had a really good sail down to Dominica. Flat seas, and a good wind from the east, and it was hot and sunny— you couldn't have asked for better sailing weather. Erica and I enjoyed the trip, which was topped off by seeing pilot whales at the entrance to Prince Rupert Bay. We spent three days exploring the town of Portsmouth. It was a very poor town, but most of our time was spent doing the tourist thing. We did a bus tour, went hiking up in the hills and swam in the hot springs. If we got bored, we'd hang out on the beach, swimming and snorkelling, looking to catch a lobster for tea.

From Portsmouth, we headed south, sailing down the coast of Dominica to the capital. In Roseau was the Anchorage Hotel, and just off the hotel was a very small area where you could anchor safely. I dropped the anchor in fifty feet of water, one hundred feet from shore. After blowing up the dinghy, I took a stern line ashore and tied it to a tree.

Back on *Seefalke*, looking over the bow, I could see the anchor; the water was crystal clear. When I snorkelled down to check the anchor had dug itself in, I was surprised to find the water was cold.

Getting around Roseau was cheap using the local buses. We spent most of our time snorkelling off Scotts Head. The water was beautifully clear, with bubbles coming up from the seabed. It was like swimming in champagne.

***

Sunday 14th June

Barbados was a hundred miles east of the other Windward Islands, meaning we would be fighting the prevailing easterly wind and current. It was good having Erica on board, and it made the trip a bit easier for me. Leaving Roseau, I turned south towards Scotts Head. With the wind and current against us, we had to tack back and forth, slowly working our way out of the channel between Dominica and Martinique. Once clear and away from the lee shore of Martinique, we had an easy sail to Barbados, with the wind unexpectedly on the beam.

I sailed into the deep-water harbour. I knew what to expect this time, and with Erica's help, it was a lot easier. After we cleared customs, we sailed around to Carlisle Bay and anchored off the Boatyard. We went ashore and had a beer at happy hour. All my old friends from the Hash House Harriers were still there; it was good to catch up with them again.

Erica spent a week with me in Barbados. I talked to her about the prospect of sailing down to Brazil, but she was not keen and decided to catch her flight home. That was the end of 'Erica's Caribbean Adventure'.

The football World Cup was on in France, and the Boatyard had a few TVs set up around the bar. How long I stayed in Barbados would depend on how long England stayed in the tournament. It was a lot of fun watching the football with my old friends and ex-pats from around the world. The decision to leave Barbados was easily made when England, having made it to the last sixteen, were knocked out by Argentina, losing on penalties.

During the time I was in Barbados, the trip down the east coast of South America was in the back of my mind. It would be tough. Reading my Admiralty passage planner, the old sailing ships would head west towards the Azores until they hit the favourable south-flowing current and the northerly prevailing winds. This was their cue to start heading south. They would carry on south to ten degrees north, before heading towards the South American coast.

Seefalke had a much better sailing performance than those old ships, especially to windward. With my new sails, I planned to sail straight down the east coast of South America, sailing against the one-and-a-half knot current and into the prevailing wind. This was a more direct route than sailing halfway to the Azores first, and I would avoid the North Atlantic hurricane season.

With England out of the World Cup once more, the next day was spent clearing Barbados customs, getting my supply of fresh food and water, and washing clothes, ready for the 1700 nautical mile trip to Fortaleza. Feeling confident I'd be able to sail a hundred nautical miles a day, I estimated that the trip would take approximately seventeen days, but I decided to work on twenty-two days to allow for stronger than expected currents and periods of poor weather.

A couple of friends from the Hash wanted a sail on *Seefalke* before I left, and the next day was their only chance. Checking the weather forecast during my last happy hour in the Boatyard, the weather was settled for the next few days with a favourable trade wind.

***

Wednesday 1st July

I left Barbados with my friends from the Hash House Harriers. It was a lovely morning, sunny and warm. As I had a crew, I put my no.1 genoa up with a full mainsail and enjoyed an exhilarating sail. The guys wished me luck as I dropped them off close to a beach on the south side of the island. I hate to think what the people on the beach must have thought to see a yacht sail close in, two people jump into the water and swim ashore, only for the yacht to turn around and head back out to sea. I was lucky I didn't get stopped by the Coastguard.

It was a good feeling to be sailing alone again and getting some more sea miles under my belt.

12:00. Pos. 12°52'N 059°26'W

Logged 17NM from Bridgetown.

The wind was set and had been picking up from the east all afternoon. I changed down to a no.2 genoa. The no.1 was too big for me to handle on my own, and I couldn't see around it. The no.2 also reduced the weather helm, which made it easier for George to hold a course. A good result all round. Course 150° mag.

18:00

A good start to the trip. I had logged 53NM—not too bad after the messing around that morning.

The further south I sailed, the darker the clouds became. I had to reef the main and change down again to my no.3 genoa.

22:00

I sailed into a big rain squall, which came with a lot of thunder and lightning and an increasing amount of wind.

***

2nd day at sea
Thursday 2nd July

00:05

The night sky was lit up by thunder and lightning—great to see, but frightening. The wind was up and down, leaving the sea in a very confused state.

06:00

Overall, it was a poor night, not improved by me getting no sleep. To make matters even worse, I'd dropped the mainsail into the water while trying to reef it. I really struggled to get the wet mainsail back on board the yacht, and for some reason, I couldn't hoist it back up. I suspected another loose screw in the mast track, but even when I got my torch, I couldn't see the problem.

To finish things off, I lost the topping lift. The broken end wrapped itself around the top of the mast, leaving a right mess. I ended up sailing most of the night on just the no.2 genoa. It was a pretty miserable night all round.

After breakfast and my morning coffee, I got the broken topping lift off the mast and found the offending loose screw in the mast track. Soon after, I had the full mainsail back up, along with the no.2 genoa.

12:00. Pos. 11°16'N 058°31'W
Logged 110NM in the last 24 hours.

Even after last night's trials and tribulations, I had managed to log over a hundred nautical miles, which was good. Next up, George broke another tiller line, which I was getting used to fixing. I couldn't solve the root problem as it was an inherent design fault causing the line to rub on a screw. I had no way of fixing that at sea; it was something I'd have to live with.

18:00
The wind had dropped and the sea was flat. Wind southeast, force 3. Barometer 1016mb. Course 160° mag.

Curry and rice for tea, brandy in my coffee as a nightcap. It was a lovely clear night, and without any light pollution, the sky was full of stars. Brilliant!

***

3rd day at sea
Friday 3rd July

06:00
The wind had shifted to the east in the night and had picked up to force 4/5. I took advantage of the flat sea, and with the wind on the beam, I had enjoyed a few hours of easy sailing on a reach, the yacht moving easily at hull speed. Barometer 1013mb.

12:00. Pos. 10°00'N 057°33'W
Logged 95NM in the last 24 hours.

The wind remained in the east, bringing with it a lot of squalls blowing through all day. The yacht was leaking a bit but not too badly. This was something I had grown used to, but still, I needed to keep an eye on it.

***

4th day at sea
Saturday 4th July

06:00
Wind easterly, sea state moderate. I had another squally night.

12:00. Pos. 08°43'N 056°46'W
Logged 90NM in the last 24 hours.

I had covered some good ground over the previous 24 hours; the trouble was I'd only logged 90NM. I sensed that I had sailed into a stronger foul current. The wind had shifted to the south-east and forward of the beam. I decided to tack, with George steering an easterly course.

18:00
The force 3 wind was shifting all the time, meaning I had to keep tacking on each wind shift. My course kept changing depending on what tack I was on.

***

5th day at sea
Sunday 5th July

06:00
I sailed past a ship, which gave me the chance to call them up and get a weather forecast. There was a big tropical wave 21° north 33° west, travelling west at 35 miles an hour. A tropical wave is the first sign of a new hurricane forming.

Now that I was sailing below 12° north, thankfully, hurricanes were no longer an issue for me. My main problem was lack of wind, as I was approaching the Doldrums!

12:00. Pos. 07°57'N 055°58'W
Logged 66NM in the last 24 hours.

This was a very slow morning, and my last 24-hour run had been even worse. Progress was poor. The wind had returned to the prevailing south-east direction, meaning I was back to sailing hard on the wind. I was hoping for a better wind direction to take me through the night.

***

6th day at sea
Monday 6th July

00:05
I awoke to find the sky filled with dark black clouds and more squally weather. The wind was fluctuating in speed and direction, making it difficult for George to steer a constant course. All told, I had another miserable and long night sitting in the cockpit.

06:00
The new day brought further changes in the weather. The wind had become very light and variable. I was back to sailing with a full mainsail and no.2 genoa, in whatever direction kept the yacht moving and comfortable.

12:00. Pos. 07°15'N 055°12'W
Logged 62NM in the last 24 hours.

From my midday position, I was 75NM away from Paramaribo on the coast of Suriname. It was a shame I didn't have a chart of the area or any information on the harbours and their approaches.

18:00
The wind finally picked up after what had been a slow, hard day. Finally, I got a break. With the wind on the beam, *Seefalke* was sailing along nicely in flat seas at hull speed for the first time in days.

***

7th day at sea
Tuesday 7th July

06:00

The good breeze I'd had last night had gone, and once again, I was becalmed, with dark, squally clouds all around me.

10:30

I managed to take a shower in a rain squall that came through with no wind in it, which was a bit of a surprise. As I was drying myself off, I looked over the stern only to see a huge gust of wind coming towards me. With no time to put any clothes on, I quickly took the helm and eased out the sails. Then I had a very exhilarating alfresco downwind ride for the next ten minutes until the squall passed me by and I became becalmed once more.

12:00. Pos. 06°29'N 054°31'W

Logged 60 NM in the last 24 hours.

This had been my worst 24 hours since leaving Barbados. *Seefalke* was drifting along in a south-easterly direction with hardly any wind. What little progress I had made I put down to having picked up the south-easterly current that was flowing down the coast, which I didn't expect.

18:00

The calm conditions did offer some benefits. I was able to make some bread during the afternoon, which turned out well. For tea, I had peanut butter sandwiches. By this time, the wind had dropped to nothing, so I decided to take the sails down to prevent them from getting damaged, as they made a horrible noise when they flapped back and forth in the uncomfortable swell.

In the previous six hours, I had only logged two nautical miles; I had lost my favourable south-easterly current.

***

8th day at sea
Wednesday 8th July

06:00
The wind picked up early that morning. I was sailing again with full mainsail and no.2 genoa, heading east, looking for the favourable current again.

12:00. Pos. 06°44'N 054°09'W
Logged 26NM in the last 24 hours.

The wind returned to light and variable, and I was still stuck in the north-west-flowing current, which was taking me back up the coast. This was pretty demoralising.

I could see where the current changed to flow south, but I didn't have enough wind to sail into it. I was tantalisingly close, which made it all the more frustrating.

As there wasn't anything else to do but wait for better conditions, I decided to start reading a new book: *Zen and the Art of Motorcycle Maintenance* by Robert M. Prising. During my time in Israel, a friend of mine had raved about this book. However, after a hundred pages, it made no sense to me at all. So, for the first and only time, I threw a book over the side without reading another page.

18:00
This trip was becoming a real struggle. With adverse currents and little wind, it felt like a game of snakes and ladders: one minute I would make some progress and then the next, I was back to square one.

***

9th day at sea
Thursday 9th July

06:00
Last night, I was becalmed in the middle of a fishing fleet. Another very long night, with no sleep.

12:00. Pos. 07°06'N 054°07'W
Logged 22NM in the last 24 hours.

During the morning, the wind increased to a force 4 south-easterly. Finally, I was sailing again hard on the wind and into a choppy sea. I had green water rolling down the deck. The yacht was not comfortable in these conditions and was being pressed hard, but I really had to try to make some progress.

Course of 100° mag with one reef in the mainsail and the no.2 genoa.

18:00

I was hoping to maintain this course for a day or two, in the hope that the north-westerly current would start to weaken the further offshore I got and eventually, I would sail into the favourable counter-current taking me down the coast.

***

10th day at sea
Friday 10th July

06:00

After a very wet night, the wind had steadily increased to a south-easterly force 5/6, resulting in a much bigger swell. In order to make *Seefalke* more comfortable, I put a second reef in the mainsail.

12:00. Pos. 07°50'N 052°25'W

Logged 110NM in the last 24 hours.

From my midday fix, I wasn't where I expected to be. I had been sailing hard on the wind in rough conditions, resulting in quite a bit of leeway. Consequently, I hadn't broken free of the north-westerly current, which was severely hampering my progress. This was day ten and I was only 530NM from Barbados. Progress was painfully slow, only 53NM a day on average, and the conditions were taking their toll on me and the yacht.

14:30

I got hit by a big squall and the wind shifted to the south, so I could maintain a south-easterly heading, although there was a lot of wind and very choppy sea.

15:00

I couldn't believe it, but within half an hour, the wind had dropped to nothing, and I was left wallowing in the still very choppy sea. What an absolute joy this trip was turning into.

18:00

I was back to sailing in an easterly direction, with one reef in the mainsail and the no.3 genoa. George was holding a steady course despite the rough conditions. The wind was south-easterly force 4/5. The only benefit of sailing due east was that it was taking me out of the adverse, north-west-flowing current.

Seefalke had started to leak badly again; she didn't like being pushed so hard to windward in the rough conditions. I was back to pumping her out every hour, which was tiring work.

***

11th day at sea
Saturday 11th July

06:00

The yacht was sailing well, although we were still hard on the wind. It felt like I had started to pick up the favourable current again, which was running parallel to the coast. My speed over the ground was greater than my speed through the water.

12:00. Pos. 07°37'N 052°57'W

Logged 68NM in the last 24 hours.

The wind went back to an easterly force 4, and while I was still sailing hard on the wind, I was now back to sailing in the right direction with a favourable current.

18:00

The wind seemed to be holding steady and set for the night.

***

12th day at sea
Sunday 12th July

06:00

This was the first morning in days where I was greeted with a flat sea, sunshine, blue sky and a lovely warm breeze. It was great to be sailing on full mainsail and no.2 genoa for a change, holding a course of 140° mag.

12:00. Pos. 07°30'N 050°43'W

Logged 133NM in the last 24 hours.

I was sailing in the right direction for the second day in a row, which was good news, although my position was showing I had a lot of leeway. The wind had dropped, and I was still enjoying good sailing in flat water, still holding a course of 140° mag.

While I was trying to search for the BBC World Service on my short-wave radio, I managed to pick up the start of the World Cup final, to my pleasant surprise. I listened to the whole game. France beat Brazil 3–1 to win the World Cup. It's a shame I wasn't in a Brazilian bar watching the game.

***

13th day at sea
Monday 13th July

06:00

The wind had dropped right off, and I was becalmed all night. However, at first light, my lack of progress was offset by the sight of dolphins playing all around the yacht. I enjoyed watching them while topping up my tan. It was far better than watching TV, although once the dolphins departed, there wasn't much to do apart from trying to whistle up some wind.

12:00. Pos. 07°15'N 49°55'W

Logged 50NM in the last 24 hours.

By mid-morning, the wind had picked up from the east, back to force 4. I was once again sailing in the right direction. This was great sailing and more akin to the conditions I wanted.

18:00

I enjoyed a really good day sailing hard on the wind in flat water. *Seefalke* was eating up the sea miles and the dolphins stayed with the yacht for hours. I spent most of my day standing on the bow, watching the dolphins riding the bow wave. It was great to see them having so much fun. This was a magical experience.

***

14th day at sea
Tuesday 14th July

06:00

I had a really good sail during the night, and I watched the sunrise. This was the start of another glorious day.

12:00. Pos. 05°24'N 048°19'W

Logged 146NM in the last 24 hours.

After recording my best 24-hour run so far on this trip, I was a bit disappointed when the wind started to drop off in the afternoon. I was still making way, but only just. However, it wasn't all bad; I was still in the favourable current, which was continuing to carry *Seefalke* down the coast.

18:00

Despite 'ghosting' along for most of the afternoon, when I turned on my GPS, I was surprised to find I'd still managed to get 30NM closer to my destination in the last six hours, which must have been due mainly to the current.

***

15th day at sea
Wednesday 15th July

06:00

I had another squally night, although progress remained positive. It was funny—I got caught in one really big squall with lots of wind and rain one minute and then absolutely nothing the next.

For a time, the sea was like glass; the moonlight was reflecting so brightly on the water it seemed almost daylight. Just sitting there with the sails hanging from the mast was a surreal experience. Ten minutes later, all hell broke loose, with the wind and rain filling in from a totally different direction.

At first light, I noticed the sea around the yacht had changed to a muddy brown colour. After consulting my chart, I found I was 180NM east of the Amazon River. Despite being a long way offshore, the flow of the river was still having a strong impact on the speed and direction of the current. There was also a surprising amount of debris being washed out to sea, and I had to keep a close eye on submerged objects such as logs and trees.

12:00. Pos. 04°16'N 047°35'W

Logged 80NM in the last 24 hours.

From my midday position fix, I was well into the Intertropical Convergence Zone (ITCZ), commonly known as the Doldrums. I continued to experience really strange weather. Wind, no wind, flat seas, big seas—this was becoming a really hard sailing trip.

But this had been another hot, sunny morning. The sea was flat, with a good breeze, and I was really enjoying the sail. The yacht was gently heeled over and maintaining six to seven knots through the water. This was great sailing. Despite enjoying these lovely conditions, I had only managed to sail 12NM in the last three hours. I went from being really happy to feeling very frustrated in a heartbeat. I was back in the north-west-flowing current, which was devastating.

18:00

It had been a long day. The wind had dropped once again to a light breeze, and I could not keep *Seefalke* sailing on the correct course. In order to keep the yacht moving, I found myself chasing the wind, which was really frustrating and pointless.

***

16th day at sea
Thursday 16th July

06:00
The wind picked up early that evening and remained steady. My sixth sense woke me up with pins and needles in my toes. Out on the horizon, I could see two ships heading towards me. I quickly put *Seefalke* about and then stayed on deck until they had both passed. I then tacked back onto my original course before returning to my bunk.

06:00
The wind was a light south-easterly, and it was shaping up to be another lovely day.

12:00. Pos. 04°13'N 046°33'W
Logged 62NM in the last 24 hours.

The yacht seemed to be making good progress during the morning, despite the sea being very confused. It was all very weird. Luckily, I found the south-easterly current, which was taking me closer to my destination. It was really important that I stayed in the south-flowing stream this time.

To pass the time, I decided to make some fresh bread.

18:00
The afternoon brought more good sailing, and the current continued to carry me south. However, it wasn't all good news. The bread was a complete flop; the sea was too rough for the dough to rise.

I tacked again, and my new course fluctuated between 160° and 180° mag.

***

17th day at sea
Friday 17th July

06:00
I didn't wake up once that night. The yacht had slipped through the water almost silently.

The seawater had finally gone back to a blue colour. One more danger avoided.

12:00. Pos. 03°38'N 044°57'W
Logged 120NM in the last 24 hours.

I was sat on the coach roof, in the shade of the mainsail, reading my book, when my sixth sense told me that something was up. I looked up from my book, to find a yacht half a mile away, directly opposite me, with a guy sitting on the coach roof, reading a book. I looked at his sails; he had the same sail set-up as me. Sailing to windward, but on a completely opposite course to mine. Strange. We looked at each other, gave each other a wave, and then, we both carried on reading. Funny. It illustrated just how fickle the wind and currents were along this coast.

18:00
The wind had returned to squalls, blowing from all directions, I was back to sailing in a very short, sharp, confused sea. Out on the horizon, I saw very large, menacing black clouds with wind and rain under them, all heading my way.

***

18th day at sea
Saturday 18th July

06:00
I experienced a very long, hard, noisy night, and I ended up with no sleep at all. There was a recurring theme of lots of wind one minute followed by none the next. At first light, I experienced one last, large squall, before the weather cheered up and the wind stabilised. I had blue skies and favourable wind; it was good to be alive. The yacht was once again tracking along nicely.

12:00. Pos. 02°36'N 043°56'W
Logged 73NM in the last 24 hours.

The wind had shifted to the north-east and picked up. For once, the wind was behind me, and I was enjoying some great downwind sailing. Any wind direction other than south-easterly was good news. I was now only 500NM from Fortaleza, or five days away, if these conditions held up.

18:00
I had another change in the weather, with more squalls coming through. One brought with it very strong wind, and I ended up having to sail west for a period. I was glad that I had taken the early decision to put in the third reef before it got dark.

***

19th day at sea
Sunday 19th July

06:00
The wind was back in the south-east and had been blowing force 5/6 all night. The best course I could make was 080° mag hard on the wind, which was rubbish for the direction I was heading in. I was punching into big seas, and if these conditions prevailed, the last five hundred miles were going to be punishing. The wind gods certainly hadn't made this an easy trip at all.

By mid-morning, the wind had backed to the east, leaving a very confused sea. I changed course to 135° mag and at the same time reduced sail to a no.3 genoa and put two reefs in the mainsail. *Seefalke* was much better balanced, but I was still encountering lots of wind and big seas. The deck was underwater most of the time, and I was pumping the yacht out every half an hour.

12:00. Pos. 02°01′N 043°08′W
Logged 59NM in the last 24 hours.

Sailing down the coast had once again turned into hard work. The basic issue was that I was experiencing strong prevailing south-easterly winds, together with rough, confused seas. Unfortunately, the laws of physics prevent yachts from sailing directly into the wind—even the latest America's Cup boats haven't cracked this. In order to maintain a reasonable speed and to nurse *Seefalke* along, I was only able to sail around forty-five degrees into the wind. In perfect conditions, *Seefalke* would have been capable of sailing a lot closer.

On top of this, I was suffering around ten degrees of leeway due to the conditions. Leeway is the yacht effectively being pushed sideways through the water, away from the desired course. This is caused by a combination of wind and waves. The cumulative effect of the leeway was a track through the water of 55 to 60 degrees either side of the south-easterly wind, and ultimately my destination. In simple terms, the passage to Fortaleza was taking twice as long as expected.

My GPS provided speed over the ground (SOG) data. Using this and the true wind direction, I could work out my VMG (Velocity Made Good), the correlation between optimum boat speed and the best angle for sailing into the wind. By understanding my VMG, I could choose the best tack for taking me closer to my destination. Without the GPS, it would have been a lot harder for me to work out which tack to take at any given point in time. It was important that I made the correct decision to tack or not each time the wind shifted. Anything more than a ten-degree adverse change in the wind direction, and I would tack, but if I stayed on the wrong tack for too long, the north-west current and adverse effects of the wind shift would negatively impact my course, and once more, I would start sailing away from my desired destination.

18:00

I was encountering more big seas. Everything was wet. I stayed below deck, pumping out the yacht every hour.

***

20ᵗʰ day at sea
Monday 20ᵗʰ July

06:00

It was a long night, but I awoke to blue skies and big seas. The wind was blowing a steady force 5/6 from the southeast.

12:00. Pos. 00°57'N 042°45'W
Logged 68NM in the last 24 hours.

From my midday fix, Fortaleza was 380NM away. The prevailing south-easterly wind remained strong. This constant headwind was making my progress frustratingly slow.

Having to work out the 'making tack' all the time was becoming mentally draining, and having to tack on a regular basis was soul-destroying. I'd become really demoralised with the constant alteration of course and the hours upon hours of pounding to windward. In an attempt to find better sailing conditions, I decided to take a leg out into the Atlantic, heading east. I hoped that at some point, the wind would back to the east and enable me to tack. Then all I would need to do was pray that I could lay a course to Fortaleza on one long port tack.

18:00

Cooking my tea had become a challenge; I had to hold the pan on the stove to prevent it ending up on the cabin sole. I had plenty of food, but fresh water was running low. Sleeping at night was getting harder with the noise of the yacht constantly bashing to windward in big seas. The sound of green water running over the deck and rushing down the side of the hull wasn't helping either.

***

21st day at sea
Tuesday 21st July

06:00

I awoke to the sound of water sloshing around inside the yacht. I had been using the automatic bilge pump to allow me to sleep for two hours at a time. It had flattened my batteries, which weren't being fully charged—as I found out later, one of my solar panels had packed up.

The weather was the same as the previous days. Big seas, wind south-easterly, force 5/6. This was starting to feel like Groundhog Day.

12:00. Pos. 01°36'N 041°45'W
Logged 70NM in the last 24 hours.

I was still pushing the yacht hard to windward and was continuing to sail away from my destination, which was utterly demoralising. The wind seemed to be blowing constantly from the south-east with no sign of any change. To make matters worse, the north-westerly current was pushing *Seefalke* back up the coast.

***

22nd day at sea
Wednesday 22nd July

06:00

Without any power, I was back to pumping the yacht out by hand every hour, which was exhausting and made for another long, sleepless night. I was greeted by more of the same: big, short seas and a steady force 5 south-easterly wind. The yacht was getting swamped, with green water rolling down the deck.

12:00. Pos. 02°06'N 040°46'W
Logged 67NM in the last 24 hours.

I desperately needed the wind to shift to give me some respite and allow me to tack onto a heading that would at least take me closer to Fortaleza. Instead, I was still heading away from the coast in the same very challenging conditions.

18:00

Wind and seas had abated slightly, although my course remained unaltered. I shook the third reef out of the mainsail but stayed with the no.3 genoa. The yacht seemed balanced and comfortable.

***

23rd day at sea
Thursday 23rd July

06:00

At first light, I awoke to the same nightmare. The conditions were pretty much the same as the day before: south-easterly winds, big seas, and wet. I had run out of dry clothes and was continuing to pump the yacht out every hour.

12:00. Pos. 02°36'N 039°16'W
Logged 95NM in the last 24 hours.

The wind had dropped during the morning and finally became variable. I decided to tack in anticipation of the new breeze. My heading was 160°mag—at last, I was on a heading taking me towards Fortaleza, which was still 380NM away.

It was a lovely day for a change: blue sky, hot and perfect for drying clothes. To top it all off, I had dolphins all around the yacht. Maybe my luck was about to finally change.

18:00
I was making further progress towards Fortaleza still joined by lots of dolphins, which had really lifted my mood.

***

24th day at sea
Friday 24th July

06:00
I awoke to another overcast day. All night I had experienced short, sharp, steep seas, with the wind fluctuating between east and south-east, allowing me to set a southerly course. The one positive factor was that the dolphins had stayed with me the whole time, which had buoyed my mood throughout the night.

12:00. Pos. 01°17'N 039°11'W
Logged 80NM in the last 24 hours.

I had 300NM to go. After my brief reprieve, the wind had picked back up and so had the sea. All this sailing to windward wasn't doing the yacht any good; she was now leaking badly. I had been trying to fix the leaks, but it was impossible from inside the yacht. Also, the port top shroud had started to fray, and I was keeping a very close eye on this. If it failed altogether, I was almost certainly going to lose the top section of the mast.

18:00
Still moving, still sinking.

***

25th day at sea
Saturday 25th July

06:00
Wind and seas and course remained constant, with yet another overcast sky.

11:05
I had been looking at my GPS all morning, watching the latitude numbers on the screen getting closer to zero until I crossed the equator. There was no celebration, but I did wonder whether the water would now turn in an anticlockwise direction when I pulled the plug out of my sink.

12:00. Pos. 00°03'S 039°11'W
Logged 80NM in the last 24 hours.
Sadly, the South Atlantic didn't bring any respite or more favourable conditions. In over a week, there had been only one day's break from the constant south-east wind.

18:00
The wind had been shifting all afternoon between 180° and 135° mag. It made the sailing challenging, tacking on each wind shift to maintain my best COG (Course Over the Ground).

***

26th day at sea
Sunday 26th July

06:00
I'd had another long night, with the force 4/5 wind fluctuating between south and south-east. Once again there were big seas. I was sailing with two reefs in the mainsail and the no.3 genoa. I tried sailing on just the full mainsail,

but the yacht was over-pressed and kept rounding up into the wind, dropping my speed to three knots. My speed over the ground was virtually zero; the yacht's speed was being cancelled out by the adverse current.

To add to my misery, the jib halyard snapped in the night. Luckily, I had a spare already rigged on the mast—what fun. The joys of sailing.

12.00. Pos. 01°08'S 039°05'W
Logged 65NM in the last 24 hours.

I was still trying to bash my way south. The yacht was taking an absolute pounding. It was clear that the weather gods weren't on my side.

***

27th day at sea
Monday 27th July

06:00
The conditions deteriorated overnight, with the sea being whipped up by the force 7/8 southerly wind. I put the storm jib up at first light. The weather was really starting to take its toll on the yacht. It was leaking badly; I was now pumping her out every half hour. The port top shroud was also getting worse, so overall, things weren't great.

12:00. Pos. 01°38'S 038°55'W
Logged 31NM in the last24 hours.

It really was tough sailing. The conditions remained the same—very rough, very wet—and I was still sailing hard to windward, with the leeward rail constantly underwater.

18:00
The wind finally eased, and the sea started to moderate. I shook two reefs out of the mainsail and hoisted the no.2 genoa. I was now making good on my southerly course.

***

28th day at sea
Tuesday 28th July

06:00

I didn't get much of a reprieve; the wind had gone back to the south-east and was back up to force 6/7. Despite the short, sharp sea, I tried to maintain a southerly heading.

I had been watching three red things on the horizon for about an hour before I finally worked out they were sails. I managed to sail close enough to give them a wave. They were local fishermen sailing on what looked like windsurfers—one man and a boy, sailing on twenty-foot-long skiffs, with only six inches of freeboard carrying a huge red mainsail. They were only wearing T-shirts and shorts; they were crazy. There I was, on a forty-foot yacht, sailing with a reefed mainsail and genoa, wearing my full waterproofs, cold and wet from the spray.

How those fishermen were going to get back to the beach from which they departed was completely beyond me.

12:00. Pos. 02°56'S 039°26'W

Logged 84NM in the last 24 hours.

For the first time in twenty-eight days, I sighted land. The wind was still blowing from the south-east, force 5/6. I was now sailing to windward on a starboard tack heading east. Fortaleza was now only 72NM away. It felt like my hell was finally ending. This trip had been a nightmare from the start.

18:00

The wind dropped to nothing, and thankfully the sea flattened off too. *Seefalke* and I got a much-needed break from sailing in those brutal conditions—we had been beating to windward for almost a month in strong winds and heavy seas. Despite the let-up in the wind, the rain squalls returned. What joy!

***

29th day at sea
Tuesday 29th July

06:00

During the night, I had put my head down for five minutes at midnight and suddenly awoke to the sound of water sloshing around the yacht. I had been asleep for four hours and the cabin sole was awash. After I pumped the water out, which took an age, I checked the compass. *Seefalke* was sailing north.

It looked as though the wind had gone around in a circle and George had done the same, given that we were still in the same position as when I went to sleep. This was hopeless. The only consolation was we hadn't sailed west and hit that big lump of rock commonly known as Brazil.

12:00. Pos. 02°28'S 038°50'W

Logged only 45NM in the last 24 hours.

During the morning, the wind shifted to the east then north-east, and dropped to a force 2/3. I took advantage of the wind shift and sailed straight towards Fortaleza. My new course was 150° mag. I was fully powered up with a full mainsail and no.1 genoa. There was still a big sea to contend with, but at least the wind wasn't on the nose for once, so I decided to push *Seefalke* hard. Fortaleza was only 76NM away. My finish line was finally in sight, thank goodness.

18:00

The wind was slowly dropping off. Course 150° mag.

***

30th day at sea
Thursday 30th July

06:00

If I'd written a novel about this trip, I don't think anyone would have believed the story. After thirty days of bashing into big seas, battling against the prevailing wind and current, I spent the whole night becalmed with only rain fronts passing through. Early in the morning, there was more of the same cloudy, overcast conditions, with lots of rain but no wind.

12:00. Pos. 03°06'S 038°37'W

Logged 41NM in the last 24 hours.

The wind started to freshen during the morning, once again from the south-east. It was back to a force 5/6 with more big seas. I was back to sailing hard on the wind but maintaining a course that was taking me directly towards Fortaleza. I was really pushing the yacht, with plenty of green water coming over the deck.

It was a make-or-break day—the port top shroud was getting worse by the hour and needed urgent attention.

18:00

The wind and waves started to abate as I got closer to the coast. I could start to make out Fortaleza, which was some ten miles away. It was going to be dark by the time I got to the harbour. However, with the direction of the wind and current off Fortaleza, I had no choice but to make an approach. If I didn't seize this opportunity, I could be out at sea for another couple of days.

21:00

I was pretty apprehensive about approaching an unfamiliar harbour at night. There was lots of background light from the town, making it hard to pick out the leading lights for the harbour entrance. I was sailing on just the mainsail, to slow the yacht down and provide increased visibility.

Despite all my efforts, I somehow managed to sail the wrong side of the harbour breakwater. I only saw the large concrete breakwater when I was less than a hundred feet away from hitting it. This summed up the whole blasted trip.

After a quick turnaround, I sailed back out on a reciprocal course and managed to pick out the light at the end of the breakwater leading into the harbour. This was the first time I had been in tranquil conditions in weeks.

I finally dropped anchor by two cargo ships at twenty-two hundred hours. I had been at sea for thirty days. Both the yacht and I badly needed some rest and recuperation.

***

Friday 31st July

I slept straight through that night, which was the first time I had slept properly for a month. My chart had referred to two wrecks in the harbour which were unlit, but all I could see when I'd dropped the anchor were the two ships I had anchored close to. With the benefit of daylight, the two wrecks were clearly visible, and I had sailed straight past them on the way to my anchorage without even noticing them. I had been lucky not to hit them.

I spent the morning relaxing on the yacht, looking at the harbour around me. By midday, I started trying to contact the marina, which, based on the information in my cruising guide, was adjacent to the Marina Hotel, but other than that, the guide provided very little additional information.

I tried calling the marina using the VHF radio on channel 16 to obtain further information but to no avail. I did, however, get a call back from the Coastguard service. The lady spoke very good English, which enabled me to ask for the information I required.

Five minutes later, she called me back and gave me the position of the Marina Hotel. She said she had spoken to George, the marina manager, and he was expecting me to call him up. At last, I felt like I was finally getting somewhere and thanked the lady for her considerable help.

It wasn't until I marked the position of the marina on the chart that I realised that something was wrong. The position given to me was thirty miles north of Fortaleza and twenty miles inland. I had no option but to call the Coastguard back and query the position that I had been given.

My new friend contacted George again and then called me back to confirm where I was moored.

I said, "I'm anchored in Fortaleza Harbour by the two ships—can you see me?"

She replied, "I should explain that I am sitting in Rio. Not Fortaleza!"

"Oh," I said.

The Coastguard operator got hold of George again and passed on some more instructions that were just as useless as the position I'd been given earlier. I thanked her for her help.

I then saw the harbourmaster's launch and called him over. Thankfully, one of the crew spoke English.

"Are you okay?" he asked. "Are you in any trouble?"

"No, I just need to find out where the Marina Hotel is."

"Okay. When we finish work later, we will show you."

By now it was four o'clock. I was going to stay where I was, happy to be at anchor in calm water.

Half an hour later, a man sailing a Hobie Cat came alongside. His English was pretty poor, but I did manage to understand the words "yacht club follow me".

On mainsail only, I followed the man on the Hobie Cat. He advised me to anchor about two hundred feet off the yacht club.

The yacht club was huge. I could see an Olympic-size swimming pool, a large, manicured lawn and a view over the harbour. The waiters were dressed immaculately, and the restaurant was set out for about five hundred people. Everything looked very expensive, and certainly out of my league. The funny thing was there were no other yachts around apart from mine.

After my first hot shower in over a month, I was asked by one of the waiters if I wanted to eat. I advised that I had no Brazilian currency, and the waiter replied, "Just run a tab."

I had to decline the offer. From what I could see, the yacht club looked way too expensive for me.

My friend with the Hobie Cat found an English-speaking waiter. He explained that the port captain would take me to the marina the following day, which was great. He also told me to be vigilant that evening because I had moored up next to a very, very poor fishing village, which was right on the beach.

Before it got dark, I went back out to the yacht. I slept well until 1 a.m., I then got up, had a good look around, put the cabin lights on to make it look as if I was awake and then crashed out again.

Early the next morning, the port captain came alongside in his harbour launch to confirm that he would tow me into the marina that evening after he finished work. I had a relaxing day sunbathing, and in the early afternoon, the port captain returned as promised. I was towed astern of the launch; I lashed the tiller amidships and then started getting the fenders and mooring lines ready in preparation for getting the yacht into a marina birth. I had left the anchor on deck, just in case I needed it.

The port captain slowed the harbour launch down to ask me a question: "How much water does the yacht draw?"

"Two metres."

"How fast can we tow you?"

"Six knots."

He then panicked when *Seefalke* kept her way on and nearly smashed into the engines on the back of their launch. I realised the crew had never towed a yacht before. After half an hour, the small harbour came into view. I could see the yacht masts sticking up above the dock wall.

I thought, *Great—a nice, easy upwind tow into the marina.* All was going well until I realised too late that the harbour was in two parts. The outer harbour was into the wind, which I thought would help the port captain to slow down and put the launch alongside *Seefalke* and safely manoeuvre me onto a berth. The marina itself was in the lower, downwind part of the harbour.

Before I had a chance to do or say anything, the port captain had other ideas. He turned the launch quickly towing me straight into the marina at six knots. Panic set in. Going downwind at speed, there was no way I was going to stop *Seefalke* apart from hitting the back of their launch or hitting the dock wall—which was getting closer by the second. I tried to shout a warning to the port captain and his crew, who were blissfully unaware of the panic I was in. Great. Oh, what fun you have sailing a yacht with no engine.

I had no choice. I ran forward to the bow, dropped the tow line and threw the anchor into the water at the same time. Luckily for me, I had the chain made fast on the capstan—there was no way I would have been able to hold it or stop it running out by hand when the anchor dug in. Thankfully, *Seefalke* spun round, stopping with her stern only ten feet off the harbour wall. I breathed a big sigh of relief. The thought of writing the yacht off after thirty days of bashing way to windward to get there wouldn't have been great for my soul.

Getting onto a berth wasn't a problem. A guy rowed over in a dinghy and introduced himself as Andre.

"I watched you getting towed in here," he said. "Do you have engine problems?"

"It's more like I don't have an engine."

"Well, it looked like you had fun getting in."

"Yes, no thanks to the idiots in the launch."

Andre took my stern line ashore, and with his help, we managed to get *Seefalke* safely moored up. Before I had time to thank him, he walked off, only to return a few minutes later.

What a boy—he handed me a cold beer. My first in a month. This was the best beer I had ever tasted. After the performance of nearly losing the yacht in the marina, I needed it. In fact, I needed lots of beers.

Andre Delius and his crew were South African. They were trying to deliver a yacht to Cape Town, and it had taken them fifty-seven days to get to Fortaleza from St Martin. Andre told me another yacht had come in just after them and it had taken fifty-six days to get here—my thirty days was good.

I asked, "Does the strong south-easterly wind ever stop blowing?"

The reply was not what I wanted to hear: "We've been here a month and it hasn't stopped blowing yet."

That evening I partied with Andre and his crew, meeting the rest of the small group of sailors in the marina. I had a great night. I played my guitar, drank too much—it was simply good to be around people again. Every sailor had their own story to tell about how they got there. That evening, I also met Peter and Terry Lattimore, a lovely Australian couple who were sailing around the world on a thirty-four-foot steel ketch with their two kids.

Chapter 18
Looking Around Brazil

The next morning, with a thick head, I finally met George the marina manager. He spoke some English and was friendly, pointing out that there was an ATM in the hotel.

George also told me where I would have to go to find the immigration department, which was a short walk away from the marina in Fortaleza. I decided to postpone my visit to immigration until the following morning.

After thirty days at sea, I had a lot of basic chores to do. First, I disposed of all the plastic I had kept, then I sorted out my laundry at the marina. While I waited, I filled up my water tanks from the dock water supply. Outside the hotel, I found a small post-office-like shop where I could make an international phone call, and called home. There was also a petrol station where I could get my batteries charged, which was really handy. More importantly, it sold a range of basic goods like food, beer and ice. I owed Andre quite a few beers following the party.

The next day, I was up early and on a mission to sort out my immigration and customs paperwork. With my clearance papers from St Martin in hand, I walked into town.

I soon noticed that all the shops were selling the same thing: bikinis. This seemed to fit with my other observation, which was that there were a lot of young, fit, tanned people around.

I found my way to the immigration office, which was closed, I deduced from the opening times on the door that the staff were on their lunch break. Instead of venturing back out into the midday sun, I decided to wait the half an hour in the shade of the really impressive immigration building.

As I waited, another guy turned up, and we got talking. John was an American on passage back to the States; he had anchored just outside the immigration office and was planning to move his yacht into the marina once he cleared immigration. I agreed to help him once our paperwork was sorted. John was very grateful for the help. Like me, he hadn't had any joy in contacting George at the marina.

The immigration officer turned up on time and spoke perfect English. He invited us both into his office and asked if we'd arrived together.

"No," I said.

"Well, who was first?"

"That would be me," I said.

I handed him my passport and yacht papers.

"Are you British?" he said. "Welcome to Brazil." He stamped my passport, saying, "I have given you a ninety-day visa. It's free. If you want to stay longer in Brazil, come back and see me."

"That's great, thanks," I said. "Do you mind if I wait here for my friend?"

"No," the officer replied.

I sat on a chair, expecting John to be sorted out just as quickly as I had been. John handed over his passport and yacht papers to the friendly immigration officer, who I heard say, "American, are you?"

"Yes, sir," was his reply.

"Come here, please."

John was fingerprinted, his photo was taken, he had three lots of paperwork to fill in, and to cap it all, he was asked for two hundred and fifty dollars for his ninety-day visa. I looked on in disbelief. Finally, after paying the cash, John, got his passport stamped.

I opened the door leading out of the office, allowing John to go first. Before I left, I looked at the immigration officer.

"What was that all about?" I asked.

He shrugged his shoulders and said, "That's the way we Brazilians get treated in America, so we treat them the same when they come here. You British have no restriction on us travelling to the UK, so you have no problem in Brazil."

As I watched, he grabbed John's paperwork, screwed it up and threw the whole lot in the bin. We both started to laugh.

"What are you laughing about?" asked John.

"The immigration guy has just lobbed all the forms he made you fill in into the bin," I told him.

"I'm not surprised," John said. "We're not much liked by our southern neighbours—America hasn't exactly helped them over the years."

I helped John move his yacht up to the marina, and over a few beers, we had a good laugh at his immigration fiasco.

Over the following week, I scoured the town for a yacht chandlery, but to no avail. I concluded that the concept of sailing and cruising yachts had not yet reached this part of Brazil. There were no yacht facilities at all, and I couldn't find the parts I needed to fix my rigging. My top shroud desperately needed replacing. In a moment of dread, I even contemplated ringing Deadloss to get him to make two new ones and have them shipped over to me.

Andre gave me a spare Sta-Lok fitting, and with some galvanised chain, I managed to repair the broken cap shroud by way of a crude jury rig. All my other jobs had been slowly ticked off, meaning I could move on again if I wanted to, but before sailing any further south, I needed a different weather system to move in, hopefully bringing more favourable winds and better conditions. The weather was really consistent: hot and sunny, with constant strong south-easterly winds.

To pass my time, I spent lazy days on the beach drinking beer, taking in the lovely scenery and watching the kids play football. I must admit, the beaches were great.

Periodically, a beggar would come up to me and ask for money. I would say no, at which point the beggar would quite happily wander off with no offence taken. On one occasion, someone came up to me trying to sell a painting that had to be at least six by four feet in size. I couldn't help but admire the guy's entrepreneurial spirit. The more run-of-the-mill salespeople focused on the easier sale of nuts or ice cream.

One really bizarre sales pitch I received while sat on the beach was from a boy who asked if I wanted to buy a starter motor for a Volkswagen Beetle. I had to laugh.

During my time at Fortaleza, I spent a lot of it helping Andre put his yacht back together. After fifty-seven days at sea, it was in a right state. The yacht had a number of issues which slowly we managed to fix.

Andre had to get the yacht to Cape Town and had decided to try to break out of Fortaleza. Over a beer, he told me that he planned to motor straight into the wind close to the coast until he picked up more favourable winds. I helped him leave the marina the next morning and wished him lots of luck—he was certainly going to need it!

Another morning, Peter came over and asked if I could help him fix his roller furling gear. I was extremely pleased to help.

A roller furling system provides the means to reef a headsail by rolling the sail around the forestay and, in doing so, reducing the overall sail area. Furling gears are a common sight on cruising boats as they negate the need to go forward to the bow to conduct headsail changes—something you don't want to be doing when you're short-handed in bad weather. I could have used a furling system on *Seefalke*.

As I walked down the dock to Peter's yacht, I met Terry, who was off shopping with their older son, Mike. Peter had agreed to stay behind to look after their baby boy, Darcy, who was only two. When I arrived on board, Peter was sat in the cockpit with Darcy, who had his short little legs sticking out the bottom of his shorts; he reminded me of Calvin from the *Calvin and Hobbes* cartoon. I could see that Darcy was going to be a real handful in the not-too-distant future.

The roller furling gear was sitting in the cockpit where I needed to work, so Peter put Darcy below in the cabin, quiet and happy.

Looking at the roller furling gear, I asked Peter what had happened to it and whether he had the manual. He said that a bearing had collapsed in the roller mechanism and thankfully, he had managed to buy a replacement from town, although he didn't have the manual.

Peter had already tried putting the gear back together, without success. I took it apart again, checked out all the components, which looked okay, and then put it back together. Still didn't work. After my third attempt, I managed to get it working properly. Peter was delighted with my help and relieved that he could carry on sailing. After we refitted the furling gear to the mast and slid the sail back up the foil, we returned to the cockpit to relax with a cold beer. Just as we sat down, Darcy climbed up to the top step of the companionway ladder and stuck his little head out into the cockpit. He then lent over the washboard, picked up his football and started to bounce it. Each time the ball hit the deck he said, "Fuck."

The two of us were crying with laughter, Darcy kept repeating the word.

"Fuck, fuck, fuck."

"Oh my god—where did he get that from?" Peter said

"He must have heard me say it!"

Of all the words we'd used that morning like "split pins", "plyers", etc., the only one Darcy had picked up was a damn swear word. I couldn't help laughing at the prospect of Peter trying to explain to Terry how he had managed to teach their two-year-old a really bad swear word in the brief time she had been shopping. Peter was going to be in the doghouse for sure.

Peter and Terry were keen to carry on their trip north; their next stop was going to be Trinidad. Now that the roller reefing was fixed, you would have thought the Australians were free to carry on sailing. However, there was a far greater crisis preventing them from leaving Fortaleza: they had run out of crunchy peanut butter and couldn't find anywhere that sold it. This was a major issue, and without restocking their supply, the future of their trip looked to be in jeopardy. This called for an all-hands-on-deck approach, and so it was agreed that the crews of the five neighbouring yachts would split up and scour the town in search of crunchy peanut butter. This was a mission of the utmost importance.

I walked into my allotted supermarket, only to find that the whole floor space was taken up with boxes upon boxes of chocolate. There was no food at all on the ground floor of the shop. How could this country be occupied by so many young, fit, attractive people, when all you could see was chocolates? The complete set-up seemed crazy to me.

I got back to the marina just as Andre was sailing in. I gave him a hand to tie up and presented him with a beer, which couldn't have come any sooner. When I asked him about his trip, he said it was just relentless.

He'd encountered constant strong headwinds and a short, sharp sea, making life very unpleasant. Andre had really started to worry about how he was ever going to make the passage to South Africa without having to bash his way to windward for half the trip, which was thousands of miles. He couldn't sail into the North Atlantic until November, as it was still the hurricane season.

I had the same problem.

I'm sorry to report that our mission to track down crunchy peanut butter ended in failure. Peter and Terry decided to leave anyway, agreeing to make do with a very poor substitute—smooth peanut butter. We had a few beers with them that night, which enabled us to swap a few books. I desperately needed some fresh reading material, as I'd read all the books I had during my thirty-day trip to Fortaleza.

After two weeks, I decided to have a go at leaving myself. The wind was just as bad as it had been on the way in, and the seas were as big. The yacht started to leak badly, with all the bashing and pounding to windward. In 24 hours, I sailed 90 nautical miles over the ground, but according to my GPS, I only managed a demoralising thirty nautical miles against my south-easterly track. If I'd carried on, I would have ended up in real trouble, so I ran back, sailing downwind to the safety of the marina. This time, I managed to sail in without issue.

The next day, as I sat on the beach pondering, I watched a local fisherman struggling to drag his skiff up the beach. I went and gave him a hand. His skiff looked more like a windsurfer than a fishing boat.

After catching my breath, I asked him, "When do the south-easterlies stop blowing, or at least die down?"

The answer I received wasn't great. The fisherman explained that the earliest the wind could change was September, although it could be as late as Christmas or not at all. Some years, the south-easterlies had been known to prevail the whole year.

I was in a real quandary. In terms of heading south, I could either wait until the wind hopefully dropped or changed direction, or I could sail halfway across the North Atlantic after the end of the hurricane season, to pick up the more favourable southerly airflow. Neither of these options was financially viable, and so I either needed to find work locally or head back north.

There was a commercial boatyard adjacent to the marina, so I went to talk with the yard manager about securing some work. The manager seemed very interested in the idea and gave me a tour of the workshops. The company had just finished building a one-hundred-foot-long motorboat for a wealthy American, which I had the pleasure of looking over. Before I left the boatyard, the manager told me the first sea trial was in the morning and to call back in the afternoon.

I took the opportunity to watch the first sea trial of the motorboat. From a bench in the park overlooking the harbour, I watched as the motorboat left the harbour with the Stars and Stripes flying proudly from the stern. The boat looked magnificent, although embarrassingly, the huge flag was flying upside down. I had to laugh.

After my morning of entertainment, I returned to *Seefalke*. Although I was berthed in the marina, I had to access the yacht via my dinghy, which had been in the water for three weeks and was starting to turn green. I could also see that the bottom needed a clean, so I decided to get the dinghy out and give it a spruce up. On closer inspection, the bottom was covered in thousands of small barnacles. Following the rudder episode, this filled me with dread, and so I promptly decided to have a quick snorkel and inspect the underside of the yacht. To my dismay, the bottom was also covered in barnacles.

I had to ask myself: if I stayed and worked in Fortaleza for a year or two, would I still have a yacht to sail on?

No, I thought, so I never went back to the boatyard.

Decision made: sailing south was out of the question due to the relentless south-easterly winds and adverse current, but I couldn't stay here any longer due to the barnacles. I spent my last days in Fortaleza getting the yacht ready to sail again. The friendly immigration officer was surprised to see I was leaving so soon; I had only been in Brazil for twenty days.

With fresh food and water on board, I was ready to move again. That evening, I met up for a beer with Andre, who was also leaving the next day and kindly agreed to tow me out. Andre's latest plan was to head north-east on a reach for a week or two before starting to head south. It sounded like he might succeed this time, although he would have to sail a lot further.

***

Friday 28th August

I was up early. With a wave, I thanked Andre for the tow out and wished him well. He would need all the luck he could get.

I hoisted the no.2 genoa, and for once, I had the strong south-easterly wind and current behind me and I was making excellent progress.

In the first two days, I covered 300NM effortlessly. It was hot and sunny, George had everything under control, and there was very little for me to do other than sunbathe and read. Going through my recently acquired books, I saw *Papillon*, a story about Henri Charriere's imprisonment on an island. I'd read it before but decided to read it again.

I sailed up the coast for about a week before I entered the Doldrums, which proved as big of a pain as on the way down. There was no wind, and worse still, there were plenty of rain squalls: the perfect combination for dire sailing in a yacht without an engine.

When I plotted my midday position on the chart of 5°N 50°W, I was pretty close to the small group of islands that formed the Îles du Salut. I recognised these islands from somewhere, then it clicked—it was from the book I was reading. I wasn't in a rush to go anywhere fast, and there looked to be a bay on the southern side of Île Royale that I could anchor in, so I decided to investigate further.

There was not much wind when I drifted up the coast towards the islands. The first thing that struck me was just how lush and green they were. The islands were a tropical paradise, although that hid an altogether more sinister past. France used these islands as a notorious penal colony from 1852 and only closed it in 1953.

The Îles du Salut is a group of three islands. Saint-Joseph Island has the prison on it where Papillon (Henri Charriere) was imprisoned for nine years before his escape. Île Royale is where the guards and their families lived. The most famous island of them all is Devil's Island, infamous for the imprisonment of Captain Alfred Dreyfus from 1895 to 1899. He was the only person ever to be imprisoned on the island.

I anchored in a beautiful, sheltered bay. The view from the yacht was of a flat green clearing with painted wooden houses around it. There wasn't a beach, just a wooden dock wall two feet high, with palm trees all around. I was eager to go ashore and explore.

I rowed ashore only to be greeted by a French police officer (gendarme).

"Good afternoon. Passport and yacht papers please," he said. "And how long are you staying?"

"Only three or four days," I said.

"Okay. I will need to keep your passport until you leave. If you need to find me it's not hard; I am the only gendarme on the island. One more thing: You cannot go to Devil's Island."

As I explored Royale and spent time talking with the locals, I found that there was no record of Papillon ever being on the island. There were, however, references to him being on another island further south, which was a leper colony at the time. This made sense to me—there were a lot of other mistakes in the book. It's still a brilliant book to read and a really interesting story.

I got lucky again: the BBC had a film crew on the islands, making a documentary. I spent most of the day hanging out with them and enjoyed a beer and their company in the evening. They were planning to film on Saint-Joseph the following day, subject to gaining permission from the French Foreign Legion, who had a base on the island.

When I joined the BBC for breakfast, I was told the Legion had agreed to let the film crew on to the island, and I could go too, which was fantastic. We got a lift across the sound with the help of the French Foreign Legion. I was surprised that the water between the two islands was quite calm—not the shark-infested rough passage depicted in the book.

Once on the island, I started walking along the nicely swept path and came across a very fit-looking Foreign Legion officer who had his top off and was quite happily sweeping the path.

"Good morning," I said.

In a strong Liverpudlian accent, I got a "good morning" back.

"You must be off that really nice-looking yacht anchored in the bay?" he said.

"Yes, that's mine. I'm sailing single-handed without an engine."

"That's brave."

I asked the guy his name; all I got back was his new Foreign Legion name—John-Paul—which was to be expected, so I said jokingly, "So, you've been a bad boy and run away to join the French Foreign Legion?"

John-Paul gave me a big smile, and as he put his top back on, he asked, "Have you seen the prison yet?"

"No," I replied

"Okay, I'll give you the grand tour."

The prison was on the top of the island. The solitary confinement cells were tiny; they measured the width of the door one way and about six feet the other. There were no windows or natural light.

In the main part of the prison, the cells had steel bars around them and were about six feet square. Each had one wooden bench to sleep on and a bucket.

John-Paul explained the bench would be lifted up at 6 a.m. in the morning. The prisoners would not be able to sit down or talk to each other until the bench was put back down at 6 p.m. in the evening. The top of the cell had an open metal grating, which armed guards would walk back and forth on while wearing soft shoes so as not to make any noise, meaning they could keep a constant check on the prisoners. The prison must have been hell, especially with all the bugs and tropical diseases that would have been about at that time. The worst part for me was, as I sat in one of the cells, I could hear the waves breaking on the shore. It must have been incredibly challenging for the inmates both mentally and physically.

The strange thing was, with the modern medicine we have today, this place could be paradise. There wouldn't be any need for a lock or key—who would want to escape from a beautiful tropical island?

After my tour, John-Paul took me to the base, where I rendezvoused with the BBC film crew. John-Paul bought me a few beers, and as I gazed out to sea, I could see a long line attached to a large red buoy. Under the buoy, four or five sharks were circling. I queried this with John-Paul, who told me the guys stationed at the barracks caught the sharks for a bit of sport.

During this conversation, John-Paul also said that when the captain of the base returned from France, they were going to attempt the seven-mile swim to the mainland. They planned to carry out the swim at night, as they believed there would be less current. I put him straight by saying the current would be the same whatever time they did the swim. I also told him they were mad to be doing the swim at night and pointed out that mako and tiger sharks are mainly night feeders. I made it clear that I thought John-Paul and his mates were completely bonkers for even contemplating the idea.

My parting comments to him were, "You've got bigger balls than me, if you try it."

Shortly afterwards, I returned to Royale with the film crew for an evening beer, and one of the crew told me he was planning to swim to Devils Island the following day.

I said, "That shouldn't be too hard. What time are you planning to do your swim?"

"Around two p.m.," he said.

"You're mad," I said.

"Why?"

"Well, when we crossed to Saint-Joseph this morning, the water was calm and very rough coming back; there was plenty of current at two p.m. If I was you, I'd do the swim at slack water, which I reckon will be around ten a.m."

The next morning at ten past ten, a red flare went up, and shortly afterwards, I saw the Legion's Zodiac rushing up the sound towards Devil's Island.

That evening, I met up with the BBC crew again. My new friend had made the swim. He said the Legion weren't very happy with him but my advice about doing the swim at slack water had been spot on.

It was time for me to move again. The next morning, I went ashore and found the solitary gendarme, who handed me back my passport, with a very nice stamp in it.

The next stop on my island-hopping tour was Tobago, 600NM to the northwest. My sail there was idyllic. I didn't encounter any bad weather; the sailing conditions were perfect.

I anchored in Tobago on 14th September and went ashore to check in with immigration, a now familiar routine. I found the office, which was in the middle of the main street. As I climbed the stairs to the first floor and entered the office, there on the wall was a picture of Barry Harbour. The Geest container ships used to bring bananas from the Caribbean into Barry docks.

The police officer asked what I wanted, so I explained that I had just arrived on a yacht and needed to get my papers stamped.

"I need to find my stamp," the police officer replied rummaging through his drawer, he said, "Hold this," and placed a 9mm Browning handgun in my hand, which came as a bit of a shock.

"I found it," he said.

Needless to say, I very quickly handed him back his gun and made a swift exit once my papers had been stamped.

I spent only three days looking around the island. It was very hot, and with little breeze to keep me cool, the conditions were pretty uncomfortable. Tobago is, however, a lovely island, with a lot of history and very friendly people. Had the weather been a bit cooler, I would have liked to have stayed for longer.

I left Tobago on 17th September to sail south to Trinidad. I was expecting a short sail with favourable winds and currents to assist my sixty-mile passage. However, soon after leaving Tobago, the wind died, although I still had three to four knots of favourable current. My plan was to sail into Chaguaramas Bay via the Bocas del Dragón Channel, but each time I got close, I lost the wind. After three attempts, I gave up. It was getting dark, so I headed back out to sea and spent the night tacking back and forth, just stemming the current on the mainsail alone.

After a few hours of sleep, I got up at first light to a wet, squally, overcast morning with very little wind. It took me most of the morning to sail back to the Bocas del Dragón. Each time I tried to sail through the mouth of the channel, the wind died on me. It wasn't until late afternoon, when a big rain squall came through with plenty of wind under it, that I finally managed to enter the Gulf of Paria.

Once the squall passed, I was left with no wind once more and was at risk of being sucked back down the channel I had just spent two days getting through. I had little option but to anchor at my current position. It was safe to anchor there— my problem was when I looked at the chart, I found out that I was in fifty metres of water. To give my anchor the best chance of holding, I needed all my spare warp to bend onto the end of my anchor warp. For rope, the prescribed length of warp is six times the depth of water. I was pretty sure I didn't have enough rope for that but hoped what I did have would be sufficient.

I deployed the anchor from the bow, praying I would be able to recover the weight of the warp and chain when it came time to retrieve it. The anchor warp hung straight down. Even though I had plenty of line out, I couldn't be sure the anchor was going to hold.

As I could not rely on the anchor, I decided to stay on watch all through the night, so I wrapped my sleeping bag around myself and sat in the cockpit. The next thing I knew, there were Coastguard officers waking me up. When I looked around, it was daylight, and the yacht was close to the shore. Straight away, I realised that the anchor had dragged—so much for my vigilance.

I was sitting outside the Coastguard station of Teteron Barracks, and the Coastguard were pretty upset. After searching the yacht, they told me that I had to leave the area straight away. I pointed out that I had no motor and there was no wind. They didn't cut me any slack, I was still told to leave. After hauling the mainsail up, I managed to pull myself forward on the anchor in order to move further out into the bay. Despite my best endeavours, I continued to drift around in the channel, in front of the Coastguard station.

Finally, I flagged down a local fishing boat, who towed me for a mile towards Chaguaramas before dropping me off in shallower water. The fishermen said I would be okay to anchor there, and if I was still there when they came back from fishing, they would tow me into Chaguaramas. Great, I thought—I needed all the help I could get. I had no wind, and the conditions were very hot and humid. I was, however, relieved to be away from the Coastguard base.

As I scanned the shoreline, my eyes were immediately drawn to a large building with lots of flags around it and a dock in front of it, which was situated about three hundred feet in front of me. In no time at all, I had another Coastguard rib tied alongside with more irate officers on the yacht telling me I couldn't anchor where I was. I tried to explain that I had no engine, and without wind, I was going to just drift back and forth on the tide. In an attempt to save them a job, I advised that my boat papers had already been checked and the yacht searched an hour ago by the Coastguard station further down the channel. Despite this, they insisted on searching the yacht again and towed *Seefalke* onto their dock.

From the cockpit, I watched as the commanding officer came marching down the dock with six heavily armed Coastguard personnel, each with an M16 assault rifle plus handguns. After five minutes of poring over the yacht, they were satisfied and told me I could leave. For the third time, I tried to explain that there was no wind and I had no engine, which was why I'd been anchored where I was in the first place. My attempts to reason with them were futile, and I was asked to leave immediately.

I untied *Seefalke*, pushed the bow out towards the channel, hoisted the mainsail, and that's where I sat—six feet off the dock. I went below and made myself a coffee and a sandwich. As I returned to the cockpit, the commanding officer started to shout at me, telling me to leave the dock at once.

"I have," I said. "You can see from my sails that there's no wind."

After a further ten minutes of shouting at me, he gave up and marched back to his office, taking his six guards with him. The boat crew who remained on the dock were creased up at the situation. I had a good laugh too; it was like a scene out of *Life of Brian*—the Monty Python film. After a further hour of being becalmed, the wind finally filled in and I was able to sail away from the dock and into Chaguaramas, where I found a safe place to anchor.

Once again, my first stop was to sign in with customs and immigration. The boat's papers and my passport were checked for the third time that day, which was a new record.

There was no town at Chaguaramas. The place centred around large boatyards, with over two thousand yachts on the hard there. I did manage to get two top shrouds made to replace the ones on *Seefalke*. There were a few pubs and a supermarket, but not much else.

Port of Spain, the capital of Trinidad, was a local bus ride away. I found it a dangerous place to hang around. I did meet up with Peter, Terry and little Darcy again (no "f*ck" this time). The roller furling gear had worked well during their trip from Fortaleza. They were waiting in Trinidad until they could make their way to Panama, and then once through the canal, they were homeward bound back to Oz.

I found the constantly changing climate in Trinidad quite challenging. The weather seemed to alternate between hot and humid and still lashing down with rain, and after ten days in Trinidad's muggy weather, it was time to carry on my island-hopping theme. I decided to go in search of more settled weather and explore the small Venezuelan islands of Los Testigos, which were about a hundred miles west.

Chapter 19
Sailing North

On the morning I planned to leave Chaguaramas, there was no wind. This was completely characteristic of my stay in Trinidad. Having to wait again for the breeze to fill in was really frustrating and served as another stark reminder of the reality of sailing a yacht without an engine. It was early afternoon before I had enough breeze to sail down the Boca de Monas passage and out into the Caribbean Sea. Once clear of the coast, a fresh prevailing easterly breeze kicked in, and with a strong favourable current behind me, I was on for an easy run towards the Los Testigos Islands.

As dawn broke, I got my first glimpses of this small group of islands. I couldn't make out any of the lights referenced in my pilot book, so I decided to proceed with caution. Closer to the coast, I dropped the genoa and got the anchor on deck in case I needed it in a hurry.

The pilot book advised that there were six main islands in the group. Only two were inhabited by small fishing communities, and there was one police officer who presided over the islands with whom I needed to sign in on my arrival.

I approached the anchorage by sailing past the two main islands of Los Testigos and Isla Iguana. Between the islands was a fast-flowing current running through the channel. The anchorage was in a small bay on Isla Iguana, where I could see a solitary concrete building on the beach.

I sailed around a very small island that protected the entrance to the bay and dropped my anchor close behind it. After a quick tidy up, I sat in the cockpit and took in my surroundings. In the small gap between the small island I had anchored behind and the main island, I noticed a three-foot-high step in the water caused by the sheer volume of water that was trying to pass through. It was an incredible sight and reminded me of a mini waterfall. The forces involved must have been immense.

Happy that I had successfully set the anchor, I blew up the dinghy and went ashore to clear immigration. The rest of that day was spent exploring the island. The fishing community lived in rough wooden shacks on the beach. There were no bars or shops on either island. Food, drink and fuel were all brought in by the fishermen from the Venezuelan island of Margarita, some fifty miles away. The locals seemed geared up for this facet of island life and used big, open wooden boats, powered by large outboard motors.

That evening I wandered back to the yacht before it got dark. It seemed strange, being on a Caribbean Island and not being able to wander into a bar for an evening of music and a drink.

I didn't sleep well that first night. Every time I woke up, all I could hear was the sound of the gushing water.

The next day was spent hiking to the island's highest point. The view over the other six islands was breathtaking—I couldn't believe how good the visibility was. Far in the distance, I could make out the Venezuelan mainland, and to the west was Margarita: my next stop. I had seen all that the Los Testigos Islands had to offer. However, I must admit that sitting on top of the island was mesmerising. I enjoyed a lovely few hours topping up my tan and reading my book.

Early the following morning, after my coffee and breakfast, it was time to carry on with my summer adventure. It looked like it was going to be another beautiful day, hot and sunny, with a force 3 to 4 easterly breeze. The sea was flat between the islands, which was ideal for *Seefalke*. I pulled the no.2 genoa up, sheeted it in and tacked her over the anchor. Once *Seefalke* was pointing in the right direction, towards the channel, I recovered the anchor. I tacked my way out of the channel and once I was a safe distance off, I brought the yacht head-to-wind and walked to the mast to hoist the mainsail. I got the sail two-thirds of the way up, but with the boom still sitting on the deck, the sail jammed.

I couldn't move it up or get it back down. The mainsail was flogging furiously in the wind, and it wasn't long before the bow inevitably fell off to leeward. I was now being pushed by the current, sideways towards the waterfall. I didn't have enough sea room to try and gybe nor the speed to tack the yacht through the wind with just the genoa up. The waterfall was getting closer and closer and louder and louder by the second. I didn't know what to do. I had the idea of trying to steer the yacht through the gap and over the waterfall. Which would have ended my sailing adventure, with me in tears.

Thankfully, in the nick of time, I came to my senses. I grabbed the sheeting lines for the second reef and pulled on them with all my strength, which took all of the sag out of the mainsail. With one foot on the tiller, I managed to gain enough windward performance to skirt the islands by about twenty feet.

I can honestly say I was too close for comfort. Thank goodness there were no outlying dangers, otherwise my summer tour would have ended.

Once I had plenty of sea room, I brought *Seefalke* back into the wind, and this time the mainsail went up without any issues. After making everything fast, I got George steering a course for Margarita, and soon the islands were fast disappearing behind me. I took a moment to reflect on what had just happened and breathed a big sigh of relief, realising I'd had a very lucky escape.

After I had calmed down and relaxed, I realised what a beautiful day it was and how perfect the sailing conditions were. In front of me were two other yachts on the same course but motoring, which I couldn't understand, given the superb conditions.

As I got closer to the island, I studied the pilot book. There were two anchorages: one in the port of Porlamar, where the customs office was, and the other in Pampatar, a small fishing village and harbour. I sailed past the entrance to Pampatar to have a good look at the approach and to make sure I could safely sail in and drop the anchor. All I could see were a few local fishing boats, the same ones I had seen in Los Testigos, and luckily no visiting yachts, meaning that there was room for me.

I sailed into the harbour under just the mainsail with the anchor ready. The only thing I wasn't sure about was whether there was enough water for *Seefalke*'s six-foot draft. As I sailed through the harbour entrance, I dropped the mainsail. It wasn't long before I felt *Seefalke* slowing down. As she gently kissed the sandy seabed, I dropped the anchor.

I had arrived. Luckily, there was very little tide to worry about, and after stowing the mainsail, I rowed a kedge anchor out to stop *Seefalke* swinging around or blowing any further into the harbour. I was in safely and decided to have a well-earned beer after my harrowing experience of nearly losing the yacht. I decided not to worry about how I was going to get the yacht back out of the harbour. That was a matter for another day.

As I looked around the harbour, on the beach I saw a massive sign saying 'Talamar Restaurant'. What a glorious sight. There was nothing I wanted more than some good food and a beer. I didn't have a lot of money, but bugger the expense—I fancied a treat. Decision made, restaurant it was.

I needed a shave, a J-cloth wash and something decent to wear before going ashore. After a good rummage in my waterproof winter clothes bag, I found a pair of jeans and a shirt that Wattsy and Bowmer had left behind after the Classics. They looked clean to me and didn't smell too bad, so all was well. I had a job to remember the last time I had worn these clothes, which was before I left Antigua, I think? With a pair of deck shoes, I'd be ready for a good meal and some beer. I quickly checked my wallet. There was one lonely five US Dollar note which wasn't going to get me very far, maybe a beer or two? I decided to bend the credit card a bit more.

I landed on the beach in front of the restaurant and made the dinghy painter fast around a big log. After dusting my feet off, I put on my only pair of deck shoes and wasted no time in walking up the beach to the restaurant. My mind started to focus on what I was going to have to eat. As I looked up, I could see a waiter stood in the restaurant doorway. The guy was impeccably dressed, wearing smart black trousers and a bright white shirt, with a freshly pressed white towel neatly folded over his arm.

As I walked towards him, in perfect English he said, "Nice yacht you have there."

"Thank you," I replied

"I have never seen a yacht in here before—how long is she?"

"Thirteen metres."

"It's a bit big for our small harbour."

"I know. It's going to be fun leaving in the morning."

"What can I get for you this evening, sir?"

"Meat. if you've got some?"

"Well, sir, you have come to the right place. Welcome to the Talamar Restaurant. I recommend the sirloin—it's especially good tonight. It comes with freshly baked bread and fries."

Result! I thought. "That sounds great to me. Can I also get a beer? And please just keep topping me up when you see the bottle is empty. Thank you."

My latest friend found me a table at the back of the restaurant. The restaurant was spotless, which came as a surprise considering it was on the beachfront in a small fishing village. As I sat drinking my first beer, the place started to fill up quickly. The men were all wearing sharp suits and the women looked incredibly glamorous. They wore beautiful dresses that looked very expensive, with matching bags and shoes. Suddenly, I felt very underdressed, which explained why I was sitting at the back of the restaurant out of sight.

After two or three beers, my steak arrived. I was gobsmacked. It looked like I had half a cow on my plate— the steak was massive. The slab of beef was at least an inch thick and covered the whole of the large dinner plate. The really thick, homemade fries came on another plate the same size and then a loaf of bread turned up on a third. Anyone would have thought I was attending the last supper. As I took a bite out of the perfectly cooked steak, it just melted in my mouth—it was just the best. On top of this, every time I put an empty bottle on the table, a new beer turned up in seconds. The service was outstanding.

Just as I was forcing down the last mouthful of food, the waiter was back with another beer and asked if I would like dessert. The guy must have thought I looked malnourished or had a bottomless pit for a stomach. I politely declined the offer of any more food and sat sipping my beer for fear that a large gulp would tip me over the edge. I had visions of my steak ending up all down the front of my nice white shirt. After taking the time to let my dinner go down, I asked the waiter for the bill, bracing myself for what was about to come. Ten minutes later, the waiter returned with the bill and stood at the table while I checked it.

My eyes immediately went to the total at the bottom, which read two thousand four hundred bolivars. When I was in Trinidad and thinking of sailing to Venezuela, I'd looked up the exchange rate. One British pound was equal to twelve hundred bolivars. It suddenly dawned on me that my amazing meal and beers had come to the grand total of three US dollars. What an absolute steal; I couldn't believe it. I handed the waiter my five-dollar bill and told him to keep the change. The waiter had the biggest smile you had ever seen; he couldn't believe his luck and thanked me for my generosity by handing me another beer as I left the restaurant.

"Thank you again for the tip!" the waiter shouted as I walked down the beach.

"No problem!" I called back. "Thank you for the brilliant meal and excellent service."

"How are you going to get that lovely yacht of yours out of here tomorrow?"

"I will worry about that in the morning. Thank you once again."

The waiter stood on the beach, watching as I dragged my dinghy into the water and climbed in. I slowly sculled back to *Seefalke* with the oar in one hand and my beer in the other.

If I could dine in top-notch restaurants every night and get away with spending five US dollars, including the tip, then I certainly wanted to see more of South America. I reckoned I could travel around the place for a couple of months on three hundred dollars and live like a king. The more I thought about it, the more I liked the idea.

I started thinking ahead as to what I might do in the future and kept coming back to two options. The first was to sail to the Chesapeake on the eastern seaboard of the States, where I would be able to sell my much-loved yacht and buy an inexpensive motorbike to explore more of South America. Or, I could go back to Antigua and carry on where I left off.

Leaving Pampatar the following morning was a lot easier than I had expected. I recovered the main anchor and turned the yacht around using the kedge anchor. The bow was now facing the right way to sail out with the wind behind me. I lifted my kedge anchor and quietly sailed out of the harbour on my no.2 genoa. Next stop was Porlamar, a short hop down the coast, where I could clear customs.

Porlamar had a large natural harbour, and I was able to anchor quite close to the beach. There was a very cosmopolitan feel, with yachts flying flags from all over the world. Clearly, this was the place to come if you wanted cheap living while riding out the hurricane season. This seemed like an ideal base if you wanted to sail around the Caribbean or explore the Eastern Seaboard.

My pilot book recommended that I call an agent who would help me check into Venezuela. The cost for this service was sixty US dollars, which I thought was steep. I could have twelve good meals for the same money, and so I decided to check in myself. After consulting with some of the other yacht owners, I reached the conclusion that this was going to be a day out of my life that I wouldn't get back. The advice was just to relax and not get too stressed over the time-consuming and complicated process.

The next morning, I set off early to clear immigration, prepared for a day of pain. First up, I withdrew cash from the ATM, then as instructed, I visited the police station. After that, the town hall and to Guardia Civil. This little exercise took five hours, and I had to complete a myriad of forms. Finally, I was ready to visit my last port of call, the customs office, to show them all my completed forms and hopefully get my papers stamped.

Just to add to my day of fun, the customs headquarters was a good mile's walk out of town, up the hill on the headland overlooking Porlamar. After I found the place, I was met by a young customs officer who spoke some English. I handed him the pile of forms I had completed, together with the boat's papers.

He said, "All your paperwork is correct, sir."

Brilliant, I had finally finished.

"I just need your stamps."

Stamps? This was the first time all day I had heard anything about stamps.

"What stamps?" I asked.

"The stamps from the post office."

"What stamps from the post office?" I said, looking really confused.

"Sir, you need to get fifteen thousand bolivars of stamps from the post office, which I will attach to your paperwork. Then I will stamp your passport."

"Oh. The stamps, can I get buy them here?"

"No, sir."

I knew it was a stupid question. It wouldn't have been that simple.

"So, where can I buy the stamps?"

"Sir, are you driving?"

"No, walking."

"Okay—it's easy, then. As you walked up here, you passed a wooden shack at the bottom of the hill by the beach, yes?"

"Yes," I said.

"You can buy your stamps there."

"Okay, thanks," I said.

As I turned to leave, he said, "Sir, one last thing. You had better be quick—we close in an hour."

"Great."

I ran back down the hill to the wooden shack, where I met a woman who spoke not one word of English. It felt like I was playing charades. I was using sign language, stamping my feet, stamping my hands pointing up the hill, and finally, after showing her my passport, she twigged and gave me stamps. What a day. I was exhausted.

I swore every step of the way as I ran back up the hill. The customs officer was waiting for me as I burst into his office with sweat pouring off me. Finally, after a very long and frustrating day, my papers were stamped. Getting all this completed in a day was by all accounts something of a record and a real triumph. I couldn't wait to go through the whole harrowing experience again when it came time to leave.

Very tired, I turned to leave, but the customs officer said, "If you wait a minute, I'll give you a lift down the hill."

The guy very kindly dropped me at a beach bar. My timing was perfect—happy hour was in full swing, meaning beers were two for the price of one, providing me with the ideal opportunity to rehydrate while telling the other yacht crews about my nightmare day.

After two really great weeks on the island, enjoying the weather, the people, their culture, and very cheap living, I'd caught the bug and wanted to see more of South America. However, my funds were running low, and I needed to crystalise my plans and decide what I was going to do next.

The one thing I was sure about was the urgent need to boost my bank balance, so whatever the next chapter looked like, I had to find work. My three options were:

Sail back to Antigua, and work for Piggy and Flemming at Seagull Services again. I'd really enjoyed my three years in Antigua but had the urge to move on.

Sail to St Martin, secure a job there and then stay for a year or two.

Sail to the Chesapeake, sell the yacht, get a motorbike and head south.

The last idea was the most appealing. I had really enjoyed the yacht, the adventure, but felt it was time to move on and start a new chapter in my life. Going to America wouldn't be a problem. I had a visa, which I'd picked up when I first arrived in Barbados in 1995.

My mind was made up, I had a plan. First, I needed to head back to St Martin and look for work. If I got lucky, I would stay for the sailing season, if not, I would restock *Seefalke* with food and water, replace and fix everything that was broken and head north to the Chesapeake Bay.

I endured the same painful experience clearing immigration as when I'd arrived. However, on the flip side, I enjoyed another happy hour in the same bar as before, with the added excuse of needing to get rid of all my bolivars, as I wouldn't be needing them again for a while.

Sailing out of Polamar, I felt motivated and excited about my next adventure. Once I cleared the eastern end of the island, I set George up to take us north. I had a reef in the mainsail with the no.2 up. The sea was flat with a strong force 5 prevailing easterly breeze. *Seefalke* was romping along in the near-perfect conditions.

It wasn't long before Margarita disappeared over the horizon. The weather together with the exhilarating sailing made for a fantastic day, and my spirits were high—until I started seeing dead fish on the surface of the water. I sailed through them for miles. This was really disconcerting and upsetting. I immediately wanted to know what had caused this to happen and assumed that there had been some major pollution incident. It was eerie; all the fish were of the same species and there were no signs of any contamination in the water. I couldn't come up with any explanation for this weird phenomenon. The whole experience left me quite disturbed. After fifteen miles, I finally passed through the last of the dead fish and my mood started to lift. Something major had happened to cause so many fish to die, but it remains a mystery to me.

Before I crashed out for a few hours' sleep, I had one last look to check if there were any ships around. Setting my two alarm clocks for two hours, I knew it would not be long before I would be fast asleep. Sailing at hull speed never created any noise below deck. There was no wind noise or any sound of water passing down the side of the hull; the silence was surreal. I think I fell asleep before my head even hit the pillow.

I remember having a strange dream. I could see a very bright light in the night sky. It reminded me of the searchlights you'd see when watching an old black-and-white WWII film on a Sunday afternoon. Even being asleep, I somehow knew that the bright light was from a Coastguard vessel. Finally, with pins and needles in my toes, my sixth sense woke me up.

As I poked my head out of the main hatch, I could see the silhouette of a big freighter. Her navigation lights confirmed that she was heading east, away from me. Despite having eyes on the ship, my sixth sense told me that there was another vessel out there. As I peered into the darkness, I could see another big black shadow, but couldn't make out what it was—although my dream had confirmed it was a Coastguard vessel. I listened out for any traffic on VHF channel 16 between the freighter and the other vessel. Over the radio, I heard the American Coastguard operator talking to a Spanish vessel. The communication between the two was very clear, so I presumed the freighter I could see was the vessel that the Coastguard were talking with.

The freighter asked if the Coastguard wanted to board them, to which the Coastguard replied, "No."

They told the freighter that their interest was in a small yacht that was sailing at speed in a northerly direction with no navigation lights on. I had a good look in all directions to see if I could see any other yachts. There was nothing. I quickly realised that they were referring to me, and I knew the vessel was close by.

I decided to call the Coastguard on channel 16 and quickly turned my navigation lights on.

My conversation with the Coastguard went something like this:

"American Coastguard vessel, I'm calling from sailing yacht *Seefalke*, my position is—"

Before I could tell them my latitude and longitude, a big searchlight like the one in my dream shone on the yacht. It blinded me for a few seconds. I could tell the powerful beam was coming from the direction of the black shadow I had noticed earlier. Instantly, the ship turned all its lights on and lit up like a Christmas tree. As my eyes adjusted, I could tell that this was a very impressive US Navy warship.

"I heard that you were interested in talking to me?" I said again.

"That's correct, sir," said the radio operator in a monotone American accent. "We are the American navy vessel *Eagle*, supporting a detachment of the US Coastguards."

"Hi, how can I help you?"

"Sir, can I get some information from you?"

"No problem."

They asked me for the yacht's position, my name and passport number and the yacht's British registration number, which I willingly gave them. They said they would check things out and get back to me.

It was a lovely warm night with a bright, clear, star-studded sky. I made myself a coffee and sat on deck, admiring the brightly illuminated USS *Eagle*. I watched as the vessel moved towards me, before running parallel to my track, sitting about a mile off my starboard beam.

After about half an hour, a call came through on the VHF.

"Sailing vessel *Seefalke*, this is the American naval vessel *Eagle*."

"Yes, *Eagle*. How can I help you?" I replied.

"Sir, do you mind if we come over and board your boat?"

"That's not a problem. But I would like to warn you the yacht's moving very fast," I said.

"It's not a problem, sir. We are very experienced at boarding boats."

I was a bit annoyed that he kept calling *Seefalke* a boat, but I decided not to correct him. I didn't want to annoy him.

"We will deploy a small Coastguard rib shortly, sir."

I went below to put some clothes on before my unexpected guests arrived. I used the time to clean up below. I noticed that my chemical toilet was full and there was a very unpleasant smell coming from it. It definitely needed emptying. The smell was rather nasty, but I thought, sod it—I'd leave it. Maybe it would deter the Coastguards and they would leave quickly.

Back in the cockpit, I could see a lot of activity on the USS *Eagle*. I watched the lights on the rib come on as it was lowered into the sea and came towards me. As it got nearer, I saw there were three people on board. The rib looked to be about twenty-five feet long with two bloody great outboard motors on the back. It got to within about fifteen feet of *Seefalke*, when the helmsman suddenly altered course and did a lap around the yacht before returning to the ship, where the rib was lifted out and placed back on deck. I found the whole exercise confusing and really bizarre.

Suddenly, the VHF radio came back to life.

"*Seefalke*, USS *Eagle*."

"Yes, *Eagle*, how can I help you?" I said again.

"You are sailing extremely fast," said the operator.

"I know—I told you that."

"Sir, please can you sail into the lee of our ship?"

"I can't do that—I'm an engineless yacht. I will risk damaging my yacht if I sail too close."

"Sir, we do need to come aboard."

"Right. The only thing I can do is slow the yacht down when your boys are ready to board."

"Okay, sir. We will send the rib back across now."

"Okay, I'll wait—I'm not going anywhere."

I sat on deck for ages, but nothing happened. Being tired, I called *Eagle* up to find out what the hell was going on.

"*Seefalke* calling *Eagle.*"

"Yes, *Seefalke?*"

"I'm going to get my head down for an hour. Please give me a call when you guys are ready, and I will get up."

"Yes, sir."

I went and got some sleep before the radio went off. A quick glance at the alarm clocks told me two hours had passed. God knows what they had been doing. I'd had a really nice nap, though, safe in the knowledge I had an American warship as an escort.

"USS *Eagle*, calling *Seefalke.*"

"Yes, *Eagle?*"

"Sir, do you mind if we come on board?"

"That's fine. It's no problem."

"Okay, sir."

"But just tell your boys: when I slow the yacht down, it will be quite dangerous as the boom will be flopping around and it's a big one and very heavy."

"Sorry, sir, what's a boom?"

Back in the cockpit, I watched the rib get lowered down the side of *Eagle* and slowly make its way over to *Seefalke*. Again, they did a lap of the yacht before trying to come alongside. I slowed the yacht down by easing out the sails, causing the boom to swing back and forth across the deck.

Those Coastguard officers were pretty much useless. On the first attempt to come aboard, they were too far away, and motored alongside *Seefalke*. On their second attempt, they got closer. On their third attempt, I was standing on deck shouting instructions to the guy on the helm, telling him what to do. The rib finally got close enough for them to hang on the side of the yacht. The guy in the bow of the rib was struggling, trying to clamber over the guard wires to get on board. I leant over the side and grabbed his arm to help haul him on deck.

With him safely standing by the mast, I told him to hold on to the rigging and watch out for the boom. By now, the other officer had managed to get himself on board and into the cockpit. He tried to stand up.

"Be careful," I said. "Watch your head on the boom."

The same question as earlier got repeated. "Sir, what's a boom?" Followed by, "Sir, have you got a gun in your hand?"

"What?"

I started to laugh. Surely, they didn't think I was going to shoot them and then try and outrun their battleship?

"Sir, have you got a gun on the boat?" the guy repeated.

"No, I haven't."

"Do you know why we are on the boat, sir?"

"I have no idea," I said with a shrug.

"Sir, we are on the boat to make sure it is safe for us to be on the boat."

"Right," I said in disbelief.

I caught myself doing the sign for 'dickhead' by putting my thumb and index finger to my head, pretending I was stroking a small dick. Lucky for me, it went over their heads.

"Look," I said. "I need you two to sit down in the cockpit, as I need to get the yacht moving again. It will be safer for all of us. It really isn't safe on deck with the boom swinging around."

With the two Coastguard officers safely sitting in the cockpit, I pulled in the mainsail to get *Seefalke* moving again. Sheeting in the genoa, I picked up the winch handle to help me pull in the last bit of the flapping sail, when I heard one of the officers shout, "Jim! Jim, watch out—he's got a weapon."

What planet were these two idiots from? I put the winch handle back in its holder.

Safely sailing again, conditions on board became a lot calmer and safer. I also got George back on course. Happy, I directed my gaze to the two men sitting in my cockpit.

Both men were big, young and fit, both over six feet tall. It was hard to tell how heavy they were; both were wearing what looked to be black bulletproof jackets, with lots of pockets containing assorted items. Around their waists, they each had a belt with a torch, walkie-talkies, a baton sort of thing, etc. You name it, they seemed to be carrying it. Last but not least, both men were carrying a 9mm Browning pistol. On their feet, they had really big, heavy combat boots. To my surprise, they only had very small inflatable lifejackets. With all that gear on, I wondered if they would be able to float if they fell in the water—I wasn't convinced they would.

"Sir, have you got a knife on the boat?" one of them asked.

"Yes, of course."

"Why are you carrying a knife?"

"I have a knife in case I need to cut one of the many ropes or the sails you can see around the yacht," I said.

"Where is the knife kept?"

"I keep it on top of the companionway steps leading to the cabin." I pointed to where it was stowed.

"Sir, do you mind if one of us goes below to have a look around?"

"Not at all." I was feeling glad that I hadn't emptied the heads.

"Sir, how do I get below to look around the boat?"

"Go through the main hatch and climb down the companionway steps," I said, pointing to the main deck hatch.

"Sir, that's a really small hole."

Stating the bleeding obvious, I thought.

"Yes," I said. "It's only two-feet square. It's designed to be small in order to keep the seawater from going down inside the cabin."

"Sir, I am not sure I can fit through the gap," said Jim, the smaller of the two men.

I shrugged; I didn't know what to say. It took several attempts, but he finally managed to get himself below deck. It would have been easier if he hadn't been wearing so much gear. Each time he tried, a piece of his kit would get caught. I hoped his bloody gun wouldn't get caught and go off.

"Sir, have you got a lifejacket?" he shouted.

"Yes, it's in the cupboard under the chart table. It's bright red; you can't miss it."

"Sir, we would also like to see your passport."

"That's no problem."

I got up to go below to dig out my passport, when the other Coastguard, who was left in the cockpit, started shouting, "Jim! Jim, watch out—he's coming below!"

I turned around and looked back at him in disbelief.

I said, "Is it okay if I go and get my passport."

"Yes, sir, that's fine," he said, regaining his composure.

As I joined Jim below deck, he was almost green. I thought he might have to use my heads himself, which would have been an interesting experience for him. I showed him my passport, and he quickly confirmed that it was in order. I think he was keen to get out of the confined space and re-join his colleague in the cockpit for some much-needed fresh air.

"Sir, it's very small down here."

I didn't know what to say, apart from, "No, Jim, it's you who's too big."

"I can't even stand up in here."

"Well, it's fine for me."

"Do you have a watertight bulkhead on the boat?"

"No, there aren't any."

"What's in that space down there?"

"That's the quarter berth, where my guitar, sails, fenders and spare ropes are stowed."

"Do you play guitar, sir?"

"Well, yes," I said. "Would you like me to play you a tune?"

"No, sir, that's okay. What's further back down there?"

"That's the counter of the yacht—sorry, I mean the back of the yacht."

"I'm going to have to take a look down there."

"Jim, I think you're too big to go down there."

"Sorry, sir, I am going to have to look down there."

I hauled out all my stuff from the quarter berth, which took a while, as the berth was full. Once I'd emptied everything, Jim flashed his torch around the berth twice and shook his head.

"I don't think I will be able to get down there."

"I told you that, Jim."

We both went back up on deck. I slowed *Seefalke* down again so their rib could come alongside. Jim and his mate transferred back to the rib. For some reason, the rib reversed away from *Seefalke*, nearly ripping George off the back of the yacht.

As they made their way back to the USS *Eagle*, I heard Jim say, "I think we should have checked his guitar."

Why the Coastguard came on board, I really don't know.

Chapter 20
What to Do

From Margarita to St Martin was approximately four hundred nautical miles. Even with the distraction of the American Coastguard and being becalmed for six hours in the lee of Guadeloupe, it only took me three days. All things considered, it was a really quick trip.

I arrived in St Martin on 18th October, and luckily, I managed to pick up a tow into Simpson Bay lagoon. There were a lot of yachts holed up there, many of them waiting for the end of the hurricane season before carrying on with cruising around the Caribbean or pushing further north to the States.

I spent a week looking for some work with no luck, so my first option had gone. The other options were America, or back to Antigua. I still fancied a new adventure—the USA it was going to be. If I didn't like it in the States, I could always sail back to the Caribbean.

Looking in my Admiralty pilot book for advice on the best time to sail north, it advised me to leave the Caribbean by the end of October, after which point hurricanes are rare. The pilot book also advised me to arrive in the States before the 20th of November, which is when the north-east storms start to track up the Eastern Seaboard. A lot of this information was based on historic data collated from old sailing ship captains. Marking my planned route on my chart of the East Coast of America, I worked out that it was roughly twelve hundred miles from St Martin to the Chesapeake Bay. It had taken me three days to do the four hundred miles from Margarita, so I figured the trip would take nine or ten days, if I had the same easterly prevailing wind.

While I was in St Martin, Hurricane Mitch started to form in the Gulf of Mexico on the 22nd of October. Despite this, I continued to plan my trip. Most Hurricanes that start in the gulf head north until they hit the coast around the New Orleans area, where they dissipate over the land, fizzling out in four or five days. Which was around the time I planned to leave.

I spent my time in St Martin getting the yacht ready to leave. One of the problems that had developed recently was that my batteries kept going flat, so I wasn't able to put my navigation lights on at night. To fix the problem, I bought a cheap car battery to leave on the cabin sole and connect straight to my small solar panel on top of the cabin. I used the battery to power the automatic bilge pumps, leaving the house battery for the navigation lights. I also repaired my big solar panel.

My last job before I could leave was to fit a new spare genoa halyard up the mast. I didn't fancy trying to climb up the rig again on my own, so I asked a Dutch girl who I knew from Antigua to help. With her safely in my climbing harness, I winched her up to the top spreader. Five minutes later she was safely back on deck with the new halyard rigged. It would have taken me hours to climb up the mast on my own using Prusik knots. As a thank you, I arranged to meet her in the pub to buy her dinner and a few beers. I was a huge fan of this beer bartering system.

Now that the yacht was ready to go all, I needed was to find someone who would be kind enough to tow me out of the lagoon. It didn't take me long to find a skipper who was leaving the following day, and after buying him a few beers, he agreed to give me a tow out of the narrow channel once the bridge opened in the morning. My beer bartering had been successful once again.

My first job in the morning before I left was to check the weather, which was displayed in the yacht chandlery window early on Monday 26th October. Hurricane Mitch, with a barometer pressure of 926mb and a wind speed of

145mph, was a class-five storm heading for Honduras in Central America, where I thought it would most probably die out over land. Honduras was a long way from St Martin and a long way from my planned route north. There were no other depressions in the North Atlantic, so I was good to go.

I decided to do all the last-minute provisioning by getting fresh food on board, like cheese, bread, bacon, eggs and potatoes. I had already stocked up on enough canned food for fifteen days, which was plenty to get me to the Chesapeake Bay. The water tanks were full, and I had cleared customs.

Back on board with everything stowed below and my dinghy rolled up and lashed to the cabin top next to my spare, I was ready to leave when the morning bridge opened. Relaxed and excited, I waited with a cup of coffee for my tow to turn up.

Chapter 21
Sailing On

Monday 26th October 1998

The skipper who'd promised to tow me out was just in time for the morning bridge opening. Once we got the green light, *Seefalke* was towed out of the lagoon and into Simpson Bay. Although the lagoon was a safe place to stay and anchor, it was also full of thick, black, smelly mud. I dropped my anchor and chain overboard just so I could snorkel down and get all the mud off and then gave the deck a good wash down in the clean water of Simpson Bay. I also managed to give the hull a quick clean while I was at it. After a quick shower on deck, I sat in the cockpit with a cup of coffee, going over everything one last time. Oncc I was satisfied I hadn't forgotten anything, it was time to get going.

With the anchor back on deck, I got the no.2 genoa up, sheeted it in and set George on a course straight out of the bay, while I got on with stowing the anchor and chain, thinking the next time I'd need it would be in the Chesapeake Bay.

Once clear of Simpson Bay, I sailed up the western side of St Martin until I was clear of Péninsule des Terres Basses. I got the mainsail up and set George on a northerly heading—next stop: the States. I was on my own again in open seas, with fresh bread and cheese on the menu for tea, followed by a coffee with a tot of brandy. Life was feeling pretty good.

Just northwest of Anguilla are a couple of small islands, which I needed to leave to starboard. The Prickly Pear Cays is a marine park, made up of these two small islands and a long reef. While it's a protected conservation area, I always thought it would be a wonderful place to have a beach bar. To the west, there is the larger Dog Island, which I safely cleared early that evening.

***

2nd day at sea
Tuesday 27th October

06:00

I stayed up all night avoiding cargo and cruise ships, plus a number of small fishing boats. I cleared Sombrero Island and sailed back into the North Atlantic just after midnight, which was my last obstacle until the Eastern Seaboard.

My course was 320° mag, and the barometer was stable at 1008mb. Wind south-west 2/3. I managed to get an update on Hurricane Mitch from the BBC World Service. It was still slow-moving over Honduras.

12:00. Pos. 19°24'N 063°33'W

Logged 85NM since leaving St Martin.

I was pleased with my early progress and enjoyed another lovely day with light winds and George doing all the work. Apart from keeping an eye out for ships, there wasn't much else to do but relax and read my latest book—*Alaska* by James Mitchiner.

18:00

For my evening meal, I had chilli, rice and fresh bread with butter. I was back on my standard sailing routine. I found it easier to make two meals at a time. My winning formula was to open two tins of chilli and cook a big pot of rice. I'd eat half the first night and then just heat up the other half the following evening. This had the added benefit of saving my cooking gas and limited water supply. I topped off my chilli and rice with my usual coffee and tot of brandy. It was a warm, tranquil evening with a light, force 4 easterly breeze that looked set for the night. With no ships on the horizon, I decided to turn in and get some sleep for a couple of hours.

***

3rd day at sea
Wednesday 28th October

06:00

The wind dropped off as the sun came up, and we were becalmed, with the yacht wallowing in the swell. I dropped the sails to save wear and prevent them from being flogged to death. A light breeze filled in around mid-morning, which was enough to get me sailing again, although George was struggling in the light conditions, so I had to resort to taking a turn on the helm.

12:00. Pos. 20°10'N 063°52'W

Logged 50NM in the last 24 hours.

My midday position put me further north than expected, meaning I was getting a favourable current coming out of the Anegada Gap. It was some much-needed good news to compensate for the poor sailing conditions and the fact I was having to steer, which was quite annoying.

18:00

The wind had picked up early in the afternoon from the north-east, force 3. My course had altered to 340° mag. The barometer was still on 1005mb. While I was making progress, a bit more wind would have been nice.

***

4th day at sea
Thursday 29th October

06:00

For the first time on this trip, I had wind all night, which was really good.

12:00. Pos. 21°38'N 065°11'W

Logged 115NM in the last 24 hours.

My best noon-to-noon run so far. The wind had picked up and shifted to the south-east and increased to force 4/5. George was back in the game as we sailed straight downwind, leaving me to enjoy the lovely, hot, sunny day and read my book. Things were looking up.

18:00

I sensed there was a ship nearby. Although I couldn't see anything at first, I stayed on deck to keep a watch. Finally, I saw a ship on the horizon on a reciprocal course. As it passed, I called it up on the VHF and asked for a weather forecast. There were no new hurricanes in the Atlantic, which was really good news.

***

5th day at sea
Friday 30th October

06:00

I was treated to a beautiful sunrise with a warm, force 4 wind still blowing from the south-east. Life was good; I had nothing to do—the yacht was all set up for effortless sailing. On deck, I carried on reading my book, topping up my tan at the same time.

12:00. Pos. 23°26'N 066°28'W

Logged 130NM in the last 24 hours.

I had entered the infamous Bermuda Triangle, having had my best 24-hour run of the trip so far.

18:00

I spent most of my day on deck reading my book and thinking of what I was going to eat for tea, as I had used the last of my fresh food.

***

6th day at sea
Saturday 31st October

06:00

The wind had shifted to the north and dropped off overnight, although there was still enough for George to maintain a course. I had the full mainsail up and, due to the lack of wind so far on this trip, was using the no.1 genoa even though it was hard to handle on my own and see around.

12:00. Pos. 24°18'N 067°29'W
Logged 76NM in the last 24 hours.

From my latest position, the current had started setting me to the west, which was helping my cause, given that there was only the slightest breath of wind—force 2 from the west. At least I was moving and happy to be on deck.

When I looked up from my book to do a check for any shipping, I saw a small black dot on the horizon. *A ship,* I thought. *Great—I can get an up-to-date weather forecast.* I kept an eye on the ship, as it could have come over the horizon and been on top of me in twenty minutes. It did not take too long for me to realise that this ship was stationary. It was only me sailing closer to it that had brought us together.

For some strange reason, when I was approximately half a mile off the stern of the ship, it suddenly got cold and overcast. The light breeze stopped completely, leaving me becalmed again.

This ship looked old. My first thought was it was a World War II Liberty ship like I'd seen in old war films. I could clearly see that the propeller was not turning. The plimsoll line was clearly above the water, meaning the ship was floating very high without a cargo on board. When I looked through my binoculars, the ship looked very tired, with a very rusty hull, and even at this close range, I could not make out a name on the stern or the bow or see any flags flying. What made the whole experience worse was I couldn't see any life on board either.

I tried to call the ship up a few times on VHF channel 16, the international distress frequency, which everybody at sea is supposed to listen to, but there was no answer. The ship was acting very strangely: there was nothing happening at all, no radio contact, no movement. It was all a bit spooky. As I was in the Bermuda Triangle, could I have been looking at a ghost ship?

18:00

Finally, the wind picked up and I managed to leave the ghost ship behind. So far, the day had been a write-off; I had only made 8NM in a north-westerly direction. But without the wind, what could I do? Oh, the joys of sailing on an engineless yacht.

***

7th day at sea
Sunday 1st November

06:00

During the night, a light northerly breeze prevailed, and George had managed to keep the yacht sailing west, just about. The barometer was stable at 1016mb, only dropping slightly from the previous day. I was praying for more wind, as my passage plan was going out of the window.

I took advantage of the conditions and baked two fresh loaves of bread and some potatoes at the same time. There is nothing like the taste and smell of fresh bread when you are at sea.

12:00. Pos. 24°15'N 068°00'W

Logged 28NM in the last 24 hours.

The barometer had dropped to 1013mb; my wish for more wind had been granted. I got to work on setting the yacht up to make the most of this opportunity before returning to the shade of the coach roof to carry on reading my book.

18:00

The wind picked up a little more during the afternoon. It shifted to the west and looked set for the rest of the day and night. I continued to sail north on a port reach.

***

8th day at sea
Monday 2nd November

06:00

I had a good sail overnight, although just before dawn, my senses warned me of the presence of a ship. On sticking my head out of the hatch, there was nothing immediately visible. After daybreak, as it started to get light, I saw a ship about two miles away that looked remarkably like the Liberty ship I had seen two days earlier.

The situation was spookily similar. Half a mile off the stern of the ship, it got colder, with a very sudden drop in the wind. I was back to being becalmed. I thought to myself, *I have been here before*. The ship had the same markings on it. The plimsoll line was high out of the water. The propeller was not turning. The ship was covered in rust with no visible name on the bow or stern or any flags flying. And no sign of life aboard. I still couldn't raise the ship on the VHF.

What was scary was that I had sailed north in the last two days. Maybe I was seeing things—there have been many accounts of people seeing strange things in the Bermuda Triangle. I was happy when the wind filled back in from the south, allowing me to sail away from this ghost ship.

12:00. Pos. 25°33′N 068°04′W

Logged 78NM in the last 24 hours.

As I sat on the deck eating a peanut butter sandwich, I saw a gold light coming off the sea. I could clearly see the line of light, which I took a photograph of. Although it was very pretty, I decided to sail along the edge of the light. This phenomenon was giving me an uneasy feeling. The Bermuda Triangle was turning into a very weird and unnerving place.

18:00

The wind remained light, but I managed to maintain three knots through the water and on the right heading. I was listening to the BBC World Service, which advised that Cuba, 460NM south-west of my position, was in for some severe weather. I was far enough away not to be affected. I desperately needed to make contact with the next ship I saw in order to get an up-to-date weather forecast.

***

9ᵗʰ day at sea
Tuesday 3ʳᵈ November

06:00

The wind was still light, and I continued to plod on in the right direction, but my boat speed had dropped to below three knots. I could have walked to the Chesapeake Bay quicker. One positive to take from this situation was the yacht wasn't leaking, so I didn't have to do any pumping out, which was a bonus. I also saw some dolphins, which was another positive and cheered me up. It's supposed to be a sign of good luck to see dolphins, so I hoped my sighting would soon result in more wind.

12:00. Pos. 26°16'N 068°49'W

Logged 58NM in the last 24 hours.

I still had a light south-east breeze and continued to maintain a course of 340° mag. It had been another demoralising day, with only 12NM covered in six hours. I had been at sea for nine days, meaning I should have already been moored up in the Chesapeake Bay. My average daily run was around 60NM, which was painfully slow, although there was nothing I could do about it, given the constant lack of wind. I was still less than halfway to the Chesapeake Bay, and this was turning into another frustrating trip.

18:00

I had been in radio contact with a passing ship—this one was moving and did respond when I called it. I managed to get a weather forecast. It was more of the same: high pressure and light winds, with no new storms in the Atlantic, which was good. The radio operator did not mention anything about the weather in Cuba.

***

10th day at sea
Wednesday 4th November

06:00

Thankfully, the breeze had picked up to a force 4/5 and gone round to the south-west. I had a reef in the mainsail and changed down to a no.2 genoa. George was holding a course of 320° mag. I had been keeping an eye on the barometer, and the pressure had been dropping all morning.

12:00. Pos. 27°14'N 069°35'W

Logged 70NM in the last 24 hours.

Course 320° mag. Barometer was 1012mb. I enjoyed good sailing that morning, and the yacht was up to hull speed; the barometer also seemed to have stabilised. With George in control, there wasn't much for me to do other than read my book and keep a lookout for shipping or anything floating I could hit.

18:00

The wind was set for the night. I had a larger tot of brandy in my nightcap to celebrate.

23:00

I had an evening of exhilarating sailing, with a strong breeze, pushing me towards Norfolk, which felt really uplifting.

***

11th day at sea
Thursday 5th November

06:00

I awoke before dawn with pins and needles in my toes. I had a quick look around on deck, but I couldn't see any ships. I half expected to see my ghost ship again.

I stayed on deck with a hot cup of coffee and watched another beautiful sunrise. It was going to be another hot day, although the wind from last night had disappeared. I was back to being becalmed in a flat sea.

In the light of day, I saw a yacht a mile off my port beam. We had passed each other in the night, but I didn't see any navigation lights on the other yacht. Maybe he too was having problems with his batteries?

It was a dark-blue-hulled ketch with just the mainsail up, pointing south. I tried calling them up but got no response. I had a good look at the yacht through my binoculars but couldn't make out a name or any signs of movement. She was quite far away though.

I remained bewildered by the fact that, out of the millions of square miles of ocean, two yachts could end up almost hitting each other in the middle of the Bermuda Triangle. What were the chances of that?

12:00. Pos. 28°56'N 070°12'W
Logged 110NM in the last 24 hours.

This was a better noon-to-noon run, considering I had been becalmed most of the morning. The wind had started to pick up around 10 a.m., coming in from the south, which enabled me to sail clear of the other yacht. I did contemplate sailing over to the ketch, but in the end, I decided to continue heading north. In reality, if something had gone wrong on board the ketch, there was very little I could have done to help anyway. I had no engine to assist with close-quarter manoeuvring.

As the day progressed, the weather had slowly become cloudy, overcast and a lot cooler on deck. Given the chilly conditions, I spent a couple of hours below messing about playing my guitar and trying to write a song.

I first sensed something was different when the motion of *Seefalke* changed. I felt her starting to wallow in a large swell. By five o'clock, the wind was back to a southerly 5/6. With the barometer at 1008mb and dropping, I put a second reef in the mainsail but left the no.2 genoa up. George was coping well, and the boat speed had improved dramatically, which was welcome, given how far I still had to go.

18:00
The barometer had dropped again, to 1005mb. The wind had picked up, and there was now a twenty-foot swell

running, although the waves were spaced a long way apart. These were the largest seas I had seen for some while.

I decided to have an early tea before it got too rough to cook. I expected a long night of pumping the water out every hour.

21:00
The barometer had dropped by a further three millibars to 1002mb. The wind was now up to a constant force 7 and periodically gusting 8 to 9. *Seefalke* was starting to surf down the face of the waves, which wasn't good. There was a great big 'rooster tail' forming in *Seefalke*'s stern wake, which looked really impressive, but the yacht was going too fast for the conditions. Urgently, I shortened the sail before I ended up pitchpoling the yacht. I put a third reef in the mainsail and changed to the storm jib before the conditions got any worse. I was heavily relying on George to look after me and the yacht at this stage, which he had done before.

22:00
There was a clear, star-filled sky, further lit up by the moon. The wind had continued to increase and was now howling. I dropped the mainsail and lashed it to the boom, which was a real struggle given the conditions and the constant spray that was now coming over the yacht, making it hard for me to see.

The barometer had dropped to 996mb, another six millibars in two hours. My sailing instructor, John Hart, had told me to expect bad weather if the barometer dropped by more than three millibars in an hour. The last time I had seen my barometer drop so quickly was when I got caught out sailing down to Lisbon, crossing the Bay of Biscay.

Despite the high winds and big waves, the yacht was quite comfortable. The mainsail was lashed to the boom and I was sailing only with the storm jib up, which provided enough speed for steerage. This meant the yacht was moving at the same speed as the huge waves.

After several hours of running before this storm, I was confident that *Seefalke* was handling the conditions well and George was in control despite the challenging conditions. Based on this, I decided to get my head down and try to get some much-needed rest.

***

12th day at sea
Friday 6th November

01:00

The wind continued to increase, and I could sense that the waves were continuing to build. Trying to get some rest was impossible. The noise of the wind was deafening and frightening, and anything below deck that could rattle and make a noise did. I was pumping the yacht out every half an hour.

I had become fixated on my barometer, which continued to drop at three millibars an hour. At this point, I kept praying that it was broken. Periodically, I plucked up the courage to look at the waves through the cabin porthole. They were monstrous. They had very steep faces and breaking crests—this was the stuff of nightmares. I knew I was in a very dangerous situation and couldn't do anything about it. Venturing out on deck was no longer an option.

Suddenly, everything went silent, and straight away I knew something was very wrong. I jumped off my bunk, stood up quickly and braced myself against the cabin sides. I looked out of the port-side porthole and all I saw was a wall of black water, followed by the sound of a breaking wave quickly followed by a thump, and the next thing I knew, my entire world was upside down. Anything that wasn't bolted down broke free, including the twelve-volt battery, which was sitting loose on the cabin sole. The battery smashed into the coach roof, followed by my diving bottle. All my tools, plates, bread knives, cutlery, cups, pots, and pans flew across the cabin, followed by cooking oil, flour, salt, yeast and vinegar. Everything—books, charts, clothes—all ended up on the cabin roof, or in the bilge.

Luckily for me, the world righted itself, and the cabin lights stayed on; the house batteries were still working. I could see the mess and the amount of water in the yacht. The floorboards were floating around. Looking at the battery I saw the connection post had snapped off, leaving two big holes in it. I had to get rid of the battery fast before it spilt acid into the bilge water, which would give off chlorine gas. Without too much messing around, I threw it over the side.

I quickly checked myself all over. I had one small cut on my forehead about a quarter of an inch long.

To empty the water out of the yacht as fast as possible, I turned on both electric bilge pumps. Luckily, they still worked. Everything was in the bilge, and I had to clean it out to stop the bilge pumps from getting blocked. There were toilet rolls, digestive biscuits, bread, broken plates and cups, paper, charts, logbooks, knives, forks, eggs—everything. If it was broken, I threw it over the side.

With the water level dropping, I quickly checked inside the rest of the yacht for damage or leaks. Thankfully, I could not find any.

I had to venture on deck out of necessity to check for other damage. With a waterproof jacket on and my safety harness clipped to the jackstay, I crawled out of the main hatch into the cockpit. I experienced the full brunt of the howling wind for the first time. I had never witnessed conditions like this before; I was incredibly frightened.

As I surveyed the mast, I saw one of the lower spreaders was broken, leaving the mast unsupported and whipping around wildly. My first job was to try to support the mast as best as I could. Crawling on my hands and knees, I tried to go forward, which was incredibly hard with the amount of white water breaking over the yacht. I finally made it to the mast and attached the spare halyards to any anchor points I could find on the deck, before winching them up tight. I hoped that the halyards would function as extra stays and help stabilise the mast. After getting my breath, I watched the mast for a while. The halyards seemed to have done the trick.

Making my way back to the cockpit, I saw that the boom and the mainsail had been washed over the side. I had to leave them where they were—it was too dangerous, and they were far too heavy to haul back on deck given the conditions. Poor old George had been in the wars too. He had lost his vane, which had snapped clean off. This was something else I was going to have to deal with after this savage storm had abated.

To keep sailing, the only thing I could do was sheet the storm jib in tight and lash the tiller into the centre of the yacht, allowing the yacht to sail downwind and straight down the waves.

Once I'd fixed everything I could, I went below and tried to find some dry clothes. Of course, there weren't any. Everything was soaked.

After pumping the water out again, I lay on my bunk in my wet clothes with my wet sleeping bag on top of me, trying to rest.

Suddenly, it went silent again. I jumped up and braced myself against the cabin sides. Looking out the port porthole, all I could see was another wall of black water, followed by the sound of another breaking wave.

BANG, another thump, and I was upside down once more. This time it was much quicker. I rolled for about two seconds. All the things I had put away an hour ago were back in the bilge. Luckily, nothing hit me. The main cabin lights went out, so I had to find a torch. It was still in its holder next to the chart table. Looking around the cabin, I was back to square one: there was carnage everywhere, and the floorboards were once more floating around. This time, I had no electric bilge pumps; I had to pump the water out by hand and clear out the bilge at the same time.

After I cleaned up the mess, I had a quick check around, looking for any leaks. The forepeak was a right mess—the anchor had broken free—but thankfully, after a thorough inspection of the parts of the hull I could get to, there were no visible signs of any leaks.

I put my waterproof jacket back on and clipped myself to the yacht for the second time. I crawled back on deck. Looking around the yacht, the sight was devastating. The mast had snapped, leaving a short stump sticking out of the deck. The rest of the mast was hanging over the side in the water, still attached to the yacht by the rigging.

Both my dinghies had been washed off the cabin top, taking the handrails with them. The stanchions had all snapped, leaving the guard wires hanging loose. *Seefalke* had been totally battered. The one piece of good fortune was that the mainsail was still wrapped around the boom, which was lying against the side of the hull, stopping the broken part of the mast from hitting the hull and knocking a hole in it. If that had happened, I would be in Davy Jones' Locker and just another mystery in the Bermuda Triangle. I knew then the gods were still looking after me.

I retreated below decks as there was nothing else I could do at this point. The conditions were too dangerous, and the yacht was full of water again. It took ages pumping by hand to get the water back out.

Checking again inside the yacht for water leaks, I found that most of the water was coming in through the deck head. Four stanchion bases that had been bolted through the deck had been ripped out as the mast went over the side, leaving three-inch square holes in the deck. Water poured in every time a wave broke over the deck. I pushed rags into the holes to try and reduce the flow of water, but this didn't make much difference. Separately, there were holes left from the screws that held the coach roof handrails on, creating a shower-like effect in the main saloon as water was forced in. Thank the gods for small mercies—at least the hull hadn't been breached.

It went quiet again and then black, BANG! and thump. With my mast hanging over the side, we didn't roll this time. For the rest of that fateful night, I had to pump the yacht out every fifteen minutes.

***

13th day at sea
Saturday 7th November

06:00

For breakfast, I had two old Mars bars that I found in my survival grab bag. The wind had dropped to a mere force 7/8, although the seas were still massive and very confused—there was lots of angry white water everywhere. A few times in the night, I heard a thump when the broken part of the mast hit the hull. I simply couldn't afford for the yacht to get holed below the waterline, and I needed to do something about this ASAP.

I had bought a rigging cutting tool years ago, for a situation just like this. In daylight, I put my waterproof jacket back on, and ventured back on deck, taking the cutters with me. I crawled to the bow and, hanging on with each wave that broke over me, managed to cut away the forestay, with the no.3 genoa still attached. The broken part of the mast was pulled away from *Seefalke*, the sail acting as a drogue.

My next problem was the self-steering paddle was hitting the mast in the water. I crawled to the stern and managed to lift the paddle out of the water. I was able to take a closer look at the four big holes left from where the mast went over the side and ripped out the stanchion bases. I tried to block the holes from the top with more rags. This didn't work either. There were too many waves coming over the deck for me to stop the water forcing its way below.

There was nothing much else I could do safely on deck. I had to wait for the storm to abate some more before trying to fix anything else. On a positive note, the yacht was still floating, even though I had to pump it out for ten minutes in every fifteen.

12:00
Lunch was a bag of dehydrated food from my survival grab bag with a coffee to warm me up. The waves were still very confused, coming from all over the place, making it difficult to hold the kettle on the stove. I had to look on the bright side: the sun was out, although the wind was still blowing very hard. There was not much I could do but wait for the storm to subside. My main priority was staying afloat. There was no point in trying to keep a lookout for ships; I couldn't do anything to avoid them. Also, any captain with any sense would have run for shelter.

When I wasn't on the bilge pump, I spent time making a quick inventory, to take stock of my situation. *Seefalke* was in a very sorry state indeed. The mast was broken; the boom and mainsail were still lying over the side. Without a mast, I had no navigation lights, and my main VHF radio wouldn't transmit without an antenna. I didn't know if the solar panels and batteries would still work. I found my two electric alarm clocks in the bilge, so they got thrown out with all the other broken items. Both dinghies had gone—I couldn't abandon ship even if I wanted to.

The good news: I still had two handheld GPSs, and both were working. I had my small, handheld, rechargeable VHF radio, some flares and my EPIRB rescue beacon, if I felt the need to use it. The yacht wasn't leaking through the hull, and if I could fix the holes in the deck, I was in with a reasonable chance of getting her watertight.

18:00

Feeling hungry and tired from pumping the yacht out, I had to find something warm to eat. Without the mast to counterbalance the keel, the yacht had a very different motion, making it difficult for me to cook a tidy meal for tea. Scrabbling around in the bilge, I found a tin of vegetable soup, which I opened. Trying to hold the pot of soup over the stove as it swung back and forth without getting burnt or spilling it was fun. I lost some of the soup, but what I had left, I ate straight out of the pot. I also found some dry bread and a lump of cheese.

I managed to stay warm by working out on the bilge pump all day. However, I desperately need to get out of my wet clothes as my core temperature was going to start dropping. After I crossed the Atlantic, I had put my warm clothes in a dry survival bag. The last time I'd looked in there was when I had my great meal in Pampatar. Digging the bag out, I found the top two or three layers had got wet at some point and were very rotten and smelly. However, I found some jumpers towards the bottom. These were still smelly, but at least they were dry and warm.

***

14th day at sea
Sunday 8th November

06:00

I had been up most of the night pumping out the water. At one point, I fell asleep only to be woken up by the sound of water inside the yacht. The floorboards were floating again.

Overnight, the weather had improved. The wind had eased, and the sea state had flattened off quite a bit. The other good news was that the barometer was continuing to rise slowly. It was still rough, but the waves weren't breaking anymore, and they were getting further apart, meaning there was a lot less water on deck and consequently less down below.

My first job, after a coffee, was to get the broken mast away from the hull, where it was still attached by the rigging. With my waterproof jacket and harness on, I worked my way up to it. Using a hacksaw, I first cut a copper pipe, which had been placed in the centre of the mast to act as a conduit for electric cables to be run up inside. This must have been installed when the mast was originally made. Working my way slowly around the deck, I undid the split pins and removed the clevis pins from the rigging screws that were attached to the chain plates. I didn't want to cut the rigging in case I need them for a jury rig later on.

I left the backstay attached in the hope I could save the mast later. With the mast floating a long way behind the yacht and the storm jib being dragged even further behind, I now had a very effective makeshift drogue, which made the yacht more comfortable. Every so often, I could feel the yacht starting to surf down the face of a wave only for the mast to subsequently stop that from happening.

My next job was to recover the mainsail before I lost it. I started by tying a line from the boom to what was left of my mast. This was to keep the boom close to the hull. Next, I leant over the side and slowly untied the mainsail, taking off each reefing line. I slowly recovered the sail on deck and pushed it down the main cabin hatch as I went. The foot of the sail was still attached to the boom by the sail slides, and I had to cut each sail slide off, avoiding the boom each time the yacht rolled. I was hampered by having to stop what I was doing every half an hour to carry on pumping out the yacht. Consequently, recovering the mainsail took me most of the morning. Finally, using the line I had attached from the boom to the mast stump and hauling in the yacht's mainsheet with some brute force, I managed to get the boom over the stanchions and back on the deck. This was a huge result and a massive relief, as it was no longer possible for the hull to get damaged by all the debris hanging over the side.

12:00

All the work had taken a lot out of me, and I was hungry. I still had some dry bread from the last time I had baked. From cleaning the bilge, I managed to find a small packet of butter, the ones used in cafés. Where it had come from and how old it was, I had no idea. I had one last piece of cheese and an unbroken egg, all the ingredients for a fried egg and cheese sandwich. What an absolute winner.

The frying pan had also ended up in the bilge, so after giving it a quick clean, I put in a drop of oil and cracked my last egg. Hanging onto the handle, I watched as the egg slowly cooked. It looked lovely. Suddenly, the yacht lurched as another big wave slammed into it. I watched in horror as my last egg slid out of the frying pan, across the stove and onto the cabin sole. Without a second thought, I picked it up, washed the dirty bilge water off it and stuck it straight back in the frying pan. My dinner was the best fried egg and cheese sandwich I ever tasted.

That afternoon, I cut up a plywood hatch cover from my quarter berth into four six-inch-square patches. This was great fun with the yacht rolling all over the place, but I finally managed to get the job done.

I screwed the plywood patches over the holes in the deck, using plenty of silicon sealer to provide a watertight seal. My temporary fix worked, and thankfully, the water stopped coming through the deck and into the bilge. This was a major achievement. For the first time in days, I didn't have to pump the yacht out every half an hour, and going forward, I would be able to get a lot more sleep each night. Everything was starting to look a little rosier.

With the two major jobs completed, my next task was to make a full list of the provisions I had left on board. I went through every locker and cupboard on board in search of food and rations. I put everything I found on the chart table, which didn't amount to much at all. I had the following:

- Four tins of baked beans.
- Four tins of corn beef hash.

- One tin of chilli.
- Six packets of soup.
- One unopened box of cornflakes.
- Three one-meal packs of porridge.
- One packet each of rice, pasta and mashed potato.
- One half-eaten jar of peanut butter.
- One tin of powdered milk.
- Half a jar of coffee.
- Half a bottle of brandy.
- A few potatoes, some oranges and an apple.
- A few teabags I had bought when I left Wales.

Additionally, I had some dehydrated food in my survival grab bag, which I kept in case I had another emergency or storm where it would be hard to cook. All told, this was not a lot of food to continue this trip, which had already taken much longer than I had expected.

I had nine tins of food, and if I used one a day this was not going to be enough. I was pretty sure I was going to be at sea for a lot longer than nine days. If I had any chance of getting through this ordeal, I was going to have to start rationing food, in what was now a survival mission. If I used half a can for each main meal a day that would give me eighteen days, and in addition, I could have porridge and cornflakes for breakfast. By adding rice and pasta to soup, I'd have a few more meals and a few more days of food to keep me going.

I wasn't worried about gas for cooking—I'd refilled my gas bottles in Margarita. I had plenty of water and could always catch rainwater as a backup. I felt a bit happier now I had a plan and rations for at least twenty days. My next task was to work out where the nearest port was that I could realistically sail to, with what was going to be a very small jury rig.

Turning on my GPS, it gave me a position of 29°41'N 71°06'W, which I plotted on my chart. I worked out that Bermuda was approximately three hundred and sixty miles away to the north-east, and initially I thought that this might be my best option but decided against it after a more detailed look at the charts. Bermuda is surrounded by reefs and had a reputation for being expensive. It would be hard to find work there and get the yacht fixed. Going back to

St Martin was off the table. It was too far, and I would be sailing against headwinds and adverse currents. The wind had also been very light during the initial stages of my trip, which was why I was in the mess I was now in. I ruled the Bahamas out too for similar reasons as Bermuda. There were too many islands and reefs to contend with, especially as I was probably only going to be able to reach or sail downwind.

I decided my best option was to head for Moorhead City, USA, which was approximately four hundred and twenty miles away. It was a lot closer than my original destination of the Chesapeake Bay. The only snag was that I didn't have any large-scale charts to get into Moorhead City. All I had was a small drawing in my guidebook.

I was hoping for a further improvement in the weather to enable me to set up a jury rig and start sailing again. With a prevailing easterly wind and west-flowing current, I felt the conditions would enable me to sail around thirty nautical miles a day. Based on this fag-packet assumption, I estimated that it would take me fourteen to seventeen days to get to Moorhead City, with a bit of luck.

That night, I had a whole tin of corned beef hash, as I hadn't eaten properly in the past four days. Feeling a bit happier about everything, I had coffee and a tot of brandy as a treat—my diet would have to start in the morning. I spent the rest of the evening trying to work out the best way to rig something out of what was left of my mast and sails.

***

15th day at sea
Monday 9th November

06:00
I enjoyed a much quieter night when compared to the last few. I got a lot more sleep, as I didn't have to pump the yacht out half as much, and awoke to a much better day. The sea had dropped right off. The wind was still blowing force 7, even though the barometer was rising more slowly.

I started my rationing. For breakfast, I had half a packet of porridge and one cup of coffee, instead of my usual two.

I guess I already knew it, but in the cold light of day, my mast was in a very sorry state. Although I still had approximately eighteen feet sticking out of the deck, it was unsupported and was flapping about very precariously. To make matters worse, there was a nine- or ten-foot split in the middle of it, leaving very little strength in what was left.

First up, I needed to lash the split in the timber. I tied a piece of rope in a loop around the top of the split, and using the spreader as a lever, I was able to twist the rope up until the lashing was properly tensioned. Once the split was closed up, I tied the rest of my rope around it all to stop the spreader from unwinding and releasing the tension. Next, I needed to find a way to support the short mast with a forestay and two lower shrouds. As part of this exercise, I also needed to rig a main and jib halyard. Using a piece of rope, I made up a jury rig to use as a forestay, with two blocks for halyards attached.

Taking my boat hook, which I had luckily stowed below when I left St Martin, I stood precariously on top of the mast winches. This made things really challenging, but with the boat hook with jury rig attached to it in one hand, I could just about reach the top of the mast. As the yacht rolled in the swell, I was getting continually swung around the mast. After a lot of struggling and swearing, I finally managed to get the forestay jury rig up and around the top of the mast. It took me a hell of a long time, and I was covered in bruises by the end of it. Finally, I tied the forestay to the bow, leaving me with two halyards I could use to pull the sails up with.

For the lower shrouds, I tied two ropes with slipknots in them around the mast as high up as I could reach then tied the ends onto the aft chain plate. My short, stubby mast was now supported. Next, I removed the damaged sail track and the mangled copper pipe, and finally, I had a mast and rig I could use to set up a jury rig. Great news.

12:00

After a break for lunch and a cup of soup, I needed to work out how I was going to make my sails fit the new, shorter mast and decide what to do with the other thirty feet of mast still being dragged behind the yacht. I decided to keep it in case I could use it somehow later on, which meant I needed to get the section back aboard.

With me safely clipped on to the yacht, I pulled on the backstay until I could reach the first part of the mast. I attached a separate rope to this section and made it fast so I could keep the mast alongside. Leaning over the side, I stripped the remaining rigging and stowed it safely, thinking it might come in handy later on.

Once all the rigging was removed, the mast was much lighter and easier to manage. To my utter surprise, it only took a few attempts to get it back aboard. On my first attempt, however, I lifted the end out of the water and gave it a big tug. As the yacht rolled to starboard, the mast came flying towards me, nearly hitting me in my crotch. Thankfully, I moved out of the way just in time.

After a couple more goes, I managed to get the mast back on deck. I removed the final bits of standing rigging, the spreaders and the diamond, which I kept. I then secured the mast to the deck with sail ties. This was a major achievement, and I felt well pleased with myself. I was another step closer to getting myself out of this mess. I'd had a really tough but productive day, at the end of which I was mentally and physically drained. For tea, I had half a tin of corned beef hash mixed with some pasta, and a coffee with a small tot of brandy.

I spent the rest of the evening giving more thought to the most effective sail plan I could come up with that would get me to Moorhead City.

***

16th day at sea
Tuesday 10th November

06:00

I was blessed with light winds, a flat sea, and the sun was out. This was a good day to get all my wet clothes dried. Before having half a packet of porridge and a coffee, I spread all my clothes out across the deck.

Once breakfast was out of the way, I had one last job to complete before I could start getting some sails up, and that was to get the boom working. The goose-neck fitting had been ripped off, so all I could do was lash the boom to the mast as best I could. I got the mainsheet working, which gave me a functioning boom. I was all finished and could now focus on getting some sails up and starting my long trip towards land.

I attached the trysail to the boom and hoisted it up. Next, I rigged the storm jib to the forestay and got that hoisted too. I sheeted both sails in, and slowly *Seefalke* started to move forwards. I fixed the self-steering by replacing the vane with the spare I'd made before I left Wales. With George back up and running, it felt like old times again.

12:00. Pos. 30°15'N 072°03'W

After an orange for lunch, I turned on my GPS. I had a midday position. I had been pushed sixty miles to the north-west by the wind and current since I last checked two days ago, which was good news. Getting that little bit closer to land helped my limited food supply.

According to the GPS, my speed over the ground was roughly one and a half knots, which wasn't brilliant, but I was moving. With the help of a bit of current, I hoped I could cover between 36 and 50 miles a day. This was still going to make for a very slow passage, and if I could coax a bit more speed out of my set-up, it would make a huge difference. I had done enough on the rig for one day, though, and so I decided to leave this little challenge. I was just content with being back sailing again.

My afternoon was spent repairing the solar panels. One had blown a diode, which was unrepairable with the equipment and spares I had on board. The other one, however, looked more promising. A wire had been pulled out. Once I emptied the water out of the connection box, sprayed it with WD40 and let it dry in the sun, I managed to get it working again. This was another big result on my road to recovery. I could now recharge my batteries and, more importantly, my handheld VHF radio. I would also now be able to use the electric bilge pump at night, if needed.

18:00

I had the same for tea as the previous day, corned beef hash and pasta, followed by coffee with a tot of brandy.

***

17th day at sea
Wednesday 11th November

06:00

I enjoyed my first good night's sleep in ages and felt really refreshed when I woke up. I had porridge again for breakfast and sat in the cockpit with my coffee, enjoying the early rays of sunshine, although it was still quite chilly.

There was still a light easterly breeze and flat sea. With this in mind, I turned my attention to improving my sailing performance. After sitting on the coach roof for a while, contemplating the problem, I came up with the idea of cutting down my oldest no.2 genoa. I cut the sail roughly in half and fixed the bottom half to the forestay, then I trimmed the foot until it cleared the deck and then attached two sheets at the leach. Next, I took the trysail down and replaced it with the top half of the genoa. This needed to be trimmed to improve the shape. Once I was happy, I cut holes in the foot and luff and attached it to the mast and boom using sail ties.

My new sail set-up made me laugh. The boom was longer than the mast was high. Laughs aside, when I checked the GPS, my new sail configuration had breathed fire into the yacht. I was now doing an electric three knots over the ground, which was unreal. At this speed, I could reasonably expect to cover in excess of 75NM a day, subject to the wind remaining constant. While this was unlikely, having the capability to cover more ground meant getting in somewhere was now a real prospect.

12:00. Pos. 30°56'N 072°37'W

Logged 50NM in the last 24 hours.

A bloody good start. While sitting on deck eating my last apple for lunch, I sensed that there was a ship in the area. After scanning the horizon, I picked it up. I tried to call it on my handheld VHF, with no luck.

I watched the ship change course, and it started heading towards me. She was called *Asphalt Champion*, and as she closed in on my position, she circled the yacht.

I waved at the ship holding my radio. Two minutes later, the ship's French captain, called me on the radio.

He asked, "Is everything okay?"

"Yes, I'm fine. I got rolled and lost part of my mast, but the hull is sound. I'm making slow progress but think I will be able to make it to a suitable port."

I also told the officer of the watch that I had enough food and water for twenty-two days.

"Do you need any more food?" he asked.

"No, but I need a beer."

"I cannot help you there. We are a dry ship."

"Just my luck, a dry ship," I replied.

"Did you get caught out in that storm?"

"Yes, it came from nowhere. I knew nothing about it until it hit me. It rolled the yacht twice."

"You are very lucky, my friend. The BBC World Service radio reported that eleven thousand people are dead or missing in Honduras. Separately, a windjammer tall ship is missing with the possible loss of thirty-one crew."

"Bloody hell. Did the storm have a name?"

"Yes, Hurricane Mitch. It was a class five hurricane when it hit Honduras."

I nearly fainted, Mitch was the hurricane that had formed before I left St Martin. It seemed inconceivable that I could be caught out by it thirteen days later.

I asked the captain if he could call my mother and tell her I was okay and that I would be a bit late getting into port.

After I passed on the phone number, he said, "I will do that right away."

"Thank you. Also, can you call the US Coastguard and inform them of my situation, position and intended destination of Morehead City?"

"Yes, no problem."

Before leaving, the captain asked if I was all right again. I said I was fine; sailing at three knots meant it shouldn't take me too long to get into port.

Wishing me luck, *Asphalt Champion* turned and headed south.

Really, I didn't want the US Coastguard to turn up. They would make me abandon the yacht—the only thing I owned.

For supper, I had rice with half a tin of beans mixed in, and a coffee with a tot of brandy as my nightcap.

***

18th day at sea
Thursday 12th November

06:00

Had a quiet night. Got up a few times and had a look around. We'd made northerly progress all night, which was good. For breakfast, I enjoyed half a packet of porridge with a cup of coffee. It was another nice morning, so I spread my clothes, my sleeping bag and my book out on deck, trying to dry everything off. I also plugged the holes in the coach roof and did a better job of resealing and refastening the stanchion bases. With the refitting of the stanchion, and with the guard wires tightened up, *Seefalke* was starting to look like a yacht again.

12:00. Pos. 31°24'N 073°38'W

Logged 58NM in the last 24 hours.

This was progress. The light wind had returned following the storms of the previous week.

For lunch, I ate my last orange, together with a teaspoon of peanut butter. This didn't really fill a hole, though, and I was still hungry.

I spent the rest of the afternoon on deck, ripping out the wet pages of my book, making sure I had read each page, before I threw it over the side. Most of my afternoon was taken up agonising about what I was going to have for tea.

Supper was rice and beans, finishing off an already opened can of beans, with coffee and a tot of brandy to round things off.

***

19th day at sea
Friday 13th November

06:00

The wind had picked up overnight and had been blowing quite hard from the north. I awoke to the sound of sails flapping around like mad. The forestay, with all the halyards, had fallen down the mast. I spent a good hour standing on the boom, hanging on to the mast with one hand with the boat hook in the other, trying to get the forestay back up the mast.

12:00. Pos. 31°53'N 074°22'W
Logged 48NM in the last 24 hours.

What a result: three days sailing around 50NM. I was sailing better under jury rig than I had with a full set of sails at the start of the trip. I was maintaining a course between east and north-east, whichever was best for George.

I had spent most of the day below deck reading my book. Conditions outside the yacht were not very good: foggy and cold with a very light north wind.

I had an uneasy feeling, so I got up to scan the horizon. Peering out of the main hatch, I saw a white ship in the distance. I tried to call it on my handheld VHF Radio to get a weather report, but again without any luck. The ship proved to be a bit of a distraction. When I picked my book up, I saw a wet page, so I ripped it out and threw it over the side, only to find I had been holding the book upside down. I had thrown the last page of a one-thousand-page book away. Just my luck. Although I was gutted, I decided to continue reading it.

18:00
Supper consisted of half a tin of corned beef hash, fried with my last potato, and coffee with a small tot of brandy to finish.

***

20th day at sea
Saturday 14th November

06:00
Around midnight, the wind had picked up, and the forestay and sails had fallen down the mast again. I had to drop the sails and tie them to the deck. The yacht was rolling around in the small, choppy seas. Bloody great. It had been too difficult to try to get the forestay back up in the dark.

Looking out through the porthole, I saw an overcast, cold-looking day, with a fresh breeze. Before I got the yacht moving again, I made myself a cup of coffee to celebrate my birthday. For an extra treat, I put a tot of brandy in it.

Climbing up the companionway ladder, I placed my coffee cup on top of the coach roof. With my head sticking up through the hatch, I looked towards the bow and saw the dorsal fin of a huge whale. It surfaced right under the bow. The back of the whale came out of the water, well above the deck. If I had been standing at the bow, I would have been able to touch the whale; it was that close. The dorsal fin was black and looked to me to have the same shape as a killer whale.

I quickly made my way to the mast and clipped my safety line around it and watched as the whale disappeared below the surface. Looking around, I saw three whales swimming around the yacht. They seemed very curious. One by one, each whale swam straight towards the yacht and dived beneath it. Sometimes they would roll over and swim inverted with their belly up underneath the yacht, coming from every direction. Amazing to watch, but too close for comfort. I did think of putting my snorkelling gear on and jumping over the side to get a better look at them, but in the end, I decided against it.

After an hour, the three surfaced behind the yacht and swam in a line only thirty feet off the portside, lifting their big heads out of the water to look at the yacht and me before disappearing below the water for the final time.

What a birthday present. I wondered what Prince Charles got for his?—We have the same date of birth.

After the whales departed, I needed a J-cloth shower. I was soaking wet from them blowing off close to the yacht. I had also managed to get the rigging back up the mast, sailing again before I had my half packet of porridge and another coffee. I realised that, for the first time, I was running low on coffee.

I remembered being given, at some point in the past, a book to log any whale sightings in the North Atlantic. I found it still dry and in one piece, which was a surprise. Looking through the book, I couldn't accurately identify which species of whale I had seen. I could not match the dorsal fin to any whale in the book. My best guess was they were either Bryde's whales or right whales. The description was the same for both.

Gentle and very curious creatures, both species are capable of reaching fifty feet in length and weighing up to fifty tons. In the front of the book was a warning advising that it's illegal to sail or motor to within three hundred metres of a whale. Someone should have told the whales that. On another note, I don't know why I clipped myself to the mast. If one of the whales had touched the yacht, *Seefalke* would have been matchwood.

12:00. Pos. 32°08'N 074°40'W
Logged 20NM in the last 24 hours.

With too much wind hampering progress the previous night and the distraction of the whales during that morning, I thought 20 miles was a respectable 24-hour run, it was better than I had expected. For lunch, I savoured a teaspoon of peanut butter. By taking my time to slowly lick the spoon, I made this nutritious feast last half an hour.

While I sat on the deck that afternoon, a seabird landed in the cockpit. It looked absolutely knackered. Its head was down, and its wings were splayed. I think it was an oystercatcher. I tried to pick it up, but as I got closer, it scrambled to the counter and got stuck in the self-steering guide wires. I went to help it, only to watch it set itself free and fly into the sea. Once in the water, it lay head down with its wings extended out. I watched as it was carried away by the sea. The bird died, and I felt very sad. There was nothing I could do to save it. I thought if a tired bird landed on the deck again, I would leave the poor thing alone.

Tea consisted of half a tin of corned beef hash and pasta, coffee, and a very small tot of brandy, which was also running low. I was going to miss my nightcaps once I drank the last of it.

***

21st day at sea
Sunday 15th November

06:00
I had a really rough night. The barometer had dropped to 1011mb, with the wind blowing force 5/6 from the southwest, bringing a big sea with it. Once again, all sails had fallen down.

I got the forestay back on top of the mast, and I decided to make my rigging sturdier. Using a thin rope, I put a figure-of-eight knot in one end, putting the loose end through the knot to make a noose, All I had to do was lasso the top of the mast. This was quite difficult to do, but once I had the lasso around the top of the mast and over the forestay, I put the rope around the mast winch, pulling it tight. With the forestay trapped at the top of the mast, it looked a lot better and stronger, and with the mainsail and genoa sheeted in, my boat speed picked back up. I hoped I'd fixed this annoying problem for the last time.

12:00. Pos. 32°46'N 075°02'W
Logged 42NM in the last 24 hours.

I was steering a course of 320° mag with a force 3 southerly breeze. I'd started to notice a pattern in the wind direction. One day the wind would be northerly, and I'd sail west; next day the wind would be in the east, and I'd sail north; then south, and I'd sail north-east. The net effect of all of this was a course made good of roughly 320° mag when I averaged out my respective headings over the three-day cycle. Although I was wandering around a bit, I was generally heading in the right direction, which was all good.

The further north I sailed, the colder it got. I had to dig out my old winter jumpers that I hadn't worn since leaving Wales. For lunch, I licked another teaspoon of peanut butter for half an hour. Psychologically, it felt like I had eaten more than I actually had.

18:00
The wind had started to die and was down to a light, south-westerly force 1/2 breeze. The barometer had risen to 1020mb, meaning I was sailing in a high-pressure system. It was a real struggle trying to keep the yacht moving in any direction.

For tea, I had beans and rice, followed by coffee with my last tot of brandy.

***

22nd day at sea
Monday 16th November

06:00

I awoke to fog and more light wind. Breakfast consisted of another half a packet of porridge. With coffee in hand, I went on deck to do my checks on the sails, rigging and George. Just as I finished, I noticed a ship in the distance, probably less than two miles away on my starboard bow. I could just about make it out in the lifting fog. It looked like a white Coastguard vessel, heading away from me on a similar course. I tried calling it up on VHF channel 16, without any luck. I couldn't make the name out—it was too far away to see, particularly given the misty conditions. I continued to watch the ship until it disappeared into the distance.

12:00. Pos. 33°06'N 074°52'W

Logged 22NM in the last 24 hours.

Another poor 24-hour sail. But the good news was, from my midday position, I was only one hundred and thirty miles away from Moorhead City. Two or three days of good sailing and I could get into port, with a bit of luck. However, I had a big problem looming. Having studied my pilot book and chart, I could see that I would soon pick up the Gulf Stream, which ran in a north-easterly direction, taking me away from my planned destination.

All day, the wind was blowing from the south-west. The best course I could make, given the wind direction, was 315° mag, which meant I was pointing straight at Moorhead City.

What I really needed to do was to start sailing on a westerly heading, to compensate for the anticipated effects of the north-easterly current. The good news was the Gulf Stream carried warmer water, so I decided to check the bilge. The water was still cold, so thankfully I wasn't in it yet. And if the wind followed its three-day cycle, I had a very good chance of sailing west, into Moorhead City.

18:00

For supper, I had another half tin of beans in rice, with a coffee. My brandy tot had finished. I sorely missed my one evening treat.

I crashed out early. I was bored, and with nothing else to do, I started to think about my next problem: the Gulf Stream.

I'd only been in bed for ten minutes when I had an uneasy feeling. When I stuck my head out of the hatch, there was another ship in the distance. It was really cold on deck. I hunkered down on my favourite top step to keep myself warm and kept eyes on the ship until it passed and sailed into the distance.

***

22nd day at sea
Tuesday 17th November

06:00

The wind was blowing hard from the southwest, force 6/7, which was not good news at all. My course was taking me north of Moorhead City. Sailing past my destination was fast becoming a reality. The barometer was also down to 1005mb, which wasn't good either.

Breakfast was the last of the porridge.

12:00. Pos. 34°10'N 075°10'W

Logged 66NM in the last 24 hours.

My best 24 hours to date, better than most days when I'd carried a full sail area at the start of this trip. Despite my record run, it wasn't a particularly nice day. The strong wind was biting, and with no sun to warm things up it was pretty miserable and overcast. The sea had also built up, but thankfully there were no breaking waves. I dropped the genoa to help George and make the yacht more comfortable. We were sailing very slowly northwest on the mainsail alone. The problem was I needed to sail a more westerly course if I still wanted to make it to Moorhead City. However, I couldn't afford to take any risks with the jury rig, so I just made the best course I could in the hope that the wind direction would change.

As I got closer to the coast, I started to see a lot more birds, which was quite heartening. Some landed on deck, and others circled the yacht.

Bored, with nothing much for me to do, I decided to finish reading my thousand-plus-page book. I really wished I hadn't thrown the last page away. I also took advantage of a rain squall that came through and had a bloody cold shower, although it was good to feel clean and get the salt off me.

For lunch, I had the last spoonful of peanut butter. I licked the jar clean.

18:00
For supper, I changed things up a bit with half a tin of corned beef hash with mashed potato and a coffee to wash it down.

***

24th day at sea
Wednesday 18th November

06:00
The wind had gone round to the west and continued to blow strongly overnight, which compounded my problems further. The seas were pretty big too. The change in the wind direction meant that I was now sailing north, which was no good at all.

After days of eating porridge for breakfast, I was now on to cornflakes with powdered milk, the breakfast of champions. Also, I was down to my last grains of coffee, so things were getting pretty grim.

12:00. Pos. 34°35'N 075°02'W
Logged 25NM in the last 24 hours.

The wind eased off in the mid-morning, to a southerly force 3/4, bringing warm, wet and misty weather with it. I immediately put the foresail back up and altered course to 270°. My midday fix left me with a real sinking feeling. I was now a long way north-east of my track, and this could only mean one thing: I was in the Gulf Stream, which was effectively taking me back out to sea. I checked the water in the bilge, and it definitely felt warm, which confirmed my fears.

Even though I was sailing west in an attempt to try and sail across the Gulf Stream, when I checked my COG with the GPS, the current was taking me north-east at 4.5 knots, which was an absolute nightmare.

18:00

Supper was more of the same: half a tin of corned beef hash, with mashed potato and a coffee.

***

25th day at sea
Thursday 19th November

06:00

Breakfast consisted of more cornflakes with the last of the coffee.

As I walked around the deck doing my checks, I saw a sperm whale swimming past the yacht, about three hundred feet off the port side. It showed no interest in the yacht or me, unlike the whales I saw on my birthday. The whale stayed on the surface and was swimming at pace in a westerly direction. It truly was a magnificent sight.

12:00. Pos. 35°26'N 074°54'W

Logged 51NM in the last 24 hours.

Even though I had been sailing west for the last eighteen hours, the north-east flow of the Gulf Stream had cancelled out my westerly course. My latest fix confirmed my worst fears: I had been carried past Moorhead City and was now 32 miles east of Cape Hatteras, which wasn't great news all round.

I was at a really low ebb. Having battled to get this far on sheer drive and determination, I couldn't understand why I wasn't getting a break. Just a couple more days of south or south-easterly winds, and I would have been home and dry.

Instead, I was now heading further north and entering a really dangerous stretch of water known as the "Ships' Graveyard". My pilot book warned that the area off Cape Hatteras was prone to sea mist and strong storm-force winds caused by the warm air of the Gulf Stream interacting with the colder air coming off the coast. In addition to the mist and high winds, the shelving nature of the seabed meant that the area was also susceptible to very short, sharp wave patterns. This is why it's estimated that there are over a thousand shipwrecks in the area.

One small piece of good news: the bilge water felt cold again, and so I was confident I had managed to work my way out of the Gulf Stream. I decided that the only thing I could do now was go back to my original plan and continue on to the Chesapeake Bay. It was roughly 110 miles to Cape Henry at the southern end of the Chesapeake Bay. Initially, I'd need to continue heading north-east until I cleared Hatteras Island, and then run northwest up the coast.

The wind had picked up from the south, the sea was flat, and I was in a better mood. My boat speed was up, and to celebrate, I had a whole packet of soup for my lunch.

18:00

I saw a big school of dolphins directly in front of the yacht. The water was a hive of activity; the pod must have consisted of a hundred dolphins or more. It was a fantastic sight, watching the dolphins playing in the yacht's bow wave. If I'd leant over the side of the yacht, I could have touched them.

I was less rash at suppertime and reverted to half a tin of beans with rice. I tried drinking black tea made from a three-year-old teabag. It tasted horrible, and I decided to give it a miss.

23:30

I was fifteen miles north of Cape Hatteras, becalmed. I could still see the loom of the lighthouse to the south of me. I could also see lights coming from the fishing boats in the area. I heard the engine on one boat with whom there was a risk of collision. To alert the boat to my position, I shone a torch onto the mainsail. This was my only means of drawing attention to the yacht. They saw my illuminated sail and changed course until they had dropped behind me. Given the amount of traffic in the area, sleeping wasn't feasible; I needed to maintain an effective lookout.

***

26th day at sea
Friday 20th November

06:00

The wind quietly started to fill in from the south-west. I had about eight to ten knots of wind, which was allowing George to steer a course of 335° mag. I also managed to contact a ship, who gave me a much-needed weather update. The outlook was looking quite good. A light southerly breeze was expected to remain in place for the next three days. I also asked the officer of the watch for any advice on sailing into Pamlico Sound and then on to Bodie Island, both of which were nearby. I didn't have any large-scale charts of the area, nor any information in my pilot book. The guy kindly agreed to look into this for me and said he'd call me back. Half an hour later, he was back on the radio.

His first question was: "What's your draft?"

"Six feet," I said.

"It's too shallow for you. There's a very narrow, winding approach channel, with lots of sandbanks either side, which are constantly shifting with the currents. You'll be better off heading up to Norfolk."

Thanking him for his advice, I watched as he continued heading north.

Looking around, I could see lots of sport fishing boats. None of them showed much interest in me, apart from one who slowed down and had a look at the yacht. The guy driving the boat stopped to ask if I needed help. I said I was fine and told him my plan to sail up to Norfolk. He too went off, wishing me luck.

12:00. Pos. 35°49'N 075°23'W

Logged 33NM in the last 24 hours.

As well as the sports boats, I was sailing in the vicinity of four trawlers. One of them was quite close. I tried calling it up on the VHF but to no avail. I even stood up in the cockpit waving the damn radio at him, hoping he would see me and make contact. I called the trawler repeatedly as it got closer. By now, I could see her blue hull and the name *Genny* painted on the bow. I found it really strange that *Genny's* skipper didn't seem bothered about responding; I would have thought my jury rig would clearly indicate I'd had some major problem. *Welcome to the good old USA,* I thought.

Finally, I did manage to raise *Genny's* skipper on the radio. He was a really grumpy guy. However, he did advise that there was a Coastguard base at Bodie Island. I subsequently called the Coastguard and gave them my current position and situation. They advised me to continue on to the Chesapeake Bay, saying the entrance to Bodie was tricky, which confirmed what the ship had told me. I also got a further update on the weather, which was largely the same: light winds from the south, force 3, for the next three days.

I had one last question for the Coastguard officer, which was the range of the tide in the bay. If it was half of the tide of Barry, it would be a real nightmare getting into the bay. The answer I had back put a shine on my day.

Two and a half feet.

This cheered me up. I was now in contact with the Coastguard and there were lots of boats around who could help me if I had any further difficulties. Furthermore, with only 75NM to go, I expected to be in the Chesapeake Bay in just over two days, which was fantastic news. The end to this adventure was finally in sight!

18:00

It had turned into a lovely day with a good breeze. I had been steering the yacht myself most of the afternoon, trying to get to the Chesapeake Bay a bit quicker.

For supper, I had chilli and rice, eating the whole tin in one go—what a treat, I had been saving the chilli for my last night at sea. I felt full, happy, and confident that I would be standing on dry land soon.

22:00

I had been sailing really well for the last ten hours, and a quick check-in with the GPS told me that I had logged 30NM and was continuing to sail at three knots. The southerly wind was warm, and George was doing a decent job of steering the yacht. The barometer was steady at 1020mb, and the forecast remained good. There was only one trawler in the area, and he was keeping clear after I had made visual contact with him.

The last two nights had been tiring, with no sleep. After checking there were no other ships around, I went below to put my head down for a twenty-minute power nap. I fell asleep pretty quickly, for how long I have no idea—all I know is my sixth sense was soon screaming at me to get up. I awoke to the sound of howling wind and rain, which was completely out of kilter with the forecast. Quickly, I put my waterproof jacket on. Without zipping it up, I rushed into the cockpit.

Everything was wrong. The yacht was sailing south; the wind was blowing hard from the north; it was raining and very foggy. As I peered over the bow into the gloom, I could just make out three faint navigation lights, which I sensed weren't coming from the trawler that had been following me earlier.

With a sense of imminent danger, I knew this was all wrong, very wrong. I unhooked the self-steering, pushing the tiller away from me with my foot. I eased out the mainsail and the genoa sheets and steered back out to sea to the east on a reach.

Thirty seconds later, out of the mist high above me, I saw a white light followed by the bow of a ship. I had been on deck less than one minute. I saw clearly the letters K.S.R.E.A.M painted on the hull. The letters were fifty feet high. I frantically shone my torch into the mainsail and towards the bridge of the container ship in the hope that someone on the bridge would see me. In one minute, the ship had passed, and I watched in a state of shock as its stern light vanished into the fog. The ship clearly hadn't seen me, and who knows what would have happened if my sixth sense had not woken me up at that exact moment in time.

Still shaken, I decided to continue sailing east out into the Gulf Stream for the rest of the night, leaving all the sails up. I wanted to get away from the shipping lanes as fast as possible.

Before I got my head down to get some more sleep, I checked the barometer. It had dropped to 1005mb. Now I starting to understand why the weather in that area was so unpredictable and why Cape Hatteras was called the "Ships' Graveyard".

***

27th day at sea
Saturday 21st November

06:00

I had slept for far longer than I should have but still felt knackered after my latest ordeal. I had been sailing east all night. At first light, with the wind still blowing a good force

6/7 from the north, I dropped the genoa to make the yacht comfortable and tacked onto a course towards Cape Henry.

Breakfast consisted of another bowl of cornflakes with powdered milk.

12:00. Pos. 36°15'N 075°03'W
Logged 30NM in the last 24 hours.

From my midday position, I was only 65 miles away from Cape Henry, although the Gulf Stream had taken me away from the coast. I had more to do than I wanted but just had to get on with it.

The barometer was starting to rise again, and the wind was dropping and slowly going back around to the south. I changed course to 310° mag and put the genoa back up.

For lunch, I had cornflakes again.

18:00
I was heading back into the shipping lanes again. I needed to make sure I stayed awake and kept a better lookout this time. I couldn't afford another episode like last night. The weather was a lot nicer though, and there was a beautiful bright sky, signalling that it was going to be a very chilly night. I sat on the top step of the ladder, with all my warm clothes on.

For tea, I had half a tin of beans and rice again but still felt hungry after I had eaten it.

***

28th day at sea
Sunday 22nd November

06:00
The barometer was up to 1040mb, nearly off the scale. It had been bitterly cold last night, and I was quite happy when the sun came out to warm me up. As the sun rose the breeze picked up from the south. There were a lot of ships around the yacht, a few miles apart and heading in the same direction as me.

I had cornflakes for breakfast again.

In the morning sun, I was back on deck, checking the rigging and sails. In the water, I saw a gannet, trapped by some fishing line. I watched it struggle. There was nothing I could do to help it.

12:00. Pos. 36°25'N 075°41'W

Logged 33NM in the last 24 hours.

I had been sailing west all morning, working my way through the shipping lanes. I could now see the coastline clearly.

For lunch—cornflakes again.

18:00

I was only 5NM off the coast by this point, and though I could see a surf line that was being caused by water breaking over a sandbank, I decided to sail on a more northerly course and head away from the coast.

I ate the last packet of soup and rice for supper.

23:00

It was another lovely night. I was sailing quietly up the coast towards the Chesapeake. I could make out the loom from the Cape Henry light, which was roughly fifteen miles north of my position. I was now too close to the coast to be sleeping.

***

29th day at sea
Monday 23rd November

06:00

It had been a long night. The wind died to the point where I had to helm. As day broke, George and I were sailing past Cape Henry, at the southern end of the Chesapeake Bay. For the first time, I could see the Bay Bridge and tunnel complex. I carried on sailing north until I could see the two gaps in the bridge. This made it easy for me to then pick up the well-marked channel along the Thimble Shoal into the bay.

The real highlight of that morning was the American Air Force putting on an air show for me. There were a couple of F-14 Tomcats flying overhead.

As I sailed closer to the bridge, I could see a large gap. The bridge sections came out from the land on either side of the bay, and at the seaward ends of the sections were white buildings which looked like terminals. The buildings were in fact situated at each end of the tunnels that connected the various sections of the bridge. This was an ingenious design that allowed large ships and sailing vessels to pass through the bridge without having to worry about any height restrictions.

There were a lot of sport fishing boats around, although none of them showed any interest in me. There was quite a bit of shipping traffic too. As I made my way up the channel, the American Navy joined the air show with a submarine motoring alongside me. It was an evil, sinister-looking thing.

I realised that getting into the bay wasn't going to be easy. My pilot book recommended entry via the southern channel, following the Thimble Shoal. The pilot book also advised me to take note of the strong currents in that part of the bay, which could run up to three knots, with particular reference to the area around the bridge.

With only a light southerly wind to sail in on, I needed to try and stay out of the strong outgoing tide, as this would cancel out my progress into the bay.

I got lucky with the outgoing current. It was flowing against me but nothing like three knots. Still, the only way I could sail through into the bay was to start out close to the bridge on the port side and try to sail crablike across the current at an angle. I had to sail out of the narrow channel a few times to avoid large ships, which were constrained by their draught and ability to manoeuvre. Finally, on my fourth attempt, I managed to sail up the channel past the bridge complex into the Chesapeake Bay. I carried on sailing on the same course until I was safely away from the bridge complex and the shipping lane.

That's it, I thought. I had achieved my goal, and it was now time to make contact with the Coastguards and get them to tow me in.

I called them up on VHF channel 16. They asked how they could help me.

I explained my whole story, including the nutritious diet of cornflakes I had been on for the last three days and the fact that I was exhausted from only getting three hours' sleep in the past seventy-two.

The radio officer asked, "Sir, are you okay?"

I said yes.

The Coastguard advised me to sail to Little Creek.

I had no information on Little Creek at all. I had to ask for the latitude and longitude in order to work out where it was.

My GPS position put me five miles away, and to get there meant sailing across the shipping lane again.

The southerly breeze was very light and coming out of Little Creek. With my jury rig, I could only sail at around sixty degrees to the wind, meaning I had no windward performance. It was going to take an age to get in unless the wind direction changed.

As I approached the Thimble Shoal Channel, I saw a ship in the distance, which I didn't think was moving. I set a course to cross the channel, and as I reached the halfway point, the ship gave a loud blast on its horn. In a bit of a panic, I carefully studied the ship through my binoculars. I could see a small bow wave, confirming that this huge ship was slowly heading towards me.

All I could do was try and sail out of the channel as quickly as possible, which took a good fifteen minutes. Meanwhile, the ship was getting ever closer. Breathing a big sigh of relief, I sailed out of the channel just in time to watch the ship pass astern of me. I was pretty relieved.

The Coastguard called me on the VHF every hour to check on my progress and to check if I was okay. Each time I confirmed that I was okay and still sailing towards Little Creek.

I tried for an hour to sail into the wind by tacking back and forth towards Little Creek, with very little progress being made, as I had no windward sailing performance. It was during this period that I had another scare. Due to the wind direction and adverse current, I got swept towards the bridge complex and the shipping lane. After managing to sail clear of these dangers, I decided to drop my anchor. Trying to sail into Little Creek was proving far too stressful. Happy that the anchor was holding, I ate the last of my cornflakes and got my head down for an hour.

I only awoke when the Coastguard called me up on the radio asking if I was okay.

I passed my latest position and reminded them that it was about to get dark and I did not have any navigation lights.

After my sleep, I felt more refreshed. On returning to the cockpit, I realised that the wind had picked up. I quickly recovered the anchor and started sailing on the mainsail alone, which allowed me to point higher and sail closer to the wind. Although sailing slower with less leeway, I was still against the wind and current. This relatively short trip was still going to take forever.

I had to keep a good lookout for any sports boats coming close. To warn them of my presence, I shone my torch either at them or the mainsail. I got shouted at a few times for sailing without navigation lights. There was nothing I could do but keep a lookout.

Closer to the shore, I made out the lights of Little Creek. It wasn't too far away. I'd be there soon.

22:00

I was finally off the approach channel into Little Creek. The Coastguard came back on the radio and asked, "Sir, will you sail into Little Creek?"

I'd had enough of sailing around the Chesapeake all day getting nowhere, and in the dark, it was getting dangerous, so I replied, "No."

I explained again that I didn't have a chart for Little Creek.

Very tired, I told the Coastguard officer that I was going to sail close to the beach and drop the anchor for the night. Once anchored, I agreed to update the Coastguard with my exact position. During this conversation, I also advised that I could not display an anchor light or any other forms of navigation lights.

I remember the Coastguard coming back and saying, "Sir, why don't you have navigation lights?"

Repeating myself again, I reminded them that I had lost my mast when the yacht got rolled and consequently lost my masthead navigation lights. I don't think they were getting the picture.

When I finally dropped the anchor. I passed my position to the Coastguard as simply as I could, telling them I had dropped my anchor in front of the third house from the end, about two hundred yards from the beach, abeam of the port-hand channel marker into Little Creek.

It was during this conversation that they finally agreed to launch a rib to tow me in. After double-checking my position, they confirmed that they would be with me in half an hour.

I couldn't believe that it had taken them all day to agree to help. If I had been in the same position in the UK, the RNLI would have been out to help far more quickly, I am sure.

I was sat on the coach roof waiting, keeping an eye out for the rib, when I suddenly heard a boat coming towards me at speed. I flashed my torch into the sky, and instantly I was blinded by the beam from a very powerful searchlight. Carefully, the skipper of the rib brought the craft alongside. The three crewmen were in disbelief when they saw the state of the yacht.

They had lots of questions to ask me.

"Sir, what's happened to your mast?"

"I lost it in the Bermuda Triangle, together with my navigation lights and life raft."

"Sir, your yacht got rolled?"

"Yes."

"Sir, how many days have you been at sea?"

"Twenty-nine, I think?"

"Sir, if you had told us your condition earlier, we would have come out straight away—you kept telling us you were okay."

I tried to explain the contrast from being out in the Atlantic with no mast to being in the safety of the Chesapeake Bay. Relatively speaking, I *was* okay.

"Sir, do you have engine problems?"

"It's simpler than that—I don't have an engine."

"Sir, no engine? How did you get here?"

"I sailed in."

The Coastguards looked again at the mast and the general state of the yacht before asking, "Sir, why didn't you activate your EPIRB after you got rolled? If you had, we would have sent a ship to pick you up ages ago."

I replied, "Well, the yacht wasn't sinking. I had food and water. I figured I could rig something up that would get me in here."

They looked at me and shook their heads in disbelief.

"Okay?" I asked.

"Sir, we can only tow you into Little Creek if you are wearing a lifejacket. Do you have one?"

"Yes, I'll put it on."

In a cupboard under the chart table, I found my lifejacket. It was still in the bag from when I bought it, with even the price tag still on. Thinking about the challenges I'd faced and given that the majority of my sailing had been done single-handed, I'm not sure what good wearing a lifejacket would have done. The chances of me floating around and getting picked up by someone would have been pretty slim.

The Coastguard passed the tow line, which I made fast to the Samson Post. I was then asked how fast they could tow me and how much *Seefalke* drew.

"Six knots, and six feet," I replied. "Also, please bear in mind that the yacht tends to carry her way, so be careful when you slow down. Otherwise, I'll end up in the back of you."

"Don't worry, sir. We have plenty of experience moving yachts around."

I thought, *I've heard that before.*

As we made our way up the channel, I dug out my fenders and dock lines. Looking around, I realised Little Creek was huge. There was a large naval base on the port-hand side, with a number of warships moored to large concrete jetties. I could have easily sailed in had the conditions been more favourable. As we approached Little Creek Marina, the Coastguard slowed down and brought *Seefalke* into an alongside tow, ahead of manoeuvring us onto the dock. Everything went really smoothly. Those guys knew what they were doing.

I had to thank them all for what they had done. They did an excellent job of getting me onto the dock. Before they left, they said, "Welcome to America. Customs and immigration will be around in the morning to see you—also you've arrived in time for Thanksgiving."

"What do you mean?"

"The last Thursday in November is Thanksgiving, and you, my friend, have a lot to be thankful for."

I was finally standing on land at 2330 hours, on Monday 23rd November, after twenty-nine days at sea. My legs were a bit wobbly, but I was extremely happy, relieved and tired all at the same time. After the Coastguards left, I sat in the cockpit, . thinking about everything I had been through and the resolve I had shown to overcome the adversity I'd faced. This was the first time I had properly reflected on the enormity of what I had just achieved. I remember being quite emotional.

As I sat surveying my surroundings, a guy walked down the dock. He had a bit of a wobble on. When he saw the yacht, he walked over and had a look at the state she was in. Then he noticed me sitting in the cockpit.

"Hi, bud. Looks like you've had some fun?"

"Oh, yes. Come aboard and I'll tell you all about it."

"My name is Kevin," he said. "Give me a minute, and I'll get us some beers from my yacht."

I sat with Kevin for an hour, having my first proper conversation with someone for a month. After the ordeal of finally getting in, drinking a few beers was just what I needed. My impressions of the USA were fast improving. I had only been on dry land for thirty minutes and I had already made a new friend.

When Kevin left, I climbed into my very salty sleeping bag for the last time, knowing that I could relax and enjoy a proper night's sleep for the first time in a month, without worrying about bad weather, ships, fog, whales or the sails falling down.

When I awoke the next morning, I could see a small crowd of people on the dock, who were all looking at and talking about the yacht. They were curious to know what had happened. I climbed out of the hatch, keen to meet them and tell them about my adventure. At the same time, Kevin asked if I wanted a coffee. I didn't need asking twice, and shortly afterwards, he returned with a large black coffee for me.

After my welcome committee had dispersed, Kevin told me where I could find the local 7-11 store, which also had an ATM. After drawing some money out, I bought everything I needed for a full English breakfast. I wanted the works—bacon, eggs, sausages, beans, fresh bread and coffee. I also picked up washing powder and some razor blades. I hadn't had a shave in thirty days.

After breakfast, I sat on deck with a coffee and reflected again on everything that had happened to me. I thought about all the twists, turns and setbacks I had endured, and then how I had made decisions to overcome the problems that ultimately resulted in me and the yacht making it safely to port. I was feeling pretty chuffed with myself; I had learnt a hell of a lot about my resolve and resilience during the past thirty days.

Travelling to Oz at the age of four had given me the travel bug. Living by the coast had taught me to respect and love the sea. Travelling around Europe in my teens with my parents had shown me there were other cultures out there which I had wanted to see.

If my apprenticeship hadn't ended when it did, my story might have been different. But even then, I'd had the courage and initiative to find work in Germany. In the eighties, the British economy was on the floor, and I'd had to travel to find work. My trade and a lack of money had led to me not wanting to rely on anybody to fix the yacht; instead, I learnt how to work and repair yachts myself. My grandmother dying when she did led me to seeing *Seefalke* for the first time.

Fate?

When I first moved *Seefalke* to Ray Harris's yard, it was outside in the wind and rain. A year later, Ray had built a large aircraft-type hangar and moved *Seefalke* into it. Only Ray's encouragement gave me the belief that I could restore the yacht—not my mother, who never thought I would ever sail across the pond. Even my best mates never thought I would get past Lundy Island.

When I left Barry, I had a cheap GPS, a yacht with no engine, and a homemade self-steering system that initially didn't work very well. I guess one of the biggest life-defining decisions I made was deciding not to put an engine in *Seefalke*.

Many will argue that had I put an engine in the yacht, I would have been able to get into harbours and rivers more easily, and still made progress when the wind died. An engine would have allowed me to maintain better speed when the wind was light and maintain better headings when the wind was against me.

Most probably, I would have had a shower with hot water heated by the engine, a modern flushable toilet, and an iron. I could have carried bigger batteries and an SSB radio, so

I would have been able to get up-to-date weather forecasts and made better contact with other vessels and Coastguard facilities. With all those creature comforts, I might have met someone who would have been keen to sail with me. Every woman I'd met who expressed interest in sailing with me went a green colour when I told her I didn't have a shower or a fixed toilet and the living space was only eight-feet-six wide by twelve feet long.

And I would be without a story to tell.

I had no regrets about not having an engine. If I'd motored everywhere, it wouldn't have been any fun. Sailing a forty-foot engineless yacht was a big part of my adventure.

1998 started with the euphoria of winning the Antigua Classic Yacht Regatta, followed by the marathon slog down to Brazil and then finished off with the events of the last month. All told, it had been a pretty character-building and exciting year.

I shouldn't deny the fact that I'm incredibly lucky to still be alive to tell my story. Looking back, if only a couple of things had been different, my story wouldn't be getting told. I learnt more about living in 1998 than most people do in a lifetime.

I have never been religious, nor believed in a god or fate. I believe everybody is in control of their own destiny, making their own life choices. After my last month's sailing adventures and all I had been through, though, I had to wonder if there was someone looking after me, and if so, why?

In my hitchhiking days, maybe St Christopher had been looking after me, as I'd had no bad experiences?

When I had a motorbike and went diving, like most young adults, I really pushed the limits. I could have been killed a few times, but somehow, I am still here. The gods of motorbikes and divers were definitely looking after me.

While sailing, Prince Henry the Navigator looked after me. When I sailed around the small fishing boat as I came out of the Lisbon River, I knew the gods of sailing were looking after me all the time I was at sea.

It seems to me my journey through life has been in the lap of the gods, or was my nan's father really looking after me?

My reflections and thoughts about the past and the choices I'd made were brought to an abrupt end when customs and immigration turned up. I was pretty familiar with the routine by now, and true to form, they asked me the usual questions.

"What happened when you rolled?"

"What happened to the mast?"

"How long have you been at sea?"

One officer said he could smell the salt inside the yacht. After an hour, I was stamped into the USA. This was good news, as I could start making plans for my future. Later that day, I went to the marina office to check in. I paid for a month to give me some time to sort myself and the yacht out. After the marina, I started on the usual chores that needed doing after reaching a destination. I desperately needed to wash all my clothes, which were stinking, then I needed to wash myself, as I, too, was stinking, and have a good shave. An hour later I was starting to feel human again, and good to be wearing clothes that weren't caked in salt. Having washed and dried my sleeping bag, it was time to find a payphone and ring my mum.

I called home, by reversing the charges. Mum was surprised to hear from me, and after she stopped crying, she said the skipper of *Asphalt Champion* had called her to say I would be delayed getting into the States as I was experiencing engine problems. Apparently, he had made no mention that I had snapped my mast and was sailing under a jury rig.

Mum told me that she'd known something else must have been wrong because she knew *Seefalke* didn't have an engine. She started crying again when I told her about my eventful trip. She kept saying that if she had known that I was in so much trouble, she would have done something to help me. I told her not to worry and reminded her that she still had her "Sun" in her life.

The last thing Mum told me to do was to go and buy myself a decent steak, to put it on my credit card, and she would pay for it. I'd thought Mum paying for the call would leave her crying again, let alone a steak as well.

On my first evening ashore, I found a local bar, and as I walked in, I asked the bartender for a beer.

"What beer?" he asked.

"What's the most popular? I asked back.

As he started to pour me a pint, he said, "You must be from that yacht with the broken mast that the Coastguard towed in last night."

"Yes, that's my yacht. How did you tell it was me?"

"Just a guess from your accent. Everybody has been talking about you and the condition of the yacht—I'm surprised you haven't made the local news."

He handed me the pint in a frosted pint glass. It looked great. I was really looking forward to my first pint in a pub for nearly a month. I took a big gulp, looking forward to the taste of nectar, but instead, the beer was bloody awful. I spat it out all over the bar.

"What's this stuff? It tastes like dishwater?"

"It's Budweiser."

"You must have something better?"

He looked shocked, he told me to sit down, saying, "Sorry, you must have had a bad pint. I have my own private collection in the fridge out the back. I'll go and get one of those for you."

The beer from the bartender's fridge tasted much better, and as soon as I finished it, he replaced it straight away. After drinking a few beers, I ordered steak and chips. Each time I had an empty glass, the bartender came over with another beer. That's American service for you.

I finished my steak and chips, and the bartender came over with yet another beer for me. He looked at me and said, "You still look hungry; do you want another steak?"

"Yes, please."

After the second steak, I sat at the bar feeling fat and happy. I then started to recount my story to the bartender as I worked my way through his selection of beers. I paid the bill with my credit card—I'd worry about my financial situation another day. I made my way back to the yacht pretty drunk, content and looking forward to my dry sleeping bag, which wasn't wet, stinking and covered in salt.

Chapter 22
My Next Adventure

Kevin and I became close friends. We were the same age and shared the same interests—sailing, playing the guitar, drinking beer—and like myself, Kevin was looking for work. I had spent three weeks in Little Creek Marina looking for work, without much luck. Little Creek was a big US Navy base housing Navy staff and was quite a poor area.

One lovely day, I was working on the yacht, when Kevin joined me for an afternoon beer. He had some good news and wanted to know if I was interested in joining him. "There's a marina in Willoughby Bay, which is being developed," he said. "I know the marina manager, Jim, and he's looking for people to work there. Jim is willing to pay ten dollars an hour—are you interested?"

"Damn right," I immediately replied.

"Right, finish your beer and let's get over to see Jim."

We got offered jobs, and as a bonus, Jim agreed that we could moor our yachts in the new marina for free. A week later, Kevin towed *Seefalke* to Willoughby Marina.

We started work on building and fitting the new pontoons. The marina office was already finished, with a clubhouse, showers and toilets. I had landed on my feet.

During the first six months in America, I made a whole lot of new friends from around the marina, mostly by working on their yachts. I was living the American dream; I had a car, and a new companion in my life—a Border Collie puppy, who I named Dylan. Everything was working out really well.

As I had not seen my mother for over a year, I decided to have a holiday and fly back home to Wales.

Once back in Ogmore, I had a fun time. It was lovely spending quality time with Mum, having a few beers and hanging out with the boys from Barry. Bowmer, Spud and Karl were all on good form and not taking life too seriously, as usual.

After catching up with everyone, I decided to go back to work in Willoughby. On my way to Heathrow, I stopped off in Reading to have a beer with Martin, who I hadn't seen since 1997.

I flew into Philadelphia. As I passed through immigration, I got stopped. They wanted to know how I'd got into the country and what I was doing there. I explained I had arrived on a yacht that had been badly damaged in a hurricane, and I had come back to fix it. I also explained that I hadn't been able to sail out of America, as it was the middle of the hurricane season, none of which got through to them, and as a result, I got marched off for a lengthier interrogation. After getting photographed and having my fingerprints taken, it was decided that I should be deported. My ten-year unlimited B1/ B2 visa was ripped out of my passport and cancelled. Despite this treatment, I do think the immigration officer felt sorry for me. He asked me if I had a credit card, and before I could answer yes, he said no, and I got a free flight back to the UK.

Martin was surprised to see me on his doorstep when he returned from work, as was my mother.

So, I was back home after my three-day round trip to the States, and on the dole. I now had to wait for my new passport to arrive. I used this time to see more of the boys in Barry and generally just hang out. This also gave me time to work out how I was going to get back into the USA and be reunited with the only things I owned—*Seefalke* and Dylan.

To pass time, my mother gave me a *Reader's Digest* magazine for me to read. In it was an article on the new Bill Bryson book, *A Walk in the Woods*, which was about walking the Appalachian Trail. So, I found a bookshop and bought the book. In the shop at the same time, I also found the book that I had inadvertently ripped the last two pages out of when I was sailing to the States. I wanted to find out what happened at the end. Why I bothered, I do not know.

I read the Appalachian Trail book with interest. Walking the trail captured my imagination—it seemed like a fantastic way to see more of America. I would get to pass through fourteen states during this two-thousand-mile hike. I would be starting at Springer Mountain in Georgia and ending up, five or six months later, in Katahdin, Maine. How cool would that be?

Not too long after I read the book, I was rock climbing with Karl and started talking to him about the book and the trail. As soon as I got back into the States, the Appalachian Trail was going straight on my to-do list.

I had already started to plan my return to the US. The best plan I could think of was to fly into Canada and then find a yacht delivery back to the States. My other option was to walk down the Appalachian Trail. But before I could put any of my plans together, my mother had a phone call from an American immigration lawyer, which went something like this, as explained by my mum.

"Ma'am, can I speak to Lynn Roach, please?"

"Sorry, he's out. Can I pass on a message?"

"Yes, Ma'am. I'm an American immigration lawyer. Can you tell Lynn that if he tries to fly back to a northern state, like New York, he will be red-flagged and stopped? However, if he flies into a southern state, like Florida, he could walk straight back in, as the computers in the southern states don't talk and are not linked to their northern counterparts. Can you pass that message on to Lynn for me, please? Thank you, Ma'am, and have a nice day."

My problem was solved. I booked a return flight to Orlando in Florida. On arrival, for some reason I got stuck at the immigration desk with the longest queue. I soon realised the officer was young and very thorough at his job. Thinking of changing to a quicker desk with a less keen immigration officer, the keen guy looked down the queue and made eye contact with me. I had no choice but to wait.

I was stuck at the back still waiting when all the other lines had cleared. As I waited, slowly getting closer to the front, I noticed a man sweeping the floor. With only two groups of people left to clear, the man with the brush called me over to where he had opened another line, just for me. After a very quick chat on how long I intended to stay in Florida, and what I did for a living, I was in. What a result! I knew I would be asked questions about my occupation, and I'd already rehearsed my answer. I told the officer that I was a toolmaker, working in a factory in Wales making hip joints. He praised me for doing such a worthwhile job! Once outside the airport, I hired a car and drove myself back to Willoughby Bay, Virginia.

Kevin had done an excellent job of looking after the yacht and Dylan while I had been away. All I had to give him was a hundred dollars for the dog food he'd bought. It was really nice to be back amongst my American friends, with my old job back. While I had been at home, my friends in the marina had all donated some money to buy a second-hand mast for the yacht. Even though it was deck-stepped, I was overwhelmed by their thought and generosity.

It took me a while, but after a few months, I had the mast ready to go on the yacht. With Jim operating the marina crane we used to move the pontoon sections around, *Seefalke* had a new mast, and I could now go sailing again, which felt fantastic!

I made a few new friends at the marina. John Sherwood was a retired reporter who, after hearing part of my story, wanted me to write a book about my adventures. He tried very hard to teach me to write and helped me understand the English language.

The best story John told me was when he wrote an article related to prostitution in New York. John had interviewed a woman in her flat. A few weeks later, John was in a bar in the same area, and after drinking way too much, he walked back to the woman's flat and knocked on the door. When the door opened, he said, "Are you open for business?"

I had to laugh.

Another character living on a yacht was Jim Grey, a big drinker and smoker whose yacht I had done a lot of work on. I mentioned to Jim that I was planning to walk the Appalachian Trail in March 2000. To my surprise, Jim was well keen to join me on my next adventure. Instead of paying me for the work I did on his yacht, he bought me the gear that Dylan and I would need for the trail, which worked out really well. From reading the Bill Bryson book, I knew everybody should have a trail name. Jim's was Detox, even before we started.

Once Kevin agreed to look after our yachts for the summer, the last piece of the jigsaw fell into place.

In March 2000, with Kevin, we drove Jim's car to Springer Mountain, Georgia, where he took a photo of us. We were stood next to the sign pointing in the direction of Katahdin, Maine, 2162.2 miles away.

Dylan led the way, carrying his own backpack with his food in it. Jim, aka Detox, followed, with me bringing up the rear.

I'd been walking for a month before I was given my trail name. Detox and I were hiking with another friend, a Welsh lad with the trail name of Vince of Wales. On this fateful day, we'd walked a couple of miles off the trail into town to pick up food for the next three days or sixty miles of walking.

After shopping and back on the road, Vince of Wales and Detox started to walk back to the campsite. I said, "Hang on, boys—let's hitchhike back."

As you can imagine, we were really weighed down with our rucksacks plus two shopping bags each full of food. Additionally, I had the dog.

My idea was met with hoots of laughter, with them both saying I had no chance of getting a lift. The two agreed we didn't stand a chance in hell but agreed to give me ten minutes to try.

The first car to pass was a big pickup truck, which to my disappointment did not stop.

The second car was a huge American Cadillac driven by an old lady, who I knew would not stop.

The third car was a young woman in a very small sports car. She stopped and said, "Get in, boys." To my surprise, I noticed there was a baby in the front seat as well.

Vince of Wales looked at me and said, "Bloody hell, mate. You must have a magic thumb."

Vince of Wales and Detox climbed into the back seat with all our rucksacks. I climbed into the boot with all our shopping bags of food, together with Dylan. Finally, I had my trail name, which would become the only thing other walkers on the trail ever knew me by:

Magic Thumb.

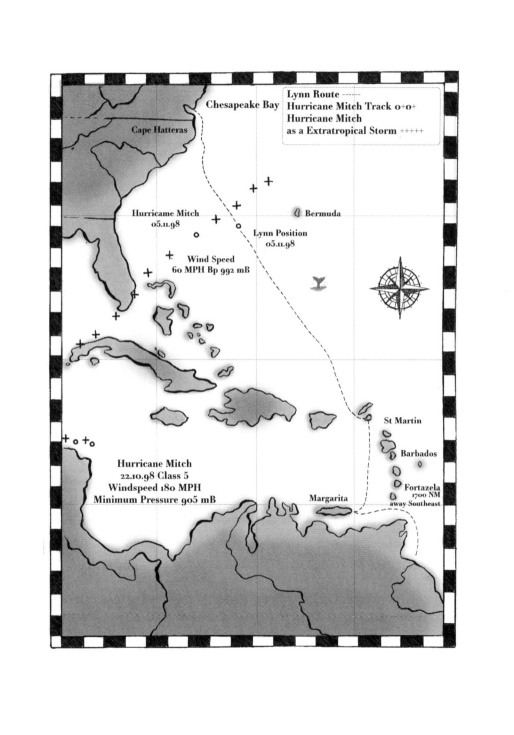

Author Profile

In school, I struggled with very poor English skills. Years later, I found out I was dyslexic.

I completed an apprenticeship as a toolmaker, which gave me the ability to travel. In Australia, I learned to scuba dive, which led to me buying a yacht.

This book is about my passion to restore that yacht, the fun I had sailing her and meeting people along the way, and the adventures I got up to with my mates.

In the 2000, I walked the Appalachian Trail, taking my Border Collie, Dylan, with me. It took me five months to walk 2167.2 miles.

In my sixty-third year, I walked out of the house, down to the beach and turned right, onto the Welsh coastal path. I walked to north Wales, where I picked up the Offa's Dyke Trail before walking back to the house twelve weeks later, taking my Springer Spaniel, Dotti, with me. A total walking distance of 1050 miles. I met some great people along the way, and it was a great way to see my homeland.

My dyslexia has not held me back. If I can travel the world and write a book, you can as well. I hope you will enjoy the read.

What Did You Think of
Living in the Lap of the Gods?

A big thank you for purchasing the book. It means a lot you chose to read it. I hope you enjoyed it.

If you are able to spare a few minutes to post a review on Amazon, that would be much appreciated.

Publisher Information

rowanvale
books

Rowanvale Books provides publishing services to independent authors, writers and poets all over the globe. We deliver a personal, honest and efficient service that allows authors to see their work published, while remaining in control of the process and retaining their creativity. By making publishing services available to authors in a cost-effective and ethical way, we at Rowanvale Books hope to ensure that the local, national and international community benefits from a steady stream of good quality literature.

For more information about us, our authors or our publications, please get in touch.

www.rowanvalebooks.com
info@rowanvalebooks.com

Printed in Great Britain
by Amazon

11777677R00237